The Renaissance in National Context aims to dispel the commonly held view that the great efflorescence of art, learning and culture in the period from around 1350 to 1550 was solely or even primarily an Italian phenomenon. A team of distinguished scholars addresses the development of art, literacy and humanism across the length and breadth of Europe – from Rome to the Netherlands, from Poland to France.

The book demonstrates that the revival of letters, and the generation of new currents in artistic expression, had many sources independent of Italy, meeting numerous local needs, and serving various local functions, specific to the political, economic, social and religious climates of particular regions and principalities. In particular the authors emphasise that while the Renaissance was in a fashion backward looking, recovering the culture of Greece and Rome, it nevertheless served as the springboard for many specifically modern developments, including the diplomacy of the 'new princes', the spread of education and printing, the growth of nationalist feeling and the birth of the 'new science'. Bridges of cultural transmission are given equal emphasis with the barriers which were to generate increased separation of linguistic and cultural domains. Three essays on major Italian centres do, moreover, demonstrate that the diversity of the Renaissance applies to the peninsula no less than to the rest of Europe.

D0141320

THE RENAISSANCE IN NATIONAL CONTEXT

Volumes edited by Roy Porter and Mikuláš Teich

Already published

The Enlightenment in national context
Revolution in history
Romanticism in national context
Fin de siècle and its legacy
The Renaissance in national context

In preparation

The national question in Europe in historical context
The Scientific Revolution in national context
The Reformation in national context (with R.W. Scribner)
The Industrial Revolution in national context:
Europe and the USA

THE
RENAISSANCE
IN
NATIONAL CONTEXT

EDITED BY

ROY PORTER

Senior Lecturer in the Social History of Medicine,
The Wellcome Institute, London

MIKULÁŠ TEICH

Emeritus Fellow, Robinson College, Cambridge

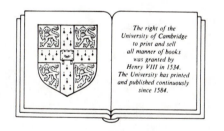

The right of the
University of Cambridge
to print and sell
all manner of books
was granted by
Henry VIII in 1534.
The University has printed
and published continuously
since 1584.

CAMBRIDGE UNIVERSITY PRESS

CAMBRIDGE
NEW YORK   PORT CHESTER
MELBOURNE   SYDNEY

Published by the Press Syndicate of the University of Cambridge
The Pitt Building, Trumpington Street, Cambridge CB2 1RP
40 West 20th Street, New York, NY 10011, USA
10 Stamford Road, Oakleigh, Melbourne 3166, Australia

© Cambridge University Press 1992

First published 1992

Printed in Great Britain at the University Press, Cambridge

British Library cataloguing in publication data
The Renaissance in national context.
1. Italian civilization, 1300–1494
I. Porter, Roy, 1946– II. Teich, Mikulas
945.05

Library of Congress cataloguing in publication data
The Renaissance in national context/edited by Roy Porter and Mikuláš
Teich.
p. cm.
Includes bibliographical refererences and index.
ISBN 0 521 36181 8 (hardback). – ISBN 0 521 36970 3 (pbk)
1. Renaissance. I. Porter, Roy, 1946– . II. Teich, Mikuláš.
CB361.R387 1991
940.2′1–dc20 90-2561 CIP

ISBN 0 521 36181 8 hardback
ISBN 0 521 36970 3 paperback

940.21
R29p

93–1168

12/1/93 - MW

CONTENTS

Notes on contributors		*page* viii
	Introduction MIKULÁŠ TEICH AND ROY PORTER	1
1	The uses of Italy PETER BURKE	6
2	Florence ROBERT BLACK	21
3	Rome NICHOLAS DAVIDSON	42
4	Venice RICHARD MacKENNEY	53
5	The Low Countries ELSA STRIETMAN	68
6	Germany JAMES OVERFIELD	92
7	France DONALD R. KELLEY	123
8	England DAVID STARKEY	146
9	Hungary TIBOR KLANICZAY	164
10	Poland ANTONI MĄCZAK	180
11	Bohemia and Moravia JOSEF MACEK	197
	Index	221

NOTES ON CONTRIBUTORS

ROBERT BLACK teaches Italian Renaissance history at the University of Leeds. American by birth but a resident of Britain since 1968, he was educated at Chicago and London. He is the author of *Benedetto Accolti and the Florentine Renaissance* (1985) and of articles on Italian humanist historiography, Renaissance schools and universities, and Machiavelli. He is now completing a book on education, society and humanism in Florentine Tuscany, 1350–1500, and a register of documents regarding the University of Arezzo in the Middle Ages and in the Renaissance.

PETER BURKE is Reader in Cultural History, University of Cambridge, and Fellow of Emmanuel College. His books include *The Italian Renaissance* (1972, 3rd edn, 1987), *Popular Culture in Early Modern Europe* (1978), *The Renaissance* (1987) and *An Historical Anthropology of Modern Italy* (1987).

NICHOLAS DAVIDSON is Lecturer in History, University of Leicester. He is the author of several articles on the social and religious history of early modern Italy, and of *The Counter-Reformation* (1986). He is currently completing a study of the Venetian inquisition in the sixteenth century.

DONALD R. KELLEY is James Westfall Thompson Professor of History, Rutgers University, and is Executive Editor of the *Journal of the History of Ideas*. His publications include *Foundations of Modern Historical Scholarship* (1970), *The Beginning of Ideology* (1981), *Françoise Hotman* (1973), the translation (with J.H. Hexter) of Claude de Seyssel, *The Monarchy of France* (1981), *History, Law and the Human Sciences* (1984), and chapters on historical thought in *A Critical Bibliography of French Literature*, ed. R. La Charité (1984), *Renaissance Humanism*, ed. A. Rabil (1988) and *The Cambridge History of Renaissance Philosophy* (1988).

TIBOR KLANICZAY is Director of the Centre for Renaissance Research at the Hungarian Academy of Sciences, Budapest.

JOSEF MACEK was Director of the Institute of History at the Czechoslovak Academy of Sciences until 1969. He is the author of eight books on a range of Renaissance/Reformation subjects. *Il Rinascimento italiano* (1972), *Jean Hus et les traditions hussites* (1973), *Machiavelli e il machiavellismo* (1980), *Histoire de la Bohême* (1984) and *Michael Gaismair* (1988) are among his foreign-language editions.

ANTONI MĄCZAK is Professor of Early Modern History, University of Warsaw. He has published books on Polish economic history, on the history of travelling in Europe, and on clientage. In 1984 he was coeditor, with Peter Burke and Henryk Samsonowicz, of *East-Central Europe in Transition*.

RICHARD MACKENNEY is Lecturer in History, University of Edinburgh. His research centres on the economic, social and cultural history of the city of Venice, and his publications include *Tradesmen and Traders: The World of the Guilds in Venice and Europe, c.1250–1650* (1987). He is presently working on the relationship of the economic and religious life of the city.

JAMES H. OVERFIELD has taught since 1968 at the University of Vermont and is currently Chair of the Department of History. He has published articles on German humanism and the pre-Reformation German clergy, and is the author of *Humanism and Scholasticism in Pre-Reformation Germany* (1984). He is presently working on a study of the church and society in late medieval Germany.

DAVID STARKEY teaches early modern English history at the London School of Economics. He is the author of the *Reign of Henry VIII: Politics and Personalities* (1985) and editor of *The English Court from the Wars of the Roses to the Civil War* (1987). His previous essay on the cultural history of the period, 'The age of the household' in Stephen Medcalf (ed.), *The Later Middle Ages* (1981), employs a more socio-political approach.

ELSA STRIETMAN is Lecturer in Dutch, University of Cambridge, and Fellow and Tutor of New Hall. Her main research is in the drama of the medieval and sixteenth-century Low Countries, and her publications include both articles on and translations of the drama of the Low Countries. She is currently writing a book on this subject.

INTRODUCTION

MIKULÁŠ TEICH AND ROY PORTER

Grasping the relations between the particular and the universal, the interplay of part and whole, is one of the historian's perennial challenges. This book forms part of a series focusing upon major constellations of ideas, culture and action, and attempting to ascertain their general features, their local and national aspects, and the links between the two, which historians commonly find both fruitful and fraught. The volumes which have already appeared in this series upon the Enlightenment, upon Romanticism, and upon the *fin de siècle* have shown how each of those key moments in European culture possessed certain common characteristics, a programme jointly held by, or spreading amongst, thinkers and activists from many lands; but they have also shown that their manifestations and meanings were importantly differentiated between (say) Spain and Sweden, Bohemia and Britain, determined by local circumstances and distinctive ideological needs.

The same clearly applied to the Renaissance. This movement obviously constituted a great turning-point in the history of the West. This has never been put more eloquently than by Engels. Looking at the concatenation, in the sixteenth century, of the new culture, the new religion, the new economic formations, the New World, and, not least, the new science, Engels argued that 'it was the greatest progressive revolution that mankind had so far experienced':

The bounds of the old *orbis terrarum* were pierced; only now was the world really discovered and the basis laid for subsequent world trade and the transition of handicraft to manufacture, which in its turn formed the starting-point for modern large scale industry. The spiritual dictatorship of the Church was shattered; . . . amongst the Latins a cheerful spirit of free thought, taken over from the Arabs and nourished by the newly-discovered Greek philosophy, took root more and more and prepared the way for the materialism of the eighteenth century.[1]

Valuably, Engels emphasised that it would be artificial to draw sharp boundaries between the Renaissance as a cultural force and the associated religious and scientific movements it helped unleash ('natural science too was

I

moving in the midst of the general revolution and was itself thoroughly revolutionary'). Following Engels, it is crucial to take the broad view. But it is also vital – with the Renaissance as with the Enlightenment and Romanticism – to examine local soils and specific differences. Indeed, with the Renaissance, the problems involved in seeking an understanding in terms of cultural affinities and spacial diversities are exceptionally complex. This may, *prima facie*, seem surprising, for every schoolboy knows that the Renaissance began in Italy and spread out thence, through the agency of visitors to the peninsula, through a diaspora of Italian scholars and artists, and through the accelerating circulation of manuscripts and printed books. Yet delineating the 'national contexts' of the Renaissance is more than a matter of pointing to an Italian well-spring and to the various mechanisms of transmission and channels of diffusion connecting Italy to other parts.

For one thing, as Peter Burke's chapter on Italy, and the local essays by Robert Black, Nicholas Davidson and Richard Mackenney emphasise, it makes little sense to speak, with respect to the Renaissance period (from the mid-fourteenth century to the close of the sixteenth), of a homogeneous 'Italy'. There was a plurality of polities in the peninsula, with sharply divergent socio-economic structures and opposing forms of government (which themselves, notably Florence, changed radically over the centuries). If, as commonly happens, the case of Florence is taken as normative, then what are we to make of Venice, which, as MacKenney insists, shared few of the philosophical and historical preoccupations of Florentine humanism yet produced a stunningly brilliant visual and verbal culture?

Similarly, it often seems convenient to include the efflorescence of painting, music and other arts in the Burgundian territories of the fifteenth and sixteenth centuries, the Low Countries and also some German-speaking areas under the umbrella term 'Renaissance'. In most instances, it is far from obvious that such musicians and artists derived their inspiration in any direct or overriding sense from contemporary ferments of thought taking place in the Mediterranean world (though most composers gravitated South).

In other words, it may be less valuable to concentrate upon the channels – which indisputably did exist – whereby ideals, outlooks and skills spread from Italy to the four corners of Europe, than to inquire into those elements common to many regions and polities, elements which combined to stimulate an extraordinary outburst of cultural and material production; a great leap forward in literacy and education; a profound desire to break with the immediate past – to be rid of what were perceived as the dead hands of clerical and ecclesiastical domination, of scholasticism, of feudalism – and to fashion new models of living, a new sense of self, with the aid of a selective, mythic, reconstruction of the past.

Common to all the contributions to this volume, therefore, are certain perceptions about broader European developments – and hence the shared facets of different societies – in the 'Renaissance centuries'. It was an age in which, in many regions, feudal bonds of lordship and economic organisation were breaking up; when capitalist expansion and rapid urbanisation (particularly in the commercial heartlands of Italy and the Low Countries) were proceeding at an unexampled but uneven rate, creating social disruption and change, both requiring and authorising new models of political association and goals of civility; when the rise of the 'modern prince' meant the invention of those glittering courts which, as Elias has stressed, were the growth-points of a 'civilizing process',[2] and, at the same time, centres for a new educated and cultured class of official servants and courtiers, who would be the ornaments and ideological mouthpieces of the 'new monarchies'; when Luther was shaking the foundations of that religious unity which had been, for over a thousand years, the greatest cohesive force within Latin Christendom; when, finally, but far from least, the invention of movable-type printing was radically expanding – indeed democratising – the scope of written culture, and thus affording the medium for a popular awareness of those religious changes just mentioned, of the discovery of the New World, and of notable breakthroughs in science, technology and industry, in mathematics and machinery.[3] In all these respects, the Renaissance needs to be conceptualised as more than the rediscovery of Livy and Cicero and the export of art and rhetoric from Italy. If, as Tibor Klaniczay puts it in his essay upon Hungary, the close of the fifteenth century finds 'Plato in Pannonia', we must look not just to the Platonic Academy in Florence but to Pannonia itself for the explanation.

Thus there were many fields of force in Renaissance Europe. But it is above all when we concentrate upon the politics of the Renaissance that the tremendous complexity of the problem of its 'location' becomes plain. For if Italy was, in some sense, its centre, it was not the Italy of the Quattrocento, but the Italy of perhaps 1,500 years earlier. In other words, to scrutinise the Renaissance in national context it is necessary to examine the different ways in which Europeans – those people who, it seems, were increasingly becoming aware of themselves as the French, the Poles or the English – also related themselves, admittedly through the mediation largely of Italian scholars – to ancient Rome, to its Latin culture, to the system of Roman law, to its *imperium*; and related themselves, through Rome, to Greece as well, and to ancestors and authorities even further back in time. The central national context of the Renaissance is thus *temporally* 'at a distance' from the Renaissance itself, the spiritual presence of Rome, still, of course, incarnate in many forms in early modern Europe, not least in the 'Holy Roman Empire'. The immediate decisions that thus faced early modern scholars, legists, historians, and, of course, all those aspiring rulers who, directly or indirectly, were motivating and sponsoring them, lay in devising 'usable histories' which did not merely relate their nations to their neighbours and to Italy present (itself often a taxing problem, especially after 1517, because Italy was the home not just of advanced culture but of the Pope), but also to Italy past.

Ancient Rome, the Romans and their Latin culture could be admired as the true model for a modern polity, a virtuous people and an enviable civilisation. More than that, the authority of Rome could serve very specific legitimising purposes. In those territories that once had constituted part of the empire of Augustus or Marcus Aurelius, jurisconsults and historians were eager to represent modern rulers as directly inheriting the mantle of Roman *auctoritas* and *gloria*. But the argument cut both ways. For Rome could be represented – not least by scholars enamoured of the tools and techniques of humanist scholarship – as the great oppressor, tyrannising over peoples born free.

As Donald Kelley in particular demonstrates in his examination of humanist ideological warfare in France, the political, legal and diplomatic quarrels of the early modern era – both internal and international – were conducted with the ghost of the Roman Empire. (*Mutatis mutandis*, the same may still be true: British, American, and, no less, Russian 'imperialism' likewise dominate and perhaps mystify the language of politics in the third world today, though there the demonic oppressor is at least more contemporary.) It is because of the intense ambiguity of this 'love/hate' relationship with Rome and all it symbolised that, as many contributors insist, we must see the Renaissance as far more than a matter of a humanist desire to recover pure Latinity, the syntax of Cicero: out of its ideological matrix arose no less the urge to promote vernaculars as the equals and successors of Latin (for was not Latin the Roman vernacular?), to emulate and excel the Ancients, but in one's own way.

The role of humanism is thus exceedingly complex. It represented Graeco-Roman culture. Yet it was also a pack of practical literary techniques, ready to be applied to the utilitarian purpose of government. Thus, as David Starkey emphasises in his essay on England, humanism was not merely characterised by its national context; it could become the language of the nation. Yet this was not universally so. Examining Bohemia and Moravia, Professor Macek notes that Renaissance humanism existed basically as a subordinate current in cultural life. This was due, he argues, to the preponderance of the ideology of the Czech Reformation, poised ambivalently between radicalising religious life and resisting cultural progress.

Even when thus distancing themselves, the poets, philosophers and painters of the Renaissance spoke face-to-face with the Ancients. The intimacy, the urgency of the rapport with the heroes of old – Robert Black quotes Machiavelli's famous account of his self-transformation into a Roman senator – indicates the intense excitement generated by the recovery of a rich and many-sided culture, apparently long lost though never entirely forgotten, a culture of expressions and images that seemed particularly happily suited to enhance the stature of modern educators, academics, moralists and men of letters, and the elites they served.

Jacob Burckhardt's classic claim that the Renaissance effected the discovery of Man in his full individuality can no longer be accepted without severe qualification.[4] As the essays in this volume abundantly show, the ethos of literate humanism was one far more disposed to venerate the authority of the past than to champion innovation; and the particular past being revered – above all, the Livian, Catonic and Ciceronian idealisation of the Roman Republic – was one which elevated the *virtù* of the community almost to sacred proportions, and stressed its moral priority over the individual. Renaissance is, after all, a matter of *re*birth.

Yet the recovery of a pristine past – or, as we might say, this invention of a historical past – was in its own way the most profound of all acts of emancipation, a break from the positivism of feudalism, from ritual deferral to custom, and from the tutelage of the church. The recovery of learning, and its accompanying recovery of nerve, restored the idea of the autonomous moral polity, and thus sanctioned, albeit indirectly, the cultured diversification of the succeeding centuries, blazing a trail for the intellectual innovations offered by the New World and the New Science. If there was only one Rome, it had a multiplicity of representations in the distinctive Renaissance of different nations.

NOTES

1 Karl Marx and Friedrich Engels, *Selected Works* (London, 1968), 339.
2 Norbert Elias, *The Civilizing Process*, vol. I: *The History of Manners* (New York, 1978); vol. II: *Power and Civility* (New York, 1982); vol. III: *The Court Society* (New York, 1983).
3 Little is said in this volume about the Reformation and Scientific Revolution. This is not, of course, because we believe they are in any way movements with no connection with the Renaissance. It is simply because they form, in their own right, the subjects of further volumes in this series.
4 Jacob Burckhardt, *The Civilization of the Renaissance in Italy* (Oxford, 1981; first edn, 1859).

ONE

𝕀𝕁

THE USES OF ITALY

PETER BURKE

The Renaissance was an international movement. The enthusiasm for antiquity, especially Rome, and the determination to imitate and to rival its cultural achievements, ideas once (in the late fourteenth century) virtually confined to a handful of Florentines, were shared in 1600 by a large part of the European upper class. Italian culture was fashionable. It was becoming the custom for young aristocrats from different parts of Europe, from Britain to Poland, to learn Italian, to visit Rome, Florence, Venice and Naples as part of the 'Grand Tour', to return with works of art in their baggage, and, later in life, to build houses in Renaissance style, often following the patterns illustrated in the famous treatises on architecture by the Italians Sebastiano Serlio and Andrea Palladio.

If a movement is international, however, it does not follow that it is homogeneous. Spain, Switzerland and Scotland all participated in the Renaissance, but their local renaissances were very far from carbon copies of one another. The point seems obvious as soon as it is made. All the same, it is hard to find many studies which take it seriously, or make it a starting-point for research.[1]

In 1981, a volume of essays was published by Cambridge University Press under the arresting title, *The Enlightenment in National Context*. The editors of that volume, Roy Porter and Mikuláš Teich, criticized the approach to the Enlightenment as a system of 'socially disembodied ideas', noted that 'comparatively little has been written about its geographical, social and political *location*', and offered their readers thirteen national case-studies, 'ranging from England to Bohemia, from Russia to America, from Italy to Sweden'. The thirteen essays presented the different national enlightenments as adaptations to local circumstances or even new creations, rather than as mere mechanical copies of a model made in France.

It is obvious that the Enlightenment is not the only great cultural movement which can and should be considered in this way, paying attention to all its regional varieties. If it is misleading to see the Enlightenment as a purely

French product, it is equally wrong to see the Reformation as solely German or the Renaissance as entirely Italian. In order to be intelligible, these movements too need to be located in a variety of geographical, political and social contexts.

On the other hand, what might be called the 'national context' model itself requires adaptation if it is to be diffused more widely and employed in situations for which it was not originally designed. The Renaissance did not spread in exactly the same manner as the Enlightenment. For example, the system of communications was not the same in the two periods. The journals which played such an important part in the diffusion of 'enlightened' attitudes did not yet exist in the fifteenth and sixteenth centuries. Consequently the time-lag between the development of new ideas or practices in the centre of the movement and their adoption on the periphery was greater in the sixteenth century than in the eighteenth.

Again, in social and political structure (to say nothing of mentalities), the Europe of the Renaissance differed in important respects from the Europe of the Enlightenment. The sense of national identity, for instance, was weaker in the sixteenth century. National consciousness was also expressed in different ways and took different forms from those which it assumed in the eighteenth century. The purpose of this introduction is to reflect a little further on these two problems, the problem of reception and the problem of the nation.

The problem of reception

Traditional accounts of the European Renaissance sometimes discuss what they call its 'reception' outside Italy, a term which seems to have been coined on the analogy of the 'reception' of Roman law in Germany and elsewhere.[2] The term may suggest that non-Italians were passive, mere 'receivers' of cultural goods from abroad, while Italians, on the other hand, were always active and creative. If it is understood in this way, the term 'reception' is extremely misleading, in three ways.

In the first place, the conventional binary opposition between Italy and the rest ignores the obvious fact that Italy was not culturally homogeneous, that the Renaissance took different forms in Florence, Venice, Rome, Naples and so on, and that these differences need to be located in their own geographical, social and political contexts. This point will be developed in detail below in the chapters by Robert Black, Nicholas Davidson and Richard MacKenney, so there is little need to dwell on it here.[3]

In the second place, the sharp division between a creative Italy and a passive 'North' ignores a good deal of evidence about the movement of cultural 'goods' in the reverse direction. Certain Flemish painters, such as Jan van Eyck and Rogier van der Weyden, were much appreciated in fifteenth-century

Italy; indeed, the technique of painting in oils on canvas was one which the Italians learned from the Netherlands.[4] The italianised name 'Giambologna' hides the fact that one of the greatest sculptors active in sixteenth-century Italy came from Douai. Among the most famous musician-composers in Renaissance Italy were northerners such as Josquin des Près, Heinrich Isaak and Adriaan Willaert.

Even the development of humanism took place outside as well as inside Italy, in Avignon for example, a papal city but far from the Papal States.[5] Contemporary translations into Italian suggest that the literature and ideas of the Spanish Renaissance in particular received a warm welcome in Italy. Among the most familar examples of this interest in Spanish culture are the play (or dramatic romance) known as the *Celestina* (translated into Italian in 1506) the neo-stoic moral treatise *The Dial of Princes* (1543) and the picaresque novel *Lazarillo de Tormes* (1622).

Most important of all, the reception of the Italian Renaissance outside Italy involved adaptation to local circumstances. The messages which Italian artists and writers sent were not always or exactly the messages which the foreign audiences received. The changes, whether conscious or unconscious, may be regarded as a kind of creative misunderstanding, or better, as a process of appropriation, adaptation or cultural translation. The process is common enough, and it has recently attracted the attention of a number of cultural theorists, in France, Germany, the United States and elsewhere, two groups in particular.

The first group, led by H.R. Jauss, views literature from the point of view of the consumer rather than the producer. It is concerned with the ways in which readers perceive texts, their 'horizons of expectation' and their responses.[6] Some members of this group would argue that the 'real' meaning of texts is constructed by these responses, not by the so-called authors. Whether this is the case or not, 'reception theory', as it is often called, is extremely relevant to the history of the reception of the Renaissance.

The second group, associated with the late Michel De Certeau and others, is concerned not only with texts but with a wide range of artifacts and performances, but once again stresses the creativity of audiences and spectators. According to De Certeau, consumption is itself a form of production.[7] Consumption may also be regarded as a symbolic act, in the sense that consumers define their identity by the objects they acquire and the ways in which they use them. This approach to the 'appropriation' and assimilation of objects has inspired a number of anthropologists and also some historians, notably Roger Chartier in his work on the history of the book in the seventeenth and eighteenth centuries.[8]

It remains to be seen how far this approach will illuminate neglected aspects of the Renaissance, for example by examining the ways in which different social groups in different parts of Europe defined themselves by their attitude to the new cultural products, whether they welcomed or rejected them. To complicate the issue, the historian of the Renaissance has to deal not only with responses to Italy, but also to Italian responses to and transformations of classical culture. The importance of mediators was particularly great on the periphery of Europe. In Scandinavia, for example, a number of architects and sculptors from the Netherlands were at work, so that the influence of classical antiquity was doubly filtered before reaching the Swedes. Local responses to the Renaissance varied with the dominant religion – Protestants were generally more suspicious than Catholics of ancient Rome and modern Italy – and even with the climate – since Italian architecture with its open loggias and its lack of chimneys was better suited to the south of Europe than to the north.

A survey of the reception of the Italian Renaissance needs to discriminate not only between regions but between media and genres as well. Humanism was a more thoroughly international movement than the arts, based on a consensus about the importance of recovering and imitating the classics of ancient Greece and, more especially, ancient Rome. Compared to this basic consensus the differences between the so-called French and Italian methods of editing texts were relatively unimportant.[9] Again, Latin literature, modern as well as ancient, the lyrics of Pontano for example, or the historical narrative of Leonardo Bruni, was relatively easy to imitate. Print made the texts accessible, and they could be followed as closely as later poets and historians wanted.

Drama, on the other hand, is a collaborative art, and even if a French playwright decided to imitate Ariosto (say), local acting traditions might produce a rather different effect. A similar point might be made about architecture. Although the treatises or pattern-books of Serlio and Palladio made the plans and elevations of Italian palaces and churches accessible all over Europe, most patrons had to rely on local materials and on local craftsmen, trained in rather different traditions, for the execution of the designs. In central Europe, for example, Renaissance decorations, such as obelisks, might be added to traditional medieval gables.

The reception of the Italian Renaissance abroad is therefore a proper subject for comparative history, provided the historian attends to differences as well as similarities and discriminates between regions and media. A good starting-point for such a comparative investigation might well be the enthusiasm for Italy and things Italian expressed by artists, intellectuals and members of the upper classes in the fifteenth and sixteenth centuries. This enthusiasm was not a matter of rhetoric alone; a good many Europeans expressed their preferences with their feet, by visiting Italy, generally to study. The scholars who did so add up to a long and impressive list, including the

Spaniard Antonio de Nebrija, Netherlanders such as Rudolf Agricola and Erasmus, Germans such as Johann Reuchlin and Conrad Celtis, Frenchmen such as Jacques Lefèvre d'Etaples and Guillaume Budé, Rabelais and Montaigne, Englishmen such as Linacre, Grocyn and Colet.

A substantial number of artists also visited Italy. Jean Fouquet is known to have lived in Rome, Justus of Ghent in Urbino. Dürer visited Venice and Bologna. The graffiti on the walls of a famous Roman ruin, the 'Golden House' of Nero, include the names of foreign artists such as Maarten van Heemskerck, Frans Floris, Hendrik Goltzius, Karel van Mander and Bartolomeus Spranger.[10] Other artists who are known to have spent some time in Italy are Hans Holbein, Jan Scorel, Pieter Brueghel, and the architects Philibert de l'Orme, Jacques Androuet de Cerceau, John Shute and Inigo Jones.

As for Italian artists, they were in demand almost all over Europe. Torrigiani and Zuccaro worked in England, Masolino in Hungary, Luca Cambiaso and Pellegrino Tibaldi in Spain, Jacopo Sansovino in Portugal, Arcimboldo in Prague, Morando and others in Poland. The demand seems to have been greatest in France, more especially at the French court, which employed (among others) Leonardo da Vinci, Rosso, Primaticcio, Cellini, Niccolo dell'Abbate and Sebastiano Serlio. Italian craftsmen were engaged to work on building sites from Munich to Zamosć. Italian actors performed at the courts of France, Spain, Poland and elsewhere.

From the point of view of the reception of the Renaissance, what matters is not so much the number of cultural exchanges of this kind as their significance. We therefore need to study the ways in which foreigners perceived Italian culture. The surviving documents do at least allow a few glimpses of the situation. Maarten van Heemskerck's Roman sketchbook has survived, allowing us to identify the buildings which most interested him, including medieval–Renaissance structures like old St Peter's as well as classical ruins. Dürer's journal has also survived and records the artist's admiration for his Venetian colleague Giovanni Bellini.[11] Montaigne's journal of his visit to Italy shows little sign of interest in Renaissance art, but considerable evidence of enthusiasm for Italian literature, including prose as well as the poetry of Ariosto and Tasso.

On the other side, Cellini's autobiography, even after we discount its boasting and exaggerations, remains valuable testimony of contemporary enthusiasm for Italian culture at the court of Francis I. We can also follow the migration of works of art, the interest in Italian painting shown, for example, by Philip II (whose correspondence with Titian survives) or Francis I (who owned works by Leonardo and Raphael).

In an essay concerned with the process of reception, the obvious strategy is to concentrate on the periphery of Europe, the regions where what might be called the 'cultural distance' from Italy was greatest, in order to see the processes of incorporation and assimilation at work more clearly than is possible elsewhere.

A few extreme cases may be worth a brief mention, partly to show how wide was the diffusion of the Italian Renaissance in the fifteenth and sixteenth centuries. Renaissance art was not unknown in the Ottoman Empire, where Mehmet II, the conqueror of Constantinople, invited Gentile Bellini to his court, while the great sixteenth-century architect Sinan Bey is said to have studied in Venice.[12] It was known in the Americas, notably in Mexico and Peru, as the churches of the colonial period testify to this day.[13] The architect Aristotele Fioravanti of Bologna worked in Muscovy, where the tsar, Ivan III, asked him to design a new cathedral – along the lines of the twelfth-century cathedral at Vladimir. Ivan IV, 'the Terrible', has been presented as a 'Renaissance prince', in whose time copies of works by Perugino were brought to Moscow and an official printing house founded.[14] A similar claim to being a Renaissance prince has also been made for an Irish nobleman, Manus O'Donnell, who was, among other things, a magnificent patron, a politician, a poet and a biographer aware of the importance of primary sources.[15] However, the evidence for the reception of the Italian Renaissance, humanism in particular, is much richer for Scotland than it is for Ireland.[16]

Scandinavia was also on the periphery of the Renaissance. There seems little to say in this respect about Finland, Norway or indeed Iceland, where it was only after the Reformation that a few theology students at the university of Copenhagen discovered the existence of humanism.[17] In the case of Denmark and Sweden, however, the evidence is considerably richer.

Two sixteenth-century kings of Sweden, Erik XIV and John III, have a good claim to be regarded as Renaissance princes. Erik XIV (reigned 1560–9) knew Italian, and he was apparently familiar with the work of Machiavelli and Castiglioni (a French translation of The Courtier was presented to the king by a visiting English merchant).[18] Erik was able to draw and to play the lute. As for his successor John III (1569–92), his enthusiasm for architecture, nourished by a reading of Serlio, is evident both in his correspondence and in a cluster of buildings erected during his reign. These buildings, some designed by a Milanese family of architects known in Sweden as the Pahrs, include castles at Vadstena and Svartsjö (the latter inspired by the pentagonal Farnese fortress of Caprarola). The style of these buildings was a blend, or at least a mixture, of Renaissance and Gothic, of Italian patterns and Swedish traditions. John III's tomb in Uppsala cathedral, the work of the Netherlander Willem van der Blocke, is a work of the northern Renaissance with reminiscences of Italy in general and more particularly of the Sansovino tombs in the church of Santa Maria del Popolo in Rome.[19]

In Denmark too there was royal interest in the Renaissance. Christian II

(1513–23) commissioned paintings from leading northern artists, notably Jan Mabuse, Quentin Massys and Albrecht Dürer, and he promoted the translation of a book on politics which may well have been by Machiavelli.[20] However, it is surely Christian IV (1588–1648) who has the strongest claim to be regarded as the Danish Renaissance prince for his munificent patronage of the arts. In his early years the king was advised by the nobleman Henrik Rantzau, who erected a pyramid on his Holstein estate in memory of Christian's father Frederick II, and corresponded with the young king about Italian treatises on architecture. Christian IV was an enthusiastic collector of paintings, such as the *Fall of the Titans* by the Dutch Mannerist Cornelis van Haarlem. He commissioned a splendid fountain, representing Neptune, from the sculptor Adriaen de Vries (a Netherlander who lived at the court of Rudolf II in Prague).[21]

Christian's name is most closely associated with the construction or reconstruction of three splendid castle-palaces in or near Copenhagen, Frederiksborg, Rosenborg, and Kronborg. Like Johan III of Sweden, Christian owned a copy of Serlio, but his palaces did not follow Serlio's model. They were built of red brick, not stone, in a northern style inspired by a French pattern-book (the *Livre d'Architecture* by Jacques Androuet du Cerceau), but executed by Netherlanders and Danes.[22]

It is rather more controversial to suggest that Spain and Portugal were on the periphery of the Renaissance, but they were rather remote from Italy, and in architecture in particular, the synthesis, or at least the mixture of Italian Renaissance motifs with local traditions, is particularly visible. In the case of Spain, the result is known as 'plateresque', because of its apparent resemblance to the work of silversmiths, or *mudéjar*, because many projects, from Alcalà to Seville, were executed by Moorish craftsmen accustomed to the architectural traditions of the world of Islam, notably to the richness of non-figurative decoration.[23]

In the case of Portugal, the distinctive architecture of the Renaissance is called 'Manueline' after King Manoel I, who reigned from 1495 to 1521. It owes something to local Moorish traditions and something to the example of Spain, but these elements are fused to form a highly distinctive style. The rich decorative vocabulary of the Manueline style, employed, for example, in the Torre de Belem, just outside Lisbon, and in the neighbouring Jeronymite monastery, includes stone ropes, sails, coral and seaweed, maritime references appropriate to the age of the making of the Portuguese seaborne empire.[24]

These examples suggest that in the case of the visual arts, at least, there is a case for dividing Renaissance Europe into zones. The Iberian peninsula, with its Muslim traditions, would be one. East-central Europe would be another (with Russia on its periphery). A third zone might centre on the German- and

Dutch-speaking part of Europe, with Scandinavia (and possibly Britain) on its edge. In the case of humanism, on the other hand, we need to distinguish between form and content. It has already been suggested that the humanist skills and techniques were relatively uniform all over Europe. On the other hand, humanist researches into the past supported (if they did not construct) local identities, civic, national and imperial.

The problem of the nation

What has the Renaissance to do with the nation? To what extent, and in what sense of the term, did the nation exist in fifteenth- or sixteenth-century Europe? These problems will recur throughout the volume and different contributors will resolve them in different ways. All the same, some preliminary reflections on the topic may have their use.

The international movement of Italophilia has already been mentioned. The Italian language was fashionable, at court for example, as well as Italian literature and art. Italophilia was matched, however, by an international movement of Italophobia, evident from England to Poland.[25] Anti-Italian proverbs were in circulation, such as 'Inglese italianato è diavolo incarnato' ('the Italianate Englishman is the devil incarnate'), modified in Germany to 'Tedesco italianato. . .'[26]

These anti-Italian sentiments were fuelled by the visibility of Italians at certain courts, notably in the France of Catherine de'Medici, but they also reveal a backlash against the Renaissance, perceived by some as the mere 'aping' of foreign ways. It was said, for example, that Englishmen 'corrupt their natural manners (by their climate created perfect)' in order 'to italianate the course of their newe ledde life'.[27] The French humanist printer Henri Estienne was a particularly eloquent critic of what he was the first to call the *italianisation* of the French language and culture, mocking affected people who say 'à bastanse' (from 'abbastanza') when they should say 'assez', or 'la strade' (la strada') when they should say 'la rue').[28] Machiavelli is an obvious example of an Italian who was viewed by many non-Italians as a stereotypical villain, stepping on stage in Marlowe's *Jew of Malta* to declare that 'I hold religion but a childish toy/And think there is no sin but ignorance.' Castiglione was associated with affectation, despite the fact that this form of behaviour is explicitly condemned in his *Courtier*. Ladies who followed Italian fashions were said to look like 'the courtesans of Venice'.[29]

Italophobia was stronger among Protestants such as Estienne and Ascham than among Catholics, and it is clear that the Renaissance was contaminated by association with Rome and the papacy. Like other forms of xenophobia, however, the denunciation of things Italian also reveals something about the social identity of the denouncers. The English humanists Ascham and Cheke were enthusiastic for their native vernacular, and Cheke argued that 'our own tongue should be written clean and pure, unmixt and unmangled with borrowing of other tongues'.[30] The positive side of Estienne's hostility to italianisation, for example, was his passion for his native language, revealed in his treatise on the primacy of French, written he claimed, in defence of 'the honour of his nation' ('l'honneur de sa nation') and arguing that the French language had no less gravity and grace than Italian and that it was 'more capable of eloquence or capable of more eloquence' than other languages.[31]

In a similar way, Cristóbal de Castillejo's criticism of Spanish poets such as Garcilaso for writing in Italian metres was associated with a defence of the traditional Spanish coplas and villancicos, just as Du Bellay's Défense et illustration de la langue française was associated with a defence of traditional ballades and rondeaux.[32] Humanists outside Italy did not always denounce the Middle Ages; they sometimes praised their native medieval traditions.

It was actually in the Renaissance that the Middle Ages became a subject for serious historical research, more especially the medieval traditions of the writer's own community. Vasari's famous biographies of artists, first published in 1550, go back as far as Cimabue in thirteenth-century Florence. The Recherches de la France by the lawyer Etienne Pasquier discuss the history of old French and of medieval literature as well as that of legal and political institutions.[33] A discussion of the history of English literature from Chaucer onwards can be found in the treatise attributed to George Puttenham on The Art of English Poesie, published in 1589.[34]

The humanist historians showed particular interest in early medieval history, that of the 'barbarians' who resisted Roman conquest or invaded and settled so many parts of Europe when the Roman Empire began to decline. Vercingetorix, for example, Julius Caesar's opponent in the Gallic wars, was praised in a history published in the 1550s.[35] The importance of Vercingetorix and other barbarians was that they were ancestors. The French claimed descent from the Franks and the Gauls, the English from the Angles and Saxons, the Dutch from the Batavians, the Swedes and Spaniards from the Goths, the Jutes from the Cimbrians, the Poles from the Sarmatians, the Hungarians from the Huns.[36] Many volumes were written in defence of these claims; among them were Jacob Wimpheling's Germania (1501); the History of All the Kings of the Goths and the Swedes by archbishop Johannes Magnus (1554); François Hotman's Franco-Gallia (1573); and Richard Verstegen's Restitution of Decayed Intelligence (1605), which considered the German descent of the English as a matter of 'National Honour'. This concern with a 'romanticised history', as it has been called, seems to have been particularly strong in Sweden in the late sixteenth and early seventeenth centuries, when that country was about to become a great power.[37]

Their interest in their ancestors encouraged Englishmen like archbishop

Matthew Parker to learn Anglo-Saxon, French and German scholars to write admiringly about the Druids, Scandinavians to study the runes and the cult of Odin, the Dutch East India Company to rename Jakarta 'Batavia' when they took the city in 1619, and scholars all over Europe to publish early texts such as the *Germania* of Tacitus, the *History of the Goths* by the sixth-century bishop Jordanes, or the *History of the Kings of the Danes* by Saxo Grammaticus.

Some scholars tried to trace the national ancestry still further back. In the Renaissance as in the Middle Ages, many attempts were made to connect different peoples with the Trojans (and so, via Aeneas, with the Romans). Since the time of the twelfth-century bishop Geoffrey of Monmouth (if not before), the British had claimed descent from Brutus the Trojan. In similar style, from the later Middle Ages onwards, the French claimed descent from Francio the Trojan, the ancestor of the Franks, and the hero of Ronsard's unfinished epic the *Franciade*.[38] The humanist abbot Johannes Trithemius claimed Trojan ancestry for the Saxons, the Bavarians and indeed for the Habsburg family.

Even the Trojans were too recent for some students of origins. In his *History of the Scots* (1526), Hector Boece, for example claimed Egyptian descent for his countrymen, from Scota, the daughter of one of the Pharaohs. Some Germans identified themselves with the descendants of Tuisco, son of Noah. The Portuguese, or Lusitanians, claimed descent from Lusus son of Bacchus, which is why Luis de Camões called his epic poem on the exploits of Vasco da Gama *The Lusiads*. Languages were traced back still further, to the origins of mankind. Some scholars argued that Adam and Eve spoke German in the Garden of Eden, others that they spoke Dutch (in the seventeenth century, a claim would be filed for Swedish).

The myths of eponymous heroes and heroines such as Brutus, Francio and Scota and their Trojan or Egyptian origins were not accepted by everyone. Such humanists as Polydore Vergil and Beatus Rhenanus were sceptical of these claims, which sometimes involved the fabrication of documents. Ronsard's preface to his *Franciade* warned his readers against taking the story literally. However, myths of this kind had a considerable appeal during the Renaissance. What exactly was their significance?

Today, historians often use the term 'myth' as a synonym for inaccurate history. It would, however, be useful to follow the lead of literary critics and social anthropologists and to look at myths (in the broad sense of stories about the past) in rather more positive terms, emphasising their uses for the people who tell them or listen to them. Stories about ancestors play an important role in the creation and maintenance of a sense of identity; who we are depends on what we were, and also on the contrast between us and 'them' which the myths often present in dramatic terms. Myths about the past are also used to justify (or as sociologists say, to 'legitimate') contemporary customs and institutions. In the Renaissance as in the Middle Ages, 'legitimation by descent' was one of the most common and persuasive means of justifying claims of different kinds, including claims to nationhood.

At this point it is necessary to grasp the nettle. Nations are problematic entities, or better, cultural constructions. They have not always existed. What we have to discuss now is whether it is illuminating or simply anachronistic to speak of nations, national consciousness or national identity in fifteenth- and sixteenth-century Europe, or to try to place the Renaissance in national (rather than merely local) context.

The case against the 'national' view of Renaissance Europe may be summarised quite briefly. It states essentially that nationalism is a modern idea, essentially the creation of the age which followed the French and Industrial Revolutions, and depending on the political, social and cultural changes of that period, from the abolition of aristocratic privilege to the rise of the railways, and above all on the centralised, unified, bureaucratic state.[39]

On the other side, there is also a case to be made. We have already seen the term 'national honour' employed by sixteenth-century writers such as Henri Estienne and Richard Verstegen. We have discussed the importance in the Renaissance of myths of national origin, from Portugal to Poland (or more exactly, from the Lusitanians to the Sarmatians). To this might be added the adaptation to different nations of Europe of the Old Testament myth of a Chosen People. In the Middle Ages, the French already claimed to be a Chosen People; in the sixteenth century, the English sometimes viewed themselves as the 'elect nation', while the new Dutch Republic claimed to be the new Israel.[40] A number of national histories were produced in the course of the Renaissance. The Italian humanists Paolo Emilio and Polydore Vergil wrote the histories of France (more exactly, 'of the French') and of England respectively, while Francesco Guicciardini's *History of Italy* wove together the stories of the different states after the French invasion of 1494.[41]

At this point conventional historical tactics suggest that we say that 'the truth is between the two extremes'. It is not easy to identify a middle point between the statement that nations existed during the Renaissance and the counter-statement that they did not. It may be more useful to rephrase the question. The fruitful question to ask is not, Did nations exist during the Renaissance? but, What were the dominant forms of collective identity?

If we examine our own sense of identity, we are likely to find that it is multiple.[42] I would identify myself as English (or as British), as a European, as male, middle-class, a member of the international academic community, and so on. In the sixteenth century, there is also clear evidence of multiple identities. The family component of identity was obviously important, especially for the upper classes; an individual was 'a' Medici, a Guise, a

Mendoza. Nobles identified with their order, craftsmen with their guild or craft. Civic identity was important to many of the inhabitants of Venice, Lyons, Antwerp, Barcelona and so on; indeed, the term *patria* in a sixteenth-century Italian text is more likely to refer to a city-state than to the peninsula. Regional identity also mattered; Ronsard, for example, described himself on the title-page of his verses as an 'Angoumois', in other words an inhabitant of the province of Angoulême. Religious identity was also important. The wars of religion in France were more than a simple conflict between Catholics and Protestants, but recent research has shown the strength of religious identification among ordinary townspeople at that time, expressed in acts of violence against the 'other'.[43]

Our problem, then, is to discover how the nation fitted into this cluster of identities. A first step, we might say that national identity was weaker then than now relative to its competitors, but we have also to take account of different conceptions of the 'nation'. It might be said that this conception was negative rather than positive. Xenophobia was strong, as the examples of anti-Italian sentiment quoted above may have suggested already, but the sense of kinship with the inhabitants of other regions within the same kingdom was weak. National identity was less closely associated than today with the 'state' which was in any case a new concept in the sixteenth century, one which had not had time to take root. Some of the myths of the origin of peoples discussed earlier in this essay refer to groups either smaller or larger than those which (for historical rather than natural reasons) we happen to regard as nations.

On one side there was civic or regional identity. The sixteenth-century cult of the Etruscans, for example, was a prop to the identity of the Tuscans, that is (more or less) the inhabitants of the Grand Duchy of Tuscany, dominated by Florence. The myths of eponymous heroes like Brabo the founder of Brabant or Friso the founder of Friesland hindered rather than helped the formation of a 'national' identity for the seven provinces of the Dutch Republic or the seventeen provinces of the Netherlands taken as a whole. Towns, too, had their myths of origin. The city of Rheims claimed to have been founded by Remus; the city of London, to be a 'new Troy'.

On the other side, we must not forget the importance in the Renaissance of what might be called 'imperial identity'. When the Venetians called themselves 'New Romans' the comparison expressed pride not only in the city but also in its empire, the maritime empire (Crete and Cyprus, for example) as well as the so-called *terraferma* (Padua, Vicenza, Verona and so on).[44] Jacob Wimpheling's treatise *Germania* is focused not so much on Germany as on his native city of Strasbourg and on the Holy Roman Empire. In Spain, too, we can find this combination of a civic with an imperial identity. On one side, Seville, for example, boasted that it was a 'New Rome'.[45] On the other, the supporters of the Castilian language, such as the leading humanist Antonio Nebrija (in a grammar published, appropriately enough in 1492) argued that languages shared the destinies of empires and that Castilian was fated to spread as the Spanish Empire expanded, as Latin had done in the days of Rome.[46]

To sum up. To understand the Renaissance we certainly need to put it into context, to look at its geography as well as the social and political history of the movement. In some instances, however, this local context is regional or imperial rather than national. There was a sense of nationhood – among some social groups at least – in many parts of Europe in the fifteenth and sixteenth centuries. This form of collective identity has a rather complicated relationship to the movement we call the Renaissance. It is hard to say what is cause and what is consequence, what is a help and what is a hindrance. On one side, the widespread fashion for everything Italian and the tendency of humanists to think of themselves as part of an international 'commonwealth of letters' discouraged the sense of nationhood. On the other, the resentment of Italian cultural dominance was sometimes expressed in Renaissance forms, from the patronage of works of art which would surpass their Italian prototypes to the writing of treatises on the noble origins of 'nations' other than the Romans.

NOTES

1 Among the distinguished exceptions are J. Białostocki, *The Art of the Renaissance in Eastern Europe* (London, 1976) and H. Oberman and T. Brady (eds.), *Iter Italicum* (Leiden, 1975); E.Rosenthal, 'The diffusion of the Italian Renaissance style in western European architecture', *Sixteenth-Century Journal* (1978). A colloquium on 'die Renaissance im Blick der Nationen Europas' took place at Wolfenbüttel in 1987, organised by the art historian Prof. G. Kaufmann. On humanism, see A. Rabil Jr (ed.), *Renaissance Humanism, vol. II: Humanism beyond Italy* (Philadelphia, Pa., 1988).

2 I have discussed this problem recently elsewhere in *The Renaissance* (London, 1987), ch. 3, and in 'Humanism outside Italy' in A. Goodman and A. Mackay (eds.), *Renaissance Humanism* (London, 1990). In the pages which follow I have tried to use different examples.

3 On Naples, see J. Bentley, *Politics and Culture in Renaissance Naples* (Princeton, N.J., 1987).

4 Classic studies of this phenomenon are A. Warburg, 'Flandrische Kunst' (1902) and 'Scambi' (1905) in his *Gesammelte Schriften* (Leipzig and Berlin, 1932).

5 The importance of Avignon for humanism has been emphasised by F. Simone, *The French Renaissance: Medieval Tradition and Italian Influences in Shaping the Renaissance in France*, trans. M. Hall (London, 1969).

6 H.R. Jauss, *Literaturgeschichte als Provokation* (1974: English trans. *Toward an Aesthetic of Reception* (Minneapolis, Minn., 1982). On the movement as a whole, R. Holub, *Reception Theory* (London, 1984).

7 M. De Certeau, *L'Invention du quotidien* (Paris, 1980).

8 A. Appadurai (ed.), *The Social Life of Things* (Cambridge, 1986); R. Chartier, *Lectures et lecteurs dans la France de l'ancien regime* (1987; English trans., *The Cultural Uses of Print in Early Modern France*, Princeton 1987).

9 A. Grafton, *Joseph Scaliger*, vol. 1 (Oxford, 1983), esp. chs. 2, 3.

10 N. Decos, *La Découverte de la Domus aurea et la formation des grotesques à la Renaissance* (London and Leiden, 1969), 141.

11 A. Dürer, *Nachlass* (Halle, 1893).

12 F. Babinger, *Mehmet der Eroberer und seine Zeit* (Munich, 1953).

13 V. Fraser, 'Architecture and imperialism in sixteenth-century Spanish America', *Art History* 9 (1986), 325–35, discusses the relation between the form of the buildings and the political context of conquest and domination.

14 M. Cherniavsky, 'Ivan the Terrible as a Renaissance Prince', *Slavic Review* 27 (1968), 195–211 (which deals with general similarities, Italian contacts, and the concept of *terribilità*); J.H. Billington, *The Icon and the Axe* (New York, 1966), 95.

15 B. Bradshaw, 'Manus the Magnificent: O'Donnell as a Renaissance prince', *Studies in Irish History presented to R. Dudley Edwards*, ed. A. Cosgrove and D. McCartney (Dublin, 1979), 15–37.

16 J. Durkan, 'The beginning of humanism in Scotland', *Innes Review* 4 (1953), 5–24; D. Hay, 'Scotland and the Italian Renaissance' (1983 rpt in his *Renaissance Essays*, London 1988, ch. 15).

17 K. Hastrup, *Nature and Policy in Iceland 1400–1800* (Oxford, 1990).

18 I. Andersson, *Erik XIV* (3rd edn, Stockholm 1948), 219f.

19 A. Hahr, *Studien i Johan IIIs Renässans I. Arkitektfamilie Pahr* (Uppsala and Leipzig, 1907); *idem, Studier i Nordisk Renässanskonst* (Uppsala and Leipzig, 1913).

20 Andersson, *Erik XIV*, 220

21 Details in the exhibition catalogue *Christian IV and Europe* (Copenhagen, 1988), 342f.

22 On Serlio and Androuet, J.A. Skovgaard, *A King's Architecture: Christian IV and his Buildings* (London, 1973), 65.

23 G. Kubler and M. Soria, *Art and Architecture in Spain and Portugal* (Harmondsworth, 1959), 2ff.

24 *Ibid.*, 101f.

25 On Poland, H. Barycz, 'Italofilia e italofobia nella Polonia del '500 e '600', in *Italia, Venezia e Polonia tra umanesimo e rinascimento*, ed. M. Brahmer (Wrocław, 1967), 142–58. See also A. Mączak's chapter below, pp. 180–96.

26 The English version is cited by Roger Ascham (among others), the German, by Barthlomeus Sastrow.

27 W. Rankins, *The English Ape* (London, 1588), 3.

28 H. Estienne, *Deux dialogues* (1578) ed. P.M. Smith (Geneva, 1980), 35–6, 92.

29 Rankins, *English Ape*, 23

30 J. Cheke's letter is printed in T. Hoby's translation of Castiglione's *Courtier* (London, 1561).

31 H. Estienne, *Précellence de la langue française* (1579), ed. E. Huguet (Paris, 1896), 1–2, 29, 57f.

32 C. de Castillejo, 'Reprensión contra las poetas españoles que escriben en verso italiano', in *Obras*, ed. J. Dominguez Bordona, vol. II (Madrid, 1927), 226–36.

33 E. Pasquier, *Recherches de la France* (Paris, 1560); later editions contain much new material. Pasquier moved in the same circle as the poets of the Pléiade. Cf. D. Kelley, below p. 133.

34 G. Puttenham, *The Art of English Poesie* (London, 1589).

35 R. Ceneau, *Gallica historia* (Paris, 1557).

36 There is a considerable secondary literature on this aspect of the history, but no synthesis. See especially F. Borchardt, *German Antiquity in Renaissance Myth* (Baltimore, Md., and London, 1971); C.-G. Dubois, *Celtes et Gaulois au 16e siècle* (Paris 1972); C. Beaune, *Naissance de la nation France* (Paris, 1985); K. Johannesson, *Gotisk Renässans* (Stockholm, 1982).

37 J. Nordström, *De Yverbornes Ö* (Stockholm, 1934), especially 55f., 'Götisk Historieromantik och Stormakstidens Anda'.

38 Beaune, *Naissance*.

39 See the brilliant and controversial essays by B. Anderson, *Imagined Communities* (London, 1983), and E. Gellner, *Nations and Nationalism* (Oxford, 1983). On the sixteenth and seventeenth centuries, the best discussion I know is to be found in the seven essays in *National Consciousness, History and Political Culture in Early Modern Europe*, ed. O. Ranum (Baltimore, Md., 1975).

40 J. Strayer, 'France: the Holy Land, the Chosen People, and the Most Christian King' in *Action and Conviction in Early Modern Europe*, ed. T. Rabb and J. Siegel (Princeton, 1969), 3–16; W. Haller, *The Elect Nation* (London, 1963); H. van de Waal, *Drie eeuwen vaderlandsche geschieduitbeelding* (The Hague, 1952), pp. 22f; G. Groenhuis, 'Calvinism and national consciousness: the Dutch Republic as the New Israel' in *Britain and the Netherlands*, vol. VII, ed. A.C. Duke and C.A. Tamse (The Hague, 1981), 118–33; S. Schama, *The Embarrassment of Riches* (London, 1987), esp. ch. 2, 'Patriotic Scripture'.

41 P. Emilio, *De rebus gestis Francorum* (Paris, 1517); P. Vergil, *Anglica Historia* (written 1513); F. Guicciardini, *Storia d'Italia* (posthumous, Florence, 1561–4).

42 For a development of this argument, see P. Burke, *Language and Identity in Early Modern Italy* (Århus, 1989).

43 N.Z. Davis, 'The Rites of Violence' (1973), rpt in her *Society and Culture in Early Modern France* (London, 1975), ch. 6.

44 D.S. Chambers, *The Imperial Age of Venice* (London, 1970), 12–30; M. Tafuri (ed.), *Renovatio Urbis: Venezia nell'età di Andrea Gritti* (Rome, 1984); and below, pp. 53–67.

45 V. Lleó Cañal, *Nueva Roma* (Seville, 1979).

46 A. de Nebrija, *Gramatica* (1492), ed. I. González-Liubera (Oxford, 1926), 3, 6.

꙰

TWO

FLORENCE

ROBERT BLACK

The importance of Florence

Unlike Rome itself, Florence had no unique connection with classical antiquity. Its classical remains or pseudo-remains, such as the Baptistry; its Roman foundation, whether under the Republic or the Caesars; its spurious famous citizens in antiquity, such as Claudian – these kinds of claims were easily matched or surpassed by many other Italian cities. In the early phases of the Renaissance classical revival – the late thirteenth- and early fourteenth-century world of Niccolò Pisano, Lovato Lovati, Albertino Mussato, Geri d'Arezzo and Benzo d'Alessandria – Florence had a relatively minor role,[1] and Florence and the Florentines were of little interest to Petrarch. Petrarch's great contemporary, Boccaccio, was Florence's first citizen to achieve prominence in the revival of classical learning, but it was only with the next generation, the group of scholars and humanists who gathered round the great chancellor, Coluccio Salutati (d. 1406), that Florence took the lead in the revival of antiquity – a position not to be relinquished until the sixteenth century.

In the years between 1375 and 1550, Florence was one among many contributors to the cultural life of Italy. If the Renaissance, however, is taken to mean not the sum total of Italian culture but the attempt to turn away from the recent medieval past and return to the ways of ancient Rome and Greece, then Florence's particular contribution was little short of astounding. The most striking examples of this movement to revive antiquity in Renaissance Florence are still visible today. Brunelleschi's loggia for the Foundling Hospital, the interiors of the churches of San Lorenzo and Santo Spirito, and the chapter house for the church and convent of Santa Croce (now usually known as the Pazzi Chapel) are the first landmarks of Renaissance architecture. If Brunelleschi's visual sources were not so much actual ancient Roman buildings as the many surviving examples of Tuscan Romanesque,[2] nevertheless he consciously rejected the Gothic style still prevailing in early fifteenth-century Italy, substituting what he and his contemporaries believed was the antique manner. His attempt to build a free-standing dome for the Florentine cathedral, inspired by classical precedents, led to innovations of engineering without direct classical models, but what was entirely classical was the use throughout his work of a simple system of arithmetic proportions, taken from Vitruvius. In this, as in so many other respects, he pointed the way for future Renaissance architects.

In painting, too, Florence was the cradle of the Renaissance, and Brunelleschi, although not a painter, was a decisive influence. His own studies of Vitruvian architectural theory and visual experiments led to the invention of line-point perspective – again an innovation without classical precedent but inspired by the desire to bring the mathematical ordering of space – which was the fundamental principle of classical architecture – to a flat surface. The first painter known to have adopted this system was another Florentine, Masaccio, whose frescoes in the churches of Santa Maria Novella and especially of the Carmine became a school for future Renaissance painters. From Masaccio's example they could not only learn to give the precision of classical architecture to the space they were depicting, but also gain skills of lighting and shading, about which hitherto there had been only the testimony of ancient authors, such as the elder Pliny. In Masaccio's work, the courtly graces of the international gothic style, so much the vogue in early fifteenth-century Italy, were rejected in favour of classical *gravitas*; here the direct copying of classical models blended effortlessly with the revival of an earlier style of monumental Florentine painting established by Giotto and his immediate followers, but allowed to lapse in the second half of the fourteenth century.

Florentine sculpture was equally influenced by the spatial studies of Brunelleschi, as is clear in the work of another founding father of the Renaissance, Lorenzo Ghiberti. His bronze relief carvings for the Florentine Baptistry show the growing use of perspective to create the illusion of depth in an incredibly difficult medium. Ghiberti never fully turned his back on the felicities of the international gothic, but his statues for the niches of Orsanmichele in Florence were an important milestone on the road to re-establishing the monumental style of classical sculpture. Ghiberti's achievement in relief carving was equalled by his younger compatriot, Donatello, who, however, left Ghiberti far behind in the other sculptural genres. Donatello was the first not only to recapture a full sense of classical *gravitas* in his statues, but also to re-establish the classical art of large-scale bronze casting. Donatello was the first artist since antiquity to make a serious study of anatomy; his new-found knowledge of the human body was put to use not only in a series of free-standing sculptures, a practice which had waned since antiquity, but also in the representation of the nude, another lost classical art which Donatello similarly revived.

The immeasurable influence of the Florentines on the future development of the visual arts in the Renaissance is widely known, but their decisive influence on the course of Renaissance letters and thought deserves equal notice. In the field of handwriting, for example, it was in Florence that Gothic script, with its angular crowding of letters, was rejected in favour of a more rounded and generously spaced form of lettering, known as humanist miniscule, which has become the basis of modern Roman printed lettering. Like many of Brunelleschi's architectural innovations, this new script was not actually based on ancient models, but on pre-Gothic examples; nevertheless, it still represented a conscious attempt to reject the immediate medieval past in favour of what was thought to be a return to antiquity. Despite its post-antique origins, Florentine humanist script, like early Florentine Renaissance architectural style, was of decisive influence for the future, setting the trend for later Renaissance developments in writing and printing.[3]

In the revival of the Latin language during the Renaissance, the first steps were taken outside Florence; it was the pre-humanists in such centres as Padua, Arezzo, Bologna and Verona who began to reject medieval vocabulary and orthography, seeking instead the purer forms of classical authors such as Virgil and Cicero. This renovation of the Latin language was carried further in the fourteenth century by Petrarch, again outside Florence, and Florentines did not become prominent in the revival of latinity until the early fifteenth century, when a group of scholars began advocating a type of language which was immediately recognisable as different from medieval Latin. These humanists – Poggio Bracciolini, Niccolò Niccoli and, at first, Leonardo Bruni – formed a circle of followers round the old chancellor of Florence, Salutati; although inspired by his vast classical learning, this young avant-garde rejected his latinity, formed as it had been by the older generation of Petrarch and Boccaccio, in favour of more exclusively classical vocabulary, spelling and grammar.[4] Especially important was their attempt to abandon medieval syntax in subordinate clauses of purpose and result, as well as in reported speech, and to revive classical diphthongs, almost entirely abandoned in the Middle Ages. This latter innovation was probably connected with the presence in Florence at the turn of the fifteenth century of a new teacher, the Greek, Manuel Chrysoloras, who criticised contemporary Latin spelling on the basis of comparison with Greek, in which the use of diphthongs had never fallen into abeyance.[5] The attempt to revive diphthongs had an importance which far transcended merely improved Latin orthography; indeed, it was an obvious and prominent sign of one-upmanship, of the distance betweeen the avant-garde and their forerunners, of the superiority of the new classicism, which helped to define the identity of the movement to revive antiquity and to establish Florence as the capital of the Renaissance and the trend-setter for the rest of the fifteenth century.[6]

Florence gave the first real impetus to another of the most significant developments of Italian Renaissance learning – the revival of the study of Greek in the West. Greek had not been a feature of the medieval school or university curriculum and hence had become almost a dead language in the Latin West during the Middle Ages. There had been a number of false starts in its revival during the fourteenth century, and it was only Salutati's scholarly group in Florence at the very end of the fourteenth century who provided a solid base for the development of Greek studies. The key figure again was Chrysoloras, who taught Greek first in Florence and then elsewhere in Italy.[7] Among his pupils, who included almost all the principal figures of the first Greek revival in Italy, was Leonardo Bruni, the central protagonist of early fifteenth-century Florentine humanism. Not only did Bruni's translations of Aristotle's *Politics* and *Ethics* displace the standard medieval Latin versions by William of Moerbeke to become great Renaissance best-sellers; he also established a new style of humanist translation, in which the medieval method of word-for-word rendering was replaced by an attempt to provide the overall meaning of the text in standard, Ciceronian Latin.[8]

Bruni's importance as a pioneer of the Renaissance went beyond his work as a translator, significant though that was. As an historian, he was the first to revive the Livian model of the history of a city-state with his *History of the Florentine People*. This work set the precedent for innumerable humanist civic histories. Previous medieval and early humanist histories had either retained medieval chronicle form, albeit sometimes incorporating classical elements on the model of Sallust, or had been cast in the form of biographies of famous men or of epic poems. It was Bruni who first undertook a fully classicised historical narrative: a classical genre, the history of a city-state, was given a fully Livian form, with an introductory book on the origins and early history of the city followed by a detailed account of internal and external events, organised as a year-to-year narrative and grouped into books.[9] Moreover, Bruni initiated the great revival of the Ciceronian dialogue in Renaissance literature. In the Middle Ages the dialogue form had been a rarity, and even in the hands of Petrarch, it had remained an abstract form, lacking the realistic setting and spontaneous atmosphere of Cicero's dialogues. Bruni's *Dialogues to Pietro Paolo Vergerio of Istria* not only had all the Ciceronian features of genuine conversation, but even imitated Cicero's *De oratore* in organisation, with the second dialogue featuring the main speaker's recanting a line of argument that he had vigorously defended on the previous day.[10] The Ciceronian dialogue was to become one of the most characteristic forms of Renaissance literature, and, like so much else, its revival began in early fifteenth-century Florence.[11]

Bruni's original contribution to the history of political ideas has sometimes been exaggerated. It was once argued that he and his followers initiated the republican strain of thought which became a feature of some – though by no means all – Renaissance political thought.[12] However, the doctrine that republics are superior to monarchies was first revived in the political theory of the Italian city-states during the thirteenth and early fourteenth centuries, to be developed further in the Florentine chancery under Salutati in the last quarter of the Trecento.[13] The classical texts at the disposal of medieval civic republicans had been limited largely to Aristotle's *Politics* and Cicero's *De officiis*; Salutati had begun to enlarge the Ciceronian armoury and it was Bruni's contribution further to exploit the Roman republican tradition. Similarly, Bruni's commitment to the merits of the active over the contemplative life can be overstated. It is true that he went further than many of his predecessors in championing the active life of the citizen, but like previous thinkers he did not see the question in black and white terms, as is clear from one of his most significant assessments of the problem, the *Introduction to Moral Doctrine*, where he states: 'Each of these ways of life has its own qualities worthy of praise and commendation.'[14] This kind of qualified judgement has its source in the tenth book of Aristotle's *Nicomachean Ethics*, an analysis which Bruni approached even more closely at the end of his life in a letter to the Venetian humanist Lauro Quirini of 1441;[15] Bruni's vacillations and qualifications echo the complex analysis of the problem found in the writings of his mentor, Salutati, as well as in the thought of Aquinas, who actually went very far in justifying the active life. Bruni has claim to some originality in the energy with which he sometimes puts the arguments for the active life, but the overall pattern of his political thought on this question is a development of Aristotelian thinking, along the lines already established by St Thomas and Salutati.[16]

Florence witnessed precocious advances in other fields of Renaissance learning and thought, such as ecclesiology,[17] legal scholarship[18] and historiographical theory,[19] but it was inevitable that with the spread of the Renaissance throughout Italy in the fifteenth century other centres would take the lead in many fields of Renaissance studies; thus Rome, once again the residence of the popes after 1443, became the undisputed capital of Latin philology, as well as of Greek scholarship and translation, not to mention antiquarian and medieval historical studies, in the mid-fifteenth century. Similarly, Milan, Ferrara, Mantua, Naples and Venice established themselves as great cultural centres of the Renaissance. However, under the patronage of the Medici in the second half of the century Florence regained some of the lost ground. In the field of Latin philology, Poliziano reached new heights of professionalism and scholarly precision and originality, setting a standard unequalled until the emergence of the great series of non-Italian philologists in the sixteenth century;[20] Florence was also the home of the great revival of Platonic philosophy and scholarship, led by Marsilio Ficino and his followers, loosely known as the Platonic Academy.[21] Other centres in Italy may have

taken the lead in such areas as architecture, archaeology and education, but
Poliziano and Ficino guaranteed pride of place to Florence in at least these
two fields until the end of the Quattrocento.

In the early sixteenth century, Florence's pre-eminence was even harder to
preserve; Florentine giants such as Leonardo and Michelangelo, although
creating high Renaissance style, nevertheless were lured away from the city,
producing many of their masterpieces abroad. Florence's greatest original
achievements in political thought and historiography, however, were saved
for the sixteenth century; Machiavelli created in Florence his new realistic art
of political thought, according to which, as he stated in the *Discourses*, men
would no longer simply admire the achievments of the Ancients, but actually
attempt to put the Roman model to real practical use.[22] Meanwhile his friend
and occasional critic, Guicciardini, wrote, in retirement from active political
life, his monumental history of Italy, the first masterpiece of modern
historical writing, a work which combined the immediacy of the Florentine
vernacular tradition with the erudition and precision of humanist philological research.[23] The classical academies of ducal Florence did not always offer
the most fertile soil for original and influential reinterpretations of the
classical tradition, although the merits and contribution of the Florentine
mannerists and academicians have often been far undervalued. Nevertheless,
it was under the Medici dukes that Vasari was encouraged to become the first
historian of art, creating a new genre out of the disparate classical models of
ekphrasis, rhetorical history and Ciceronian historiographical theory;[24]
moreover, higher education in ducal Florence received a level of support
unheard of under the republic, providing an academic environment capable
of rearing a genius of the calibre of Galileo.[25]

The revival of the antique: the political background

It is possible to suggest many reasons why Florence in particular emerged as
the first capital of the Renaissance. Florentine enthusiasm for the antique
outstripped the achievement of the rest of Italy in the years after 1390, and it
was probably no coincidence that this burgeoning of culture occurred in a
period when the Florentine ruling class was in a particularly buoyant and even
triumphant mood. Florence had long been controlled by an oligarchy of
merchants and landed gentry, but their predominance had been repeatedly
challenged in the course of the fourteenth century; the lower-class threat had
reached its climax in 1378, when a revolution by the politically disqualified
wool-workers (Ciompi) was followed by the establishment of a much more
broadly based regime. When this more popular government was toppled in
1382, the patrician class, restored to greater security than ever before, felt a
sense of unqualified and victorious relief. The high spirits of the Florentine

elite were further bolstered by a series of successful foreign wars. The threat of papal expansion, met by Florence in the War of the Eight Saints from 1375 to 1378, disappeared in the years of the Great Schism. An even greater danger was posed by the Visconti of Milan; this challenge was resisted, at great financial cost to the Florentines, until 1402, when the death of the duke of Milan, Giangaleazzo Visconti, resulted in the temporary collapse of the Visconti empire. The Florentines were equally fortunate in the timely death in 1414 of Ladislas of Naples, who had posed yet another threat over the previous five years.

Moreover, the flowering of the early Florentine Renaissance coincided with the creation by Florence of a great dominion in Tuscany, of a territorial empire to rival the domains of the dukes of Milan or even the kings of Naples. In the early fourteenth century, Florence had established itself as the dominant power of Tuscany; nevertheless, most of the neighbouring cities remained independent until mid-century, when first Prato, then Pistoia, San Gimignano, Colle di Val d'Elsa and Volterra fell into Florentine hands. Even this expansion, however, was small in comparison to the rapid growth of Florentine rule at the end of the fourteenth and in the early fifteenth centuries. Florence's former rival, Arezzo, fell in 1384 and Florentine expansion to the south-east went even further when Montepulciano was taken in 1393; growth to the east culminated in the surrender of Cortona in 1411, but Florentines were most jubilant over their expansion to the west. Florence's great rival, Pisa, was taken in 1406, soon to be followed by Livorno.[26]

The heady atmosphere of imperial Florence – triumphant at home and abroad – was faithfully reflected by Leonardo Bruni, so often the accurate spokesman of the Florentine ruling class, in the preface to his history of Florence, written in 1415. For Bruni, the victory over Milan, the capture of Pisa and the defeat of Ladislas marked the stages by which Florence had grown from a mere city-state to a great empire whose influence was felt throughout Italy, from the Alps to Apulia, extending even to ultra-montane Europe; for him, Florence deserved comparison with Rome after the victory over Carthage.[27] This period of renewed oligarchic rule after 1382 went down in the annals of Florentine history as a golden age:

Florence was successful both at home and abroad; at home, because it remained free, united, and governed by the well-to-do, good, and capable men; abroad because it defended itself against powerful enemies and greatly expanded its dominion. Florentine successes were so great that this government is deservedly said to be the wisest, the most glorious, and the happiest that our city had had for a long time.[28]

The triumphant self-assurance of the ruling class of imperial Florence may have helped to create a climate in which artistic and scholarly innovation could flourish, but there were also specific Florentine political experiences, as

well as particular features of Florence's political system, which made the
revival of antiquity so attractive in the late fourteenth and early fifteenth
centuries. Florentine mettle had been put to an extreme test in the long series
of foreign wars waged in the forty years following 1375. In the course of this
struggle, the Florentine chancellor, Coluccio Salutati, in his capacity as
official spokesman for the republic, had developed an ideology particularly
well suited to the defence of Florentine independence.[29] At first Salutati
carried on the well-established republican thought of the Italian city-states. In
developing the argument that republics were superior to monarchies, which
was the cornerstone of his defence of Florence first against the papacy and
then in the early years of the struggle against Milan, Salutati used a limited
range of classical sources – mainly Sallust and the republican implications of
Cicero's De officiis. But as his study of the classics deepened, so was he able to
find more classical texts to support Florence's republican ideology. Thus his
rediscovery of Cicero's Familiar Letters in 1392 inspired him to write to
Genoa condemning both Caesar and Augustus as initiators of 'perpetual
servitude';[30] more study of Sallust and perhaps of Cicero's second oration
against Catiline enabled him to show that Florence had republican origins,
founded by veterans of Sulla's campaigns;[31] his study of Livy allowed him to
contrast the true liberty enjoyed by Romans under the republic with the
licence prevailing under the kings of Rome;[32] his reading of Cicero's letters
permitted him to vindicate Cicero's condemnation of Caesar.[33]

Bruni did not assume the mantle of Florence's official apologist until 1410;
he gave up the chancellorship after less than a year's service in 1411, not to
reassume office again until 1427. Nevertheless, in these first years of the
fifteenth century he took on the role of unofficial defender of Florentine
republicanism with a vigour that equalled or even surpassed the republican
verve of his mentor, Salutati. Every drop of pro-republican sentiment had not
always been extracted from the classical sources by Salutati, but Bruni seldom
erred on the side of understatement. Salutati had not fully exploited the
republican implications of his discoveries regarding the foundation of
Florence, but Bruni showed how much such revelations from the Ancients
could enhance the arsenal of Florentine rhetoric.[34] Moreover, Bruni went
further than Salutati in his reading of Livy and the Elder Pliny to develop the
theme that Florence was heir to the Etruscans, whose civilisation collapsed
when they lost their freedom to Rome.[35] Bruni also made use of classical texts
which Salutati had not studied. Tacitus' Historiae had been rediscovered by
Boccaccio at Montecassino and had been read by various friends and
followers of Salutati, but it was Bruni who first saw the republican implications: 'when Florence was founded the city of Rome flourished greatly in
power, liberty, genius, and especially with great citizens. Now, after the
Republic had been subjected to the power of a single head, "those outstanding

minds vanished", as Tacitus says. So it is of importance whether a colony was founded at a later date, since by then all the virtue and nobility of the Romans had been destroyed', but in fact Florence had its origins 'when a free and unconquered Roman people flourished in power, nobility, virtues, and genius.'[36] Moreover, Bruni made full use of his newly acquired knowledge of Greek. He modelled his *Panegyric to the City of Florence* on Aristides' *Panathenaicus*, basing his portrait of Florence as the saviour of Italian liberty during the Milanese wars on Aristides' depiction of Athens as the bulwark of Greek freedom during the Persian wars.[37] His study of Thucydides provided another model: in his funeral oration for Nanni Strozzi, the central theme is again Florentine liberty, just as Athenian freedom was Pericles' focus in his funeral oration.[38] Yet a further Greek source for Bruni was Aristotle's *Politics*, on which he based his outline in Greek of the Florentine constitution, a brief work which highlights the republican features of Florentine government.[39]

Salutati and Bruni developed most of their republican ideology before they became Florentine citizens; as chancellors, they were constitutionally barred from political discussions and decision-making.[40] Nevertheless, the republican sentiments which they expressed received the whole-hearted backing of the Florentine elite. Not only did members of the Florentine governing class, such as Cino Rinuccini and Goro Dati, repeat Salutati's and Bruni's ideas in their own apologetic writings,[41] but the actual style of the debates in Florence's deliberative assembly changed in the early years of the fifteenth century. In the fourteenth century, the ideological content of the speeches made by Florentine statesmen in these assemblies had been sparse, but now a new style of political rhetoric prevailed, consisting of more elaborate speeches, more references to history and more citations from classical authors.[42] These debates were recorded by the chancery, and it is possible that such changes were the result of new methods of recension or elaboration of arguments by the chancery notaries;[43] nevertheless, it is an attractive hypothesis that this new style of political discourse shows the impact on the Florentine ruling class of Salutati's and Bruni's republican ideology, demonstrating the elite's appreciation of the wide uses to which the classical heritage could be put.

Classical texts could also be cited to justify the political system which Florence had evolved in the course of the fourteenth century. On the one hand, Florence was a republic in which power and office were shared amongst the citizenry. Office holders were usually selected by sortition rather than by election; tenure of the major magistracies was limited to brief periods; there were restrictions on successive or repeated terms of office for individuals and families. Such features were intended to secure a fair distribution of political honours among citizens, but there were also aspects of Florentine government which limited access to political power. Those qualified for political office usually had to belong to one of the city's twenty-one guilds, and the major guilds of large-scale merchants and professionals enjoyed a statutory right to a great majority of seats in government. Moreover, in order to be drawn by sortition for office, a citizen had first to be vetted by neighbourhood and city-wide committees, and these preliminary scrutinies tended to eliminate candidates from less prestigious families.[44] The conflicting forces of democracy and oligarchy had frequently clashed in the thirteenth and fourteenth centuries, but finally after 1382 a *modus vivendi* was established whereby it was possible to accommodate the aspirations of the wider political class to hold public office, and yet at the same time to enable a restricted oligarchy to retain a tight grip over real political power. This balance was achieved by qualifying ever larger numbers of citizens for the highest political offices, while at the same time giving preferential treatment to the oligarchs through the use of constitutional manipulations.[45]

Traditional Florentine political thought, as articulated by chancellors, poets, theorists and chroniclers, had sung the praises of both wider and narrower government, but it was Salutati who first showed how a constitution balanced between democracy and oligarchy could be justified by reference to classical authorities. In a famous passage of *De officiis* (I, 124), on the one hand, Cicero had argued for egalitarianism, stating that the private individual ought to live on fair and equal terms with his fellow citizens ('aequo et pari cum civibus iure vivere'), a line which Salutati paraphrased soon after taking office: 'cum paribus pariter vivere'.[46] Similarly, in another early letter he restated Cicero's warning not to favour any particular faction, but rather to support the people as a whole.[47] On the other hand, antipathy to the lower classes is a prominent theme in classical literature; for Cicero, for example, they were ignorant and incapable of government (*De amicitia*, xxv–xxvi), while Sallust regarded them as rebellious, envious, lazy and seditious (*Bellum Catilinae*, xxxvii). Such sentiments were frequently repeated and elaborated by Salutati: thus, in a letter of 1383 written after the fall of the popular regime, he utterly condemned the Ciompi revolt and the insane violence of the Florentine mob, a verdict which he confirmed later that year and again in 1385.[48] For Salutati, the traditional Florentine order was the ideal, the golden mean between oligarchy and democracy, a mercantile republic: neither the nobility – overbearing, proud, bloodthirsty – nor the mob – ignorant, ferocious, insatiable, bestial – should rule, but rather the middle class – pacific, satisfied, fair-minded, patriotic.[49] His words closely echo Aristotle's views in the *Politics* (IV, II): 'the city which is composed of middle-class citizens is necessarily the best governed; they are, as we say, the natural elements of a state . . . for they do not, like the poor, covet their neighbours' goods; nor do others covet theirs, as the poor covet the goods of the rich; and . . . they neither plot against others, nor are themselves plotted against.'[50]

Florentines thus learned from Salutati how effectively classical erudition could be deployed in defence of their particular political order – a lesson which was continued by his disciple, Bruni. As for Salutati, equality was, according to Bruni, the cornerstone of Florentine liberty; this connection between freedom and equality derived directly from Cicero, as did Bruni's distinction between equality before the law and equality of political rights. He uses Aristotle's system of classification to designate the Florentine constitution as popular or democratic, and his emphasis on collegiate government and short terms of office to guarantee republican liberty echoes Livy. On the other hand, like Salutati, Bruni also used the legacy of antiquity in support of the restrictive tendencies of Florentine government: his emphasis on equal hope (rather than on equal distribution) of political honours, on the selection of the most virtuous and upright citizens for office, recalls the Aristotelian preference for aristocratic regimes, as does his view that the Florentine constitution favoured 'the best and the rich'. Like Salutati, Bruni reconciled these divergent tendencies in Florence in true Aristotelian fashion, through the doctrine of the middle way. Florence was a mixed constitution of the Aristotelian mould. Short tenure of office and sortition were democratic features; approval of laws by small committees and limitations to the prerogatives of popular councils were aristocratic aspects. Exclusion of magnates from government was democratic, but the disqualification of the lowest social order was aristocratic.[51] 'Shunning extremes this city prefers men of middle condition', wrote Bruni,[52] recalling, like his mentor Salutati, Aristotle's words in the *Politics*.

The revival of the antique: social and educational dimensions

The Florentine upper classes were also not slow to appreciate the possible social advantages offered by the revival of antiquity. For centuries Florence, like the rest of Italy, had been a snobbish, elitist society;[53] the Florentines had never established a constitutionally privileged and exclusive aristocracy as in Venice, but neither had they allowed rapid and extreme fluctuations of wealth, characteristic of the medieval Italian economy, to level the gradations of the social hierarchy. In the fourteenth and fifteenth centuries, the social position of a Florentine family was determined by numerous influences. In Poggio Bracciolini's dialogue *On Nobility*, the interlocutors agreed that social rank in Florence was defined by a family's wealth, lineage and political experience.[54] In one of Europe's great commercial capitals, it is hardly surprising that money counted for so much: one Florentine patrician declared that, before he was rich, he was universally snubbed in Florence,[55] while

Alberti wrote that poverty cast a shadow over virtue.[56] Ancient lineage was always prized in Florence, all the more so when newly enriched families were constantly trying to break into the exclusive circles of upper-class society. Dante's scorn for the *nouveaux riches*, expressed at the beginning of the fourteenth century,[57] differed little from Giovanni Morelli's observation, at the beginning of the fifteenth, that 'everyone today boasts an old family'.[58] Membership of the political oligarchy too was essential for social prominence: Alessandra Strozzi, for example, was willing to contemplate a marriage alliance with the socially inferior Parenti family, in part because they had achieved a place – albeit modest – among the ruling elite of Florence.[59] Indeed, marriage was the most public declaration a family could make of its social position: as Morelli advised his descendants, 'make sure that your father-in-law . . . is rich, is from an ancient Florentine family, and is a member of the oligarchy (*nello istato*)'.[60]

Traditionally, a classical education meant little to the Florentine upper classes. What they wanted for their children was enough literacy and numeracy to carry on the family business, to maintain and improve the family's patrimony: for them, in Alberti's words, 'it is enough to know how to write your name, and to know how to add up how much money you are owed'.[61] It was along these lines that one patrician Florentine, Bernardo Manetti, provided for the education of his son: 'At a young age, he sent him, according to the custom of the city, to learn to read and write. When, in a brief time, the boy had mastered the learning necessary to become a merchant, his father took him away from elementary school and sent him to arithmetic [abacus] school, where in a few months he similarly learned enough to work as a merchant. At the age of ten he went into a bank.'[62] Another Florentine, a member of an ancient Florentine family of illustrious feudal descent, Messer Andrea de' Pazzi, gave his son Piero little encouragement to pursue his education: 'Being the son of Messer Andrea and a young man of handsome appearance, devoted to the delights and pleasures of the world, Piero gave little thought to the study of (Latin) letters: indeed, his father was a merchant and like those who have little education themselves, he had scant regard for learning nor did he think that his son would show much inclination in that direction.'[63] Traditional attitudes were reflected in the guidance given in 1415 by the Florentine dominican preacher, Giovanni Dominici, to a Florentine matron of the upper classes, who had asked for advice on how to bring up her children. He especially warned against any association with the avant-garde who were attempting to revive classical antiquity. 'In my view', he declared, 'our forbears saw the light in educating the young, whereas today they are blind, raising their children outside the faith. The first thing our ancestors used to teach was the Psalter and sacred learning; and if they went any further in school, they used' the traditional medieval textbooks – Cato, Aesop, Boethius, Prosper, Eva Columba – 'books which teach nothing wrong. Now children of this generation grow up learning all imaginable and shameful evils, studying Ovid's *Metamorphoses*, letters, *Ars amandi* – his most lascivious and sensual books and writings. Then they pass through Vergil, tragedies, and other pursuits – teachers of carnal love rather than of good behaviour.'[64] Dominici, of course, gave a religious slant to Florentine attitudes, but his suspicion of classical education was shared by many Florentines: such were the views of Bernardo Manetti, a man who was, 'in accordance with the custom of the city, more given to earning than to learning', and who therefore refused to consent to his son's classical studies.[65]

The Florentine idea of a gentleman, however, began to be redefined by the circle of patricians who had originally gathered around Salutati and who became even more influential after his death. For such men as Palla Strozzi, Niccolò Niccoli, Roberto Rossi, Antonio Corbinelli and Agnolo Pandolfini, classical learning was an essential ingredient of gentility, a necessary qualification for membership of the social elite – a view which was confirmed by further study of the Ancients themselves. The classical texts which provide the most compelling portrait of the ideal Roman gentleman – Cicero's *Orator* and *De oratore* and Quintilian's *Institutiones* – were either studied for the first time or with renewed vigour in the early fifteenth century; from such sources the Florentine avant-garde was confirmed in its view that no one should command a high social position, no one could rightfully call himself a gentleman without a classical education.

The most forceful prosletyte for this new social ideal was Niccolò Niccoli, in this as in so many other ways the trend-setter *par excellence*. His activities are vividly portrayed by a contemporary biographer:

One day Messer Piero de' Pazzi, who had never spoken to Niccolò, was walking past the palace of the podestà. Seeing that he was a young man of handsome appearance, Niccolò called to him. Since Niccolò was some one of the highest reputation, Piero immediately went over to him. When Niccolò had had a look at him, he asked whose son he was. He replied that his father was Messer Andrea de' Pazzi. He asked him what his occupation was. He replied, as do the young: 'Having a good time.' Niccolò said to him: 'Considering whose son you are, considering the good family you come from and your good looks, it is disgraceful that you do not devote yourself to Latin letters, which would give you great distinction. If you do not study the classics, you will be considered a nothing; when you have passed the prime of your youth, you will find yourself without any merit (*virtù*) and you will enjoy no one's esteem.'[66]

Niccoli gave this kind of grilling, it was said, to all the young men of Florence with any intelligence. The effect that he and his fellow classical enthusiasts had on the younger generation was summed up by a contemporary: 'At that time whoever did not know Latin letters was not considered a man nor regarded among men of worth.'[67] The social *cachet* of Latin letters for the new Florentine upper class of the fifteenth century was made clear by Alberti:

And who does not know that the first thing useful for childeren are (Latin) letters? And this is so important that someone unlettered, however much a gentleman, will be considered nothing but a country bumpkin. And I should like to see young noblemen with a book in hand more frequently than with a hawk. . . . If there is anything which goes beautifully with gentility or which gives the greatest distinction to human life or adds grace, authority and name to a family, it is surely letters, without which no one can be reputed to possess true gentility.[68]

The social advantages now attached to a classical education were not overlooked by parents of the Florentine patriciate. It became fashionable among upper-class Florentines by the early fifteenth century to employ, for their children, private tutors, usually called *repetitori*, *precettori* or *pedagogi*. Leading Florentine statesmen such as Rinaldo degli Albizzi, Palla Strozzi, Agnolo Acciaiuoli and Dietisalvi Neroni,[69] engaged a succession of tutors to live in their houses and educate their children; the list of families who employed *repetitori* – for example, the Bardi, Pazzi, Rucellai, Capponi[70] – reads like a Florentine social register. Some of these tutors were little-known grammarians, but many – Bruni, Poggio, Tommaso Parentucelli, Sozomeno, Iacopo Ammannati, Enoch of Ascoli,[71] Antonio Rossi,[72] Marsilio Ficino,[73] Bartolomeo Fonzio, Poliziano[74] – were or were to become leading humanists and men of letters.

What is particularly significant is that a private classical education became a status symbol in Florence, one further sign – like wealth, ancient lineage, public office, marriage – of a family's exclusive social position. This type of education provided upper-class Florentines with a particularly effective means of distinguishing themselves and their children from the more common elements of society. Indeed, without a private tutor, a satisfactory Latin or what was called grammar education was difficult to come by in Florence. In contrast to other Tuscan towns such as Lucca, Pistoia, Arezzo and Volterra, Florence made sparse provision for public grammar teaching.[75] Careful study of communal records has shown only occasional subsidies and appointments of grammar masters throughout the fourteenth and first half of the fifteenth centuries.[76] Florentines seem to have distrusted communal schools: as Giovanni Dominici wrote, 'if you send your son to a communal school, which gathers together a multitude of undisciplined, miserable, difficult children, badly inclined and resistent to good influences, I fear that he will lose in one year what he has gained in seven'.[77]

Primary education – reading and writing – was usually entrusted in Florence, not to a communal grammar teacher as elsewhere in Tuscany, but to a lesser breed of teachers, variously called *maestri di fanciulli, doctores puerorum* or *maestri di leggere e scrivere*.[78] These men were usually from the artisan class; they show little sign of much education themselves and probably knew almost no Latin.[79] They ran little shops (*botteghuzze*) where boys were sent to learn reading and writing.[80] The teaching provided there was very basic indeed: reading was taught phonetically, without comprehension, and there was almost no attempt to impart any knowledge of Latin.[81] This type of teaching constituted the largest sector of education in fourteenth- and fifteenth-century Florence. The most popular form of secondary education in Florence was the abacus or arithmetic school. Here a pupil learned basic arithmetic and problem-solving; the emphasis was on methods which would be of use in the commercial world, and instruction was conducted entirely in Italian.[82] Most Florentines went directly into business or a craft after abacus school; grammar was a tertiary study for the few Florentines who wished to learn Latin.[83] Even in the early fourteenth century, grammar had attracted only half as many pupils as the abacus;[84] moreover, as a subject for the general population, grammar suffered a further serious decline in the course of the fifteenth century, to such an extent that only 2 per cent of boys were at grammar school in 1480, in contrast to 25 per cent at abacus school and 29 per cent at elementary school.[85] In fact, this collapse of grammar education seems to have been unique to Florence; small towns throughout Italy maintained their commitment to Latin instruction[86] and even in other large commercial cities such as Venice or Genoa, not to mention Rome itself, grammar apparently maintained itself as the principal form of secondary education in the fourteenth and fifteenth centuries.[87]

Against this background, it is not difficult to understand why a private education in the classics was so enthusiastically cultivated by Florence's social elite. Political reversals could lead to exclusion from public office or even exile; commercial upsets could bring hardship or poverty; without riches or political position it was difficult to marry well. But, like an ancient lineage, a good education was a shield against the blows of fortune. Machiavelli was not the only Florentine who, in bad times, took solace in the sense of social privilege provided by a classical education:

I get up in the morning with the sun and go into a grove I am having cut down, where I remain two hours to look over the work of the past day and kill some time with the cutters, who have always some bad-luck story ready, about either themselves or their neighbors . . . Leaving the grove, I go to a spring, and thence to my aviary. I have a book in my pocket, either Dante or Petrarch, or one of the lesser poets, such as Tibullus, Ovid, and the like. I read of their tender passions and their loves, remember mine, enjoy myself a while in that sort of dreaming. Then I move along the road to the inn; I speak with those who pass, ask news of their villages, learn various things, and note the various tastes and different fancies of men. In the course of these things comes the

hour for dinner, where with my family I eat such food as this poor farm of mine and my
tiny property allow. Having eaten, I go back to the inn; there is the host, usually a
butcher, a miller, two furnace tenders. With these I sink into vulgarity for the whole
day, playing at *cricca* and at trich-trach, and then these games bring a thousand
disputes and countless insults with offensive words, and usually we are fighting over a
penny, and nevertheless we are heard shouting as far as San Casciano . . . On the
coming of evening, I return to my house and enter my study; and at the door I take off
the day's clothing, covered with mud and dust, and put on garments regal and courtly;
and reclothed appropriately, I enter the ancient courts of ancient men, where, received
by them with affection, I feed on that food which only is mine and which I was born
for, where I am not ashamed to speak with them and to ask them the reason for their
actions; and they in their kindness answer me; and for four hours of time I do not feel
boredom, I forget every trouble, I do not dread poverty, I am not frightened by death;
entirely I give myself over to them.[88]

Florentine political needs certainly provided a great stimulus to the revival
of antiquity, but it is important to realise too the social implications of the
Renaissance. At the turn of the fifteenth century Florentines began a
momentous process which was to continue for centuries – the re-education of
the aristocracy.[89] Before this time a practical, mercantile, in part moral and
religious, sometimes chivalraic, education had prevailed. The Florentine
humanist avant-garde decisively shifted the emphasis. Classical, literary
learning became the essential attribute of the gentleman, and once more
Florence was ahead of the rest of Italy and transalpine Europe. Hexter writes:

Before the Renaissance few people demanded or expected that a gentleman should be a
clerk . . . Yet in the sixteenth century we have a spate of words dedicated to the
proposition that all gentlemen worthy of the name must be clerks, deep in learning and
the intellectual virtues; and the words come, mind you, not merely or mainly from
clerks but from the gentlemen themselves . . . Ignorance and indifference to letters in
the aristocracy are not new in the sixteenth century; what was new and radical was the
suggestion that things should be otherwise.[90]

Hexter sees the 'earliest impetus toward education – clerkly bookish education – for the aristocracy among the nobles of Burgundy' under Philip the
Good, noting their presence in the matriculation lists of the University of
Louvain in the second quarter of the fifteenth century. A generation earlier,
however, the humanist avant-garde was demanding a classical education for
scions of the great Florentine families, and here, as elsewhere, it was Florence,
not Burgundy, which pointed the way for the rest of Renaissance Europe.

As far as aristocratic education is concerned, the Florentine example –
although the earliest – would therefore not remain unique. What was peculiar
to Florence was that a classical, humanist education should become largely
the exclusive preserve of the upper social orders. Elsewhere in Italy as in the
rest of Europe, the aristocracy came to share this latinate, classical formation

with a wide segment of the lower classes. In Venice and Genoa, for example, a Latin education was the normal fare, not only for aspiring aristocrats, but also for many would-be notaries, civil servants and ecclesiastics, not to mention merchants. This was much less characteristic of Florence, which in fact developed a two-tiered education system by the fifteenth century. For the artisan and lower commercial classes, education was almost entirely commercial and practical; Latin or humanist education was largely unknown to the humbler social orders of Florence. The Florentine upper classes had an education that was uniquely their own – a classical training usually imparted by a private tutor. This unusual feature of the Florentine education system meant that the classics achieved in Florence a kind of socially exclusive connotation not characteristic of the rest of Italy, where humanist training, often of a remarkably high standard even in small towns such as Arezzo or San Gimignano, was available, frequently free of charge, in most civic grammar schools. It is small wonder, therefore, that the Florentine patriciate gave such unique support to the classical revival in the fifteenth century. In Florence, classical learning was the distinctive preserve of the aristocracy, and so by supporting the Renaissance they were advertising the social preeminence and superiority of their own class. The elitism of Florentine society and the monopoly which the Florentine patriciate had over classical culture made Florence the first and greatest capital of the Renaissance.

NOTES

1 R. Weiss, 'The dawn of humanism in Italy', *Bulletin of the Institute of Historical Research*, 42 (1969), 1–16; 'Lineamenti per una storia del primo umanesimo fiorentino', *Rivista storica italiana*, 60 (1948), 349–66.

2 H. Burns, 'Quattrocento architecture and the antique: some problems' in R.R. Bolgar (ed.), *Classical Influence on European Culture* (Cambridge, 1971), 269–87; H. Saalman, 'Filippo Brunelleschi: capital studies', *Art Bulletin*, 40 (1958), 113–37.

3 B.L. Ullman, *The Origin and Development of Humanist Script* (Rome, 1960).

4 *Ibid.*; H. Baron, *From Petrarch to Leonardo Bruni* (Chicago, 1968), 219–23; R. Black, *Benedetto Accolti and the Florentine Renaissance* (Cambridge, 1985), 109–10.

5 Ullman, *Origin*, 70–2.

6 E.H. Gombrich, 'From the revival of letters to the reform of the arts: Niccolò Niccoli and Filippo Brunelleschi' in his *The Heritage of Apelles: Studies in the Art of the Renaissance* (London, 1976), 93–110.

7 I. Thomson, 'Manuel Chrysoloras and the early Italian Renaissance', *Greek, Roman and Byzantine Studies*, 7 (1966), 63–82.

8 Ch. Schmitt, *Aristotle in the Renaissance* (Cambridge, Mass., 1983).

9 L. Bruni, *Historiarum florentini populi libri XII* in E. Santini (ed.), *Rerum italicarum scriptores*, 2nd edn. vol. XIX, 3 (Città di Castello, 1914).

10 Bruni, *Ad Petrum Paulum Histrum dialogus*, in E. Garin (ed.), *Prosatori latini del*

Quattrocento (Milan, 1952), 44–99. On its relation to *De oratore*, see R. Sabbadini in *Giornale storico della letteratura italiana*, 96 (1930), 131ff; H. Baron, *The Crisis of the Early Italian Renaissance*, 2nd ed. (Princeton, N.J., 1966), 228–32, 510–14; J. Seigel, '"Civic humanism" or Ciceronian rhetoric', *Past and Present*, 34 (1966), 14–18.

11 D. Marsh, *The Quattrocento Dialogue* (Cambridge, Mass., 1980).

12 Baron, *Crisis*, 47ff. R. Witt, 'The rebirth of the concept of republican liberty in Italy' in A. Molho and J. Tedeschi (eds.), *Renaissance Studies in Honor of Hans Baron* (Florence, 1971), 173–99, and *Coluccio Salutati and his Public Letters* (Geneva, 1976), 77–88, has attempted to salvage Baron's scheme, but see R. Black, 'The political thought of the Florentine chancellors', *The Historical Journal*, 29 (1986), 999–1000 and n. 13 below.

13 C. Davis, 'Ptolemy of Lucca and the Roman Republic', *Proceedings of the American Philosophical Society*, 118 (1974), 30–50; Q. Skinner, *The Foundations of Modern Political Thought* (Cambridge, 1978), vol. I, 41ff, 53ff; N. Rubinstein, 'Political theories in the Renaissance' in A. Chastel *et al.*, *The Renaissance: Essays in Interpretation* (London, 1982), 153ff.

14 L. Bruni, *Isagogicon moralis disciplinae* in his *Humanistisch-Philosophische Schriften*, ed. H. Baron (Leipzig and Berlin, 1928), 39.

15 L. Mehus (ed.), *Leonardi Bruni Aretini epistolarum libri viii* (Florence, 1741), vol. II, 134ff; for the date, see Baron (ed.), *Schriften*, 215.

16 P.O. Kristeller, 'The active and the contemplative life in Renaissance humanism' in B. Vickers (ed.), *Arbeit Musse Meditation: Betrachtungen zur Vita Activa und Vita Contemplativa* (Zürich, 1985), 133–52; 'Vita attiva e vita contemplativa in un brano inedito di Bornio da Sala e in San Tomaso d'Aquino', *Essere e libertà: studi in onore di Cornelio Fabro* (Perugia, 1984), 211–24.

17 Black, *Accolti*, 204–8.

18 L. Chiappelli, 'Carlo Marsuppini e Giovanni Forteguerri precursori della scuola umanistia di diritto romano secondo un testo inedito', *Archivio giuridico*, 38 (1887), 398–410; D. Maffei, *Gli inizi dell'umanesimo giuridico* (Milan, 1956), 45; R. Black, 'Higher education in Florentine Tuscany: new documents from the second half of the fifteenth century' in P. Denley and C. Elam (eds.), *Florence and Italy: Renaissance Studies in Honour of Nicolai Rubinstein* (London, 1988), 209–22.

19 R. Black, 'The new laws of history', *Renaissance Studies*, 1 (1987), 126–56.

20 A. Grafton, *Joseph Scaliger*, vol. I (Oxford, 1983), 9–44, a revision of his earlier article, 'On the scholarship of Politian and its context', *Journal of the Warburg and Courtauld Institutes*, 40 (1977), 150–88.

21 See the bibliography by P.O. Kristeller in G.C. Garfagnini (ed.), *Marsilio Ficino e il ritorno di Platone* (Florence, 1986), 50–80.

22 Machiavelli, *Discorsi*, libro primo, proemio.

23 F. Gilbert, *Machiavelli and Guicciardini* (Princeton, N.J. 1965), 271–301.

24 S. Alpers, '*Ekphrasis* and aesthetic attitudes in Vasari's *Lives*', *Journal of the Warburg and Courtauld Institutes*, 23 (1960), 190–215.

25 C.B. Schmitt, 'The faculty of arts at Pisa at the time of Galileo', *Physis*, 14 (1972), 243–72.

26 G. Brucker, *Florentine Politics and Society*, 1343–1378 (Princeton, N.J., 1962);

'The Ciompi revolution' in N. Rubinstein (ed.), *Florentine Studies* (London, 1968), 314–56; *The Civic World of Early Renaissance Florence* (Princeton, N.J., 1977).

27 Bruni, *Historiarum . . . libri XII*, 3–4.

28 F. Guicciardini, *Storie fiorentine*, ed. R. Palmarocchi (Bari, 1931), 2–3; Eng. trans., M. Domandi (New York, 1970), 3.

29 P. Herde, 'Politik und Rhetorik in Florenz am Vorabend der Renaissance', *Archiv für Kulturgeschichte*, 47 (1965), 141–220; Witt, *Public Letters*; D. De Rosa, *Coluccio Salutati: il cancelliere e il pensatore politico* (Florence, 1980).

30 *Ibid.*, 141; Witt, *Public Letters*, 81–2.

31 R. Witt, *Hercules at the Crossroads: The Life, Works, and Thought of Coluccio Salutati* (Durham, N. Car., 1983), 246–52; 'Coluccio Salutati and the origins of Florence', *Il pensiero politico*, 2 (1969), 161–72.

32 Salutati, *Invectiva in Antonium Luschum* in Garin, *Prosatori*, 16.

33 De Rosa, *Salutati*, 159; E. Emerton, *Humanism and Tyranny: Studies in the Italian Trecento* (Cambridge, Mass., 1925), ch. 3.

34 Witt, *Public Letters*, 71, and *Hercules*, 166–9; Baron, *Crisis*, 54–5, 61–4, 74–6, 99ff, 159, 195.

35 G. Cipriani, *Il mito etrusco nel rinascimento fiorentino* (Florence, 1980), 1–13; Baron, *Crisis*, 65, 415ff, 424–5.

36 Bruni, *Laudatio florentinae urbis* in Baron, *Petrarch to Bruni*, 247–8; Eng. trans., B.J. Kohl in B.J. Kohl and R. Witt (eds.), *The Earthly Republic* (Manchester, 1978), 154.

37 Baron, *Crisis*, 192–5.

38 *Ibid.*, 412ff.

39 N. Rubinstein, 'Florentine constitutionalism and Medici ascendancy in the fifteenth century', in his *Florentine Studies*, 444–8.

40 Black, *Accolti*, 121–35; 'Florentine political traditions and Machiavelli's election to the chancery', *Italian Studies*, 40 (1985), 1–16.

41 Baron, *Crisis*, 76–8.

42 Brucker, *Civic World*, 284–95 and his 'Humanism, politics and the social order in early Renaissance Florence' in S. Bertelli *et al.* (eds.), *Florence and Venice: Comparisons and Relations* (Florence, 1979), vol. I, 3–11.

43 Black, *Accolti*, 159–63.

44 N. Rubinstein, *The Government of Florence under the Medici* (Oxford, 1966).

45 J. Najemy, *Corporatism and Consensus in Florentine Electoral Politics, 1280–1400* (Chapel Hill, N.C., 1982).

46 De Rosa, *Salutati*, 118.

47 *Ibid.*, 120.

48 A. Petrucci, *Coluccio Salutati* (Rome, 1972), 43–53.

49 De Rosa, *Salutati*, 123–33.

50 Trans., B. Jowett (Oxford, 1905), 169.

51 Rubinstein, 'Florentine constitutionalism', 444–9.

52 Quoted, *ibid.*, 447.

53 On Florentine upper-class society, see L. Martines, *The Social World of the Florentine Humanists* (London, 1963).

54 P. Bracciolini, *De nobilitate* in his *Opera* (Basel, 1538), 6ff.

55 G. Cavalcanti, *Istorie fiorentine* (Florence, 1838–9), vol. I, 97.

56 L.B. Alberti, *I libri della famiglia*, ed. C. Grayson (Bari, 1960), 267.

57 *Paradiso*, XVI, 49ff.

58 G. Morelli, *Ricordi*, ed. V. Branca (Florence, 1956), 81.

59 A. Strozzi, *Lettere di una gentildonna fiorentina*, ed. C. Guasti (Florence, 1877), 3–4.

60 Morelli, *Ricordi*, 264.

61 Alberti, *Della famiglia*, 68.

62 Vespasiano da Bisticci, *Le vite*, ed. A. Greco (Florence, 1970–6), vol. II, 519.

63 *Ibid.*, II, 309.

64 G. Dominici, *Regola del governo di cura familiare*, ed. D. Salvi (Florence, 1860); selections reprinted in E. Garin (ed.), *Il pensiero pedagogico dello umanesimo* (Florence, 1958), 72.

65 Vespasiano, *Le vite*, vol. II, 519.

66 *Ibid.*, 310.

67 *Ibid.*, 427.

68 Alberti, *Della famiglia*, 68, 70. Pier Paolo Vergerio had in mind the kind of upper-class society which he had seen in Florence when he wrote his *De ingenius moribus*, the first humanist educational treatise, at the turn of the fifteenth century: see E. Garin, *L'educatione in Europa* (Bari, 1957), 132.

69 Vespasiano, *Le vite*, vol. I, 38, 559; vol. II, 10, 143–5, 300; Archivo di Stato, Milan, Potenze estere, Firenze, 269, n. 17 (28 September 1457): '. . . Dicto Detesalvi nostro . . . trovandossi in Valle de Serchio presso a Luca in lecto cum un suo figliolo et havendo ali pedi loro uno Antonio de'Rossi, preceptor de' soy figlioli, docta persona . . .'

70 Vespasiano, *Le vite*, vol. II, 51, 236, 316, 369; F.W. Kent, *Household and Lineage in Renaissance Florence* (Princeton, N.J., 1977), 37.

71 Vespasiano, *Le vite*, vol. I, 38, 463, 539, 559; vol. II, 10, 21, 51, 145, 300.

72 See n. 69 above.

73 Kristeller, 'Ficino' in Garfagnini, *Il ritorno*, vol. I, 171.

74 A. de la Mare, 'The library of Francesco Sassetti (1421–90)' in C. Clough (ed.), *Cultural Aspects of the Italian Renaissance: Essays in Honour of P.O. Kristeller* (Manchester, 1976), 160–201; A Brown, *Bartolomeo Scala* (Princeton, N.J., 1979), 212.

75 P. Barsanti, *Il pubblico insegnamento in Lucca dal secolo XIV fino al del secolo XVIII* (Lucca, 1905); A. Zanelli, *Del pubblico insegnamento in Pistoia dal XIV al XVI secolo* (Rome, 1900); R. Black, 'Humanism and education in Renaissance Arezzo', *I Tatti Studies: Essays in the Renaissance*, 2 (1987), 171–237; M. Battistini, *Il pubblico insegnamento in Volterra dal secolo XIV al secolo XVIII* (Volterra, 1919).

76 A. Gherardi (ed.), *Statuti della università e studio fiorentino* (Florence, 1881); K. Park, 'The readers at the Florentine Studio', *Rinascimento*, ser. 2, 20 (1980), 249–310; E. Spagnesi, *Utiliter edoceri. Atti inediti degli ufficiali dello Studio fiorentino (1391–1396)* (Milan, 1979).

77 Dominici, *Regola*, in Garin, *Il pensiero pedagogico*, 71–2.

78 S. Debenedetti, 'Sui più antichi "doctores puerorum" a Firenze', *Studi medievali*, 2

(1906–7), 327–51.

79 E.g., Archivo di Stato, Florence, Catasto, 15, fol. 901r–v; 17, fol, 341r–v; 20, fol. 1103r; 45, fol. 691r.

80 Morelli, *Ricordi*, 457. Archivio di Stato, Florence, Carte Strozziane, II, 11, fol. 33r.

81 P. Lucchi, 'La santacroce, il salterio e il babuino: libri per imparare a leggere nel primo secolo della stampa', *Quaderni storici*, 38 (1978), 593–630; Ch. Klapisch-Zuber, 'Le chiavi fiorentine di Barbablù: l'apprendimento della lettura a Firenze nel XV secolo', *Quaderni storici* 57 (1984), 765–792.

82 W. Van Egmond, 'The commercial revolution and the beginnings of western mathematics in Renaissance Florence, 1300–1500', Ph.D. thesis, Indiana University, 1976; (ed.), *Practical Mathematics in the Renaissance: A Catalog of Italian Abbacus Manuscripts and Printed Books* (Florence, 1981).

83 On the basis of A. Verde's extracts from the Florentine *catasto* of 1480 (*Lo studio fiorentino 1473–1503*, 4 pts and 7 vols. (Florence and Pistoia, 1973–85), III, ii, 1011–1202', the average age of an abacus pupil in Florence was 12.8 whereas that of a grammar pupil was 14.1

84 G. Villani, *Cronica*, ed. F. Dragomanni (Florence, 1845), vol. III, ch. 94, 324.

85 P. Grendler, *Schooling in Renaissance Italy* (Baltimore, 1989), 75, based on Verde's statistics.

86 Black, 'Arezzo'; Barsanti, *Lucca*; Zanelli, *Pistoia*; Battistini, *Volterra*; V. Bellemo, 'L'insegnamento e la cultura in Chioggia fino al secolo XV', *Archivio veneto*, n.s. 35 (1888), 277–301 and 36 (1888), 37–56; F. Gabotto, *Lo stato Sabaudo da Amedeo VIII a Emanuele Filiberto*, iii: *La cultura e la vita in Piemonte nel Rinascimento* (Turin 1895).

87 E. Bertanza and G. Dalla Santa, *Documenti per la storia della cultura in Venezia. I: Maestri, scuole e scolari in Venezia verso la fine del Medio Evo* (Venice, 1907); A. Massa, 'Documenti e noltizie per la storia dell'istruzione in Genova', *Giornale storico e letterario della Liguria*, 7 (1906), 169–205, 311–28; G. Petti Balbi, *L'insegnamento nella Liguria medievale: scuole, maestri, libri* (Genoa, 1979); Grendler, *Schooling*, 78–86.

88 N. Machiavelli, *Lettere*, ed. F. Gaeta (Milan, 1961), 302–4; Eng. trans. A. Gilbert, *The Letters of Machiavelli* (New York, 1961), 140–2.

89 J.H. Hexter, 'The education of the aristocracy in the Renaissance' in his *Reappraisals in History* (London, 1961), 45–70.

90 *Ibid.*, 49.

FURTHER READING

Bec, C. *Les marchands écrivains: affairs et humanisme à Florence 1375–1434*, Paris, 1967.

Brown, Alison *The Renaissance*, London, 1988.

Grafton, A. and L. Jardine, *From Humanism to the Humanities. Education and the Liberal Arts in Fifteenth- and Sixteenth- Century Europe*, London, 1986.

Holmes, G. *The Florentine Enlightenment, 1400–50*, London, 1969.

The Cambridge History of Renaissance Philosophy, ed. C.B. Schmitt *et al.* Cambridge, 1988.

—————————— ℣ ——————————

THREE

ROME

NICHOLAS DAVIDSON

On 8 April 1341, the poet Francesco Petrarch was crowned with laurel on the Capitoline Hill in Rome. In his Oration, he explained why he had chosen to accept the invitation to be crowned in Rome in preference to another he had received from Paris:

> The honour of the Republic stirs my heart when I recall that in this very city of Rome – the capital of the world, as Cicero calls it – on this very Roman Capitol where we are now gathered, so many and such great poets, having attained to the highest and most illustrious mastery of their art, have received the laurel crown they have deserved . . . And although I hesitated for a time because of the present fame of that University [of Paris], I finally decided to come hither – why, I ask you, if not for the very reason that Vergil gives, 'Vincit amor patriae'. (Wilkins 1955, 304–5)

It may seem strange, at first sight, that Petrarch should claim to have been defeated by patriotic love of a city in the Papal States, when he had been born the son of a notary from the independent city of Florence. Admittedly, his father was in exile at the time of Francesco's birth, and on other occasions the poet did demonstrate an awareness of the common heritage shared by all Italians (Petrarch 1554, 1,194); but he was not the only outsider who viewed Rome as in some way his own. Poggio Bracciolini, who was employed by the papal curia for almost fifty years between 1403 and 1453, was also able to distinguish between Florence – his 'naturalis patria' – and Rome – his 'civilis patria' (Baron, 1938, 31). And this pride in Rome was of course, central to the Renaissance in all parts of Italy. Rome was, as Petrarch recognised in his Oration, the capital of the ancient world, and it was precisely this self-conscious interest in the achievements of the ancient world that marked off the Renaissance from the culture of the Middle Ages.

Italian scholars had already begun to commit themselves to the search for the works of classical writers in the fourteenth century. Petrarch was the first, and Poggio one of the most successful: in journeys that reached as far afield as Switzerland, France, the Rhineland and even England between 1407 and 1423, he unearthed among other treasures the texts of Quintilian's *De institutione oratoria* and the *De rerum natura* of Lucretius (Goodhart Gordan 1974, 2–3). Many of these works were either unknown at the time, or known only in corrupt versions, and the newly discovered manuscripts were therefore studied assiduously, and published in corrected editions. Pope Innocent VII proposed the establishment of Chairs in Latin and Greek literature at the University of Rome in 1406, and we know that Latin rhetoric was taught there in subsequent years by scholars as distinguished as Giovanni Ponzio, Lorenzo Valla and Francesco Filelfo (Chambers 1976, 69, 73–7). The growth of interest in literary scholarship was matched by the growth of libraries: the Pope's private library in the Vatican contained 340 works in 1447; by 1455, this figure had increased to 1,200, and by 1484 to 3,600 (Delumeau 1974, 120).

This interest in the literature of ancient Rome extended to its buildings, too: as the recurrent tag had it, 'Roma quanta fuit ipsa ruina docet' (Albertinis 1510, vivr; Serlio 1544, title-page). As early as 1375, the Paduan Giovanni Dondi dell'Orologio had made notes on the city's ancient monuments based on his own examinations of the ruins; more careful measurements were taken by Leon Battista Alberti in the 1430s for his *Descriptio urbis Romae*. The first methodical account of the ancient city was provided in the fifteenth century by Flavio Biondo's *Roma instaurata*, which was composed between 1444 and 1446 and published in 1470. This was based on an exemplary range of sources, including inscriptions, coins, and both ancient and medieval descriptions, as well as the material remains, to create an image of the development of the city itself (Weiss 1967, 115; 1988, 51–2, 65–8, 90–2). By the early sixteenth century, artists' drawings demonstrated a clear understanding of classical architectural principles (Saxl 1957, 204–6) and several private collections of antiquities – bronzes, cameos, gems and coins, ivories and intaglios, as well as statues – had been opened to students (Weiss 1988, 186–95).

The spirit of these early archaeological pioneers is manifest in a letter sent by Poggio from Rome to a sickly friend in the summer of 1416, in which he recorded a visit to Ferentino

to look for ancient remains . . . the heat was terrific . . . I wandered over the whole city . . . and searched in it for a citadel of ancient workmanship . . . On the inner side [of a carved stone was] an inscription which I am sending you because I think it will please even your sick stomach. But see that you understand the abbreviations correctly, for there are many of them, and let me know what you think of it . . . I sweated for several hours, and sweat indeed I did in the midday sun, but hard work conquers all.

(Bracciolini 1832, 219; Goodhart Gordan 1974, 127–9)

In Poggio's time, though, such commitment was rare: in the main, concern for the visible remains of ancient Rome was superficial. The Middle Ages, it seems, had lost the awareness that classical civilisation was different, and buildings like the Pantheon inspired only dread because of their association with paganism (Weiss 1988, 2–3; Buddensieg 1971, 260). They were not, therefore, systematically preserved; in the mid-fifteenth century, a Spanish visitor to the city reported that, frequently, only the tops of ancient buildings could be seen above the debris that had accumulated around them during the intervening centuries (Partner 1976, 5), and in his *Roma instaurata*, Biondo lamented the current desolation of the Capitol (Biondo 1470, 14r–v). For centuries, in fact, the people of Rome had plundered classical monuments for building materials, and had exported marbles, sarcophagi and statues, despite the occasional efforts of popes such as Pius II and Sixtus IV to protect them (Weiss 1988, 8–10, 98–101, 103–4, 112–14, 192). No licensing system was established for the sale of antiquities until the second half of the sixteenth century, and in the meantime, even the new building commissioned by sympathetic popes entailed the demolition of earlier structures (Partner 1976, 90–1; Albertinis 1510, vivr). In 1519, Raphael could still deplore the damage caused 'by those who should have defended these poor relics of Rome as fathers and tutors' (Golzio 1936, 82–3).

The cultural impulse that lay behind the Italian Renaissance was therefore from the start – in Rome at least – a minority interest. And among these admirers of classical civilisation, further intellectual and artistic advance was believed to be a product of imitation, and not of innovation. In a debate with Angelo Poliziano on the use of Latin in the late fifteenth century, for example, Paolo Cortesi, another employee of the papacy in Rome, put the argument clearly: 'not only in oratory, but in the other arts also imitation is a necessity. For all knowledge is acquired with the aid of previous learning' (Portoghesi 1972, 27–8). Cultural activities could thus be revived in the present if they reverted to the principles expounded by the ancients. The Italian language itself might even benefit from a little conscious Latinising (Shearman 1967, 37–8).

In Rome, the literary and artistic Renaissance worked closely together. The ground-floor rooms of Agostino Chigi's Villa Farnesina, for example, built next to the Tiber by Baldassare Peruzzi in 1509–11, are decorated with scenes from classical mythology drawn from Ovid's *Metamorphoses*. In one room, Raphael and his pupils were responsible for a series of frescoes recording the story of Amor and Psyche drawn from Apuleius' *Golden Ass*; according to Fritz Saxl, they here deliberately set out to imitate the artistic achievements of the ancients. 'The Amor and Psyche paintings', he says, 'represent the greatest effort to illustrate pagan myths in the spirit of the classical marbles as they reappeared from beneath the Roman soil' (Saxl 1957, 192–5). Both form and content were alike derived from classical Roman examples, one artistic and the other literary. Renaissance architects, too, derived inspiration from the surviving remains of the ancient world; Bramante's Tempietto of 1502 or later in Rome clearly echoes the temple of Vesta at Tivoli, which we know the architect had previously visited (Portoghesi 1972, 41–2). The same was true of

sculptors – so much so that Cardinal Raffaele Riario even bought Michelangelo's Cupid of *c.* 1496–7 on the assumption that it was a genuine antique!

Similar examples can, of course, be found all over Renaissance Italy. One of
the peculiar features of the Renaissance in Rome, however, is that none of the
men involved in the campaigns to rediscover and then recreate the culture of
the ancient city had been born there. Raphael, for example, came from
Urbino, as did Bramante, and Michelangelo was a Florentine. Among the
other non-Roman artists who visited or worked in the city were Ghiberti,
Brunelleschi and Donatello, Giuliano and Antonio da Sangallo, Sansovino,
Piero della Francesca and Leonardo. Masaccio died in Rome; Perugino,
Signorelli, Ghirlandaio, Rosselli, Botticelli and Lippi were all commissioned
in 1481 to decorate the Sistine Chapel. The same is true of music in Rome:
Italians played only a minor part in the history of the papal chapel in the
fifteenth and early sixteenth centuries, which was dominated by foreigners
like the Burgundian Guillaume Dufay, Josquin des Prez, who was born in
Picardy, and Francisco de Peñalosa, a Spaniard. But these figures were hardly
atypical once they had reached the city, for it has been estimated that only
about 17 per cent of the 3,000-odd householders listed in the census of 1526–7
were natives; 20 per cent were not even Italians (Mitchell 1973, 39, 45). It was,
and remained, a cosmopolitan city, and local loyalties inevitably therefore
took a rather different form to those in other Italian cultural centres. For the
majority of intellectuals and artists in Rome there could be no local patriotism
except to the idea of the city itself; and by the fourteenth and fifteenth
centuries, that idea was ineluctably associated with the Papacy.

For Rome was not only the capital of the ancient world; it was also the
capital of western Christianity, and the permanent home of the popes from
1420. Artists and scholars regularly praised the munificence of the papacy;
virtually all other potential patrons in Rome were also associated with the
Curia, and it was, of course, the prospect of clerical, and above all papal,
patronage that drew artists and scholars to Rome from their native cities
elsewhere. But that patronage had a purpose. The history of the Church in the
years before 1420 had been dominated by the Schism and the Conciliar
controversy; after the Schism had been settled, and Martin V had returned to
Rome, the common theme of works commissioned by the popes was the
reassertion of their own office and universal authority.

These two great themes – the city of Rome and the role of the papacy – are
irretrievably bound together in the history of the Renaissance in Rome, and
differentiate it sharply from the Renaissance in other Italian cities. Even
outsiders like the Venetian Domenico de' Domenichi could appreciate the
city's particular mystique: he called Rome 'a holy nation, an elect people, a
priestly city' (O'Malley 1979, 210). Rome was believed to have its own
peculiar destiny, from capital of a world empire to capital of a spiritual

empire. In a neat juxtaposition of ancient and modern, Marco Girolamo Vida could thus publish in 1535 his epic poem entitled the *Christiad*; this was clearly modelled on the *Aenead*, and sought to present itself as a prophecy from the ancient world of Rome's forthcoming greatness as the seat of the Church (Mitchell 1973, 92).

A similar juxtaposition can be found in Perugino's fresco of 1482, in the Sistine Chapel, of the delivery by Christ of the Keys of Heaven and Hell to St Peter, a Gospel story set against the wholly anachronistic background of the Arch of Constantine, which was not complete until the year AD 315. It was even possible in 1517 for Raphael to use pagan motifs from ancient Rome in his decoration of the Loggie of the Cortile of S. Damaso at the heart of the papal palace. This ornamentation was inspired in part by the discoveries at the ancient Domus Aurea in *c.* 1480; the grotesques were reproduced exactly, but put by the artists into a biblical context to suit the requirements of the site. Figures from the Old Testament, and even Christ himself, thus coexist with the gods and heroes, satyrs and nymphs of classical mythology (Dacos 1976).

At the time, this attempt to bring together the worlds of ancient and modern Rome seemed quite unexceptional. But in the same year, Paride de Grassi, the papal Master of Ceremonies voiced a deeper concern when referring in his diary to a sermon heard by the Pope in the Sistine Chapel to celebrate the feast of St John the Evangelist. This, he claimed, was 'more Gentile than Christian', for the preacher had invoked the pagan gods and goddesses (de Grassi 1884, 59). The full text of the sermon has not been found, but de Grassi's reference alone suggests an awareness by the reign of Leo X of a possible conflict between an admiration for ancient Rome and the interests of the contemporary papacy: could a committed Christian hope to revive and imitate every facet of the pagan city? Even before 1500, residents of Rome had questioned aspects of their classical inheritance. Pope Paul II had once prohibited the teaching of pagan poetry in schools, Giannozzo Manetti had criticised the obscenity and cruelty of the ancients, and Lorenzo Valla had expressed doubt about the whole of their philosophy since it was based on the unchristian assumption that men can act justly without the assistance of divine grace (Grayson 1967, 55; Trinkaus 1970, 148–50, 727–9). In 1517 – in the same year that Raphael worked at the Loggie and Leo X heard the 'Gentile' sermon – Desiderius Erasmus suggested that paganism was seeking to rise again in Rome under cover of a renascent classicism (Delumeau 1974, 146).

There is, in fact, a certain amount of evidence to lend credence to Erasmus' charge. The boundaries between the pagan and the Christian worlds were at best blurred in Cardinal Bembo's reference to the Virgin Mary as a 'radiant nymph', or in the recommendation made in 1438 by Lapo da Castiglionchio, a papal secretary, that the modern Church should follow the example of the ancients, whose idols were always gloriously decorated with gold. The confusion seems even more apparent in Paolo Cortesi's praise of St Thomas Aquinas as 'the Apollo of Christianity' (Delumeau 1974, 146; Baron 1938, 30). And some of the popes themselves could find a surprising use for classical imagery. After the military campaigns of 1506–7 that enabled the papacy to gain control of Perugia and Bologna, Julius II recreated for himself an ancient Roman Triumph, in which he was drawn through the streets of Rome, like the pagan Emperors, in a chariot drawn by four white horses. One of the arches erected on his route was inscribed with Julius Caesar's famous words 'Veni, vidi, vici', and a coin minted to mark his achievement was inscribed 'Iulius Caesar Pont. II' (Stinger 1985, 235–8, 383). Comparisons between Pope Julius and his imperial predecessor abound in the contemporary literature: it was also in 1507, for example, that Giles of Viterbo (then vicar-general of the Augustinians) reminded the Pope that Julius Caesar had ruled only half the world; since the discovery of the Americas, Julius II had ruled all of it (O'Malley 1969; cf. Albertinis 1510, Aiiiv–Biv).

The most startling example of this willingness to bring pagan and Christian together is perhaps the ceiling in one of the rooms in the Borgia apartments in the Vatican. The structure of the building had been completed before 1450, but in the 1490s Alexander VI commissioned Pinturicchio and his assistants to redecorate the interiors. Most of the rooms contain scenes from the lives of Christ and the saints, but in one room the artists have depicted the classical myth of Io, a girl pursued by Jupiter, the king of the gods. He transformed her into a cow, and his wife, the vengeful Juno, drove her from Greece to Egypt, where she was restored to human shape, took the name Isis, and married Osiris. In due course, Osiris was murdered and dismembered, only to reappear in the form of a bull as the focus for a new religion. This pagan story seems to bear little relation to the traditional Christian material in the other rooms. Admittedly, the bull was the family emblem of the Borgias, and over 200 bulls have been counted in the decoration of the Borgia apartments as a whole (Saxl 1957, 175–88); but it is difficult to give any very orthodox interpretation to the inclusion of this pagan tale in an otherwise Christian context, and the ambiguity inherent in the celebration by a Christian pope of his family emblem's association with a resurrected pagan god remains unsettling even now.

Alexander's reputation for orthodoxy has never been very secure: in 1498, Savonarola maintained that the Pope had denied the existence of God, a charge that survived his death and which has reappeared occasionally in succeeding centuries (Davidson 1991). Whether it is entirely true we may, of course, legitimately doubt; but the same charge had already been laid in 1468 against a number of distinguished humanists in Rome. In that year, Alexander's predecessor, Paul II, had suppressed the Roman Academy, which had been founded by Pomponio Leto, a professor at the University of Rome to foster the revival of classical learning and archaeology. So complete was its members' devotion to the ancient world that they even used ancient titles as forms of address. Hostility to the Academy focused on three matters above all. The first was the academicians' alleged sexual immorality; there may have been some truth in this, for at the time of the suppression, Pomponio Leto himself was imprisoned in Venice on a charge of sodomy (Zabughin 1909, 25–32, 283–4). The second was their alleged republicanism, derived, it was said, from their devotion to classical scholarship. Republicanism was indeed a recurrent feature of Roman life, and was often associated with a call for the revival of ancient forms of government. In 1347, for example, Cola di Rienzo – a student of classical inscriptions and constitutions – claimed that 'he wanted to reform the whole of Italy under obedience to Rome – as it had been in the ancient times' (Villani 1857, 494–5); in 1511, claiming inspiration from the ancient world, Pompeo Colonna and Antimo Savello 'called the Roman people to liberty' during an illness of Julius II, and declaimed 'against the domination of the priests' (Giovio 1561, 117v). There does in fact seem to be some evidence that members of the Academy were involved in a plot to assassinate Paul II (Zabughin 1909, 99, 107); but the third charge against them is perhaps the most intriguing. They were accused of neo-paganism; contemporary observers recorded their doubts about the existence of the afterlife, of the soul and of God Himself, and they certainly seem to have avoided religion as a topic of conversation at their meetings (Sabellico 1502, 55v–6v; Zabughin 1909, 45–52).

The full story of the Roman Academy may never be known; but the other examples collected here indicate sufficiently well that contemporaries were at least sometimes aware of the potential conflict between the two major themes that characterised the art and scholarship of the Renaissance in Rome. There were, however, some valiant efforts to bring the ancient and modern worlds of Rome together in closer harmony, for it had been observed since the time of the early Church that some pagan writers seemed to share a number of beliefs with Christianity: monotheism, the immortality of the soul, the afterlife and elements of Christian morality all appear in Platonism, for example. According to Giles of Viterbo, God does not distance Himself from anyone, and the truth can therefore be discovered, by the use of natural reason, outside the Christian tradition altogether. The pagan past can therefore contain elements of value for contemporary Christians (O'Malley 1968, 22–7).

A pictorial demonstration of this willingness to recognise the value of pagan thought is provided by Raphael's School of Athens in the Stanza della Segnatura of the Vatican, painted in 1509–10. This depicts Plato, Aristotle, Pythagoras and many other figures of the ancient world in a glorious classical building (reminiscent of the Baths of Diocletian), right in the heart of the

Pope's apartments. The principles of unity and harmony, in nature as in human thought, were central to much of the Renaissance (Portoghesi 1972, 32). The truth is indivisible, and even the errors of the ancient world can be explained if they are interpreted as fables or parables. Pagan poetry and mythology can thus be seen as allegories, which can be made to disclose their hidden truth by skilled and knowledgeable interpreters (O'Malley 1968, 55–7; Wind 1968, 17–21; Trinkaus 1970, xvii, 686–8).

This awareness of a *theologia poetica* was associated with a much broader belief in a *theologia prisca*, an 'ancient theology' which was known even before Christ had been born. Philosophers devised lists to show the correct genealogy of true learning, tracing its development from Noah (who had preserved everything of value before the Flood) through Moses and the ancient Greeks, such as Pythagoras and Plato. Normally it was believed that this wisdom had been preserved in ancient Egypt; but in the Papal States a separate tradition suggested that Noah had settled in Rome after the Flood, and that the 'ancient theology' had thus been passed directly to the Etruscans and Romans. The Pope was therefore Noah's successor, as well as Peter's (O'Malley 1968, 31; Stephens 1984; cf. Ettlinger 1965, 111, 115–16). It was this community of belief, shared by Jews, pagans and Christians alike, that explained the essential harmony of all religious texts, even those attributed to the supposed Egyptian sage Hermes Trismegistus (Walker 1972, 1–41). The final stage of the genealogy was represented by the Sibyls, ecstatic women who lurked at pagan shrines and prophesied the coming of Christ. The Sibyls appear frequently in Roman Renaissance art – in the Borgia apartments, for example, and most famously, perhaps, in Michelangelo's Sistine ceiling (Saxl 1957, 175; O'Malley 1968, 31; Stinger 1985, 308–10, 312).

All these examples reflect a Roman emphasis on the harmony of pagan and Christian thought, and an almost Messianic desire to see all mankind, ancient and modern, caught up in a single ideological understanding and subject to a single, papal authority. The most extreme exponent of this thinking was probably Giovanni Pico della Mirandola. He was born in 1463 at his family home near Modena, and at the age of 23 he had become so convinced, as a result of voracious reading, by the similarities between pagan, Jewish, Christian and even Muslim thought that he collected 900 theses for discussion, in philosophy, theology and science, and summoned scholars to a debate in Rome in 1487 to prove his case. The debate was never conducted, for the Pope took fright at some of his propositions and charged him with heresy; but his aspirations, at least, were not atypical of the Renaissance in Rome (Cassirer 1948, 223–54; Trinkaus 1970, 753–8; Craven 1981, 48, 57–9, 68; Stinger 1985, 300–1).

The danger of such thinking, and indeed of any attempt to bring together the worlds of ancient and modern Rome, was that Christianity's claim to an exclusive revelation of the truth might be minimised or even eliminated. Even after the sixteenth century, classicism remained the language of Roman culture and art; but its pagan influence could not survive the Counter-Reformation. Figures like Guillaume Postel and Giordano Bruno, who preached harmony on the basis of secret or new theologies, were imprisoned or executed by the Roman Inquisition, and the sternest of the early modern popes, Pius V, even expelled classical statues from the Belvedere in the Vatican Palace.

By the time of the Counter-Reformation, however, the essentially imitative approach of the Renaissance to classical Rome had already been undermined, in part, at least, by the talent of its admirers. Respect for the language of the ancients gave way to a desire to develop it: as Poliziano had explained in the fifteenth century, 'I am not Cicero . . . it is through Cicero that I have learnt how to be myself' (Portoghesi 1972, 27). In the visual arts, the impulse to surpass the achievements of the ancient world was displayed most dramatically in the career of Michelangelo, who (according to Vasari) 'broke the knots and chains of what, in line with the established tradition, everybody else had continually observed' (Vasari 1881, 193). John Shearman dates the first appearance of this more self-conscious and inventive 'Mannerist' style to about 1520 in Rome, just before a series of disasters struck the city, such as the plague of 1522 and the Sack of 1527 (Shearman 1967, 23, 35, 42–61, 70–9). In the 'Late Renaissance' world that emerged in the mid-sixteenth century, art and culture in Rome were used to maintain the devotional commitment of the faithful after the Reformation. The ancient world was still admired, but not unquestioningly; in the Eternal City, the Renaissance had by now served its purpose as a vehicle for notions of a universal papal primacy and had been superseded.

REFERENCES

Albertinis, F. de (1510), *Opusculum de mirabilibus novae et veteris urbis Romae* (Rome)

Baron, H. (1938), 'Franciscan poverty and civic wealth as factors in the rise of Humanistic thought', *Speculum*, 13, 1–37

Biondo, F. (1470), *Blondi Flavii Forliviensis in Roma instaurata* (Rome)

Bracciolini, P. (1832), *Epistolae*, ed. T. de Tonellis (Florence)

Buddensieg, T. (1971), 'Criticism and praise of the Pantheon in the Middle Ages and the Renaissance' in R.R. Bolgar (ed.), *Classical Influences on European Culture A.D. 500–1500*, 259–67 (Cambridge)

Cassirer, E. *et al.* (eds.) (1948), *The Renaissance Philosophy of Man* (Chicago and London)

Chambers, D.S. (1976), 'Studium Urbis and *gabella studii*: the University of Rome in the fifteenth century' in C.H. Clough (ed.), *Cultural Aspects of the Italian*

Renaissance: essays in Honour of Paul Oskar Kristeller (Manchester), 68–110

Craven, W.G. (1981), *Giovanni Pico della Mirandola, Symbol of his Age: Modern Interpretations of a Renaissance Scholar* (Geneva)

Dacos, N. (1976), 'Les Loges de Raphael: repertoire à l'antique, Bible et mythologie' in R.R. Bolgar (ed.), *Classical Influences on European Culture A.D. 1500–1700*, 325–34 (Cambridge)

Davidson, N.S. (1991), 'Atheism and unbelief in Italy, 1500–1700' in M. Hunter and D. Wootton (eds.), *Atheism from the Renaissance to the Enlightenment* (Oxford)

de Grassi, P. (1884), *Il diario di Leone X*, ed. P. Delicati and M. Armellini (Rome)

Delumeau, J. (1974), *L'Italie de Botticelli à Bonaparte* (Paris)

Ettlinger, L.D. (1965), *The Sistine Chapel before Michelangelo: religious imagery and papal primacy* (Oxford)

Giovio, P. (1561), *Le vite di dicenove huomini illustri* (Venice)

Golzio, V. (1936), *Raffaello nei documenti, nelle testimonianze dei contemporanei, e nella letteratura del suo secolo* (Vatican City)

Goodhart Gordan, P.W. (1974), *Two Renaissance Book Hunters: The Letters of Poggius Bracciolini to Nicolaus de Nicolis* (New York and London)

Grayson, C. (1967), 'The Renaissance in Italy outside Florence' in D. Hay (ed.), *The Age of the Renaissance* (London)

Mitchell, B. (1973), *Rome in the High Renaissance: The Age of Leo X* (Norman, Oklahoma)

O'Malley, J.W. (1968), *Giles of Viterbo on Church and Reform: A Study in Renaissance Thought* (Leiden)

   (1969), 'Fulfilment of the Christian Golden Age under Julius II: text of a Discourse of Giles of Viterbo, 1507', *Traditio*, 25, 265–338

   (1979), *Praise and Blame in Renaissance Rome: Rhetoric, Doctrine, and Reform in the Sacred Orators of the Papal Court, c. 1450–1521* (Durham, North Carolina)

Partner, P. (1976), *Renaissance Rome 1500–1559: A Portrait of a Society* (London)

Petrarch, F. (1554), *Opera quae extant omnia* (Basle)

Portoghesi, P. (1972), *Rome of the Renaissance* (London)

Sabellico, M.A. (1502), *Opera* (Venice)

Saxl, F. (1957), *Lectures* (London)

Serlio, S. (1544), *Il terzo libro di Sabastiano Serlio Bolognese, nel qual si figurano, e discrivono le antiquità di Roma* (Venice)

Shearman, J. (1967), *Mannerism* (Harmondsworth)

Stephens, W.E. (1984), 'The Etruscans and the Ancient Theology in Annius of Viterbo' in P. Brezzi and M. de Panizza Lorch (eds.), *Umanesimo a Roma nel Quattrocento* (Rome and New York)

Stinger, C.L. (1985), *The Renaissance in Rome* (Bloomington)

Trinkaus, C. (1970), *In Our Image and Likeness: Humanity and Divinity in Italian Humanist Thought* (London)

Vasari, G. (1881), *Le vite de' più eccelenti pittori scultori ed architettori*, ed. G. Milanesi, vol. VII (Florence)

Villani, G. (1857), *Croniche di Giovanni, Matteo e Filippo Villani* (Trieste)

Walker, D.P. (1972), *The Ancient Theology: Studies in Christian Platonism from the Fifteenth to the Eighteenth Century* (London)

Weiss, R. (1967), 'The New Learning: scholarship from Petrarch to Erasmus', in D.
    Hay (ed.), *The Age of the Renaissance* (London), 101–22
    (1988), *The Renaissance Discovery of Classical Antiquity* (Oxford)
Wilkins, E.H. (1955), *Studies in the Life and Works of Petrarch* (Cambridge, Mass.)
Wind, E. (1968), *Pagan Mysteries in the Renaissance* (London)
Zabughin, V. (1909), *Giulio Pomponio Leto: saggio critico* (Rome)

—————————————— ⅋ ——————————————

FOUR

VENICE

RICHARD MACKENNEY

If we are to understand the culture of the Venetians, we must employ with caution the idea of a Renaissance defined in Florentine terms. There are parallels, of course: most obviously, in terms of great achievements in the arts within the political framework of a republic. But the Venetian context can be understood only very imperfectly, if we try to force upon it a pattern of creativity dependent on individuals of genius who made audacious leaps across ages of darkness to reach the ancient world. Nor can we concentrate exclusively on a single city, for Venice stood at the centre of a maritime colonial empire and a territorial state.[1] For reasons of manageability, this chapter is largely concerned with Venice itself, but it does scant justice to what Venetians built to secure their eastern trade, to the lively and semi-autonomous culture of centres such as Verona, Vicenza and Padua, and to the civilised life-style of the mainland villas, a life-style which owed at least as much to Tuscany and Rome as to Venice, as much to princes and courts as to the serene Republic.[2]

Even if we narrow our focus to the city itself, we are faced with not one context but two: the historical and the social. For, unlike Florence, Venice had no direct link with a Roman past, and, unlike most other cities and states, Venice experienced no political revolution. Thus, our first task is to chart the history of the Venetian Renaissance: what was its chronology and how does it relate to the classical past? We must then ask what the character of the city's culture owed to a pattern of society uniquely stabilised by public institutions and by the rhythms of the economy. It might be argued that if we are to understand the culture of Venice, we should dispense with the term 'Renaissance' altogether. We might choose to look at Venice in the neutral context of two centuries: the fifteenth, when the Florentine Renaissance occurred, and the sixteenth, when that culture spread to other parts of Europe. An essay on 'Quattrocento Venice', and an exhibition on 'The genius of Venice, 1500–1600' can communicate the many-sidedness of the Venetian achievement without being tied to an inflexible notion of classical revival. However, there

amalgam, and the absence of explosive changes of character, or of crucial turning-points in the city's cultural development is matched by the city's untroubled political and social history, which brings us to our second context.

Venice's immunity to revolution used to be explained in terms of the positive action of a constitution perfectly designed and operated by a wise ruling class.[19] More recent research has emphasised the role of the corporate social structure in underpinning political stability. Certainly, the absence of an absolute ruler was symptomatic less of distaste for tyranny informed by the experience of the ancient world, than of a general suspicion of individual greatness which ran throughout Venetian society. A historical concept based upon anonymity is by nature elusive, but it serves to demonstrate how inappropriate to Venice is an idea of the Renaissance based on the achievements of the Florentines. For Vasari, the great cultural revival was to be understood in terms of the biographies of individual artists. Burckhardt devoted one of his six chapters to 'The development of the individual', and Baron sought to show how Bruni had almost single handedly revitalised the notion of republican liberty. By contrast, the political and social structure of Venice was overwhelmingly corporatist.[20]

In Venice, the individual found identity as a member of a group: the nobles in their family clans, the small citizen class as brothers within the great charitable institutions, the Scuole Grandi.[21] For the populace there were smaller confraternities, the *scuole piccole* – perhaps 200 of them in the fifteenth century – and about a hundred trade guilds which provided solidarity in work, sickness and death. Some of the foreign communities established their separateness through institutions which were quintessentially Venetian. Florentines, Slavs, Greeks and even Jews had their own *scuole*. Others – the Germans, Arabs, Turks and Persians – established great warehouses or *fondachi* to consolidate the presence of their traders. And the whole was bound together in a mesh of neighbourhood networks within the six large areas (*sestieri*) and the seventy parishes into which the city was divided.[22]

The great range of solidarities was regularly celebrated in spectacular public festivals, extravagant affirmations of the public weal. There were twelve great *andate* which gave pride of place to the Doge, but the striking feature of the Venetian festive calendar is the way in which different solidarities – sometimes the Scuole Grandi, sometimes the Arsenal workers or fishermen, the furriers or blacksmiths, occasionally a particular parish – were elevated to an equal prominence. In an important sense, Venetian processions gave substance to the myth of social harmony. The invasion of individual privacy by informers and the secret ruthlessness of the Council of Ten, once the caricatured hallmarks of Venetian government, were in reality much less significant than the celebration of political, religious and social solidarity through corporations which were elevated to public prominence even though they were denied access to executive power. The constitution gave power only to a closed and clearly defined aristocracy, but other institutions integrated the interests of state and society to an unusual degree. The corporations held the balance between rulers and ruled, enabling their members to feel part of public life in the market-place or procession, giving the government access to the subjects of the state. Moreover, they acted to sustain the public weal in the relief of poverty – the corporate structure even embraced the poor. Thus, Venetian civic ritual celebrated stability and advertised wealth in great theatrical events in which the whole city seemed to participate.[23]

The pervasiveness of a species of public life which subordinated the individual to the corporation dissolved or suppressed the tensions which so often galvanise the historical experience of other cities and states: tensions between republicanism and tyranny, church and state, between the public and private spheres, the populace and the elite. The impact of Venetian public life on Venetian culture was profound.

First of all, the character of public life helps to understand why humanism in Venice can appear artificial and alien in politics and in historical writings. A literary culture aimed at securing the position of powerful elites provided scant propaganda for the kind of social solidarity celebrated so publicly in Venice.[24] Moreover, given the stability of the city's constitutional history, commentators and politicians did not need the historical and rhetorical ammunition which the works of Cicero provided for those who sought to describe and arrest the transition of a state from republic to tyranny. Paolo Sarpi, the great ideologue and propagandist, made his attacks on Rome and his defences of Venice in a style remarkable for its lack of rhetorical ornament.[25]

Sarpi was the champion of secular sovereignty, and the second aspect of the pervasiveness of public life which must be stressed is the state's penetration of the religious sphere. The cathedral, San Pietro, stood remote and isolated in Castello. San Marco was the Doge's private chapel. The public celebrations which took place before it and wound their way through it subordinated the ecclesiastical calendar to dates in the history of Venice.[26] They were often accompanied by music, and there can be little doubt that the richness of the creative achievements in this sphere owed much to a centre of patronage which operated independent of the formal demands of the music of the Roman church.[27] Elsewhere in the city, funerary monuments and religious paintings commemorated public service and public events. The church of the Frari resembles a great Venetian pantheon with its monuments to the *condottiere* Paolo Savelli, the Generalissimo da Mar Jacopo Marcello, the Doges Francesco Foscari and Nicolo Tron, and the paintings of Bellini and Titian combined the sacred and the civic to ensure that images of the Madonna dissolved into those of Venice herself.[28]

That subordination of the private interests of individuals or families was another symptom of the way public life dominated social life. We must not, of course, be captivated by the myth of patrician responsibility and popular obedience, for we know only too well that there was plenty of self-interest and corruption amongst the ruling class, and that the populace at large was not always law-abiding.[29] At the same time, we must remark upon a striking public dimension to what might otherwise be adjudged private patronage, and perhaps admit 'a distinctive sense of mission on the part of the aristocracy'. The art collections of patricians – the antique sculptures belonging to the Grimani and the Foscari, the paintings of the Priuli and the Vendramin – were a source of civic pride.[30]

Outside the ranks of the patriciate, the commissions of the city's corporations put the wealth of private persons in the service of institutions which were often deeply involved in the life of the state through their provision of welfare to the poor and their supply of galleymen to the fleet. The Scuole Grandi combined piety and civic splendour in a powerful identification of their own needs with those of the state, and their patronage is paralleled in the modest but numerous works commissioned by guilds anxious to make some impact in the public domain.[31]

As we follow the chain of patronage from the aristocracy to the guilds we find that we can dispense with the popular/elite stereotype, and with the barriers which are usually assumed to have existed between a cultured life and everyday drudgery. Even the social realities of poverty, famine and plague did not produce an easily discernible line between popular culture and that of the elite. Studying the civilisation of Venice – a civilisation which lacked the patronage systems which billowed around absolute monarchs – prompts the idea that the court, exclusive and haughty, consciously set apart from the rest of society, was one of the most powerful influences on the emergence of a culture for the elite which was quite distinct from that of ordinary people. For Aretino, not going to court was what life was about: 'la vita è non andar in corte'. And Titian did not have to leave Venice to paint princes: they often came to him.[32] In a fundamental sense, the Renaissance in Venice was a vernacular phenomenon, which is amply demonstrated by a catalogue of the significant resonances between economic life – what primarily involved and affected ordinary people – and the cultural achievements of the Venetians.

The transformation of the marshy islands into the nucleus of a trading empire demanded constant virtuosity from the inhabitants. The early wooden buildings were often ravaged by fire and therefore continually needed renovation. Later, in the fifteenth century, the construction of great stone buildings on such unstable foundations required expertise throughout the building trades.[33] Piles had to be sunk to support structures of any weight. Different waterside contours between the hundred islands and 150 banks demanded many different types of bridge, as inspired in their design and engineering as more celebrated monuments.[34]

The waters of the lagoon could be crossed, but not drunk. The well heads which give such delight in many Venetian squares crown a system of water purification which is a triumph of engineering. The city's vernacular architecture conceals brilliant (but anonymous) solutions to a wide range of problems: and still stands to prove it. Impervious clay protected the foundations against rising damp, and above water level bricks were interspersed with transverse strata of Istrian stone. Much thought was given to privacy: a housing block might contain twelve multi-storey dwellings with separate street entrances and interior stairs. Living space was as ample as in 'a modern American inner-city flat', and there was sometimes a surprisingly large garden area.[35] Many of the solutions were taken up in the domestic architecture of Sansovino and Palladio.[36] Ecclesiastical buildings also reflected vernacular expertise. The churches of San Stefano and San Giacomo dell'Orio are like upturned boats, their vaulted ceilings dependent on engineering skills which carpenters had developed in the city's shipyards.[37] Within the city's forty belltowers chimed further reminders of the application of technological expertise to the structures of everyday life. And we know that Rizzo's Moors for the clock-tower at San Marco were cast in the Arsenal.[38]

Another aspect of economic life which gave strength to vernacular culture was an immigrant population. Writing at the end of the fifteenth century, the French ambassador, Philippe de Commynes, observed that 'most of the people are foreigners'. This is understandable. Maritime commerce did not always secure adequate grain supplies, the city's cisterns did not create immunity to disease. The ravages of famine and plague had to be made good by immigrants from throughout the Mediterranean world.[39]

The social mosaic was highly varied. There may have been 4,000 Greeks in the city in the late sixteenth century. In a list drawn up in 1531, the ironmongers' guild classified its members according to their place of origin. Only one in six was described as a Venetian, almost one-third came from Ballabio. There were casual visitors as well. Many will have stayed at the Lion Bianco, one of Venice's foremost Gothic monuments. Visitors from Vicenza, Bergamo, Londinara, Rovigo and Friuli were assigned to their own lodging houses. All the Germans had to stay at the Fondaco dei Tedeschi. Around 1500, there were 232 merchants there from the city of Nuremberg alone, although the German population was much more dispersed. In 1508, two young artists, Giorgione and Titian, decorated the walls of the Fondaco with frescoes.[40]

Both were part of the great human flood. Giorgione came to the city from his mainland home of Castelfranco, Titian from Cadore. The list may be extended. Antonello, a native of Messina, came to Venice in 1474, possibly via the workshops of Flanders, conceivably bringing with him the oil-based paints so essential to Venetian colourists. The sculptors Lombardi (Pietro and his sons Tullio and Antonio) displayed their origins in their name and were followed by almost an entire school. Antonio Rizzo, Girolamo Campagna and Michele Sanmichele came from Verona, as of course did the painter Paolo Caliari, 'il Veronese', while Arezzo is commemorated in the name of Pietro Aretino.[41]

The metropolitan economy was based on what are misleadingly called 'luxuries' – misleadingly, because 'necessities' were so rarely in evidence while inessentials abounded. Canon Pietro Casola, a pilgrim en route to the Holy Land, writing at about the same time as Commynes, remarked that 'the special products for which other cities are noted are to be found there' – and in quantity.[42] This was certainly the case in the shops which lined the Merceria between Rialto and San Marco, crammed with German metalware, pewter from Flanders, felt, jewels, caps, bonnets, veils, wedding chests – all the bric-à-brac which adorns a Renaissance interior or a scene by Veronese – from Lombardy, Tuscany, Bologna, the Romagna and Modena. There was a good living to be made in thread, buttons or feathers.[43] Other wares were made in Venice itself. Some of the shops no doubt displayed mirrors, and there was glassware unmatched in other cities, produced on Murano according to jealously guarded trade-secrets. Goldsmiths wrought not only delicate jewelry, but caskets and crosses justly described as 'architecture in miniature', so substantial is their presence.[44] The production of glass and jewelry depended on standards of training and quality set down in the statutes of the appropriate guilds. Although we would perhaps not wish to group Venetian painting with these 'lesser arts', we still need to view it in a social context which has nothing to do with courts and academies: 'In spite of the ancient aspiration of painters to the liberty enjoyed by poets . . . their art was always subject, at least in Venice, to the same laws which governed any product of commercial value'.[45] Thus, Lorenzo Lotto exhibited his wares for sale at Ascensiontide like anyone else with something to sell, and he left his brushes and equipment to the painters' guild with a view to its finding two aspiring youngsters who might make use of them. The objection that Lotto is not in the front rank of Venetian painters, which derives in part from Titian's friend Aretino, must be countered with a reminder of Lotto's collaboration with Raphael and the persuasive attribution to him of the Swiss Guards in the frescoes of the Vatican Stanze. We do not need to elevate or relegate his status as an artist, however, to set him in the Venetian context, a commercial context of guilds, apprentices, shops and market-days.[46]

What strikes us in the Scuola Grande di San Rocco is that Tintoretto's great decorative cycle is only part of the decoration. The paintings share the spirituality of the reliquaries, and their grandeur increases within the ample space of the great meeting-hall, whence the approach to the upper chamber gains majesty from the massive staircase. Once ascended, we find Tintoretto's masterworks thriving amid the dark carving which adorns the lower walls and which springs in golden dance around the ceiling paintings. The visitor to San Rocco is reminded of the skills of builders and decorators, goldsmiths and wood carvers – and is drawn to reflect on how much of the city's everyday economic life was devoted to the production and presentation of works of art.

Similar currents of economic life help us to understand why it was in Venice that a highly skilled engraver from Germany, Albrecht Duerer, encountered the powerful classicism of Mantegna, and on his next visit, in 1505, benefited from corporate sponsorship, for the *scuola* of the German community commissioned the *Feast of the Rose Garlands* for their altar in San Bartolomeo.[47] Similar commercial eddies enhance an appreciation of Venice's outstanding role in the development of modern music. The greatness of San Marco as a centre of musical culture owed much to the arrival in 1527 of Adriaan Willaert, bringing with him northern counterpoint. The Gabrieli drew inspiration from their visit to Germany, whence they returned laden with the notational techniques of Lassus, enriching the tradition which reached its zenith with the arrival of Monteverdi from Mantua.[48]

The Renaissance in Venice may be seen, then, in the context of a unique environment, peopled with immigrants dealing in luxury goods, manufactured and marketed according to the exacting demands of Venetian corporations, accompanied by the abstract traffic in styles, forms, techniques and ideas, a traffic unhindered by the social barriers imposed by princely courts. These themes are united in the most characteristic of Venetian products and the most significant contribution which Venice made to the civilisation of the Renaissance – the book trade. Even before the revolution brought about by the printing-press, the written word was something a Venetian would wish to exchange for money as well as for intellectual stimulus. The inventories of shops show formidable stocks of high value.[49] Working with words and figures was of obvious importance to a highly skilled labour-force operating in an emphatically commercial economy, but as one has sought to suggest, in the case of Venice, commercial exchange cannot be understood purely or even primarily in economic terms. Business concerns cannot be separated from intellectual activity or indeed from a search for spiritual satisfaction.

This is the background to the arrival in Venice in 1508 of an illegitimate visitor who collaborated with an immigrant from Rome. The co-operation of Erasmus and Aldus Manutius was distinctly unacademic, and we must understand Aldus as a harassed businessman seeking to sell his wares in the Merceria or asking goldsmiths to help with the preparation of type founts. The octavo format and italic print served 'to free literature from the study and the lecture room'.[50] And so did Erasmus. For in Italy, he reached his widest audience not as a humanist scholar or tolerant rationalist, but as a ribald satirist. As the antithesis of Cicero and as the champion of the laity, he was the forerunner of Aretino and – for all the difficulties involved in quantifying the influence of ideas – he was the indirect inspiration of many of the Venetian populace.[51]

The impetus provided by the printing-press gained momentum in a society where education was not the preserve of the courtly establishment. Venetian culture brushed aside the rigid social barriers which existed for political convenience. The evidence is fragmentary but suggestive. In 1442, the teacher Vettore Bonapace included the sons of a boatman and of a bricklayer amongst his clients, as well as young nobles. From a register of teachers drawn up in 1587, it would appear that there were 258 tutors and about 4,500 pupils in regular attendance, half of them in vernacular schools where the overwhelming majority of teachers were laymen. They did not receive the humanist education available in the Latin schools, but they will have read Ariosto, and even an Italian version of Beavis of Hampton. Such books as these were often in the possession of merchants and craftsmen. Some of them may have undergone a formal education, others may have learned from Giovanni Antonio Tagliente's *Libro maistrevole*. Tagliente wrote a handwriting manual for potential civil servants which went through thirty-five editions after 1524. His contact with circles in which a humanist education may have predominated did not prevent him from writing a book on business arithmetic: essential, in his words, to that 'necessity of human life, exercising the art of commerce'. The *Libro maistrevole*, however, was 'a pioneer effort aimed at aspirants to literacy in the vernacular' – especially artisans and women – to foster adult literacy for strictly secular purposes'. Literacy extended itself informally in taverns, homes, convents and shops.[52]

Erasmus and Aldus exchanged ideas in the print-shop at Sant'Agostino 'in an almost incredible mixture of the sweat-shop, the boarding house, and the research institute'. Lorenzo Lotto may have been attracted to ideas later deemed heretical in the company of goldsmiths and mercers. The archives of the Inquisition are stuffed with prosecutions of literate artisans expressing ideas in shops – usually ideas which doubted the validity of saints, purgatory, indulgences, jubilees, free will, and all the external sacramentalism so distasteful to Erasmus. We see this in the trials of Domenego the shoemaker, Francesco the grocer, Martin the goldsmith, Pasquale the turner, Zuanne the silk dealer and a host of others, and indeed that of the goldsmith Alessandro Caravia, author of a satirical poem, and the correspondent of Aretino.[53] The circle at once most famous and most typical met in the late years of the sixteenth century at the Nave d'Oro, premises owned by a member of the mercers' guild, Francesco Zechinelli, frequented by a merchant from Flanders, Daniel Nis. Here were discussed the news of the wars of religion and the character of other countries. The most avid listener and the most stimulating participant was a Servite friar, who also attended gatherings in the house of the nobleman Morosini – Paolo Sarpi. He wrote against the church's pretensions to secular power and against the prohibition of books. Like Erasmus, he stood 'between Renaissance and Enlightenment', like Erasmus, he related some of the most profound theological considerations of the Reformation era to the condition of lay society – and, like Erasmus, he found intellectual stimulus in a Venetian shop.[54]

This chapter has sought to establish a connection between economic and cultural life, a connection most obvious in the history of the Venetian press. But in what sense have we been discussing the Renaissance? If we choose to define that phenomenon as a revival of the values of the classical past in fifteenth century, then we have established no more than a marginal phenomenon. If, on the other hand, we see the Renaissance as a great burst of cultural creativity fuelled by the energies of the laity as a collectivity resistant to clerical interference – as an Erasmian as well as a Tuscan creation – then we have perhaps begun to understand the Renaissance in its Venetian context, a context which looks forward to Amsterdam as well as back to Florence.

NOTES

1 Among the most important treatments of the Venetian Renaissance are G. Piovene et al., *La civiltà di Venezia del Quattrocento*, Fondazione Giorgio Cini, *Storia della Civiltà Veneziana* (Florence, 1957); D. Valeri *et al.*, *La civiltà veneziana del Rinascimento (il Cinquecento)*, Fondazione Giorgio Cini, Storia della Civiltà Veneziana (Florence, 1958); V. Branca (ed.), *Rinascimento europeo e rinascimento veneziano* (Florence, 1967); *Umanesimo europeo e umanesimo veneziano* (Florence, 1963); O. Logan, *Culture and Society in Venice, 1470–1797: The Renaissance and its aftermath* (London, 1972).

2 On the city and its dominions, see G. Cozzi and M. Knapton, *Storia della Repubblica di Venezia dalla guerra di Chioggia alla riconquista della Terraferma* (Turin, 1986), an outstanding account based on recent research; on specific aspects, see M.L. King, *Venetian Humanism in an Age of Patrician Dominance*, (Princeton, N.J., 1986), 247; L. Puppi, 'Patronage on the Venetian mainland', in C. Hope and J. Martineau (eds.), *The Genius of Venice* (London, 1983), 21; and, in general, M. Muraro, *Venetian Villas: The History and Culture* (New York, 1986).

3 J.R. Hale, 'Quattrocento Venice' in A. Toynbee (ed.), *Cities of Destiny* (London, 1967), 48, 67.

4 T. Pignatti, 'Altarpieces' in Hope and Martineau, *Genius of Venice*, 29.

5 J. Ackerman, 'The geopolitics of Venetan architecture in the time of Titian' in D. Rosand (ed.), *Titian. His World and his Legacy* (New York, 1982), 41–71.

6 D. Howard, *The Architectural History of Venice* (London, 1980), 70–6.

7 C. Hope, *Titian* (London, 1980), 168.

8 Howard, *Architectural History*, 182–4.

9 Ackerman, 'Geopolitics', 54.

10 G. Fiocco, 'Le arti figurative' in Valeri *et al.*, *La civiltà veneziana del Rinascimento*, 190–1; J. Steer, *A Concise History of Venetian Painting* (London, 1970), 163.

11 S. Sinding-Larsen, 'The "Paradise" controversy: a note on argumentation' in D. Rosand (ed.), *Interpretazioni veneziane: studi di storia dell'arte in onore di Michelangelo Muraro* (New York, 1983), 368; P. Hills, 'Piety and patronage in Cinquecento Venice: Tintoretto and the Scuole del Sacramento', *Art History*, 6 (1983), 30–43; Steer, *Concise History*, 153.

12 P. Fehl and M. Perry, 'Painting and the Inquisition at Venice: three forgotten files', in Rosand, *Interpretazioni*, 371–86.

13 M. Muraro, 'The statutes of the Venetian "arti" and the mosaics of the Mascoli chapel', *Art Bulletin*, 43 (1961), 263–74.

14 F.C. Lane, *Venice: A Maritime Republic* (Baltimore, Md., 1974), 2–5; P. Braunstein and R. Delort, *Venise: portrait historique d'une cité* (Paris, 1971), 23–50.

15 G. Fiocco, 'L'arte a Torcello e a Venezia' in M. Uhlirz *et al.*, *La Venezia del Mille*, Fondazione Giorgio Cini, Storia della Civiltà Veneziana (Florence, 1965), 203–21; S. Bettini, 'Le opere d'arte importate a Venezia durante le crociate' in S. Runciman *et al.*, *Venezia dalla prima crociata alla conquista di Costantinopoli del 1204*, Fondazione Giorgio Cini, Storia della Civiltà Veneziana (Florence, 1965), 157–90.

16 D. Hay, *The Italian Renaissance in Its Historical Background* (Cambridge, 1970), 145–6; M. Lowry, *The World of Aldus Manutius: Business and Scholarship in Renaissance Venice* (Oxford, 1979), 74; N. Wilson, 'The book trade in Venice, c. 1400–1515' in H.-G. Beck, M. Manoussacas and A. Pertusi (eds.), *Venezia: Centro di Mediazione tra Oriente e Occidente (sec. x–xvi): Aspetti e problemi*, 2 vols. (Florence, 1977), vol. II, 381.

17 In general, see Beck *et al.*, *Venezia: Centro di Mediazione*, and A. Pertusi (ed.), *Venezia e l'Oriente fra tardo medioevo e rinascimento* (Florence, 1966).

18 For the Corte Seconda del Milion, see Howard, *Architectural History*, 36; on other contacts with the east, see G. Fedalto, 'Le minoranze straniere a Venezia tra politica e legislazione' in Beck *et al.*, *Venezia: Centro di Mediazione*, vol. I, 143–62; O. Pinto, 'Viaggiatori veneti in Oriente dal secolo xiii al xvi' in Pertusi, *Venezia e l'Oriente*, 389–401.

19 For the earliest elaboration of the myth, see G. Contarini, *The Commonwealth and Government of Venice*, trans. L. Lewkenor (1599), facs. edn (Amsterdam, 1970). Among the most important modern treatments are F. Gaeta, 'Alcune considerazioni sul mito di Venezia', *Bibliothèque d'Humanisme et Renaissance*, 23 (1961), 58–76; E. Muir, *Civic Ritual in Renaissance Venice* (Princeton, N.J., 1981), pt. I; R. Finlay, *Politics in Renaissance Venice* (London, 1980), pt. I.

20 J. Burckhardt, *The Civilization of the Renaissance in Italy*, trans. S. G. C. Middlemore (Oxford and London, 1945), 81–103; H. Baron, *The Crisis of the Early Italian Renaissance: Republican Liberty in an Age of Classicism and Tyranny*, vol. I, revised edn (Princeton, N.J., 1966), 191–272; B. Pullan, *Rich and Poor in Renaissance Venice: The Social Institutions of a Catholic State to 1620* (Oxford, 1971); R. Mackenney, *Tradesmen and Traders: The World of the Guilds in Venice and Europe, c. 1250–c. 1650* (London, 1987); D. Romano, *Patricians and Popolani: The Social Foundations of the Venetian Renaissance State* (Baltimore, Md., 1987). For a perceptive summary, see Braunstein and Delort, *Venise*, 131–93.

21 On the patriciate, see S. Chojnacki, 'In search of the Venetian patriciate: families and factions in the fourteenth century' in J.R. Hale (ed.), *Renaissance Venice*

(London, 1974), 47–90; 'Political adulthood in early Renaissance Venice', *American Historical Review*, 91 (1986), 791–810; 'Kinship ties and young patricians in fifteenth-century Venice', *Renaissance Quarterly*, 38 (1985), 240–70; 'Dowries and kinsmen in early Renaissance Venice', *Journal of Interdisciplinary History*, 5 (1974–5), 571–600; J.C. Davis, *The Decline of the Venetian Nobility as a Ruling Class, 1500–1700* (Baltimore, Md., 1962); *A Venetian Family and Its Fortune: The Donà and the Conservation of their Wealth* (Philadelphia, Pa., 1975); D. Queller, *The Venetian Patriciate: Reality vs Myth* (Chicago, Ill., 1987); P. Burke, *Venice and Amsterdam: A Study of Seventeenth-Century Elites* (London, 1974); A.F. Cowan, *The Urban Patriciate: Venice and Lübeck* (Cologne, 1986), which also contains important material on the citizen class, as does Pullan, *Rich and Poor*, especially 63–196.

22 On the guilds, see Mackenney, *Tradesmen and Traders*; R.T. Rapp, *Industry and Economic Decline in Seventeenth-Century Venice* (Cambridge, Mass., 1976). On the *scuole*, see Pullan, *Rich and Poor*; T. Pignatti (ed.), *Le scuole di Venezia* (Milan, 1981); S. Gramigna and A. Perissa, *Scuole di arti mestieri e devozione a Venezia* (Venice, 1981). On minorities, see Fedalto, 'Le minoranze'; H. Simonsfeld, *Der Fondaco dei Tedeschi in Venedig*, 2 vols. in 1 (Stuttgart, 1887); G. Perocco and A. Salvadori, *Civiltà di Venezia*, 3 vols. (Venice, 1977–9), vol. II, 771–805.

23 Muir, *Civic Ritual*; Mackenney, *Tradesmen and Traders*, ch. 4. A. Momo, 'Virtù e fortuna nel teatro veneziano del Cinquecento' in Rosand (ed.), *Interpretazioni*, 311–22, has interesting material on the theatricality of Venetian life.

24 King, *Venetian Humanism*, esp. 248, 192, 244.

25 On Sarpi's plain style, see H.F. Brown, 'Paolo Sarpi, the man' in his *Studies in the History of Venice*, 2 vols. (London, 1907), vol. II, 223, and P. Burke, 'The great unmasker: Paolo Sarpi, 1552–1623', *History Today*, 15 (1965), 430.

26 Muir, *Civic Ritual*, chs. 2–7; Mackenney, *Tradesmen and Traders*, 138.

27 E. Rosand, 'Music in the myth of Venice', *Renaissance Quarterly*, 30 (1977), 511–37; Perocco and Salvadori, *Civiltà di Venezia*, vol. III, 952–68.

28 R. Goffen, *Piety and Patronage in Renaissance Venice: Bellini, Titian and the Franciscans* (London, 1986), 64–87, 145.

29 Queller, *Venetian Patriciate*; G. Cozzi, 'Authority and the law in Renaissance Venice' in Hale, *Renaissance Venice*, 293–345; A.D. Wright, 'Venetian law and order: a myth?', *Bulletin of the Institute of Historical Research*, 53 (1980), 192–202.

30 L. Puppi, 'Patronage on the Venetian mainland' in Hope and Martineau, *Genius of Venice*, 21; A. Fletcher, 'Patronage in Venice', *ibid.*, 19; M. Perry, 'A Renaissance showplace of art: the Palazzo Grimani at Santa Maria Formosa, Venice', *Apollo*, 113 (1981), 215–21.

31 On public service, see Pullan, *Rich and Poor*, 132–56; Mackenney, *Tradesmen and Traders*, ch. 6. On patronage, see P.F. Brown, 'Honour and necessity: the dynamics of patronage in the confraternities of Renaissance Venice', *Studi Veneziani*, NS 14 (1987), 179–212; P. Humfrey and R. Mackenney, 'The Venetian trade guilds as patrons of art in the Renaissance', *The Burlington Magazine*, 128 (1986), 317–30.

32 P. Labalme, 'Personality and politics: Pietro Aretino' in Rosand, *Titian*, 121; C. Hope, 'Titian as court painter', *Oxford Art Journal*, 2 (1979), 7–10.

33 H. Burns, 'Architecture', in Hope and Martineau, *Genius of Venice*, 24–8; G. Gianighian and P. Pavanini (eds.), *Dietro i palazzi: tre secoli di architettura minore a Venezia, 1492–1803* (Venice, 1984).

34 E. Trincanato, 'Le forme dell'edilizia veneziana' in Gianighian and Pavanini, *Dietro i palazzi*, 11–23; Perocco and Salvadori, *Civiltà di Venezia*, vol. I, 242–50.

35 On cisterns, see Perocco and Salvadori, *Civiltà di Venezia*, vol. I, 270–3; on bricklaying, M. Piana, 'Accorgimenti costruttivi e sistemi statici dell'architettura veneziana' in Gianighian and Pavanini, *Dietro i Palazzi*, 35–7; on the organisation of space, J. Schulz, 'The houses of Titian, Aretino and Sansovino' in Rosand, *Titian*, 75–6; G. Gianighian and P. Pavanini, 'I Terreni Nuovi de Santa Maria Mazor' in Gianighian and Pavanini, *Dietro i palazzi*, 45.

36 Burns, 'Architecture' in Hope and Martineau, *Genius of Venice*, 24; D. Howard, 'Jacopo Sansovino's house at San Trovaso' in Rosand, *Interpretazioni*, 252.

37 Perocco and Salvadori, *Civiltà di Venezia*, vol. I, 342; Howard, *Architectural History*, 76.

38 M. Muraro, 'The Moors of the clock tower of Venice and their sculptor', *Art Bulletin*, 66 (1984), 603–9. I am indebted to Dr Peter Humfrey for his reference.

39 On Commynes, see Lane, *Venice*, 273. On demographic trends, see D. Beltrami, *Storia della popolazione di Venezia dalla fine del secolo xvi alla caduta della Repubblica* (Padua, 1954); Rapp, *Industry*, 32–48; Pullan, *Rich and Poor*, 216–19.

40 On the Greeks, see Fedalto, 'Le minoranze', 148; on the blacksmiths, Mackenney, *Tradesmen and Traders*, 112; on the Lion Bianco, Howard, *Architectural History*, 44. Information on the accommodation of visitors is to be found in *Archivio di Stato di Venezia, Giustizia Nova, busta* 5, registers 11 and 12. On the German population, see Simonsfeld, *Fondaco*, P. Braunstein, 'Remarques sur la population allemande de Venise à la fin du moyen age', in Beck *et al.*, *Venezia: Centro di Mediazione*, vol. I, 233–43; on contacts with Nuremberg, Pullan, *Rich and Poor*, 232; on Titian and Giorgione, see Howard, *Architectural History*, 56.

41 On Antonello, see T. Pignatti, *La pittura veneziana del '400* (Bergamo, 1961), 46; on sculptors, B. Boucher and A. Radcliffe, 'Sculpture' in Hope and Martineau, *Genius of Venice*, 355, and D.S. Chambers, *The Imperial Age of Venice 1380–1580* (London, 1970), 158.

42 *Canon Pietro Casola's Pilgrimage to Jerusalem in the Year 1494*, ed. and trans. M.M. Newett (Manchester, 1907), 129.

43 Mackenney, *Tradesmen and Traders*, 92–111.

44 G. Mariacher, 'Arti minori veneziane del Rinascimento: il vetro e l'oreficeria dal '400 al '500' in Branca, *Rinascimento europeo*, 319–26; H. Tait, *The Golden Age of Venetian Glass* (London, 1979); P. Molmenti, *Storia di Venezia nella vita privata*, 3 vols (Bergamo, 1927–9), vol. II, 137–72.

45 Muraro, 'Mascoli chapel', 269, n.27. See also M. Muraro, 'The Guardi problem and the statutes of Venetian guilds', *The Burlington Magazine*, 102 (1960), 421–28; E. Favaro, *L'arte dei pittori a Venezia e i suoi statuti* (Florence, 1975).

46 D. Puppulin, 'Lotto e l'arte dei dipintori' in Rosand, *Interpretazioni*, 351–8; P. Zampetti, in Hope and Martineau, *Genius of Venice*, 175–6.

47 T. Pignatti, 'The relationship between German and Venetian painting in the late

'400 and early '500' in Hale, *Renaissance Venice*, 27–92; E. Panofsky, *The Life and Art of Albrecht Duerer* (Princeton, N.J., 1971), 107.

48 E. Lowinsky, 'Music in Titian's *Bacchanal of the Andrians*. Origins and history of the *Canon per Tonos*', in Rosand, *Titian*, 195; Perocco and Salvadori, *Civiltà di Venezia*, vol III, 956–62, 695–8.

49 V. Branca, 'Lauro Quirini e il commercio librario a Venezia e Firenze', in Beck *et al.*, *Venezia: Centro di Mediazione*, vol. I, 377; H.F. Brown, *The Venetian Printing Press* (London, 1891), 429–50.

50 Lowry, *Aldus Manutius*, 8, 10, 143.

51 S. Seidel Menchi, *Erasmo in Italia, 1520–1580* (Turin, 1987) – I am most grateful to Mr Peter Burke for this reference; on the importance of Erasmian humanism, see H.A. Enno van Gelder, *The Two Reformations in the Sixteenth Century: A Study of the Religious Aspects of Renaissance and Humanism* (The Hague, 1964); on his influence upon Aretino, see C. Cairns, *Pietro Aretino and the Republic of Venice: Researchers on Aretino and his Circle in Venice, 1527–1556* (Florence, 1985).

52 Lowry, *Aldus Manutius*, 185–7; V. Baldo, *Alunni, maestri e scuole a Venezia alla fine del xvi secolo* (Como, 1977); P. Grendler, 'What Zuanne read in school: vernacular texts in 16th-century Venetian schools', *Sixteenth Century Journal*, 13 (1982), 41–53; A.J. Schutte, 'Teaching adults to read in 16th-century Venice: Giovanni Antonio Tagliente's *Libro maistrevolè*', *Sixteenth Century Journal*, 17 (1986), 3–16. J. Martin, 'Popular culture and the shaping of popular heresy in Renaissance Venice' in S. Haliczer (ed.), *Inquisition and Society in Early Modern Europe* (London, 1987), 115–28.

53 Lowry, *Aldus Manutius*, 92–4; Puppulin, 'Lotto'; V. Rossato, 'Religione e moralità in un merciaio veneziano del '500', *Studi Veneziani*, NS 13 (1987), 193–253; Seidel Menchi, *Erasmo*, 40–67; Mackenney, *Tradesmen and Traders*, 174–95. On Caravia, see Pullan, *Rich and Poor*, 119–21, 130–1, and in an inappropriate context of 'popular culture' in C. Ginzburg, *The Cheese and the Worms: The Cosmos of a Sixteenth-Century Miller*, trans. J. and A. Tedeschi (London, 1980), 23–6.

54 F. Micanzio, 'Vita del Padre Paolo' in P. Sarpi, *Istoria del Concilio Tridentino*, ed. C. Vivanti, 2 vols. (Turin, 1974), 1305–9; Burke, 'The great unmasker'; D. Wooton, *Paolo Sarpi: Between Renaissance and Enlightenment* (Cambridge, 1983). On Zechinelli's connection with the mercers' guild, see *Archivio di Stato di Venezia, Arti, busta 397, marzeri, nomi di fratelli*, lists of 1586, 'capomaestri in lettere rosse', and 1594 under 'sestier di San Marco'.

FIVE

THE LOW COUNTRIES

ELSA STRIETMAN

Introduction

The Renaissance in the Low Countries occurred, not in one, but in two national contexts. The Lowlands, present-day Netherlands and Belgium, share a medieval political past and a linguistic and cultural heritage. Paradoxically it is easier to point at shared political, social and cultural developments in the medieval history of the motley, disunited provinces and regions which were known as the Low Countries than it is to find much in common in their Renaissance and post-Renaissance development.

The Renaissance in the Low Countries can be traced, in some aspects, to beginnings in the mid-fifteenth century and fades out, in some ways, after the middle of the seventeenth century. The flowering of the Renaissance in literature and the visual arts and in architecture, occurred in the northern part of the Low Countries, the Republic of the Seven United Netherlands, in the first half of the seventeenth century, later, in effect, than in the rest of Europe.

We will need to look in detail at the political history of these lands to understand some of the reasons for this late development and we will see that the political and the cultural situation have a bearing upon each other. The national context of the Low Countries is, if not unique, then at least very distinct in the period under discussion. Two nations eventually emerged from the medieval Low Countries and it is this development that will be central in this essay. We will see that the question of nationhood provides a good example of a development in these lands that was initiated in the south, but found its full flowering in the north. In the course of this chapter we will meet such developments in literature, in the visual arts and in the history of Protestantism.

To establish the beginning and the end of the Renaissance in the Low Countries is a complex task. Each of the areas one should take into consideration, politics, religion, the visual arts, literature, music, architecture yields different evidence. Naturally, Renaissance as rebirth and renewal is

N

Noordvaark

Oostraart

Westvaark

GRONINGEN

FRIESLAND

DRENTE

Oostzee

OVERIJSEL
Deventer

Westfalen

Haarlem

Amsterdam

G
E
L
D
E
R
L
E

England

Leyden

Utrecht

Rotterdam

Lisbon-Cadiz
France

Vere

Venlo

Middelburg

Bruges

Antwerp

Calais

FLANDERS

Ghent

B
R
A
B
A
N
T

L
I
E
G
E

Ypres

Courtrai

Brussels

Maastricht

Liège

ARTOIS

HENEGOUWEM

G
E
R
M
A
N
Y

Cateau Cambrésis

LUXEMBURG

Crépy

FRANCE

0 ————— 100 km
0 ————— 100 miles

The Low Countries at the time of Charles V

used to refer to a renewed interest in classical antiquity, but there is a wider context as well: that of a different attitude to the world and its inhabitants. Evidence of this can be found in all manner of scientific developments, of which one offshoot, for instance, are the voyages of discovery, demanding, and resulting in, better navigational instruments and better maps. Evidence of a different way of observing we can find for instance in the treatment of the perspective in painting and drawing. Signs of an *ars nova* in painting can be found in the early fifteenth century in the southern Low Countries where Jan van Eyck and others made great innovations in the fabrication of paint; this, and their mastery of perspective and their attention to the individual, heralded both scientific progress and a new awareness and valuation of God's creation on earth. It is true that the changing appreciation of life on earth was still very much *sub specie aeternitatis*, but the ecstatic delight in craftsmanship, the exquisite rendering of the smallest detail of the external world, seems in itself a celebration, both conscious and unconscious, of human life and the precise observation of the natural world.

Sculpture was not a prominent art-form in the Low Countries, but Claus Sluter's monumental sculpture for the first Duke of Burgundy, Philip the Bold, in the Carthusian Monastery of Champmol,[1] was a far cry from the sober, static effigies gracing the last resting places of many medieval lords and kings. The flowing lines, the individualism in the figures of the prophets, St John, the Virgin, Mary Magdalene, can perhaps not be given the epithet 'renaissance', but that here was the beginning of a new style, is certain. The Charterhouse was meant as a sepulchre for Philip the Bold and his heirs and it was definitely a novelty of its kind. If it is possible, and proper, to detect exuberance in a mausoleum, then Champmol is lavishly exuberant.

In music, too, there were new harmonies and melodies to be heard: musical life at the Court of Burgundy was lively and a good example of the mutual learning and enrichment which Italy and other European countries bestowed upon each other: Burgundian musicians, such as Guillaume Dufay, Josquin dez Prez and Jacob Obrecht were part of the choir of the Papal Chamber in Rome, in the Court of Ferrara and in Milan Cathedral, where they made considerable reputations for themselves. Their knowledge of the Italian styles of singing and composing was a major impetus in the flowering of Renaissance music in the Low Countries in the fifteenth and early sixteenth century.[2]

Painters, musicians and scholars made the journey across the Alps to see the wonders of the new art created in the Renaissance Italian cities and this was not a one way traffic: the craftsmanship of the Van Eycks was known and appreciated in Italy, as was Rogier van der Weyden. Hugo van der Goes made quite an impression on Ghirlandaio and other Italian painters and was asked to complete the Portinari altarpiece.[3] Karel van Mander, the Vasari of the Low Countries, mentions in his *Schilderboeck (1604)* that Lorenzo il Magnifico possessed a St Jerome by Van Eyck and Alfonso I of Naples a St George.[4] Sometimes places in between benefited too: a small Austrian church in the Tirol, mercifully untouched by the Baroque craze, displays a – now somewhat grimy – altarpiece by the sixteenth-century north Netherlandish painter Jan van Scorel, on his way to, or from, Italy.

In literature, however, it is not so easy to detect early traces of changing styles and altered views of the world as early as the fifteenth century. In fact, in the canon of Dutch literature the 'early Renaissance period' is held to be the late sixteenth century. The first unmistakable evidence of Renaissance poetry is a collection by the Antwerp nobleman Jan van der Noot, published in 1567.[5] If we widen our concept of literature from *belles lettres* to *bonae litterae*, such as those of Erasmus and other humanists, then we do encounter new views long before 1567, which do indicate the changing perception of heaven and of earth which marks the Renaissance and its writings.

Charting the beginning of the Renaissance in the Low Countries is difficult, charting its ending, tracing where and when the Renaissance gives way to other forces, is also controversial. If we stay for a moment with the literary culture in the Republic of the Seven United Netherlands, then it is convenient to see the years between the Peace of Münster in 1648, the end of the struggle with Spain, and the year of Joost van den Vondel's death, 1679, as the years in which the last tidal marks of the Renaissance and the Baroque are washed away by the floods of the next change. We will return to this later in the chapter. Names and dates, after all, need their historical and geographical context, without which their significance is all but lost. That context we will examine in the next section.

The question of nationhood and the forging of a nation

It is convenient in many respects to begin a description of the period in which the Low Countries became part of Europe's Renaissance culture with the emergence of the Burgundian realm as an identifiable member of the international community and as a force to be reckoned with in Europe. To some extent this was achieved by Philip the Bold (1342–1404), but it was with the reign of the third duke, Philip the Good, from 1419 until 1467, that the majority of the loosely connected provinces of the Low Countries were forced into a federation, which was only completed however in 1543, when the Duchy of Guelders was finally incorporated into the Burgundian realm, itself then part of the vast possessions of the Emperor Charles V, Holy Roman Emperor and King of Spain. Whether the dukes[6] aimed to create a Burgundian national state, or whether their centralising efforts were anything more than a means of achieving a well-oiled machinery for financial control, is still controversial. The result was, however, that by the late fifteenth century the

Low Countries presented something akin to a national consciousness to the world and were identified to a large extent with its ruling house of Burgundy. Certainly, the arrival of Maximilian of Austria, Mary of Burgundy's husband, who after her death in 1482 became the regent for their young son Philip, was perceived as an unwelcome takeover by a foreigner.

Fate caused the House of Burgundy to be submerged by the Habsburg dynasty at the beginning of the sixteenth century. In the reign of Charles V (1515–55), very definite centralisation policies were carried out and the northern provinces, which had been part of the Burgundian realm more in name than in fact, were now subjected to a firm central government which could not do other than result in a more or less coherent confederation. Charles made the succession hereditary and drew the Low Countries together in a separate entity within his realm, the so-called Burgundian Kreits (1548).

A number of historians have pointed out that a sense of nationality amongst inhabitants of the Low Countries seems to emerge only after 1560.[7] Hoogewerff found that the thousands of students and artists who signed themselves into the registers of Italian universities in the sixteenth century abandoned a precise identification, such as 'Brabantinus' or 'Goudensis', in favour of the collective 'Belga' or 'Flamengus', meaning from the Netherlands, in the years that Spanish rule was beginning to be felt as particularly oppressive both in political and religious matters.[8] The greater consciousness of identity was not due to an increased sense of identification with the ruling house. Under Charles V, and even more so under his son Philip II, these lands chafed under what was felt to be, in many respects, a foreign, far-off, uncaring regime. This process of gradual disenchantment with the rulers was accelerated in the later half of the sixteenth century, when for both the rulers and the ruled the religious controversies between Catholics and Protestants, particularly in the southern provinces at first, but spreading rapidly to the north as well, became a focal point in a situation in which the umbilical cord connecting the God-given king and his subjects was already stretched too tautly.

Throughout the history of the Low Countries, from the emergence of the powerful trading cities in the southern Netherlands in the fourteenth century to the competitive appearance of the mighty merchant towns in the northern provinces in the late sixteenth century, there was a constant tug-of-war between the rulers who strove for strong central government and the towns which guarded their autonomy jealously. Ghent for example was punished severely in 1453 by Philip the Good as a reprisal for the town's repeated refusal to pay a salt tax to central government. In 1540 the town lost all its privileges after it refused to grant a special payment to Charles V. Ideologically, too, the town took an independent stance: in the sixteenth century it became, together with Antwerp, a refuge for Protestant dissidents. One of the early incidents relating to religious controversy in the southern provinces occurred in Ghent in 1539.[9] A drama and poetry festival organised by a number of the amateur literary guilds, the so-called Chambers of Rhetoric, which dominated the literary life in the towns, had as its main item on the programme a series of morality plays. As usual, these plays were all written around a central theme, in this case: 'What is the greatest comfort to a dying man?' Some of the plays showed Protestant influence in their answer to this question, as well as Erasmian influence, and the heresy hunters of the Spanish Inquisition placed the printed collection of the plays on the Catholic Index. Even amongst those in the town's administration who were on the same side in the struggle of all the provinces against Catholic Spain strife and dissension were never far away, as the Prince of Orange was to find to his cost several times when he tried to get all the towns and regions to present a united front against Spain. Often, at the heart of such trouble, were the notions of autonomy and liberty, not only in Ghent, but wherever and whenever regional or local government found itself threatened by other towns or regions or by a central government which tried to override or infringe local customs or privileges. Frequently such conflicts were caused by economic issues or by the overlord's demand for a financial grant. In the course of the sixteenth century the towns or provinces often refused to comply with efforts to persecute Protestant heretics, calling on their liberty to determine what measure of freedom would be allowed to dissidents. The ideal of liberty which emerged from the behaviour of the towns, was in the first place a concept of economic self-determination, and secondly a concept of at least partial political independence, such as in determining relations with England for the textile industry, or with the Hanseatic towns for those importing or exporting grain. In the course of the sixteenth century the ideal of liberty was extended to include religious self-determination and the relationship with the ultimate rulers of the Low Countries, the Emperor Charles V, and, from 1555 onwards, his son King Philip II of Spain, whose judicial and religious policies roused enormous resistance.

It is difficult to determine the relationship between the learned discourse of Europe's humanists on individual and corporate freedom and the pragmatic use of the concept of liberty by towns, regions and various groups in the society of the fifteenth- and sixteenth-century Low Countries. Some comparisons can be made with the emergence of the Italian city-states.[10] It is true that the Flemish and Brabant towns did not give rise to Medicis and Sforzas, even though the Borsselens, the Arnolfinis and others were self-confident merchants, entrepreneurs and bankers. It was not until two centuries later that a powerful patrician regent class formed itself in the northern Republic, but it never became as tyrannically powerful, nor as autonomous as the rulers of Florence and Milan. And yet, as in Italy, the bandying about of the much used and abused concept of liberty by the Flemish and Brabant towns had a simple and pragmatic origin: in the face of centralisation policies of the overlords, inspired by their financial needs, the towns fought back by quoting their privileges, won earlier from previous rulers, often exemptions from paying this or that tax. The fierce guarding of their rights to a measure of self-governance, including consent to taxation, was not based on any theoretical, political concept alone, far less on a longing for complete self-government, but on a desire to be autonomous in so far as autonomy befitted their trade and industry. They were equally fierce in their competition with other towns and sometimes with the surrounding countryside whenever their economy was threatened. For instance, when independent weavers in the villages of Flanders started to produce cheaper cloth than the unionised weavers in the towns, the village looms were destroyed or confiscated. Moreover, the towns were quick enough to call on their overlord for protection, be it against England's competitive wool prices threatening the Flemish textile industry, as happened in the 1430s,[11] or as arbiter in the squabbles between towns and provinces amongst each other. Liberty without protection was not desirable and it is clear that their concept of liberty was primarily an economic one.

In the struggle against Philip II of Spain in which all the seventeen provinces of the Low Countries were involved in the second half of the sixteenth century, liberty and autonomy were again key issues. Documents relating to the revolt of these lands against Spain, such as petitions, apologies, remonstrances and edicts, many issuing from the Prince of Orange and his advisers, were studded with these concepts.[12] So, too, were the many pamphlets and songs which spread news, exhorted to resistance, deplored defeats and celebrated victories and, above all, preached trust in God and in a divine preordained plan in which the Netherlands were, like the Israelites, fated to create their Promised Land. The role of the king, his rights and duties, the role of the subjects, their rights and duties, the relationship between king and subjects, were repeated time and again, almost as incantations. Of course, these were partisan writings and not necessarily educated writings, but it is all the more striking to find that the language, the arguments, the jargon of all these varied messages were informed by the language of the Bible, by that of the law-courts and the Court, be it French or Dutch. What we encounter here, is the reflection, in two vernaculars, of centuries of learned debate, ranging from Trecento Italy to sixteenth-century Dutch humanism, concerning the relationship between prince and subject and the freedom of the individual with regard to his religious beliefs. In these areas occurred an unprecedented breakdown in the Low Countries, reaching its peak between the 1560s and the 1580s. Just one passage, randomly chosen out of many, conveys to us, through the centuries and through its translation from the biblical tones of sixteenth-century Dutch into modern English, the vehemence and passion of those who fought for liberty as they saw it and who were perplexed that things had come this far:

Edict of the States General of the United Netherlands by which they declare that the King of Spain has forfeited the sovereignty and government of the aforesaid Netherlands, with a lengthy explanation of the reasons thereof . . .[13]

The States General of the United Netherlands greet all those who will see or hear this read.

It is common knowledge that the prince of a country is appointed by God to be the head of his subjects to protect and shield them from all iniquity, trouble and violence as a shepherd is called to protect his sheep, and that the subjects are not created by God for the benefit of the prince, to submit to all that he decrees, whether godly or ungodly, just or unjust, and to serve him as slaves. On the contrary, the prince is created for his subjects (without whom he cannot be a prince) to govern them according to right and reason and defend and love them as a father does his children and a shepherd does his sheep when he risks his body and life for their safety. It is clear therefore that if he acts differently and instead of protecting his subjects endeavours to oppress and molest them and to deprive them of their ancient liberty, privileges and customs and to command and use them like slaves, he must be regarded not as a prince but as a tyrant. And according to right and reason his subjects, at any rate, must no longer recognise him as a prince (notably when this is decided by the States of the country), but should renounce him; in his stead another must be elected to be an overlord called to protect them. This becomes even more true when these subjects have been unable either to soften their prince's heart through explanations humbly made or to turn him away from his tyrannical enterprise, and have no other means left to protect their ancient liberty (for the defence of which they must according to the law of nature be prepared to risk life and property) as well as that of their wives, children and descendants. This has often happened for similar reasons in many other countries at various times and there are well known instances of it. And this should happen particularly in these countries, which have always been governed (as they should be) in accordance with the oath taken by the prince at his inauguration and in conformity with the privileges, customs and old traditions of these countries which he swears to maintain. Moreover, nearly all these countries have accepted their prince conditionally, by contracts and agreements and if the prince breaks them, he legally forfeits his sovereignty.

In many of these documents, as in the songs and pamphlets, the provinces are referred to as *Nederlant*, in the singular, or as the 'Low Countries' and they present the States of the provinces and the States General, which had delegates of all the provinces and the major towns, as the proper representatives of the subjects to the king. It cannot be denied that especially towards the end of the sixteenth century these same States were at each other's throats many a time, but that does not diminish their sense of really belonging together when faced with a common, outside enemy.

If the emergence of a national consciousness was a feature of Renaissance Europe, then the Low Countries demonstrated this in a remarkable way: first a foreign dynasty, the Burgundians, imposed a kind of centralisation on a motley collection of provinces which fiercely defended their economic and judicial independence. Then, the second foreign dynasty, that of the Habsburgs, took over after nearly a century of Burgundian rule and those same provinces gradually more or less banded together under the flag of liberty and finally stood up conscious of their separate identity, refusing to become a money-providing, uncared-for part of a foreign realm, a part which was not allowed to decide its own political allegiance or their financial, and, more and more important, religious policies.

Almost in the very act of becoming conscious of the common weal this precarious togetherness was undone: in 1579 most of the provinces became united in the Union of Utrecht, a reaction to the Union of Arras, which had brought together some French-speaking provinces and important Catholic nobles against the Prince of Orange and his supporters, both Catholic and Protestant. The Union of Utrecht was effectively the formalisation of the resistance against Philip II and in particular against his religious policies, followed in 1581 by an Edict of the States General of the United Netherlands, declaring that the Catholic King of Spain had not fulfilled the duties of a sovereign and had therefore forfeited the sovereignty.

Thus the rebellion against Spain had the result that at the end of the sixteenth century, the mosaic unity of these lands, loosely held together by a shared language in some parts, by cultural factors to some extent, by allegiance to various overlords such as the Burgundian dukes and the counts of Holland and Zeeland, was rent apart arbitrarily by the religious controversy, the political squabbles and the military battles. Such coherence as had been achieved by the Burgundian dukes gradually dissolved, two distinct national entities came into being, though not at the same time. Fate was fickle: the fostering of the concept of the unity of the Low Countries occurred largely in the southern Netherlands, where the impact of the Burgundians was greatest and yet the nation took shape formally in the northern provinces as the Republic of the Seven United Netherlands. Even in their burgeoning nationhood, the northern and southern Low Countries were very much out of step with each other. In the early seventeenth century, whatever the internal divisions or the hopes that north and south might yet be united again, the northern provinces were welded into an identifiable entity, both to its inhabitants and to the international community of states. The southern Netherlands, however, led, as far as identity was concerned, a shadowy existence as a satellite state of the Spanish empire, then as part of the Austrian Habsburg empire, then as part of Napoleon's empire. In 1815, the Congress of Vienna effected a well-meant, but unrealistic reunification of north and south under King William I of Orange, which came to grief in 1830.[14] Thus the southern Netherlands did not really shape its own destiny as a nation until the 1830s, by which time the Republic, apart from a brief Napoleonic interlude, had had two centuries of nationhood behind it. The new kingdom of Belgium resumed the struggle for internal unity, hampered by being a bilingual state and the uneasy co-existence of a French- and Dutch-speaking culture. *Plus ça change . . .*

After the split of north and south, effectively after 1585 when Antwerp finally fell into the hands of the Spaniards and the exodus of money, intellect and artistic talent to the north drained the south, a shift of emphasis occurred in the south. Gradually, but inexorably, under the combined forces of the Counter-Reformation and of Spain's determination to strengthen its bulwark in the Low Countries, the self-confident Dutch-speaking culture, its literature and its art, which had been the glory of the medieval civilisation in the Low Countries, began to be dominated by a culture which was French-speaking and orientated towards France. The easy coexistence between the two cultures which characterised the southern provinces under the Burgundians was lost forever. It was not until the late nineteenth century that the Dutch culture of the southern Netherlands came into its own again.[15] It is, therefore, not due to an attack of xenophobia that I will focus, in the next section, ultimately on developments in the Renaissance of the north, where the new republic, with the life-blood, the capital, the know-how, the civilisation and the piety of the south, created a new culture, more 'Dutch' to the outside observer than perhaps that of any other country, yet indebted in a multitude of ways to the displaced civilisation of the southern Low Countries.

Humanism and Renaissance literature

Humanism in the Low Countries begins to be noticeable in the second half of the fifteenth century, when a special course of Latin, called 'Poetica', was established at Louvain University in 1478. Taught by native Italians this education in the *bonae litterae* seems to have been a success. At the same time a series of luxury editions of Latin authors was published by the Louvain printer Jan van Westfalen.[16]

Another impetus for a gradually changing study of the Ancients came from a less exalted intellectual milieu, that of the followers of Geert Groote (1340–84), the Brothers and Sisters of the Common Life. Their Latin schools, mainly in the northern provinces, introduced many school-children to Virgil and Seneca. Rudolf Agricola of Groningen (1444–85), the earliest internationally known humanist from the Low Countries, is always associated with these schools, as is Erasmus. However tenuous this link may have been, there is no doubt that the schools provided a high level of literacy for a significant number of children. Agricola's *De inventione dialectica* integrated elements present in the teaching of the schools of the Devotio Moderna, such as their *ora et labora* ethic and their emphasis on the moral values which one could ·

glean from a reading of the Ancients, into his own strong plea for a classical education which shaped characters, moulded morals and provided insight and knowledge in life and letters.[17]

Another Groningen humanist, Wessel Gansfort (1420–89), attempted to bring about a fusion of the piety of the Modern Devotion with the scholarly methods of the Italian humanists.[18] Agricola and Gansfort are the most famous of the humanists from the northern provinces, but they were by no means the only ones. Many of their learned friends taught in the schools of the Devotio Moderna and their scholarly activities became known through the printing presses of Deventer, the centre of the Devotio and, towards the end of the fifteenth century, the centre from which many editions of Plautus, Cicero, Cato, Virgil, Aesop and Seneca found their way into the world. By the beginning of the sixteenth century, classical and biblical humanism were well established in the Low Countries; editions of classical works came off the printing presses as early as 1475; the first Greek texts in this part of Europe were published by Thierry Martens, friend of Erasmus, in Louvain in 1512.[19]

And then, of course, there was Erasmus.[20] Perhaps he would have been rather put out to be claimed as a Dutch scholar, since he was as important for the Low Countries as he was for the rest of Europe. Apart from his role in the founding of the Collegium Trilingue, no special benefit was bestowed on the Low Countries for being the cradle of this *vir illustris*. And yet, Erasmus' spirit, his tolerance, his undogmatic thinking, his impatience with empty ceremony, all these were part of the spiritual atmosphere which has become synonymous with the culture of the Low Countries. The Erasmian interpretation of religion as a divinely inspired ethical code, to live by and let live, rather than a set of strict dogmatic rules, did not come into being only with Erasmus, but can be sensed in the writings of early reformers and humanists, such as Agricola of Groningen and in the gentleness of the adherents to the teaching of the Devotio Moderna. Erasmus' connection with the Devotio is slight and less important than is sometimes alleged,[21] but that strengthens, not weakens, the case for pointing out the similarities in spirit between the humble Brothers and Sisters of the Common Life and the most learned, most famous son of the Low Countries. It is tempting to think, in view of these shared spiritual elements, that Erasmus was formed as much by his native country as he influenced the civilisation of his fatherland and of the rest of Europe. But Erasmus' own attitude to his country of origin was ambivalent. He conceded that there were civilised fellow spirits in the Low Countries, but at the same time he needed an intellectual stimulation and fellowship which could not be found in one country. It was provided by the international community of the learned, who communicated in Latin and had little use for the vernaculars. Erasmus the polyglot did not break a lance for his mother-tongue, *die duytsche tale*,[22] even though he thought that Dutch was a formative tongue of the Germanic language family. However, many others viewed the vernacular as a worthy means of literary expression, although the attitude of Goropius Becanus' *Origines Antwerpianae* (1569) took this to extremes: Becanus was convinced that Dutch was the oldest language in the world and had therefore been spoken in Paradise.[23]

We touch here upon a concern that is central to sixteenth-century humanism: the concern with the vernacular and the battle to win it a place next to Latin as a worthy vehicle for expression: in literature, in science, in philosophy and in theology. This is a phenomenon by no means special to the Low Countries, but there it has particular features worth considering, because they are in some ways linked to the emergence of the northern republic as a separate, Protestant state and it was in the Republic that the Renaissance in all its aspects found its glorious flowering. Of course, the translations of the Bible and the Psalms, the sermons in the vernacular, were, *mutatis mutandis*, common to all those countries where the Protestant creed gained a foothold. In the Low Countries however, the struggle for religious freedom became so entangled with the struggle for freedom from Spain, that the use of the vernacular became itself a defiant statement of independence. An example of this were the *Geuzenliederen*,[24] the songs about the revolt against Spain, amongst which the *Wilhelmus*, an apologia in which the Prince of Orange states his reason for his rebellion against Philip of Spain, takes the place of honour. It is still the national anthem of the Netherlands today. Many of the *Geuzenliederen* used well-known hymn melodies as well as popular secular melodies and in spirit they are often deeply devout, equating the struggle of the rebels with that of the Old Testament Jews who fled the captivity in Egypt and established themselves in the Promised Land.

The vernacular was also the concern of scholars, poets and scientists. The influential humanist D.V. Coornhert (1522–90) wrote the introduction to the *Twespraeck van de Nederduitsche Letterkunst* (1584), a work about Dutch spelling, vocabulary and syntax by another important humanist, H.L. Spiegel (1549–1612). Here Coornhert urged a clear, incisive formulation of notions in the mother-tongue. In his own large and varied *œuvre* he practised what he preached, demonstrating that Dutch could be used to express everything, be it history, theology, philosophy and the sciences.[25] This latter use was advocated strongly by Simon Stevin (1548–1620), scientist and inventor, in his *Dialectike ofte Bewijskonst* (1585), and further evidence about the preoccupation with the vernacular came in his book about mechanics, *Beginselen der Weegkonst* (1586), which has as its preface an essay about the dignity and the value of the Dutch language. It would be too difficult, Stevin wrote, to explain the complicated scientific terminology in any language other than Dutch, which was, after all, the original language from which bastard languages such as French and Italian had developed![26] Stevin was a refugee from the south and it is remarkable that, unlike many others who were forced to flee north, he did not scoff at the uncouth language of his adopted country. On the contrary, he sees Dutch or *Hollands* as a purer form than Flemish which he thought was a corrupted version of the original language. He could not have been more wrong, but it is interesting nevertheless. Stevin's position as Professor of Engineering in the University of Leiden enabled him to spread his creed, and the result was that new technological ideas became available and effective in the Republic in a much wider circle than they would have done had they been written in Latin.

Leiden had many champions of the vernacular but, unfortunately, they did not succeed in making Dutch the language in which lectures were held. The University became the centre of an international humanist culture though not the centre in which the national Renaissance in the Republic developed: that role would be taken on by Amsterdam. Two further examples of the ambivalence of the humanist who wants to be heard internationally and yet is well aware of his own language and culture are the cases of Hugo de Groot and Daniel Heinsius. De Groot[27] (1583–1645), the great lawyer, scholar and dramatist, wrote several of his books in Dutch, amongst which was one about Dutch law. He was insistent that his mother-tongue was well suited for such a purpose and that Latin had no monopoly on clarity and force of expression. Grotius wanted to be heard by an international audience and therefore needed to write also in Latin, but, nevertheless, and even though he lived most of his life in exile, he valued his own language. Daniel Heinsius (1580–1655),[28] famous classicist, dramatist and poet, was one of the leading lights in Leiden University, which was offering ever increasing salaries in order to retain his services. Heinsius had no need to write in Dutch and yet he chose that language for a collection of poems, the *Nederduytsche Poemata* (1616), and this was seen as an enormous boost for the vernacular cause: here was a world-famous scholar who deigned to use his mother-tongue for poetry in the new style. This was particularly significant because it was seen to have originated in the bulwark of humanist-classicist learning, Leiden University. The floodgates were opened and never again was there need to apologise for not writing one's sonnets in French or Italian, one's tragedies or histories in Latin.

This brings us to another important aspect of the national Renaissance in the Low Countries, the dramatic and historiographic writings that were concerned to present a national 'image', origins and history. Of course, chronicles and annals in Latin and in the vernacular existed in plenty, but the new Republic needed some more specific justification: it had come into being as a breakaway faction and by the abjuration of its rightful king. For many Catholics this was difficult to accept but it was no easier for Protestant consciences, because obedience to the secular power was part of their

religious creed as well. Moreover, the revolt against Spain had been, and was
for many still a religious war. This just cause and the bloody and traumatic
means by which victory had been achieved were not easily reconcilable with
each other. Hence these preoccupations were central to the drama and the
historiography of the first half of the seventeenth century. There are plays
which deal with particular events: the murder of William of Orange in 1584 by
someone in Spanish pay is a much used theme,[29] while other plays and
historical writings try to present the history of the Republic as a logical, and
inevitable, series of events in which God's hand could easily be discerned.
Thus the Republic created its own mythology and fused it with the Calvinist
interpretation of its recent history, namely that God had given them, the
Elect, a new Promised Land, as he had done for the Israelites. The mythology
had been used before, too, at the turn of the previous century and was
modelled on the writings of Tacitus and Pliny in particular. Caesar's conquest
of the north had led these historians to write of the peoples in the Rhine-delta,
amongst whom were a tribe called the Batavians. They gave their name to the
area enclosed by the Rhine, Maas and Waal which had come to be known as
the Betuwe. This was the origin of the Batavian myth, first brought to the
attention of a non-Latin-speaking audience by the humanist Cornelius
Aurelius (1462?–1531), to whom is ascribed *Die Cronycke van Hollandt,
Zeelandt ende Vrieslant*, printed in Leiden in 1517.[30] Aurelius' aim was
threefold: to write a native chronicle for the people of the northern provinces
in order to make them aware of their separate history, distinct from that of the
rest of the Burgundian realm; to imitate their Italian and German humanist
colleagues' historiography; to provide the 'Hollanders' with their own
mythology and history. Towards the end of the sixteenth century, as it
became clear that out of the old Burgundian realm two separate entities were
evolving, the northern provinces gradually shaping themselves into the
Republic of the Seven United Netherlands, the Batavian myth became
Batavian history for a while. The Republic provided itself with a past as a
parvenue provides himself with a lineage. The echoes of this history appeared
in a number of diverse writings, the most important of these was undoubtedly
the *Nederlandsche Historien* (1642),[31] the monumental history of the revolt
against Spain by Pieter Corneliszoon Hooft (1581–1647),[32] statesman, historian, dramatist, poet, a true Renaissance spirit with a happy combination of
patriotic 'Dutchness' and a lively interest in international affairs, political and
cultural. The *Historien* is one of the great achievements of the Dutch
Renaissance: in the deliberate cultivation of the Dutch language, in the
elevation of the long and bitter struggle onto a level whereby it became a
divinely inspired epic of liberation, in its regard for historical accuracy and its
attempts at fairness in portraying friend and foe, in its function of providing
the nation with a background and its leaders with a *speculum*. For as much as

this was meant to be the history of a people, it was also the history of one man, William of Orange, the by then legendary ideal prince. One of the particular features of the Republic was that its princes had very circumscribed powers and were ultimately responsible for their actions to the States General. None of the descendants of William the Silent ever reached the same stature in the eyes of the people. William's example, as Hooft had depicted it, was like a lighted beacon and was meant to be a model not only for princes but for all the leaders of the Republic, commoner or aristocrat. Last, but not least, it is fitting to reflect on Hooft's veneration for and the influence on the *Historien* of Tacitus.[33] The Roman was a source of wisdom and inspiration for many who were trying to solve some of the political problems which were prominent at the end of the sixteenth and in the seventeenth century, not least the questionable desirability of an absolute monarchy. The Netherlands were among many states grappling to establish an ideal form of government, but their situation was perhaps more acute. The founding of the Republic had been almost accidental and the continuation of the republican form of government was by no means a foregone conclusion. The murderer of William of Orange had robbed them of someone who had become their natural, God-given leader and after his death attempts had been made to attract potential heads of state, none of which had proved satisfactory. William's eldest son Maurice, who became in some respects his successor, was eventually in the thick of a controversy which came very near to full-scale civil war. The Republic was technically at war with Spain until the final signing of peace in 1648, and it was only then that its continued existence was more or less guaranteed. In this sea of uncertainties the debate about the best form of government, the best type of leader, as well as the wish to establish a national identity with a proper history, was naturally prominent. In Tacitus' writings, which were incidentally an important and intensively studied subject at Leiden University where Hooft read law, many similarities with the republican situation could be found. For Tacitus the ideal form of state was a republic with a senate, but he was aware that corruption, civil war and disagreement had led to the adoption of a monarchy with a strong head, Augustus. Not an ideal, but a pragmatic solution. For Hooft, and many others, there was much too be learned from the classical past which was directly relevant to their own situation. It was not that they wanted to imitate the past, but they realized that it had an exemplary bearing on modern life. Hooft, a republican by choice, had been close enough to the disastrous kingship of Philip II, as well as to the potential strong and certainly benevolent guardianship of the Prince of Orange, not to dismiss too lightly any pragmatic solution. And, for most of his life, he witnessed the utterly destructive forces of civil disagreement at work. Peace within and without was a prime issue in the Republic as it had been with Tacitus. Thus it was Tacitus' philosophy and ideas which strongly attracted the young Hooft and later continued to fascinate the mature statesman. His biographer tells us that he read the Roman's work fifty-two times because he so admired his language and his wisdom. Hooft was readily given the *epitheton ornans* of *Hollandtschen Tacitus*.

Amongst Hooft's dramas, which in one way or another were preoccupied with matters of state and government, is one which uses the Batavian myth to supply the 'Hollanders' with the story of their origin. It will not come as a surprise that *Baeto*[34] is a portrait of the ideal ruler, who rather than cause civil war, withdraws from his rightful kingdom, though consoled by a prophecy that from his descendants a new nation will develop, that of Holland. This new and glorious nation, Hooft indicated, had found its embodiment in the Republic.

More recent history, namely that of the fourteenth century, provided Hooft with material for his drama *Geeraert van Velzen* (1613).[35] It centred on one of the vassals of Count Floris V of Holland, who, in punishing his overlord for political and personal misdemeanour, himself becomes corrupted and drags the country into civil war for his own purposes. Moreover, he involves a foreign, English, power and thus turns traitor as well. In this play Hooft showed himself to be a firm supporter of an aristocratic-republican government, without interference from foreign powers or from 'the people'. All this had familiar echoes for those who remembered the disastrous involvement of the Count of Leicester, as well as of other foreign princes in the affairs of the Republic in the 1580s and, nearer still, the turbulence that followed the interference of 'popular opinions' in the internal politics of the state. Vondel would later on use the same historical material for his drama *Gijsbrecht van Aemstel* (1637),[36] while providing a different view. In general, it should be stressed how much the Renaissance literature of the republic, particularly its drama, was preoccupied with its past and present and therefore was involved in shaping its society.

If the Renaissance of the Low Countries achieved its flowering in the Republic of the Seven United Provinces during the first half of the seventeenth century, then signs of its dissolution were to follow. A gradual 'verbugerlijking', a lessening of expansion and expansiveness, of enterprise and innovation, an increase in adherence to the rules for the sake of regulation, can be said to be the heralds of decay. The colours seem to have become muted as the century went into its final quarter. The much vaunted ideal of stability, political and social, finally exacted its price.

But early on, such stability had been no more than a longed-for ideal in the young Republic; the position *vis-à-vis* Spain was not really clear until the Peace of Münster in 1648, after which other predators appeared; religious controversy and civil war continued to be nightmarish possibilities and

sometimes realities; the social structure of the Republic was in flux, partly due
to the enormous immigration from the south, partly to changing economic
features and partly because the seven provinces each experienced difficulties
with their coexistence. In this turmoil creativity was burgeoning, economi-
cally, scientifically, in the visual arts, in literature, in law and theology. Urban
society in the Netherlands, always dominant, now expanded. The physical
expansion can still be seen today in the canal-cities such as Amsterdam and
Utrecht, in the lay-out of Leiden, Gouda, Dordrecht, The Hague, Haarlem
and other towns. Medieval town walls had given way to new fortifications in
order to withstand heavier and more sophisticated sieges; new harbours had
been built for many more, and much bigger, ships; new land was wrested from
the water to provide more safety and more food for an ever-increasing
population. Both pride and self-confidence demanded a sturdy display of
wealth: the many grachtenhuizen with their quietly beautiful façades, the
country mansions with formal gardens and within easy reach of the commercial centres, the public buildings such as the exchanges, the weighing houses,
the town halls, the meeting halls for the guilds, the theatres, and the
government buildings in the Hague. Note: just a few palaces and not many
churches!

Much of the glory of this Golden Age is well documented; the painting, the
architecture, the voyages of discovery are the subjects of scholarly[37] and more
popular interest, and the coffee-table book, much maligned, has a function
here, if anywhere: we need to see the pictures of a society that left visible
testimony to its concerns for the world around it and the prosperous common
good of daily life. But not so well known, at least outside the Netherlands, is
the literature of the Republic, which is every bit as interesting as its French or
German counterpart and as involved in the shaping of Dutch society as were
the statesmen and merchants. Indeed, those who created the literature were
often engaged in more mundane pursuits which were part of the daily and
civic life of the Republic. Vondel,[38] the greatest of them all, whose life
spanned the emergence, flowering and then the baroque transformation of the
new art in the Republic, had a shop selling stockings. Hooft, elegant and
patrician, was a magistrate; Huygens,[39] the homo universalis par excellence,
was a diplomat and secretary to two Princes of Orange. Bredero[40] earned a
living as a painter; Grotius was a lawyer, Heinsius a university professor. All
of them earned their spurs in diverse branches of the bonae litterae, they were
poets and playwrights, they wrote letters and treatises, philosophical and
historical works, and all of them were, to varying degrees, aware that they
were contributing to, and shaping, a society.

They contributed in part to one of the indisputable characteristics of the
Renaissance across Europe, in their interest in the revival of the classical past.
We have already noted that during the sixteenth century the Low Countries

had initiated a great tradition of editing, translating and publishing classical texts which made possible the philological activity for which Dutch and especially Belgian universities and scholars were and are still much respected. In the seventeenth century that activity was centred in Leiden. But the very preoccupation with the classics in that University, founded by the Prince of Orange to reward the town for its heroic resistance of the Spanish siege, caused it, ironically, to be only incidentally connected with the vernacular literature which constituted the national Renaissance. The latter was to be the creation of a number of individuals like Vondel, Huygens, Bredero and others, who were, for the most part, not university scholars. Collective efforts came from the literary and dramatic societies, the so-called Chambers of Rhetoric.[41] These had been the major centres of creativity in all of the Low Countries in the late fifteenth century and the sixteenth century and had, on the whole, not been the trail-blazers for the new art. But once the sonnet, the ode and the tragedy had become better known and found general acceptance, many of the rhetoricians turned their hands to the new art forms. The Chambers of Amsterdam, Leiden, Haarlem, Gouda and others, their ranks swelled by many sophisticated refugees from the south, became non-academic centres of vernacular Renaissance literature on a broad popular level. More elite circles there were too: the poet Roemer Visscher and his intellectual daughters were the centre of gatherings of painters, musicians, poets and others artistically and sociably inclined. Higher up the social scale were the patrician gatherings at Muiden Castle, where the High Bailiff P.C. Hooft held court for lovers of art, music and debate. At the court of the Princes of Orange, the vernacular culture was largely ignored: a curious isolation in such a small country. Almost throughout the century, including the reign of William III and Mary, the court was dominated by the English ménages of the Stuart princesses who became wives of the princes.[42] One exception, Constantijn Huygens, the courtier, diplomat, composer and statesman who was very much part of this milieu, yet managed to contribute in no small way to the glories of Dutch seventeenth-century literature whilst being equally creative in French, English, Latin, Greek, German, Italian and Spanish. Some of his sonnets in Dutch would alone bestow merit on the Republic's Renaissance culture.[43]

Beauty there was in plenty: Hooft's virtuoso poetry shows that, and the opulent riches of many passages in Vondel's tragedies, arias amidst the recitatives, Bredero's sonnets, for all that they are often translations and adaptations of French poems, yet added unmistakably Dutch gems to Dutch literature. This is the miracle of the Dutch Renaissance: that out of the plodding sixteenth-century language reform and the mixture of imported Flemish and Brabant dialects with native Hollands dialects, some mysterious process of alchemy was at work to create a new language, supple, efficient and capable of heart-aching beauty;[44] not only in poetry, but, for instance, in the Authorised Version of the Bible, which was the product of the Synod of Dordrecht in 1618; or, in Hooft's *Nederlandsche Historien* where the graft of Dutch onto Tacitus' Latin created scholarly dignity and precision; or, on a different level, in Bredero's *Spaansche Brabander*,[45] where the very awareness of the mixture of cultures and dialects created a play like a series of cartoons of Amsterdam life, whilst, on a deeper level, he treated the quixotic problem of the relationship between fiction and reality.

Beside the beauty, there is purpose, or rather, a multitude of purposes. One of the outstanding characteristics of some of the most important Dutch literature of the period was its connection with the shaping of the state in which it flourished. Not all, but many of the different strands in the Dutch national Renaissance can be found in the work of Joost van den Vondel (1587–1679).[46] His *œuvre* lends itself to a demonstration of many of the features and concerns discussed earlier in this essay. Some things he was not: he was not a love poet; Petrarch and Ronsard meant nothing to him, and the channelling of personal emotions into poetry was as foreign to him as it was natural to Hooft, Huygens and Bredero. He was neither patrician, like Hooft, nor intellectual like Huygens, or vulgarly funny, like Bredero. He was not a wit, such as Huygens and Hooft. He had no sense of humour, as did Huygens and Bredero. He was in a class of his own, idiosyncratic and yet very Dutch. His personal history was typical of the history of his country. Born in Cologne from parents who had fled from Antwerp for the sake of their Protestant, possibly Baptist, faith, Vondel grew up in Amsterdam in a modest middle-class milieu which retained the piety and the gaiety of its Brabant origins and was culturally steeped in the traditions of the Chambers of Rhetoric. Vondel's education was modest and traditional and seemingly an unpropitious start for someone who in the course of his life would acquire so much learning. Vondel's knowledge of the Bible, of the Church Fathers, of the classics, both Greek and Latin, of contemporary theories about drama, was phenomenal.

His poetry and his drama very often are concerned with his country. Every conceivable occasion of state was commemorated by him. The bitter religious controversy which ended with the beheading of the elderly statesman Oldenbarnevelt[47] caused him to write some heartbreaking poems, in which he accused Oldenbarnevelt's corrupted judges and mourned the loss of the Father of the Fatherland and of the integrity of his country. His drama, *Palamedes oft Vermoorde Onnooselheyd* (1625),[48] bravely tackled the same episode under the guise of the conspiracy against Palamedes in the *Iliad*. It nearly landed him in prison, but neither then nor later did this prevent him from speaking his mind if he deemed it necessary. From his poetry alone it would be possible to piece together the life and career of Frederik Hendrik, Prince of Orange and *stadholder* from 1625 until 1647. To Vondel this prince was a hero, a soldier who fought for peace, a leader who protected liberty, a symbol of the values Vondel wanted his country to cherish. It was a one-sided devotion: never by so much as a word or a gesture did the prince acknowledge the tribute of the poet. This did not deter Vondel: the actual Prince was a useful vehicle for the model of the ideal prince and Vondel was a great upholder of ideals. Just like Hooft, Vondel was interested in his country's past. Both poets used historical materials from the fourteenth century and wrote plays centring round Count Floris V and his entourage. Floris was murdered by his vassals in the name of liberty. The rights and wrongs committed in the name of freedom were bound to be particularly interesting to the inhabitants of the Republic. Vondel created in his *Gijsbrecht van Aemstel* (1637) a gentle hero, prepared to suffer and go into exile, rather than inflict more civil war on his people, very much as Baeto, Hooft's hero in the play of that name, had done. Both plays are prophetic, in that a great future is promised for both Hooft's Batavians and Vondel's Amsterdam. Vondel does more: he links the destruction of Amsterdam in the play with the destruction of Troy, and the escape of Gijsbrecht with that of Aeneas. The Trojan hero's new foundation, Rome, would become the centre of Christendom and that is the link with Gijsbrecht, who is portrayed as a truly Christian hero, while the new Amsterdam will rise gloriously from its ruins. A slightly more uncomfortable link for Vondel's audience was his interest in 'the old religion' and it was for that reason that the play, meant to be performed on New Years Day to celebrate the opening of Amsterdam's new theatre, was, for a short time, forbidden. Vondel did, in fact, later convert to Roman Catholicism and, though this isolated him in some measure, he entered the tradition of the Counter-Reformation which caused him to write some splendid baroque plays, such as the *Salomon* (1648),[49] the *Lucifer* (1654),[50] the *Jephta of Offerbelofte* (1659)[51] and many others. Vondel not only strove to express the concerns of state and religion, he also relentlessly tried to write the perfect tragedy, renovated and innovated his ideas about the genre, read Seneca and Sophocles. In content and in form he aimed to emulate the Ancients. The Batavian history as related in Tacitus provided him with the material for a play about Julius Civilis, the Roman-educated soldier who became the leader of the tribes who rebelled against Julius Caesar. In Vondel's hands it became a play about freedom and justice, *De Batavische Gebroeders* (1663),[52] at a time when there was a swing towards monarchical power by a large faction in the Republic, fanned by the ambitions of the circle around the young prince William III. Civil strife was yet again a real danger, as it had been in the 1620s and Vondel, who had spoken out then, did so again. These are but a very few examples compared to the many that Vondel's *œuvre* and that of others could provide of the lasting interests and concern with the affairs of the Republic. It is this engagement of art with political, religious, social and philosophical issues which gives the Dutch Renaissance its unique national context and which provided the Netherlands with an identity that is clearly discernible still today.

NOTES

1 W. Prevenier and W. Blockmans, *The Burgundian Netherlands*, Eng. trans., Peter King and Yvette Mead (Cambridge, 1986), 293–5.
2 N. Wilkins, *The Lyric Art of Medieval France* (Fulbourn, 1988), 225–58.
3 Prevenier and Blockmans, *Burgundian Netherlands*, 332.
4 *Ter Liefde der Const. Uit het 'Schilderboeck' (1604) van Karel van Mander*, ed. W. Waterschoot (Leiden, 1983), 43–63.
5 *'Das Buch Extasis' van Jan van der Noot, with a summary in English*, ed. C.A. Zaalberg (Assen, 1954).
6 R. Vaughan, *Philip the Bold. The Formation of the Burgundian State* (London/ New York, 1962); *John the Fearless, The Growth of the Burgundian Power* (London/New York, 1966); *Philip the Good. The Apogee of Burgundy* (London/ New York, 1970); *Charles the Bold. The Last Valois Duke of Burgundy* (London/ New York, 1973).
7 G.J. Renier, *The Dutch Nation: An Historical Study* (London, 1944), 15.
8 G.J. Hoogewerff, 'Uit de geschiedenis van het Nederlandsch nationaal besef', *Tijdschrift voor Geschiedenis*, 44 (1929), 113–34.
9 B.H. Erné and L.M. van Dis, *De Gentse Spelen van 1539* ('s-Gravenhage, 1982).
10 Q. Skinner, *The Foundation of Political Thought*, 2 vols. (Cambridge, 1978), vol. I, 1–65.
11 Prevenier and Blockmans, *op. cit.*, 377–8.
12 *Texts concerning the Revolt of the Netherlands*, ed. E.H. Kossmann and A.F. Mellink (Cambridge, 1974).
13 *Ibid.*, 216–17.
14 E.H. Kossmann, *The Low Countries 1780–1940* (Oxford, 1978), 48–205.
15 E.H. Kossmann, *op. cit.*, 439–516.
16 F. Baur *et al.*, *Geschiedenis van de Letterkunde der Nederlanden*, 9 vols. (Antwerpen/Brussel/s'-Hertogenbosch, 1949), vol. III, 180.
17 *Rodolphus Agricola Phrisius (1444–1485). Proceedings of the International Conference at the University of Groningen 28–30 October 1985*, ed. F. Akkerman and A.J. Vanderjagt (Leiden/New York/København/Köln, 1988).
18 E.W. Miller and J.W. Scudder, *Wessel Gansfort, Life and Writings*, 2 vols. (New York, 1917).
19 L.D. Reynolds and N.G. Wilson, *Scribes and Scholars. A Guide to the Transmission of Greek and Latin Literature*, 2nd edn (Oxford, 1974), 160.
20 M. Mann Phillips, *Erasmus and the Northern Renaissance* (London, 1959); J. Huizinga, *Erasmus of Rotterdam* (London, 1952).
21 F. Oakley, *The Western Church in the Later Middle Ages* (Ithaca/London, 1979), 100–6.
22 Baur *et al*, *Letterkunde der Nederlanden*, vol. III, 44.
23 *Ibid.*

24 P. Geyl, *The Revolt of the Netherlands 1555–1609*, 2nd edn. (London/New York, 1980), 266.

25 Baur *et al*, *Letterkunde der Nederlanden*, vol. III, 45–6.

26 *Ibid.*, 46–8.

27 W.S.M. Knight, *The Life and works of Hugo Grotius* (London, 1925).

28 P.R. Sellin, *Daniel Heinsius and Stuart England* (Leiden/London, 1968).

29 J. Duym, *Het Moordadich Stuck van Balthasar Gerards, begaen aen den Prince van Oraignen*, 1584, ed. L.F.A. Serrarens and N.C.H. Wijngaards (Zutphen, n.d.).

30 K. Tilmans, *Aurelius en de Divisiekroniek. Historiografie en humanisme in Holland in de tijd van Erasmus* (Hilversum, 1988).

31 *Episodes uit Hoofts Nederlandsche Historien*, ed. E. Verwijs, 4th edn (Amsterdam, 1919).

32 H.W. van Tricht, *P.C. Hooft* (Arnhem, 1951).

33 J.D.M. Cornelissen, 'Hooft en Tacitus. Bijdrage tot de kennis van de vaderlandse geschiedenis in de eerste helft van de zeventiende eeuw', *De Eendracht van het Land. Cultuurhistorische studien over Nederland in de zestiende en zeventiende eeuw* (Amsterdam, 1987), 53–101.

34 P.C. Hooft, *Baeto (1617)*, ed. F. Veenstra (Zwolle, 1954).

35 P.C. Hooft, *Geeraert van Velzen (1613)*, ed. A.J.J. de Witte (Zutphen, n.d.).

36 J. van den Vondel, *Gijsbrecht van Aemstel (1637)*, ed. L.M. van Dis (Groningen, 1962).

37 S. Schama, *The Embarrassment of Riches. An Interpretation of Dutch Culture in the Golden Age* (London 1987).

38 A.J. Barnouw, *Vondel* (New York, 1925).

39 J. Smit, *Constantijn Huygens* ('s-Gravenhage, 1980); L. Strengholt, *Constanter. Het leven van Constantijn Huygens* (Amsterdam, 1987).

40 J.A.N. Knuttel, Th. de Vries and J.B. de Klerk, *Bredero, Poëet en Amsterdammer* (Amsterdam, 1968).

41 E. Strietman, 'Teach yourself art: the literary guilds in the Low Countries', *Dutch Crossing*, 29 (1986), 75–94.

42 *Glorieuze Revolutie: de wereld van William en Mary: een korte biografische schets en een beeld van de tijd*, ed. R. Bastiaanse *et al*. ('s-Gravenhage, 1988). Text in Dutch and in English.

43 *Dutch Crossing*, 33 (1987) has articles about Huygens in translation (Th. Hermans), Huygens' musical activities (G. Chew), and translations of his poetry by A.F. Harms, P. Vincent and A. Lefèvre.

44 For translations of, and articles about, many of the seventeenth-century poets, see *Dutch Crossing*, 10 (1980), 11 (1980), 13 (1981), 24 (1984), 25 (1985), 26 (1985), 27 (1985), 29 (1986), 36 (1988), 37 (1989).

45 *G.A. Bredero's Spaanschen Brabander Jerolimo*, ed. B.C. Damsteegt (Zutphen, 1978); H. D. Brumble III jr, *G.A. Bredero, The Spanish Brabanter* (New York, 1982).

46 G. Brandt, *Het leven van Joost van den Vondel*, ed. P. Leendertz jr ('s-Gravenhage, 1932).

47 J. den Tex, *Oldenbarnevelt*, 5 vols. (Haarlem/Groningen, 1960-72); 2 vols. abridged English edn (Cambridge, 1973).

48 *Joost van den Vondel's Palamedes*, ed. N.C.H. Wijngaards (Zutphen, n.d.).
49 'Salomon (1648)' *De Werken van Vondel*, ed. J.F.M. Sterck *et al*, 10 vols. (Amsterdam, 1927–37), vol. v, 373–449.
50 *Lucifer (1654)*, ed. W.J.M.A. Asselbergs (Zwolle, 1966).
51 *Jephta of Offerbelofte (1569)*, ed. N.C.H. Wijngaards (Zutphen, 1976).
52 'Batavische gebroeders (1663)', *De Werken van Vondel*, vol. ix, 898–971.

FURTHER READING

General and historical background

Algemene Geschiedenis der Nederlanden, ed. P. Blok *et al*, 15 vols. (Haarlem, 1977–83), in particular:

Decavele, J. 'De Reformatie in het begin van de restauratie 1556–1568', AGN, VI, 166–85.

Halkin, L.E. 'Het Katholieke herstel in de Zuidelijke Nederlanden 1579–1609', AGN, VI, 344–51.

Janssens, P. 'Het Bestand in de Zuidelijke Nederlanden', AGN, VI, 315–24.

Mellink, A.F. 'Prereformatie en vroege reformatie, 1517–1568', AGN, VI, 146–65.

Nijenhuis, W. 'Religiegeschiedenis 1621–1648. Kerk in het meervoud', AGN, VI, 397–411.

de Schepper, H. 'De reconquista mislukt. De Katholieke gewesten 1579–1588', AGN, VI, 262–78.

van Uytven, R. *et al.*, 'Het politieke en religieuze leven na 1480', AGN, V, 419–92.

Burke, P. *The Renaissance* (London, 1987).

Duke, A.C. 'Building heaven in hell's despite: the early history of the Reformation in the towns of the Low Countries' in A.C. Duke and C.A. Tamse (eds.) *Britain and the Netherlands* (The Hague, 1981), 45–75.

van Gelder, H.A.E. *The Two Reformations in the Sixteenth Century* (The Hague, 1961).

Geyl, P. *History of the Low Countries* (London, 1963).

History of the Netherlands, 3 vols. (London/New York, 1958).

Groenhuis, G. 'Calvinism and national consciousness: the Dutch republic as the new Israel' in A.C. Duke and C.A. Tamse (eds.), *Britain and the Netherlands* (The Hague, 1981), 118–33.

Haley, K.H.D. *The Dutch in the Seventeenth Century* (London, 1972).

Huizinga, J.H. *The Waning of the Middle Ages* (Harmondsworth, 1972).

Dutch Civilization of the Seventeenth Century (London, 1968).

Israels,. J.J. *The Dutch Republic and the Hispanic World, 1606–1661* (Oxford, 1986).

Koenigsberger, H.G. 'The empire of Charles V in Europe' in G.R. Elton (ed.) *The Reformation 1520–1559* (Cambridge/London/New York/Melbourne, 1975), 301–33.

Parker, G. *The Dutch Revolt* (London, 1977).

Spain and the Netherlands 1559–1659. Ten Studies (London, 1979).

Wilson, C.H. *The Dutch Republic and the Civilization of the Seventeenth Century* (London, 1968).

Humanism, literature and arts

Bolgar, R.R. *The Classical heritage and its beneficiaries*, 5th edn (Cambridge/London/New York/Melbourne, 1977), 302–79.

Chatelet, A. *Early Dutch Painting. Painting in the Northern Netherlands in the Fifteenth Century*, trans. C. Brown and A. Turner (Oxford, 1981).

Foster, R. and P. Tudor-Craig, *The Secret Life of Paintings* (Woodbridge, 1986), 5–23.

IJsewijn, J. 'Humanism and humanist literature in the Low Countries before 1500', *Classical influences on European culture, A.D. 500–1500* (Cambridge, 1971).

  'The coming of humanism to the Low Countries', *Itinerarium Italicum. The profile of the Italian Renaissance in the mirror of its European transformation*, ed. H.A. Oberman and Thomas A. Brady jr. (Leiden, 1975), pp. 193–301.

Meyer, R.P., *Literature of the Low Countries* (Assen, 1971).

Smit, W.A.P. *Van Pascha tot Noah*, 3 vols. (Zwolle, 1956, 1959, 1962).

⁊

SIX

GERMANY

JAMES OVERFIELD

On 31 August 1492, Konrad Celtis, the German 'arch-humanist', having just commenced his career as salaried professor of poetry and oratory at the University of Ingolstadt, delivered an inaugural oration to gathered students, masters and local dignitaries. Celtis spoke with passion and feeling, for he was a man with a mission. Born into a peasant family in 1459, Celtis had studied at the universities of Cologne, Heidelberg, Rostock and Leipzig, and by 1487 had produced enough acceptable Latin verse to warrant his crowning by Emperor Frederick III as the first German Poet Laureate in the Holy Roman Empire.[1] Shortly thereafter, he embarked on a whirlwind tour of Italy that took him to Padua, Bologna, Venice, Rome and Florence. His experience was more than a bit unsettling. Although impressed by the eloquence and classical learning of the Italian humanists, Celtis was incensed by their undisguised sense of superiority and by their unwillingness to take seriously anyone, even a crowned poet, from the barbarian north.

This sojourn to Italy explains the urgency of Celtis' Ingolstadt oration.[2] He hoped to rouse his fellow Germans from their intellectual torpor and inspire them to follow the cultural paths blazed by the Italians. Germany, he told his listeners, was corrupt and decayed, to foreigners the home of 'drunkenness, barbarism, cruelty and whatever is bestial and foolish'. Germany's deterioration resulted from but one cause: a decline in learning, specifically a neglect of the great philosophers, poets and orators of antiquity. He proclaimed: 'we have neglected them like the detested spoils of the enemies, as if locked in a prison, covered with dust, untouched, and not well protected from the rain.' Among the peoples of Europe, only the Italians had embraced fully the wisdom of antiquity, and this, said Celtis, was the reason they flourished and were envied by other nations. Germans, especially German youth, now must do the same. He urged his listeners to abandon the moldy precepts which passed for learning in Germany and to dedicate themselves to the sublime wisdom of the Ancients. Then they would 'win the praises of illustrious authors' and 'procure immortality for themselves and glory and praise for the fatherland'.

Celtis was not the only German who was convinced that Germany was about to enter a period of revival and renewal. After many decades of political disintegration, economic decline and religious decay, Germany at the end of the fifteenth century was awash with reformers who had blueprints for the improvement of everything from monasticism to the constitution of the Holy Roman Empire. Among the many designs and proposals for Germany's rejuvenation set forth in the years around 1500, the conception outlined by Celtis in his 1492 oration was in certain aspects the most ambitious. The cultural and educational programme he envisaged would make the German people more eloquent in their speech and more profound in their thought. But much more could be expected. Piety would deepen, culture would be enriched, political institutions would be reinvigorated, and, as of old, Germans would be honoured, respected and even feared. Although he did not use the word *renascitio* in his speech, it is clear that in his view of Germany's past and future, Celtis fully expected a German 'Renaissance'.

Unquestionably, some of Celtis' expectations were fulfilled. Germany had a 'Renaissance', if by that is meant a conscious effort on the part of some individuals to reshape thought and culture by drawing upon the heritage of ancient Greece and Rome and by imitating certain intellectual and cultural currents that had emerged in fourteenth- and fifteenth-century Italy. This Renaissance did not, of course, fulfill the grandiose dreams of Celtis and like-minded humanists. Even without the impact of the Reformation, the givens of human nature and the realities of Germany's religious, political and socio-economic situation negated any possibility that the humanists' hopes for a transformed and culturally ascendant Germany would be realised. Nonetheless, a Renaissance occurred. In varying degrees, it affected scholarship, art, education, literature and religious attitudes, but, even in the areas of its greatest impact, it never obliterated inherited German cultural and intellectual patterns. The Renaissance in Germany, as it was throughout northern Europe, was a story of compromise and adjustment.

Architecture, sculpture and painting

Was there an artistic Renaissance in Germany? In architecture, even though there were signs of Italian influence and classical inspiration in the sixteenth and seventeenth centuries, the term 'Renaissance' seems inappropriate.[3] After the onset of the Reformation, new church construction stopped until the 1580s, and overall the number of new buildings declined. Protestants simply took over formerly Catholic churches, and suitably stripped them of papist ornaments and decorations. Catholics, on the other hand, were too damaged, both financially and psychologically, to undertake new building projects.

Some non-ecclesiastical construction continued, however, and a few efforts, not always successful, were made to introduce classical motifs. When, for example, the Palatine Elector Otto Heinrich decided to enlarge the Heidelberg castle in the 1550s, he chose an architect, whose identity is unknown, who set out to design a building immediately recognisable as classical in inspiration. His façade combined dozens of Greek and Roman architectural motifs: a Doric frieze was supported by Ionian and Doric pilasters; pediments placed over windows were supported by classical columns and contained medallions portraying ancient heroes; sculptures of mythological figures were placed between the windows. Such confused and overcrowded ornamentation was almost a parody of the restrained classicism of the Italians, Brunelleschi, Alberti and Bramante. More successful was the *Stadtresidenz* at Landshut in Lower Bavaria, built between 1536 and 1543 for Ludwig X, Duke of Bavaria-Landshut. Ludwig, having been deeply impressed by the recently completed Palazzo del Te during his visit to Mantua in 1536, imported Italian masons and stuccoists to Landshut, where they designed and completed a reasonable facsimile of the Mantuan palace. Except for these two undertakings, however, the Renaissance in German architecture for most of the sixteenth century, was little more than a system of classical ornament applied to essentially late Gothic structures. Classicism ultimately had great impact on German architecture, but only in the eighteenth century, and then by way of England and France, not Italy.[4]

Like architecture, German sculpture before the Reformation century was little affected by the Italian Renaissance. In late medieval Germany many sculptors were kept busy with commissions from ecclesiastical institutions, municipalities and private individuals.[5] Most, such as Tilmann Reimenschneider (1460–1531) of Würzburg, and Veit Stoss (1438?–1533) of Nuremberg, were Gothic artists, untouched by the Renaissance. Notable exceptions were two brothers, Hermann and Peter Vischer, who, having trained in the Nuremberg workshop of their father, Peter Vischer the Elder, were inspired by visits to Siena and Rome in the 1510s. On their return, they collaborated with their father to produce the great shrine of St Sebald in St Sebald church, Nuremberg, a work which included Renaissance elements within a fundamentally Gothic framework. Hermann died shortly after the shrine's completion, but Peter lived on to produce medals, plaques and bronze statuettes, some depicting characters from classical mythology. Except for the Vischer brothers, however, most German sculptors, while showing exceptional technical skill, adhered to traditional Gothic forms and motifs. Their works attracted little attention outside the cities that housed their workshops.

During the fifteenth century, German painting gave every indication that it would be no more creative or innovative than sculpture.[6] Germany produced a number of capable painters, but their work, strongly dependent on masters from the Netherlands and Flanders, was unoriginal. An exception was Michael Pacher (c. 1435–98), whose paintings, such as *Pope Sixtus II Taking*

Leave of St Lawrence (*c.* 1462–70) and *St Wolfgang Forces the Devil to Hold his Prayerbook* (*c.* 1481), show skill in perspective, solidity of forms and depiction of drapery that resulted from his study of Italian painters during journeys to the Po Valley from his Tyrolean home. Another exception was Martin Schongauer (*c.* 1450–91), an Alsatian from Colmar, the one fifteenth-century German artist who gained an international reputation. He was best known for his many copper engravings, which in their detail, complexity and a range of shading rivalled the work of the Italian master engravers, Mantegna and Pollaiuolo. His most famous engraving, *The Temptation of St Anthony* (*c.* 1470–5), was carefully copied by the adolescent Michelangelo when he was an assistant in Ghirlandaio's Florentine studio.

Then, around 1500, German painting took an unexpected turn. In the next three decades, Germany produced a group of spectacular painters, whose works surpassed those of the Netherlands and at least equalled those of High Renaissance Italy. Their ranks included Albrecht Dürer (1471–1528), 'the German Leonardo', Hans Holbein the Younger (1497/8–1543), one of the greatest portrait painters who ever lived, and a host of other powerful artists, among them, Matthias Grünewald (d. 1528), Lucas Cranach the Elder (1472–1553), Hans Baldung Grien (1484–1545), Hans Burgkmair the Elder (d. 1531) and Albrecht Altdorfer (1480–1538). Then after three decades, great names disappeared. From the 1530s onward, the quantity and quality of German painting plummeted to a point well below that of the fifteenth century. This sudden demise of German painting is understood only slightly better than its early sixteenth-century blossoming.

The work of the brilliant and original German painters of the early sixteenth century is sometimes referred to as 'the German School', but it is difficult to see much unity in their work. Dürer – the masterful engraver and woodcutter, the incisive portraitist and self-portraitist, the sensitive interpreter of nature, the friend of humanists and the ardent Lutheran – had no rivals in the ability to imbue art with powerful religious and intellectual meaning. He laboured to provide an intellectual underpinning to German art, and in this cause, he produced important treatises on perspective and human proportion. Holbein was a portrait specialist who painted such luminaries as Erasmus, Thomas More, King Henry VIII, four of Henry's wives and several of his major advisers. Altdorfer, a representative of the 'Danube style', was famous for his dramatic and moving landscapes. Grünewald, the 'last medieval mystic', was preoccupied with pain and suffering. Among his twenty-two authenticated paintings, there are six Crucifixions, two Lamentations of Christ and one Mocking of Christ. No painting in Christian art captures more movingly the agony of the Crucifixion than his *Isenheim Altarpiece* (1510–15). Cranach, a Saxon court artist for most of his career, drew inspiration from Dürer, Grünewald, Holbein and the Dutch painters, and presided over a workshop that produced portraits, religious works, landscapes and mythological scenes for a long list of patrons. Grien showed a special interest in correct human anatomy and had a range of subjects as wide as Cranach.

This was unquestionably an era of brilliance for German painting, but was it a 'Renaissance'? To what extent was the German achievement inspired by classical models and Italian innovations? Among the German masters of the early 1500s, only two made artistic pilgrimages to Italy. Dürer, while in his mid-twenties, went to Venice, and most likely to Padua, Mantua and Cremona in 1495. A decade later, he made a longer, two-year visit to Italy. He spent most of his time in Venice, where among other things he received the commission from the German community for his *Festival of the Rose Garden* (1506). He also visited Bologna, and possibly Milan, Florence and Rome. Hans Burgkmair the Elder, who may have travelled to Italy in the 1480s, and unquestionably did so in 1505, was the only other major German painter of the early 1500s with direct Italian experience. Holbein the Younger moved from his native Augsburg as a teenager to work in Basel and Lucerne; we know he visited Blois and Bourges in 1524, but there is no evidence that he or any other major German painter of the early 1500s travelled to Italy.

A visit to Italy was not, of course, the only way a painter might be introduced to classicism and Italian art. Prints and engravings by Pollaiuolo and Mantegna circulated throughout Germany, and through the engravings of the tireless Mercantonio Raimondi, who copied works by numerous Italian painters, especially Raphael, Germans could become familiar with a wide range of Italian artists. We know that Altdorfer's first extant work was a drawing of two muses taken from an engraving of Mantegna's *Parnassus*. Other German painters may have become interested in classical themes as a result of contacts with humanist intellectuals. Holbein painted Erasmus three times, Burgkmair painted Celtis; and Cranach, Altdorfer and Grien, who worked, respectively, in Wittenberg, Strasburg and Regensburg, all lived in cultural environments influenced by humanism. Finally, German artists of the early 1500s could catch a glimpse of the Italian Renaissance through contacts with Dürer himself or by studying his works.

As a result in part of Italian influence, German painting of the early 1500s underwent indisputable changes. Non-religious paintings, for example, became more common. Portraits by Dürer and Holbein drew on Italian (and Flemish) precedents, as did the interest of prominent patrons in having them done. The influence of Italian art and of humanism, both Italian and German, can also be seen in the numerous paintings inspired by ancient history and classical mythology. How German painters handled classical subject-matter, however, indicates some of the limitations of the 'German Renaissance' in painting. Altdorfer's most famous work, *The Battle of Issus* (1529), depicts

Joseph Krauskopf Memorial Library

the victory of Alexander the Great over Darius III at the battle on the River Issus in 333 BC. This five-foot-tall canvas meticulously details literally thousands of soldiers in medieval battle dress, fighting against a fantastic background of crumbling fortresses, cities, mountains, seas and whirling storm-clouds. The rising sun at the right and the waning moon at the upper left of the painting are locked in a battle that dwarfs the action on the battlefield. According to one interpreter: 'This sudden opening up of space, with its subordination of the human figures to the cosmic landscape, bespeaks a new view of nature, a view that will see man as an insignificant mote in an infinite universe.'[7] Thus Altdorfer's work is classical in subject, but in spirit is far removed from the Italian Renaissance sense of human dignity and power.

An interest in themes from antiquity, without a real classical spirit, also can be seen in the work of Lucas Cranach the Elder. His *Judgement of Paris* (1531) shows Paris and Hermes dressed as sixteenth-century German knights. Although more than a touch of Renaissance sensuality can be seen in his *Nymph of the Fountain* (1518), his nudes show no attempt at harmonious proportion or any serious study of human anatomy. The hearty, bearded Apollo, from his *Apollo and Diana* (1518) suggests less a god of the sun than a Saxon peasant who has just taken off his clothes.

Dürer, of all the German painters of the early sixteenth century, most resembled the great Italian masters in his personality, international fame and general approach to art.[8] Intensely conscious of his own being, he left behind self-portraits, notes, sketches, letters and diaries through which he revealed his extraordinary mind and personality. Also like the Italians, he had a deep interest in artistic theory, and he made important contributions to the study of perspective and human proportion. Most importantly, he was totally committed to the Italians' ideal of the dignity and high purpose of art, which he laboured to raise in Germany from the level of a handicraft.

Signs of Italian Renaissance influence abound in Dürer's work. His fascination with physical perfection and sculptural form can be seen in his engraving, *Adam and Eve* (1504); his mastery of perspective is evident in his engraving, *St Jerome* (1514); his acquaintance with neo-platonic philosophy is borne out in his brooding *Melancholia I*; and his ability to paint monumental and simple forms in the Italian manner is revealed in one of his last and greatest paintings, *The Four Apostles* (1526).

Dürer remained, however, a painter of the north. This can be seen in the fine line work and the closely observed, precisely outlined details evident in his paintings, woodcuts and engravings. Perhaps the greatest example of Dürer's preoccupation with an exacting detailed description of nature is his famous water-colour, *The Great Piece of Turf* (1506), so accurate that botanists can easily identify in it dandelions, yarrow, great plantain, meadow grass and heath rush. Dürer's northern roots are also evident in his love of symbolism. In his engraving, *Adam and Eve*, the two idealised figures, in poses suggesting the *Apollo Belvedere* and the *Medici Venus*, are placed against a background of a dark and threatening northern forest. At their feet and behind them are depicted a rabbit, cat, elk and ox, representing man's four humours, the sanguine, choleric, melancholic and phlegmatic. On a distant peak, a bison stares down into an abyss, and at the feet of Adam, a small mouse fails to sense the presence of a nearby cat. The bison and mouse both represent the tragedy about to befall humankind. The engraving expresses the quality of Dürer's genius – his ability to creatively draw upon the artistic innovations of Quattrocento Italy while holding true to his German roots.

In 1526, two years before his death, Dürer completed his great masterpiece, *The Four Apostles*. Donated to the Nuremberg city council to be hung in the city hall, this painting expressed the artist's commitment to the Lutheran Reformation. The majestic figures of John and Peter are on one panel, and Mark and Peter are on the other. Below them, quotations from their books, in Luther's German translation of the Bible, warn against false prophets and the perils of the age. *The Four Apostles* immediately was recognised as a work of genius, and ever since viewers have been moved by its grandeur and power. But it was also the last great work produced by the remarkable German painters of the early 1500s, and it was the only true German masterpiece that can be said to have been inspired by Lutheranism. Lucas Cranach the Elder continued as the Saxon court painter until his death in 1553, but most critics agree that as his art became more didactic and more tightly harnessed to Lutheran theological themes, it lost much of its earlier vitality.

Many explanations have been suggested for the demise of German painting after the 1530s.[9] It has been linked to Germany's economic slump, the political decline of Germany's cities, and the long absences of Emperor Charles V, who gave most of his commissions to artists in Spain and the Low Countries. The onset of the Reformation seems, however, to have been the most important factor. Clearly, the political and religious conflicts of the early Reformation created an unfavourable atmosphere for artistic creativity. Several artists, for example, were ruined because of their support for the peasant's cause during the Peasants' War in the mid-1520s. The painter Jorg Ratgeb was executed at Pforzheim in 1526, the sculptor Tilmann Riemenschneider was imprisoned and tortured by the authorities in Würzburg, and Matthias Grünewald avoided punishment by Archbishop Albrecht of Brandenburg only by fleeing in 1526 from Mainz to Halle, where he died in 1528.

In addition, the early Reformation caused a drastic decline in commissions for ecclesiastical art, a fact of obvious importance in an era lacking a strong demand for secular art. In areas under Zwinglian and later Calvinist influence, the demand for ecclesiastical art was reduced to zero. Both Zwingli and Calvin viewed images in churches as idolatrous, and were sceptical about the usefulness and suitability of art as an educational tool. Although Luther at first shared many of Zwingli's reservations about religious art, he gradually adopted a more moderate position, which accorded to 'theologically correct' art an instructional role of some importance. Nonetheless, the demand for religious art in Lutheran areas fell far below the level of the late Middle Ages. The Lutheran emphasis on proclaiming the word through preaching made the visual aspect of worship less significant, and the emphasis on faith over good works discouraged private individuals from commissioning religious art now that this activity no longer held promise of direct spiritual benefits.[10] Commissions for art also plummeted in Catholic regions, reflecting the general demoralisation of German Catholicism in the 1520s and 1530s.

As the market for art declined, artists closed their workshops and turned to other professions. Training of new artists deteriorated, and as the giants of the early 1500s died, no one replaced them. The German Renaissance in painting came to an end, an unintended victim of the Protestant Reformation.

German literature

It is difficult to develop a case for the existence of a 'Renaissance' in German literature during the fifteenth and sixteenth centuries.[11] In quantitative terms, the productivity of German writers was enormous. They poured out literally thousands of dramas, poems and prose works of every imaginable description in both Latin and in German. Within their ranks, however, there was no Petrarch or Boccaccio, no Rabelais or Montaigne, no Shakespeare.[12] Unlike the painters of Dürer's generation, no German author effectively drew upon the models of antiquity and recent Italian writing to raise medieval German literature to a higher level of force and expression. A representative figure of the age might well have been the Nuremberg cobbler, Hans Sachs (1494–1576), who in 1567 wrote a poetic inventory of his works: by that year he had composed sixteen volumes of *Gesangbücher*, containing 4,275 *Meistergesänge*, and eighteen volumes of *Spruchbücher*, containing another 1,700 poems, of which more than 200 were plays. These works show only the most superficial impact of German humanism or the Italian Renaissance, and today they have relatively few readers.

Previously during the twelfth and thirteenth centuries, the inventiveness, beauty and power of German literature ranked second only to that of France. Germany, for example, produced many excellent lyric poets, whose works, referred to collectively as the *Minnesang*, expressed the ideals of courtly love. Walther von der Vogelweide, who was born around 1170 and died around 1230, is viewed by some as the greatest lyric poet, not just of Germany, but of all medieval Europe. German authors also produced large numbers of knightly romances – longer poems, with themes mainly borrowed from France, that celebrated chivalric virtues in the context of complex and fantastic plots. The most famous example of this genre was the *Parzival* of Wolfram von Eschenbach (*c.* 1170–1220). Finally, the early thirteenth century saw the appearance of a number of epic poems based on Teutonic traditions, the most important of which, the *Niebelungenlied*, was written by an unknown Austrian cleric.

In the late Middle Ages, the *Minnesang* and other literary expressions of knightly culture declined, but Germany's literary output remained robust. The *Minnesang* gradually evolved into the *Meistersang*, a form of poetry cultivated in special 'schools' in Germany's major cities. In these 'schools', *Meistersänger* composed and performed lyric poetry that had to conform to rigid rules derived from twelve so-called masters of the early medieval period. German drama also developed during the late Middle Ages. Most of the performances were serious religious plays designed to instruct and inspire the populace. From simple playlets acted by three or four clergymen, they evolved in some places into major community undertakings lasting up to a week. Plays of a far different nature, but still connected with the liturgical year, were the *Fastnachtspiele*, or Shrovetide plays, performed just before Lent. These were brief and usually ribald comedies dealing with marital conflict, dull-witted peasants, shrewish women, fools, drunkards, corrupt clergy and general human folly.

The Renaissance of the 1400s and 1500s affected Germany's literary traditions in a number of ways. First and foremost, humanist efforts to introduce new, classical standards for writing Latin affected the German language itself. Latin had been the language of scholarship and the church throughout the Middle Ages, but the Latin of medieval schools and universities had lost its ties to literature and was studied mainly as a branch of logic and philosophy.[13] The humanists successfully expunged medieval 'speculative grammar' from the schools and replaced it with an approach to Latin teaching inspired by the best authors of ancient Rome and Renaissance Italy. Thus when learned Germans spoke or wrote Latin in the sixteenth century, it no longer was the technical, jargon-filled Latin of scholastic philosophy, but a Latin which in theory resembled the elegance and power of Cicero and Horace. Inevitably, this affected German itself.[14] Most of the Latin loan words still in use in modern German entered the language between 1450 and 1650. Latin also exerted its influence on German syntax. For the many Germans who wrote, spoke and thought in Latin in their professions, Latin usage and grammatical constructs affected their German. Furthermore, the first printed grammar texts for German, which appeared in the sixteenth century, were written in Latin and applied to German Latin grammatical structures. As a result, in the sixteenth century, imitation of Latin grammatical construction had an impact on German. Examples include the transposition of the verb to the end of a clause introduced by a subordinating conjunction or by a relative pronoun, and the use of participles in various types of absolute constructions ('Diese Arbeit vollendet, ging Ich zu Bett').[15] Thus Renaissance humanism, though not rivalling the importance of Luther's biblical translations or the appearance of the printed book, did influence the development of the German language.

Renaissance humanists also enormously expanded the literary horizons of Germans by introducing them to the full literary heritage of ancient Greece, ancient Rome and Renaissance Italy. From the very start of the German humanist movement, editing and publishing works of ancient and recent Italian authors was a major activity. Niklas von Wyle (1410–78), a town clerk and schoolmaster from Esslingen in Swabia, who hoped to discipline German by subjecting it to Latin structure and grammar, rendered into German eighteen Latin treatises by Bracciolini, Bruni, Boccaccio and Petrarch; he also translated Lucian's *The Golden Ass* into German, but from a Latin version of Bracciolini. Albrecht von Eyb (1420–75), an aristocratic churchman from Franconia, in addition to assembling his *Margarita poetica* (1459), a voluminous anthology of Latin literature from Roman, patristic and recent Italian authors, made several translations from Latin to German, including works by Boccaccio and Plautus. Heinrich Steinhöwel (1412–78), the official physician of the south German city of Ulm, is best known for his translation of Boccaccio's *De claris mulieribus* into his German version, *Von den synnrychen erluchtern wyben* (*On Wise and Illustrious Women*).[16] Among the later humanists, especially those who were university teachers, editing and publishing works of Roman authors was pursued energetically, and it is safe to say that by the 1540s, printed editions of all major and most minor Roman writers were available. Editions of works of important Greek writers, sometimes in the original Greek, sometimes in Latin translations, were also published. Some later humanists continued the tradition of von Weyl, von Eyb and Steinhöwel by publishing German translations of ancient classics. Works by Ovid, Homer, Virgil, Apuleius, Hesiod, Terence, Plautus, Seneca, Quintilian and Cicero were all translated into German and published.[17]

The greatest impact of the classics on German literature came only after the sixteenth century, however. Classical themes provided plot lines for a number of sixteenth-century plays, among them several works by the prolific Hans Sachs, a man always looking for new subject-matter. And the impact of classical literary models, especially Terence, can be seen in numerous German plays that were divided into five acts, utilised a chorus, strove to develop a dramatic plot and sought to fit language to personality and social status.[18] On the whole, however, in the sixteenth century, it is difficult to detect much true 'classicism' in vernacular German literature.

One reason for this was undoubtedly the advent of the Reformation, which fostered strong didactic and moralistic tendencies in German literature, with many Lutheran writers in particular writing mainly to discredit Catholicism. Stories based on biblical characters such as the Prodigal Son, Judith, Susanna and Joseph became increasingly popular. Following the Peace of Augsburg, religious tensions eased, and in the late sixteenth and early seventeenth century there emerged a group of poets, among them Paul Mellissus (1539–1602), Martin Opitz (1597–1639) and George Rudolph Weckherlin (1584–1653), who consciously set out to write German poetry inspired by classical models and the work of Italian and French Renaissance poets.[19] After 1618, however, Germany was plunged into the Thirty Years' War, and poetic innovation gave way to other more pressing and deadly concerns.

The rise of German humanism

In terms of its diversity, freshness and overall achievement, no facet of the Renaissance had greater impact on German life and culture than humanism. Germany's artistic Renaissance was largely limited to painting, drew but modestly on the Italian Renaissance and was over in a little more than three decades. German literature during the age was touched, but only lightly, by the new vogue of classicism. In contrast, the humanist movement owed little to Germany's medieval traditions. On the contrary, the message of humanism was that Germans must abandon their past, and embrace fundamentally new concepts of culture, scholarship and education.

It is true, of course, that the humanists did not accomplish all their ambitious goals, but the changes they effected were not inconsequential. In a remarkably short time, they redefined scholarship, inspired basic changes in Germany's schools and universities, fostered the study of Greek and Hebrew, wrote a substantial amount of praiseworthy neo-Latin literature and, in general, introduced their educated countrymen to views quite different from many of their inherited conceptions.

At one time, the origins and causes of German humanism were the subject of much scholarly debate and controversy. Konrad Burdach, the prolific scholar of medieval and Renaissance literature, argued that humanism within the empire could be traced back to the court of Charles IV in Prague in the mid-fourteenth century. There, he argued, as a result of contacts with such eminent Italians as Cola di Rienzi and Petrarch, the imperial chancellor, Johann of Neumarkt (1310–80) introduced a new Petrarchan Latin style into the chancellery and stimulated new interest in classical letters.[20] This much is clearly true, but his assertion that German humanism, indeed the northern Renaissance in general, grew from this group in Prague, is no longer given much credence. The numbers were too small, the moment too brief, and clear lines of contact with later humanists simply do not exist.[21] Other theories, too, have largely fallen by the wayside. These include the argument of Heinrich Hermelink, who saw humanism growing out of the Thomistic revival within the fifteenth-century German universities,[22] and that of Augustin Renaudet, Albert Hyma and others, who linked humanism with the schools sponsored by the Brethren of the Common Life.[23]

Despite the ink that has been spilled debating the merits of these various arguments, the facts concerning the origins of German humanism seem quite clear. It began in the mid-fifteenth century and was inspired directly by Italian models. Germans in the fifteenth century had many reasons to travel to Italy: to trade, to do business with the Curia, to study at one of Italy's outstanding universities. Among the early representatives of German humanism, the overwhelming majority was inspired by such visits to Italy. George Peuerbach and Johann Regiomontanus, who lectured on the *studia humanitatis* at the University of Vienna in 1450s before turning to astronomy, both had studied at the University of Padua.[24] Peter Luder, who introduced courses on rhetoric and poetry at the University of Heidelberg in the same decade, had spent no less than twenty years in Italy before returning north.[25] Of the three previously mentioned early translators of Italian Renaissance material into Germany, both von Eyb and Steinhöwel had started at Italian universities.

Other Germans stayed at home but were introduced to humanism by visiting Italians. In the early history of humanism, the most illustrious Italian visitor was Aeneas Sylvius Piccolomini, later Pope Pius II, who in the 1440s was called by Emperor Frederick III to serve as secretary to the imperial chancellory in Vienna. He inspired Niklas von Wyle, one of the early translating triumvirate, and three University of Vienna students, Philip Mauttherr, Paul Swicker and Johann Mandl, who in the 1450s lectured on various classics at their *alma mater*.[26] In the late fifteenth century, several other Italian humanists, none as illustrious as Aeneas, taught in Germany. They included William of Savona, who lectured at Vienna in the 1450s,[27] Petrus Antonius Finariensis, who taught at Basel and Heidelberg,[28] Jacobus Publicius Rufus, active in Leipzig and Erfurt between 1467 and 1469, and a more prominent figure, Girolamo Balbi, who spent several stormy years at Vienna in the 1490s.[29]

Italian influence was continuous throughout the history of German humanism. All the major humanists, with the exception of the conservative Jacob Wimpfeling, visited Italy. Many corresponded with leading Italians such as Marsilio Ficino,[30] and all benefited from published Italian humanist works and Italian editions of classical texts.

Aside from their shared inspiration from Italy and their common dissatis-faction with Germany's cultural and educational status quo, German humanists showed marked diversity. In terms of their social background, they included sons of peasants (Celtis and Heinrich Bebel), of urban artisans (Wimpfeling), of nobles (von Eyb, Ulrich von Hutten and Hermann von dem Busche), of urban patricians (Conrad Mutian and Willibald Pirckheimer) and of parish priests (Rudolf Agricola). A few supported themselves through inherited wealth (Pirckheimer) or the occasional generosity of patrons, but most, even those who accorded themselves the lofty title of 'poet', had to work for a living. Many sought careers as university teachers and school-masters, but others were physicians (Steinhöwel and Luder), lawyers (Johannes Reuchlin, Sebastian Brant and von Eyb) or churchmen (Wimpfel-ing and Mutian). In temperament they varied from the free-spirited Celtis, who lectured to students while inebriated, wrote decidedly erotic poems and died of syphilis at the age of forty-nine; to the prudish Wimpfeling, who fretted about the dangers of allowing youths to read non-Christian poets and once warned boys not to curl or dye their hair, because 'it makes the hair fall out, insults God the Father and frightens away guardian angels'.[31] Most importantly, the German humanists showed marked variation in their intellectual and literary activities and in their goals. Some sought nothing more than the reform of Latin language instruction; some sought poetic greatness; others dreamed of nothing less than the revitalisation of Germany's religious and political life.

Historians have proposed several chronological schemes to describe the development of the humanist movement in Germany.[32] My version is less complicated than most. If one discounts the brief flurry of interest in the classics at the court of Charles IV, then there were three turning-points in the history of German humanism. The first took place in the 1450s, when humanism was introduced to the universities and the first translations of Italian Renaissance works were made. The second took place in the 1490s, when the humanists became bolder, more ambitious and expanded the range of their intellectual and literary activities. The third took place after the onset of the Reformation, a time in which humanism achieved some of its greatest triumphs but also lost much of its exuberance and vigour.

Before sketching the development of German humanism, it is necessary to stress one of the characteristics that sets it apart from humanism in other parts of Europe. This was the close connection between humanism and the universities. Everywhere in Europe humanists sought changes in university education, and many of them held university posts; but nowhere outside Germany did universities provide such a focus for humanism's growth and direction. Humanists turned to the universities in part because there they found a youthful and what they hoped would be a receptive audience for their message of cultural renewal. Higher education in late medieval Germany was a growth industry, with no less than thirteen successful foundations in the century and a half before the Reformation. By the early 1500s, annual matriculations had reached an average of approximately 2,500, with the total number of enrolled students between two and a half and three times that number.[33] Humanists also turned to the universities out of economic necessity. Although it is true that Emperor Maximilian I and many princes were sympathetic to humanism, their resources were too limited to provide much patronage. This also holds true for the fragmented German church and Germany's relatively small and often provincial urban patriciate. Thus from the 1450s onward, many humanists sought to support themselves by gaining teaching positions at German universities, and in doing so were thrust into the milieu of late scholasticism. Much in the history of German humanism is explained by this fact.[34]

Humanists came to the universities as outsiders, usually without ties to any of the four faculties, and proposing to teach material without a place in the traditional arts-course curriculum. Based on the course of studies developed at the University of Paris in the thirteenth century, this curriculum showed remarkable uniformity throughout Germany. Instruction leading to the bachelor-of-arts degree was primarily designed to introduce students to the vocabulary and methods of scholastic discourse. This meant protracted study of logic, based largely on Aristotle, but also on one or more medieval texts that dealt with aspects of logic not treated by Aristotle.[35] New university students were also expected to study Latin grammar, a subject which by the late Middle Ages had become a sub-branch of logic and philosophy. The so-called 'speculative grammarians' of the late Middle Ages sought to discover the philosophical underpinnings of grammatical usage, an enterprise that involved a great deal of complicated logical analysis, but completely ignored the literary qualities of classical Latin and the literary potential of the language.[36] Once equipped with the basics of scholastic methodology and vocabulary, some students went on to pursue their master of arts degree, which involved the study of the scientific and philosophical works of Aristotle.

From the 1450s to the 1490s, German humanists produced no great works of history or literature and said little about scholastic theology or issues related to religious and political reform. Instead, they dedicated themselves to the more mundane task of bringing about certain changes in the universities' arts-course curriculum and in the teaching methods of secondary schools. First and foremost, they sought to convince their countrymen that instruction had to be broadened to include new disciplines, referred to by the humanists as the *studia humanitatis*. Thus Peter Luder, one of the first 'poets' to lecture at a German university, announced a basic theme of early humanism in his inaugural oration at the University of Heidelberg in 1456.[37] Luder told his listeners that although logic, physics and theology were worthy of study, for their own use and 'for the glory of their country and university', they should also pursue history, oratory and poetry. History provided a guide to living, broadened the intellect, inspired morality, and did so without the 'highest possible torments' connected with the study of philosophy. Oratory taught eloquence, God's special gift to man, and, like history, was capable of inspiring morality. Poetry, said Luder, improved one's ability to speak and write Latin, but also empowered human beings with the capability of movingly expressing the highest moral and religious truths. Quoting Cicero, Luder concluded his speech by asserting that the *studia humanitatis* 'inspire youth, give pleasure in old age, embellish prosperity, offer escape and solace in adversity and give enjoyment at home'. He urged 'the noble and studious young men' in his audience to 'devote their work, their labor and their industry to the humane studies'.

The message of Luder's speech – that the *studia humanitatis* must become a central focus of German education and culture – was hammered home by succeeding humanists in countless orations (most notably in Peuerbach's *encomium* to the *studia humanitatis* delivered at the University of Vienna in 1458[38] and Celtis's inaugural oration at Ingolstadt in 1492), pedagogical treatises (such as Agricola's *On a Plan for Studies*, written in 1484[39]), dialogues (such as Johannes Landsberger's *Dialogue for and against the Poetical Arts*, published in 1492),[40] and dozens of manuals and treatises for classroom use.

The early humanists' concerns with education meant that most of their scholarly and creative energies were directed towards pedagogical ends. One of their most important activities, for example, was the editing and publishing of texts for classroom use. Overwhelmingly, these were not original works, but rather were the better-known writings by major classical and Italian Renaissance authors. Nor were they works of scholarship in any meaningful sense. Some were simply pirated versions of works already published in Italy. Many seem to have been rushed into print to meet a deadline for beginning a semester. A suggestive example is the Leipzig humanist, Petrus Eolicus, who in 1494 and 1495 produced no less than six editions of works by classical or Renaissance authors.[41] Despite their limitations, the significance of these activities should not be underestimated. Works by Ovid, Terence, Plautus, Cicero, Quintilian, Seneca, Virgil, Valerius Maximus and other ancient authors were made available for the first time to German students and the reading public.[42]

A third area of concern among the early humanists was Latin grammar instruction. Soon after they began their efforts to instil in their students a love of literature and eloquence, they met an immediate and formidable stumbling block: their students' training in grammar made them hopelessly unprepared to appreciate their efforts. Technically, they knew Latin, but a Latin taught according to the doctrines of the medieval 'speculative grammarians'. The humanists quickly realised that if their countrymen were to achieve true eloquence, the ties between logic and grammar would have to be cut, and the doctrines of the speculative grammarians suppressed. Humanists fought their campaign against speculative grammar with several weapons. Alexander Hegius (1433–98), in his *Invective against the Modes of Signifying* (1480s), and Dietrich Gresemund the Younger (1475–1512), in his *Dialogue on the Seven Liberal Arts* (1497), were among the several humanists who published treatises which heaped scorn on the deficiencies of traditional Latin instruction.[43] Others, such as Bernard Perger, the leading Viennese humanist in the 1480s and 1490s, composed and published texts for Latin instruction. His *Nova grammatica*, first published in 1482 and subsequently reissued dozens of times, set forth grammatical rules in a straightforward manner, illustrated them with classical citations and offered practical instruction on the forms and styles of letter-writing. For his part, Jacob Wimpfeling, the prolific Alsatian humanist, in his *Isidoneus germanicus*, wrote a 'how to' manual for teachers. He stressed the importance of early grammar training and recommended utilisation of one of the many excellent grammar texts recently published in Italy.[44] Of all the German humanists, none worked harder to improve Latin instruction than the schoolmaster who taught at Halle and Chemnitz, Paul Niavis.[45] He published over twenty manuals, teaching aids and texts for Latin, and introduced into Germany the dialogue or colloquy as a means of teaching diction and grammar.

Although many municipal and cathedral schools before 1500 adopted new humanistic methods of Latin instruction and instituted courses in Latin literature,[46] at the universities, because of their institutional complexity, stronger curricular traditions and greater size, humanism made less progress. By 1500, only the universities of Ingolstadt, Tübingen, Freiburg im Breisgau and Vienna had established salaried chairs for professors of poetry and rhetoric, and even at these four institutions the traditional scholastic curriculum remained intact, meaning that courses taught by humanists were not required for degrees. Among all the universities within the empire, the only attempt at serious curricular reform took place at the University of Vienna in the 1490s. Sponsored by the university superintendent, Bernard Perger, and supported by the Habsburg court, the proposed reforms, which would have required courses in rhetoric and decreased the requirements in logic, were highly controversial and finally failed when the university senate withheld its approval. Nonetheless, by the 1490s, courses on the *studia humanitatis* had been introduced at every German university, even those in the remote north, Rostock and Greifswald. Foundations had been laid for the impressive scholarly and literary achievements of German humanism from the 1490s onward.[47]

The flowering of German humanism

Beginning in the 1490s, the tentative and timid humanism of the late fifteenth century was transformed into a movement marked by innovation, boldness and solid accomplishment in many areas. Several factors explain these changes: the groundwork done by the early humanists; continuing inspiration from Italy; increased patronage, especially from Germany's princes; the growth of the German printing industry; the progress of humanism within the universities; and finally, the efforts of humanist proseltysers such as Conrad Celtis, who, until his death in 1508, never stopped exhorting and prodding his countrymen towards an acceptance of humanist ideals.

One of the most dramatic contrasts between earlier and later humanism was in the area of literary output. Although some of the early humanists, such as Peter Luder and Samuel Karoch,[48] fashioned themselves as 'poets', their literary output was both meagre and unoriginal. Sebastian Brant's poetic satire, the *Narrenschiff*, first published in 1494, then translated into Latin in 1497 and reprinted dozens of times, was a best-seller, but it was not truly a 'humanist' work. Although Brant wrote many Latin works, and certainly qualifies as a humanist, this, his 'masterpiece', was written in German, and despite its citation of some ancient authors, is much closer to the didactic poetry of medieval Germany than the satirical tradition of ancient Rome.[49]

The first and most powerful voice of German humanist literature was Conrad Celtis. He gave promise of his literary genius in 1487, when at the age of twenty-eight, he published his moving 'Ode to Apollo', in which he implores the poet-god to leave 'fair Helicon' for Germany to dispel cultural darkness through the beauty of his verse.[50] He went on to produce a substantial amount of Latin poetry, which despite its tendency to dwell on his own highly personalised triumphs, frustrations and setbacks, is of high quality. In the one major poetic work published during his life, *Quattuor Libri Amorum*, he combined poetic descriptions of various parts of Germany with detailed and often highly erotic accounts of his love-affairs with four German women. Published after his death were another collection of odes and a collection of his epigrams, modelled on Martial, Persius and Juvenal.[51]

Between 1500 and 1520 German humanists produced many thousands of lines of Latin verse of every conceivable variety, in which they strove to match the poetic achievements of ancient Rome. How well they succeeded is difficult to say. Aside from Celtis, only the work of von Hutten has received much scholarly attention, and modern editions of the humanists' poetry are virtually non-existent.[52] There can be little doubt, however, that the humanists themselves were convinced that the poetic spirit of Apollo had indeed graced their land.

Although poetry was clearly the humanists' literary vehicle of choice, several of them earned places in the history of German theatre. Wimpfeling, for example, is given credit for writing and directing Germany's first Latin comedy, *Stylpho*, performed in connection with commencement ceremonies at the University of Heidelberg in 1480. In its simple plot, completely in character with the morally earnest Wimpfeling, the anti-hero, Stylpho, ignores his studies, seeks ecclesiastical advancement by playing politics in Rome, and ends up a pig-herder in his native village.[53] Wimpfeling set a twofold precedent by modelling his play on Terence, and by having it performed in an academic environment. We have records of several dozen similar performances, including Reuchlin's *Henno* and *Sergius*,[54] presented at Heidelberg in 1496 and 1497, Jacob Locher's *Historia de rege Franciae* and *Judicum Paridis*, both performed at Freiburg im Breisgau in the early 1500s, and Celtis' *Rhapsodia*, performed in Vienna in 1504. Previously, in 1502 and 1503, Celtis had become the first German humanist to direct plays by actual Roman authors, the *Eunuchus* of Terence and the *Aulularia* of Plautus. Humanist drama of this sort provided entertainment for the academic community and offered students an opportunity to practise their Latin speech and elocution. The only drama produced outside an academic setting was Celtis' *Ludus Dianae*, presented at the imperial court in Linz in 1501.

Although some modern critics have reservations about the quality of the humanists' literary output, there is no debate about the soundness and importance of their scholarship. It is true, of course, that of necessity, they continued to churn out inexpensive editions of classical works for classroom use. By now, however, enough general interest in the classics existed to justify publication of more expensive editions designed for permanent collections. Such was the richly illustrated edition of the works of Horace, edited and published in 1498 by Jacob Locher.[55] Humanist scholarship not only increased in quality, but also branched out into new areas. Celtis discovered and published two lost literary pieces from Germany's medieval past: the plays of the tenth-century nun, Roswitha of Gandersheim, and the anonymous *Ligurinus*, an epic poem which recounted the deeds of Emperor Frederick Barbarossa.[56] Pirckheimer made a major contribution to scholarship by translating scores of Greek works into Latin and German. Lucian and Plutarch were his favourites, but he also produced editions of works by Ptolemy, Plato, several Greek orators and three of the Greek church fathers. Although Reuchlin translated and published Greek works by Athanasius, Demosthenes, Hippocrates and Homer, his greatest contribution was as a Hebraist. His two texts on Hebrew grammar, *De rudimentis Hebraicis* (1508) and *De accentibus et orthographia linguae Hebraicae* (1518), opened up new possibilities in Christian Hebraic scholarship.

Reuchlin's work on the Hebrew language was but one sign of the diversification taking place within German humanism after 1500. Although they continued to affirm the value and importance of the rhetorical-literary studies treasured by older humanists like Luder, increasingly after 1500, Reuchlin and others were intrigued by Florentine neo-Platonism. Several visited or corresponded with Marsilio Ficino, the leader of the Florentine Platonic Academy, and, as a result, were inspired to study the Greek language, Plato and various neo-Platonists.[57] Conrad Mutian, a cathedral canon from Gotha, was easily the most daring German neo-Platonist. His highly spiritualised view of Christ and his pantheistic interpretation of nature took him well beyond the limits of Catholic orthodoxy. Perhaps with good reason, he expressed all his ideas in private correspondence and never published a single word.[58] Reuchlin was drawn to the other major representative of Florentine neo-Platonism, Pico della Mirandola, whom he met on a trip to Italy in 1490. Pico was largely responsible for Reuchlin's life-long interest in the magic and mysticism of the Cabala, about which he wrote two books, *De verbo mirifico* (1494) and *De arte cabalistica* (1518).[59] Some humanist intellectuals went farther still. Johannes Trithemius (1462–1516), the 'monastic humanist', and, even more so, Cornelius Agrippa of Nettesheim (1486(?)–1535), were deeply involved in magical and occult studies involving astrology, Cabalism, alchemy and Hermeticism.[60]

Of all the changes in humanism after 1500, none was more striking than the transformation of the humanists' own image of their role and purpose in society. The horizons of the early humanists had been largely limited to the classroom; when they spoke of 'reform', they meant comparatively minor changes in the arts course or improvements in Latin instruction. After 1500, humanists became bolder and more assertive. Within the universities they pushed hard for a major restructuring of the arts course and broadened their attacks on scholasticism to include theology. More importantly, 'reform' came to mean more than the reform of education. Many humanists became angry and persistent critics of Germany's religious establishment, the reform of which, they asserted, was the necessary first step towards any true German revival.

Humanist denunciations of clerical abuses hammered away at long-standing abuses. When Wimpfeling fulminated against simony and priestly womanising,[61] when Celtis attacked the pointless ceremonies of monks,[62] and when Mutian denounced clerical greed and ignorance,[63] they raised issues that had provoked the wrath of reformers for more than a century. Nonetheless, humanist criticisms of the church had an impact that exceeded anything achieved by previous reformers, and only in part because the printed book allowed the humanists to reach a larger audience. Unlike previous reformers, who often concentrated on one issue, such as monastic abuses or excessive clerical wealth, the humanists' criticisms were wide-ranging, encompassing everything from papal politics to popular superstitions connected with relic worship and pilgrimages. In addition, the humanists' literary training was not in vain – their attacks on the church were forceful, persuasive, readable and biting. Finally, the humanists successfully couched their appeals for reform in the rhetoric of German patriotism, a growing cultural force in the late Middle Ages, and one heavily tinged with anti-Italian sentiment. No one did this more effectively than the fiery poet and polemicist, Ulrich von Hutten (1488–1523).[64] During the 1510s, von Hutten had two lengthy visits to Italy, where his family hoped in vain that he would earn a law degree. What he saw of Rome angered him to the core, and on his return to Germany in 1517, he wrote four blistering dialogues, *Febris Primus*, *Febris Secundus*, *Vadiscus sive Tria Romana* and *Inscipientes*. They vilified Leo X and his cardinals and blamed the Roman Curia for destroying German virtue, weakening the empire, plundering its wealth, blocking the progress of good letters and undermining the German church. Von Hutten, it goes without saying, was one of Luther's earliest supporters.

Given the growing strength and aggressiveness of humanism after 1500, it is not surprising that humanists and their ideas sparked controversies, especially within the universities. Several universities, most notably Leipzig, Erfurt, Ingolstadt, Frankfurt an der Oder and Vienna, seriously debated curriculum reform, but the results were disappointing from the humanists' point of view. At Frankfurt an der Oder, in 1511, lectures on poetry became a regular part of the academic schedule, but the courses were not required.[65] At Ingolstadt, no changes were made,[66] while at Erfurt and Vienna, reform went no further than the adoption of humanist texts for Latin instruction.[67] In fact, the slow pace of curriculum reform at Vienna was the main reason behind the founding in 1502 of Celtis' short-lived brain-child, the College of Poets and Mathematicians. Independent of the four faculties, and financially supported by Maximilian I, the college consisted of two poets and two mathematicians who taught courses which made their students eligible for the poet's laurel crown, but not a university degree.[68] Celtis' project got off to a slow start, and apparently it was no longer functioning when Celtis died in 1508. Although sometimes viewed as a forward step for humanism, actually, the opposite is true. It was an attempt to gain some sort of institutional recognition for poetry and mathematics after the reformers in the 1490s had failed to effect meaningful changes in the degree programme of the faculty of arts.

The reasons for the slow pace of curriculum reform are partially revealed by the well-documented debates at the University of Leipzig, where reforms were considered in 1502, 1508 and 1511.[69] The issues were wide ranging. The place of poetry in the curriculum, the role of the salaried humanist lecturer, the suitability of various grammar texts, the adoption of new humanist translations of Aristotle, the continued use of Peter of Spain's text in logic and changes in the teaching of theology were all discussed. Although the humanist position was supported by most young arts faculty masters, by many students and in all likelihood, by Duke George of Saxony, ten years of debate resulted in only minor concessions to humanism. Further changes were blocked by a group of older arts faculty masters and theologians, who either out of self-interest or conviction, opposed any concessions to humanism. Their domination of the faculty senate and the arts faculty council gave them a position of strength that proved unassailable. That the early 1500s saw growing opposition to humanism within the universities is also confirmed by events that took place in Tübingen and Freiburg im Breisgau. In 1505, both institutions adopted statutes that rejected 'recent innovations' in Latin instruction and stipulated that only traditional texts could be used.[70]

Humanists after 1500 became embroiled in a number of other feuds,[71] but none matched the prolonged and acrimonious controversy between Reuchlin and the theologians of the University of Cologne. Lasting more than a decade, involving kings, a pope and an emperor, and inspiring a mountain of writings, including the satirical gem, *The Letters of Obscure Men*, the Reuchlin affair is an excellent indicator of the humanists' frame of mind in the 1510s.[72] Reuchlin provoked the wrath of the theologians by opposing a plan, endorsed by the Cologners, to encourage Jewish conversions to Christianity by destroying Hebrew books. Betweeen 1510 and 1513, Reuchlin and various Cologners carried on a heated pamphlet war in which they debated confiscation, and, as could be expected, attacked each other's motives and erudition. The German humanists, correctly viewing the confiscation issue as something that had little bearing on the revival of 'good letters', kept their silence. This changed in 1513, however, when Jacob von Hochstraten, a Cologne theologian and Inquisitor of Heretical Pravity in Germany, called Reuchlin before his court of inquisition in Mainz to answer charges of heresy for statements made in his 1511 pamphlet, the *Augenspiegel*.

Although Hochstraten's case was scuttled by the Archbishop of Mainz, the Dominican's accusation brought an outpouring of support for the humanist. For a variety of reasons – sympathy for the ageing Reuchlin, anger at Hochstraten's high-handed tactics, and fear that humanism itself was endangered – Reuchlin's fellow humanists responded by writing letters of support, publishing pamphlets on his behalf, lobbying rulers to support him and in the *Letters of Obscure Men*,[73] producing the great satirical masterpiece of German humanism. Largely the work of Crotus Rubeanus, an Erfurt humanist, Hermann von dem Busche, and von Hutten,[74] the work consists of bogus letters 'written' by some actual anti-Reuchlinists, but mostly by fictitious monks and scholastics, to Ortwin Gratius, a Cologne humanist who had sided with the theologians in the confiscation debate. Their 'letters' reveal the obscure men as moral degenerates and intellectual buffoons who write barbarous Latin, quibble over trivialities and have absolutely no appreciation or understanding of literature. But the *Letters* was much more than a simple defence of Reuchlin or an attack on scholasticism. Especially in the third edition of 1517, to which von Hutten added seventy new 'letters', the Roman Curia, the Pope, indulgences, relics, religious orders and church dietary rules are also held up to ridicule. Thus the *Letters of Obscure Men*, even though its coarseness offended some of the older, conservative humanists, summarised the full range of the humanist critique of German religious and intellectual life on the eve of the Reformation.

The war of words and litigation continued until 1520. Humanist pamphleteering tailed off after the appearance of the *Letters*, but Hochstraten produced no less than three ponderous anti-Reuchlin tomes, and the unfortunate Gratius took a stab at anti-humanist satire with his *Lamentations of Obscure Men* (1518). Hochstraten also doggedly pursued his case against Reuchlin in Rome. Finally, in 1520, Leo X formally condemned the *Augenspiegel*, and ordered Reuchlin to pay court costs. The verdict, which was quietly accepted by Reuchlin, evoked neither outrage from the humanists nor exultation from Hochstraten and the Cologners. For both camps, the onset of the Reformation made old controversies seem trivial.

The end of the Renaissance in Germany

Like all their countrymen, after 1517 German humanists faced the choice of siding with Luther or holding to the old faith. And like their countrymen, humanists were divided in their choices. Some like von Hutten immediately embraced Luther and his cause; some like Reuchlin and Wimpfeling quickly voiced their opposition; others agonised and vacillated. Clearly, however, the Reformation did not snuff out German humanism, even after the momentous split between Luther and Erasmus in 1525. Classical scholarship went on, Latin verse and drama continued to be written, and most importantly, fundamental changes in German education were achieved. In many respects the early decades of the Reformation era were marked by continuity, not disruption, in German humanism.[75]

The greatest humanist triumph after the onset of the Reformation was the transformation of German education in the 1520s and 1530s. Without exception, the German universities, both Catholic and Protestant, adopted curriculum reforms in these years that obliterated most of Germany's scholastic traditions, and replaced them with a programme of studies that reflected the values of humanism.[76] The pace of reform varied, with Wittenberg, Erfurt, Leipzig and Ingolstadt taking the lead in the late 1510s, and other institutions such as Cologne delaying reform until the 1530s. The end result, however, was an approach to university education, especially in the arts course, that showed remarkable uniformity throughout Germany. Aristotle's work on natural philosophy continued to be studied, but in more accurate humanist translations and without extensive commentary. Otherwise, none of the mainstays of the medieval arts course survived. In the place of the logic-soaked curriculum of the scholastics, plans of study were implemented that emphasised the *studia humanitatis* and the mastery of ancient languages. The major function of universities became the introduction of a large number of students to a wide range of disciplines, from poetry to physics. Changes in the study of theology also took place. In Protestant universities the great scholastic *doctores* were dropped altogether, and the Bible, studied in its original languages, became the primary focus of instruction. At Catholic universities, faculties of theology floundered until the 1550s, when the Council of Trent and the Jesuits began to give them a new sense of purpose and direction. Here too, scholastic theologians, except Aquinas, passed into oblivion, and more emphasis was placed on the scriptures, the church fathers and a mastery of Greek and Hebrew.

Germany's secondary schools also were reshaped by humanism during the sixteenth century. In Protestant areas, this resulted in large measure from the efforts of Philip Melanchthon, Luther's Wittenberg colleague, who fully deserves his title as *Praeceptor Germaniae*.[77] Deeply committed both to humanism and education, Melanchthon successfully worked throughout his adult life to organise schools in Lutheran Germany to provide sound classical training and inculcate Protestant values. Johannes Sturm, the administrator of the famous *gymnasium* in Strasbourg and the author of dozens of pedagogical treatises, was the other leading Protestant educator in the early years of the Reformation. He, like Melanchthon, was thoroughly convinced of the importance of training in classical languages and literature.[78] Later in the century, when the Jesuits took control of major secondary schools in Catholic areas, they too centred their curriculum around the classics.

Classical scholarship also flourished after the onset of the Reformation. Many scholars, including Melanchthon, continued the work begun by pre-Reformation humanists such as Pirckheimer, of editing and translating major Greek works. The outstanding classicist was the prolific Joachim Camerarius (1500–74), whose academic career took him from the Nuremberg *gymnasium*, to the University of Erfurt and finally to the University of Leipzig.[79] An author with 183 titles to his credit, he produced a definitive edition of Plautus and translated numerous Greek authors into Latin, including Lucian, Homer, Theocritus, Demosthenes, Sophocles and others.

In the years following the Reformation, German authors also continued to produce massive amounts of Latin poetry and drama. Drama was prized by Protestant and Catholic educators alike as a means of training students' memories, improving Latin elocution, teaching moral lessons and providing experience in public speaking. Dramas were also entertaining, but their main purpose was utilitarian. Dramatic performances became part of the academic routine at hundreds of schools, and the demand for material was enormous. According to Derek van Abbe, 'After 1540, the writing of plays became something of a mass industry'.[80] The production of Latin poetry also showed no sign of diminishing.

Clearly, humanism continued to exert a strong influence on German culture well into the Reformation era. It was a humanism, however, that in certain respects was no longer a 'movement'. Before the Reformation the disciples of 'good letters' were bound together by their common opposition to scholasticism, their collective sense of mission and their shared conviction that they were involved in a cultural movement of momentous importance for their countrymen. By the mid-sixteenth century, Germany had hundreds, even thousands of neo-Latin poets, classical scholars and teachers of rhetoric, but unlike their predecessors of the early sixteenth century, they no longer sought out each others' company in sodalities, preached cultural reform to their countrymen, worked in common for educational reform or banded together, as they had in the Reuchlin affair, to defend one of their number who was being maligned and threatened. Although convinced of the value of the classics, they no longer shared the utopian dreams of earlier humanists that a revival of 'good letters' could solve all of Germany's problems.

German humanism's loss of energy and verve was not unique; it happened elsewhere in Europe when most of the humanists' goals had been achieved. Other changes, however, were linked directly to the Reformation. Luther admired classical learning, appreciated the importance of rhetoric and was convinced that no one could be a theologian without Greek and Hebrew. But for Luther, and also for Melanchthon, Bugenhagen, Camerarius and others who shaped the intellectual and cultural world of early Protestant Germany, eloquence, poetical gifts and classical erudition were never viewed as ends in themselves, but only as one part of an educational programme designed to produce dutiful subjects and committed Lutherans. The men who taught the classics or ancient languages in the Lutheran universities and *gymnasia* had to be 'team players' willing to co-operate in disseminating the values prescribed by church and state. In the Germany of Luther and later of the Catholic Reformation, there was no room for free spirits like Luder, Celtis, Locher, von dem Busche and von Hutten, whose willingness to take on the educational and ecclesiastical establishments had been a distinctive part of early humanism.

Thus in Lutheran schools, only 'safe' classics were taught, and early humanist interests in neo-Platonism, Cabala and the occult received no support or recognition. 'Humanist' school dramas, performed by the thousands in sixteenth-century Germany, were based on acceptable religious themes, or if not, at least taught some moral lessons in keeping with the Lutheran or Catholic view of things. Latin poetry of the Reformation era also took on a distinctly religious and didactic character. Lewis Spitz has cited as a sign of humanism's post-Reformation's vitality the fact that Karl Goedeke's list of sixteenth-century published neo-Latin poets includes no less than 273 names.[81] Once one excludes elegies and other 'occasional' works celebrating marriages, battlefield victories and the like, one is quickly impressed, however, by the overwhelming preponderance of biblical and religious themes.[82] The eroticism, pugnacity and pungency that had marked the verse of earlier poets like Celtis, von Hutten, von dem Busche and Locher have disappeared.

German humanism had been effectively tamed and made respectable. If the humanists of the pre-Reformation era had been able to look down on Germany in the mid-1550s to contemplate the fruits of their early activities, it would not be surprising to find that among them all, the cautious, pious and morally earnest Wimpfeling was wearing the biggest smile.

NOTES

1 On Conrad Celtis, see F. von Bezold, 'Konrad Celtis, der deutsche Erzhumanist', *Historische Zeitschrift*, 49 (1883), 1–45; L. Spitz, *Conrad Celtis, the German Arch-Humanist* (Cambridge, Mass. 1957); and 'Celtis the arch-humanist', in *The Religious Renaissance of the German Humanists* (Cambridge, Mass., 1963), 81–109.

2 Latin text and English translation in L. Forster (ed.), *Selections from Conrad Celtis 1459–1508* (Cambridge, 1948), 36–65; another translation by L. Spitz may be found in L. Spitz (ed.,), *The Northern Renaissance* (Englewood Cliffs, N.J., 1972), 15–27.

3 Historians of architecture do certainly use the term, 'German Renaissance architecture'. The most recent survey is H.-R. Hitchcock's encyclopaedic *German Renaissance Architecture* (Princeton, N.J., 1981).

4 D. Watkin and T. Mellinghof, *German Architecture and the Classical Ideal* (Cambridge, Mass., 1987).

5 W. Pinder, *Die deutsche Plastik: Vom ausgehenden Mittelalter bis zum Ende der Renaissance*, 2 vols. (Potsdam, 1924–9); G. von der Osten and H. Vey, *Painting and Sculpture in Germany and the Netherlands 1500 to 1600* (Baltimore, Md., 1969).

6 O. Benesch, *German Painting: From Dürer to Holbein*, trans. H.B.S. Harrison (Geneva, 1966); O. Fischer, *Geschichte der deutsche Malerei* (Munich, 1942); C.D. Cutler, *Northern Painting from Pucelle to Bruegel* (New York, 1968).

7 H. de la Croix and R. Tansey, *Gardner's Art through the Ages* (New York, 1975), 558.

8 On Dürer, the following works are basic: E. Panofsky, *The Life and Art of Albrecht Dürer*, 4th edn. (Princeton, N.J., 1955); L. Grote, *Dürer: Biographical and Literary Study*, trans. H. Harrison (Geneva, 1965); H. Wollflin, *The Art of Albrecht Dürer*, trans. A. and H. Grieve (London, 1971); the vast literature on Dürer is compiled in Mende, *Dürer-Bibliographie* (Wiesbaden, 1971).

9 For a discussion of the various theories concerning the decline of German painting, see C.C. Christensen, *Art and the Reformation in Germany* (Athens, Ohio, 1979), 164–80.

10 *Ibid.*, 171, 172.

11 There are many excellent historical surveys of German literature in the late medieval and Renaissance periods. They include W. Stammler, *Von der Mystik bis zum Barock 1400–1600* (Stuttgart, 1927); A. Buck, *Renaissance und Barock* (Frankfurt am Main, 1972); H. Rupprich, *Die deutsche Literatur vom späten Mittelalter bis zum Barock*, 2 pts. (Munich, 1970, 1973); H. O. Burger, *Renaissance, Humanismus, Reformation. Deutsche Literatur im europäischen Kontext* (Bad Homburg, 1969).

12 In his article, 'German Renaissance literature', *Modern Language Notes*, 81 (1966), 398–406, Harold Jantz points out that given the impressive quantity of sixteenth-century German literature, Germany was on the brink of a literary 'golden age'. But no 'genius' appeared to carry German literature to a higher plane: 'It took only the enigmatically sudden lack of high genius to frustrate the well-prepared and promising development of literature in the German lands.' (436).

13 On the teaching of grammar in the Middle Ages, see L.J. Paetow, *The Arts Course in the Medieval German Universities with Special Reference to Grammar and Rhetoric* (Champaign, Ill., 1910); J.J. Baebler, *Beiträge zur Geschichte der Lateinischen Grammatik im Mittelalter* (Halle, 1893); and the long introduction in D. Reichling, *Das Doctrinale des Alexander de Villa-Dei* (Berlin, 1893).

14 J.T. Waterman, *A History of the German Language* (Seattle, Wash., 1966), 102–36; C.J. Wells, *German: A Linguistic History to 1945* (Oxford, 1985), 179–226.

15 Cited in Waterman, *German Language*, 121.

16 On the work of the early German humanists, see O. Herding, 'Probleme des frühen Humanismus in Deutschland', *Archiv für Kulturgeschichte*, 38 (1956), 344–89; of the early humanist translators, A. von Eyb has received the most scholarly attention. See M. Herrmann, *Albrecht von Eyb und die Frühzeit des deutschen Humanismus* (Berlin, 1893) and J. Hiller, *Albrecht von Eyb, a Medieval Moralist* (Washington, DC, 1939).

17 Rupprich, *Die deutsche Literatur*, 200–7, 370–2.

18 R. Pascal, *German Literature in the Sixteenth and Seventeenth Centuries* (New York, 1968), 61.

19 R. Newald, *Die deutsche Literatur vom Späthumanismus zur Empfindsamkeit 1570–1750* (Munich, 1951), 156–203.

20 K. Burdach, *Vom Mittelalter zur Reformation* (Halle, 1893); 'Zur Kenntniss altdeutschen Literatur und Kunst', *Zentralblatt fur Bibliothekswesen*, 7 (1891), 145–76; 432–88; *Deutsche Renaissance: Betrachtung über unsere künftige Bildung* (Berlin, 1920).

21 Many of Burdach's arguments were effectively demolished by P. Joachimsen in his 'Vom Mittelalter zur Reformation', *Historische Vierteljahrsschrift*, 20 (1920–1), 426–70.

22 H. Hermelink, *Die religiosen Reformbestrebungen des deutsche Humanismus* (Tübingen, 1907); 'Die Anfänge des Humanismus in Tübingen', *Württembergische Vierteljahrshefte fur Landesgeschichte*, n.s., 15 (1906), 319–37. His work

46 There has been no recent study of pre-university schools in late medieval Germany. Among the older works, the following are still useful; F. Paulsen, *Geschichte des gelehrten Unterrichts auf den deutschen Schulen und Universitäten vom Ausgang des Mittelalters bis zur Gegenwart* (Leipzig, 1885); J. Knepper, *Das Schul-und Unterrichtswesen im Elsass von den Anfängen bis gegen das Jahr 1530* (Strasburg, 1905); G. Bauch, *Geschichte des Bresaluer Schulwesens vor der Reformation* (Breslau, 1909); a wide-ranging collection of documents can be found in J. Müller (ed.), *Vor- und frühreformatorische Schulordnung und Schulverträge in deutschen und niederländischen Sprache* (Zschopau, 1885–6).

47 On the fate of humanism at the German universities between 1450 and 1500, see Overfield, *Humanism and Scholasticism*, 101–42.

48 H. Entner, *Frühhumanismus und Schultradition in Leben und Werk des Wanderpoeten Samuel Karoch of Lichtenberg* (Berlin, 1968).

49 Students of German literature have endlessly debated the 'humanism' of Brant's famous work. Two studies by U. Geier are worth mentioning: *Studien zu Sebastian Brants 'Narrenschiff'* (Tübingen, 1966) and 'Sebastian Brant's *Narrenschiff* and the humanists', *Publications of the Modern Language Association*, 83 (1968), 266–70.

50 L. Forster, *Conrad Celtis*, see n. 2, 20, 21.

51 All of Celtis' poetry exists in modern editions: K. Hartfelder (ed.), *Fünf Bücher Epigramme* (Berlin, 1881); F. Pindter (ed.) *Quattuor Libri Amorum, secundum quattuor latera Germaniae* (Leipzig, 1934); *Libri odarum quattuor. Liber epondon. Carmen saeculare* (Leipzig, 1937).

52 Again, von Hutten is an exception: E. Böcking, *Ulrichi Hutteni Opera*, 4 vol. and suppls. (Leipzig, 1859–64); earlier in the century, death prevented G. Ellinger from completing an exhaustive study of sixteenth-century neo-Latin literature in Germany; see, however, his 'Neulateinsiche Dichtung Deutschlands im 16. Jahrhundert', in Paul Merker and Wolgang Sammler (eds.), *Reallexikon der deutschen Literaturgeschichte*, vol. II (Berlin, 1965), 621–45.

53 H. Holstein (ed.), *Jacobus Wimphelingius Stylpho* (Berlin, 1881).

54 H. Holstein (ed.), *Johann Reuchlins Komödien* (Halle, 1888).

55 J. Locher, *Horatii flacci opera cum quibusdam annatotionibus imaginibusque pulcherrimis aptisque . . .* (Strasburg, 1498); Locher also edited works of Claudianus, Fulgentius and the church father, St Athanasius.

56 L. Spitz, *Conrad Celtis*, 96–9.

57 L. Spitz, 'The *Theologica Platonica*' in *Middle Ages – Reformation Volkskunde*, 118–33.

58 F. Halbauer, *Mutianus und seine geistesgeschtliche Stellung* (Leipzig, 1929); L. Spitz, 'Mutian – intellectual canon', *The Religious Renaissance*, 130–54.

59 J.-L. Viellard-Baron, 'Platonisme et Kabbale dans l'oeuvre de Johann Reuchlin' in J. Lefebvre and J.-C. Margolin (eds.), *L'Humanisme allemand (1480–1540)* (Paris, 1969), 159–67.

60 C.G. Nauert, Jr, *Agrippa and the Crisis of Renaissance Thought* (Urbana, Ill., 1965); N.L. Brann, *The Abbot Trithemius (1462–1516): The Renaissance of Monastic Humanism* (Leiden, 1981).

61 Wimpfeling atacked simony in his *Apologia pro republica Christiana* (Pforzheim, 1505), and concubinage in *De integritate libellus* (Strasburg, 1505).

62 Pindter, *Libri odarum quattuor*, bk. 3, ode 15, 29ff.

63 Mutian's criticisms of the church are discussed in Bernstein, *German Humanism*, 90–3.

64 The colourful von Hutten has attracted many biographers. The best scholarly account remains H. Holborn, *Ulrich von Hutten and the German Reformation* (New Haven, Ct., 1937); see also L. Spitz, 'Hutten – militant critic' in *The Religious Renaissance*, 110–29.

65 G. Bauch, *Acten und Urkunden der Universität Frankfurt a. O.*, 6 (Breslau, 1906), 39, 40.

66 A. Seifert, *Die Universität Ingolstadt im 15. und 16. Jahrhundert* (Berlin, 1973), 58–67.

67 E. Kleineidam, *Universitas Studii Erffordensis*, 2 vols. (Leipzig, 1964, 1969), vol. II, 181, 183, 187; R. Kink, *Geschichte der kaiserlichen Universität zu Wien* (Vienna, 1854), vol. II, 315, 318.

68 The charter of the Poets' College can be found in C. Celtis, *Briefwechsel*, ed. Hans Rupprich (Munich, 1934), 456–60.

69 On the Leipzig reforms, see Overfield, *Humanism and Scholasticism*, 222–7.

70 R. Roth, *Urkunden zur Geschichte der Universität Tübingen* (Tübingen, 1877), 416, 417; H. Ott and J.M. Fletcher, *The Medieval Statutes of the Faculty of Arts of the University of Freiburg im Breisgau* (Notre Dame, Ind., 1964), 119.

71 Among them was the semi-farcical conflict between the outspoken humanist Jacob Locher, on the one hand, and on the other, a Freiburg theologian, Georg Zingel, and two conservative humanists, Ulrich Zasius and Jacob Wimpfeling. Locher's personality was the major issue, but the feud did produce the only defence of scholastic theology of the early 1500s, written by the humanist, Wimpfeling. Two Leipzig academies, Konrad Wimpina and Martin Mellerstadt, traded pamphlets in the early 1500s in a disagreement that began over the relative merits of poetry and theology, but which quickly degenerated into competitive mud slinging. Several humanists were 'expelled' from university teaching posts; they included Hermann von dem Busche, dismissed from Leipzig in 1505 and Erfurt in 1507, Johannes Aesticampianus, dismissed (but only after he resigned) from Leipzig in 1511, and Tillmann Conradi, from Erfurt in 1513. These expulsions took place after the humanists had supposedly 'slandered' other faculty members or else had broken some university regulation. For summaries of these various feuds, see Overfield, *Humanism and Scholasticism*, 173–88, 235–46.

72 J.H. Overfield, 'A new look at the Reuchlin affair', *Studies in Medieval and Renaissance History*, 8 (1971), 167–207.

73 E. Böcking (ed.), *Epistolae obscurorum virorum* in U. von Hutten, *Opera*, suppls. 1 and 2 (Leipzig, 1864–9) is the best modern scholarly edition; the standard English translation is F.G. Stokes (ed. and trans.), *Epistolae obscurorum virorum* (New Haven, Ct., 1909).

74 On the authorship of the *Letters of Obscure Men*, see W. Brecht, *Die Verfasser der Epistolae Obscurorum Virorum* (Strassburg, 1904).

75 Much has been written about the fate of humanism after the onset of the Reformation. See G. Ritter, 'Die geschichtliche Bedeutung des deutschen Humanismus', *Historische Zeitschrift*, 127 (1923), 393–453; B. Moeller, 'Die deutschen Humanisten und die Anfänge der Reformation', *Zeitschrift fur Kirchengeschichte*, 70 (1959), 47–61; L. Spitz, 'Humanism and the Reformation' in *Renaissance Studies in Honor of Hans Baron*, A. Molho and J. Tedeschi (eds.), (De Kalb, Ill., 1971), 641–62.

76 Details concerning the university reforms of the 1520s and 1530s can be found in Overfield, *Humanism and Scholasticism*, 298–330.

77 K. Hartfelder, *Philipp Melanchthon als Praeceptor Germaniae* (Berlin, 1889).

78 W. Sohm, *Die Schule Johann Sturms und die Kirche Strassburgs in ihrem gegenseitigen Verhältnis* (Munich and Berlin, 1912).

79 See the collection of articles in F. Baron (ed.), *Joachim Camerarius (1500–1574)* (Munich, 1978).

80 D. van Abbe, *Drama in Renaissance Germany and Switzerland*, 19.

81 Spitz, 'The course of German humanism', in H. Oberman and T.A. Brady (eds.), *Itinerarium Italicum: The Profile of the Italian Renaissance in the Mirror of its European Transformations* (Leiden, 1975), 371–436, see 422.

82 K. Goedeke, *Grundrisz zur Geschichte der deutsche Dichtung*, vol. II. *Das Reformationszeitalter* (Dresden, 1886), 87–119.

SEVEN

ℜ

FRANCE

DONALD R. KELLEY

Nationality and revival

The 'French Renaissance' represents the intersection between two complex traditions which are also at least partly mythical constructs. One is French nationality, which can be perceived over some nine or ten centuries, but which has been vastly exaggerated by historians and has never been fully realised even in a political sense. 'The name of France', as Ferdinand Braudel noted in his last book, 'is diversity'.[1] The second notion is that of the 'Renaisance', an even more problematical abstraction which some medievalists refuse even to recognise. The old question, 'Was there a Renaissance?' is no longer of much interest, but it seems clear that any judgement about a general cultural revival must be located in the eye of the beholder, whether contemporary observer or modern historian, and depends on which aspects of culture are considered. Without the old and even larger myths of human progress and modernity, neither French nationality nor the European Renaissance carry much meaning except as very general ways of classifying and periodising political, social and cultural forms, and these qualifications should be kept in mind by any serious student of modern history.

Modern 'nationalism' in a political sense did not emerge in France until the Revolution (the word dates from 1798), but there are many forms of culture that from medieval times were 'national' (a sixteenth-century term).[2] At first, the geographical expression 'France' applied only to the areas around Paris and the Ile-de-France, but associations with the Capetian monarchy and more tenuous links with the Carolingian and Merovingian dynasties of Frankish kings (*reges Francorum*) gave a certain mythical and (which is often the same thing) legal continuity to the French peoples. The 'memory and legend' of Charlemagne were still potent in the sixteenth century, and so was royal thaumaturgy.[3] This inferred common heritage, adorned with legends of Trojan origins, pretensions to 'most Christian' status, and claims of independence from Roman domination (*francus* meant 'free' as well as 'French') found more concrete illustrations from the twelfth century in the 'customs of France'. In written form these *consuetudines Franciae* came to be recognised as the social and legal expression of the *prévôté* and *vicomté* of Paris and a 'common law' of even wider application.[4] This expanding set of feudal and bourgeois usages gave further definition to the idea of a French 'nation' as a social and cultural unit. By the sixteenth century the French *coutumes* had been officially received into royal tradition and, after due 'reformation', became a cornerstone of political unity.

By the sixteenth century, too, the kingdom of France was in the process of assuming its recognisably modern form – the medieval pentagon being reshaped, through expansion towards the Rhine, into the familiar modern hexagon. Political and dynastic expansion was accompanied by major social transformation – the economy on its way to becoming what Braudel called a *marché national*, society undergoing urbanisation and demographic expansion (the population doubled between 1500 and 1560), and royal government attempting to cope with, and benefit from, the new conditions through its own fiscal, administrative, judicial and military expansion and consolidation on the Romano-Byzantine model of 'absolute' monarchy.[5] Historians have often interpreted these changes as evidence of 'modernisation', but the price was high – an unending series of economic crises, fundamental social divisions (intensified by the religious revival produced by the Reformation) and political breakdown. All of this was conditioned by natural disasters (including famine and recurrent plague) and the ever-present enterprise of war, which continued to be the chief business of Renaissance government, and which acquired an international as well as civil scope in the course of the sixteenth century. For France 'the Renaissance in National perspective' was a mixed blessing, combining extraordinary cultural achievement, religious ferment, social and economic transformation and political upheaval; and the late sixteenth-century denouement, the wars of religion, more than counter-balanced any positive national achievements brought by putative revival.

The grand monarchy

Politically, the foundations of the Renaissance monarchy in France were laid in the generation of the first Valois king, Francis I, in 1515. The 'grandeur' of the 'grand monarchy of France' was described most comprehensively, authoritatively and influentially by Claude de Seyssel, whose treatise (part handbook of administration and counsel, part essay in political theory, part mirror-of-the-prince) summed up, for the benefit for the young King Francis I, a lifetime's experience as councillor and diplomat in secular and ecclesiastical affairs. Seyssel began conventionally enough with arguments for the superiority of monarchy, but moved immediately and invidiously to the praise of

French monarchy in particular as enjoying 'greater power and dominion' and as being 'better regulated than any other', in effect the supreme achievement of the science of politics.[6] In contrast to Machiavelli's contemporaneous *Prince*, Seyssel's *Monarchy of France* (1516; published 1519) was concerned less with the niceties of policy than with the complexity of the polity and its institutional, social and economic base – 'joining the old laws, customs and observances with the new and more recent'. Beyond the kingly office itself, Seyssel described and celebrated the three essential 'bridles' (*freins*) which enhanced and controlled as well as limited the 'force' of the monarchy. Though retrospective and in some ways idealised, Seyssel's vision of French government was based on practical experience in war and peace, and it serves conveniently to illustrate the character of the national monarchy in France during the first phase of the Renaissance and on the eve of the Reformation.

The first of Seyssel's 'bridles', religion, was manifested both in the sacred character of kingship and in its devotion to the Christian faith, and in the sixteenth century the continuing pre-eminence of France in matters of faith was reinforced by the theological authority of the Sorbonne.[7] In its more worldly aspect, 'religion' also suggested the great system of power and patronage embodied in the Gallican church – for like Machiavelli, Seyssel understood the practical functions of religion. This ecclesiastical cornerstone of monarchy had, arguably, an even longer tradition. Scholars like Jean du Tillet, Etienne Pasquier and Pierre Pithou traced the 'ancient liberties of the Gallican church' back not only to the crucial period of the Great Schism and Councils, which produced that 'charter of Gallican liberties', the Pragmatic Sanction of Bourges (1438), but also to Charlemagne (who furnished valuable precedents for a 'national church') and even to the 'primitive church', which had traditionally been divided into provinces (Gallican, Anglican, Hispanic, etc.), all enjoying parity with Rome. In the Concordat of Bologna (1516) the Gallican liberties were in effect joined to the 'grand monarchy' itself and contributed significantly to royalist ideology and power. The Reformation cast the Gallican church into a prolonged crisis. Caught between 'papist' and 'Protestant' extremes, Gallicanism struggled to preserve its independence by reconstructing its canon, demonstrating its antiquity, and thereby establishing the legitimacy of its own status as a privileged partner of the 'grand monarchy'.

The second member of Seyssel's royal trinity, 'justice', was again 'greater and more praiseworthy in France than in any other land'.[8] Like religion, too, justice displayed an institutional as well as an ideal face; for it referred not only to the royal monopoly of judgement and grace, of civil discipline and punishment, but also to the elaborate system of courts which had grown out of the royal council (*curia regis*) over the previous two centuries. The centre of this system was the 'sovereign court' of the Parlement of Paris, which claimed its own liberties and privileged estate as, in effect, the legal arm of monarchy. The Parlement was also a capstone of the legal profession in France; and the learned (university-trained and licensed) jurists who gathered in the law courts, next to the Sainte-Chapelle, themselves constituted an extraordinary lay intelligentsia rivalling the clergy and making cultural, as well as professional contributions, not only to the monarchy, but also to public and cultural life in general. Drawing on the resources of civil and canon law, the French legists celebrated the theory and practice of kingship and their own counselling and 'bridling' associations with it. At the same time they moved into the vanguard of secular scholarship, literature, philosophy and political controversy; and, in many ways, they represented the most dynamic and politicising element in Renaissance culture. As cultivators of 'good letters', they were also the creators of the language of power and partisanship, which helped to fire, as well as to illuminate, the religious and political conflicts of the later sixteenth and seventeenth centuries.

The third face of monarchy, the 'police', was defined by Seyssel as the legislative tradition of the monarchy – 'the many ordinances, made by the kings of France themselves and afterwards confirmed and approved from time to time', including the old restrictions on the 'alienation of the domain' – but, more generally, it included the administration of government and the structure of society, as well as the officers of the crown, the lawyers, the tax collectors and the military.[9] Beyond formal government, however, Seyssel sought the 'force' of monarchy in the social structure in all of its members and especially in the three orders, or 'estates'. For the old medieval convention of nobility, church and third estate, however, Seyssel substituted a more modern (and perhaps Italianate) analysis: first is the nobility, which served the king by its readiness 'to risk goods and life for the defence of the realm' (and therefore was free of all taxes); second is 'the middling estate, or the rich people', who supply the material base for 'grandeur', not to speak of most of the offices of justice – of which, Seyssel adds, 'France has more . . . than the whole rest of Christendom taken together'; and lastly, 'the estate of the lesser folk', including artisans, tradesmen, lower offices of justice and finance and the lower ranks of the army.

Such were the social foundations of the grandeur of the French monarchy. Its strength, Seyssel argued, rested not only on 'the harmony and agreement of the three estates', but also on social mobility – 'how men go from the third estate to the second and from the second to the first'. Nor did he neglect factors of population and education; for these, too, supported the final cause of his argument, which continued to be 'the things necessary for the preservation and augmentation of the monarchy of France by means of its police'. Like Machiavelli, Seyssel had his blind spots, and especially concerning the force of popular religion and ideological enthusiasms (although he spent his last months as Archbishop of Turin pursuing Waldensian heresy). In particular he was not quite prophetic enough to recognise that the social strengths of monarchy could also be weaknesses – a divided nobility feuding over royal authority, an unsettled church vulnerable to 'protest' and dissension, and a discontented 'people', both the 'middling' and the lower sort, becoming prey to various subversive forces, all leading, finally, to a condition of war – but in this case 'civil' rather than imperial and turned inwardly and destructively upon the grand monarchy and all of its estates.

French humanism

Yet – a commonplace, perhaps, rather than an irony of history – this time of social disruption, religious ferment, material concerns and military obsessions was also an age of cultural revival. The cultural roots of the French (and in part the Italian) Renaissance have been traced back to the twelfth-century revival of ancient thought and the founding of the University of Paris, and in 'national perspective' they cannot be kept separate from the intervening intellectual and artistic activities, 'medieval' as well as humanistic.[10] From the fourteenth century the cultural primacy and hegemony of Italy was undeniable; no more than the Germans or the English were the French disposed to dispute it. By the end of the fifteenth century, however, they were ready to challenge it.

In France the idea of a full 'Renaissance of learning', that is, of classical literature and its attendant styles, attitudes, methods and doctrines, was related directly to renewed contacts with Italy in the wake of the invasion of 1494. It was much reinforced by the impact of the printing-press, which had been introduced into the University of Paris in 1469 by Guillaume Fichet and Jean Heynlin, and which was hailed as a 'miracle' by some, as a fearful threat to orthodoxy by others.[11] The invention of 'impression' gave enormous impetus to the dissemination of classicist attitudes through the work not only of ancient Roman and Greek authors, but also of modern Italian imitators and interpreters like Lorenzo Valla and Angelo Poliziano, who were in effect the mentors of the first generation of French 'humanists' (a term used in this connection by Pasquier and Montaigne, among others). In general, the idea of cultural revival, born out of the literary claims of Petrarch, Boccaccio and their successors, was reinforced and 'publicised' by the commercial rhetoric of printers and scholars, and 'patronised' by ecclesiastical and secular powers for their own purposes. In this context the 'renaissance' was tied to the new world of book learning and publicity, made possible and promoted by the 'typographical revolution', and it – both the myth and the reality – became the prize and the target of church, state and other powerful interests.

It was in the context of print culture, then, that the myth of the Renaissance took shape, although by the fifteenth century the Italianate notion of cultural rebirth was projected beyond its original literary base to a wider historical scene, including the 'new' as well as the 'ancient' world, Christian as well as pagan learning, and the active as well as the contemplative life. As Louis le Roy wrote in 1575, with full reference to the authors and inventors involved:

For we now see the languages restored, and not only the deeds and writings of the ancients brought back to light, but also many fine things newly discovered. In this period grammar, poetry, history rhetoric, and dialectic [the five *studia humanitatis*, from which the term 'humanism' derives] have been illuminated by expositions, annotations, corrections, and innumerable translations. Never has mathematics been so well known, nor astrology, cosmography, and navigation . . ., physics and medicine . . ., arms and military instruments . . ., painting, sculpture, modelling, and architecture . . ., jurisprudence and eloquence, even politics . . ., and theology. Printing has greatly aided this work and has made easier its development.[12]

Le Roy also went on to notice the discoveries in the New World and the impact of the new religious ideas and what he called 'bombard', which however 'seemed invented rather for the ruin than the utility of mankind'. It was to reap the benefits of such 'progresses' (and avoid the destructive force of political 'vicissitudes') that Le Roy 'exhorted his countrymen to cease' quarrelling over religious opinions and establish civil peace.

In effect Le Roy was transforming a humanist topos into a historiographical thesis. He was one of the first to chronicle what scholars like Erasmus and Guillaume Budé had envisaged and promoted, and what was given more comprehensive formulation three centuries later by Jules Michelet – and with a similar hyperbolic invocation of the power of the press (which 'multiplied a hundredfold', he exclaimed, 'man's means to liberty'). For Michelet 'the amiable word "Renaissance"' referred not only to Italian art and to 'the restoration of the study of Antiquity': it began indeed with what he called not the invasions of, but 'the discovery of Italy', but it led beyond this, in a still more famous phrase, to 'the discovery of the world, the discovery of Man'.[13] And for him it was the historical project and destiny of France, through ordeals of conflict and war, to establish its national identity between these 'two great electric currents', the (Italian) Renaissance and the (German) Reformation. For Michelet, viewing 'the Renaissance in global as well as national perspective', 'A world of Humanity begins'. This hard-won 'identity' is also the theme of Braudel's last, unfinished book, though expressed in terms of material culture, rather than social psychology and intellectual achievement.

Political culture

Besides learning and art, Michelet recognised a third aspect of cultural revival, and this was the lesser known national effort 'to enlighten the chaos of our old customs' (p. 51) and to achieve 'the unity of civil law'. Attempts to shape and to control provincial customs went back to the earliest 'redactions' of the thirteenth century, but the 'reformation of customs' in the later sixteenth century was a much more aggressive and intrusive attack on feudal privilege aimed at bringing national unity to law and justice. This officially promoted Reformation movement was indeed a central feature of Renaissance monarchy, and it was natural for Michelet to rank this social and for him 'popular' enterprise, carried out with the consent of the three estates, above the more conspicuous claims of the monarchy to political sovereignty.[14] Once again it was printing (bringing together and giving access to civil, canon and customary laws) that made possible this impulse towards legal uniformity, and it was accompanied by scholarly efforts to uncover and to interpret medieval legal tradition on which the 'grand monarchy' also drew. In the event, of course, codification came only after the Revolution of 1789 and the imperial work of Napoleon; but Michelet and many others have recognised the seminal importance of the earlier 'Reformation and the attendant (anti-feudal, anti-Romanist) interpretations of French law – juridical nationalism' it has been called – especially by the leader of the Reformation movement, Christofle de Thou, and the greatest of French legists, Charles Dumoulin, who sought 'the union and concord of all the customs of France'.[15]

In their efforts to bring feudal custom and ecclesiastical 'liberties' under royal control, the spokesmen and champions of the last of the Valois kings (Francis I, his son Henry II and his grandsons, Francis II, Charles IX, and Henry III) worked their way towards a more general conception of absolute monarchy. Legists like Jean Ferrault and Charles de Grassaille gathered and commented on the great legacy of 'regalian rights' and royal privileges (*regalia, insignia, praerogativae, praeeminentiae*) accumulated over several centuries, and asserted them in particular against the claims of pope and emperor, especially Francis I's rival, the Habsburg emperor Charles V.[16] Among other claims, the king of France was 'most Christian' (*christianissimus, tres chrestien*), 'had no superior in temporal things' (a canonist formula indicating French independence from the empire), was 'emperor in his kingdom' (*rex imperator est in regno sua*) and possessed a wide range of feudal, ecclesiastical and extraordinary rights which, in effect, constituted 'marks of sovereignty' and the legal basis for a theory of kingship which was expressed during the reign of Francis I, though not fully (or, at least, formally) realised until that of Louis XIV. The major premise of French royalty was that neither civil nor canon law had force in France, so that the king himself (on the model of the ancient Caesars, especially Justinian, and the *plena potestas* of the pope) was the exclusive source of law – whence the famous Romanist formula that the king's will was law (*Quod principi placuit, legis habet vigorem*). This formula was given final theoretical expression in the famous definition of legislative sovereignty given in Jean Bodin's *Republic* in 1576.

French Renaissance culture revolved about and flourished in the light of the monarch (the solar image is appropriate before the time of Louis XIV). There were of course other centres besides Paris, most notably Lyon, and the universities surpassed the court in many ways; but, in the sixteenth century, learning and the arts had close ties with royal power and patronage – Mars and Minerva, as Guillaume Budé put it, being constant companions. The monarchy both promoted and benefited from the restoration of 'good letters' and, as historians were eager to argue, shared the myth of national revival. Charles VIII began the Italian adventure in 1494 and was the first ruler to receive intensive journalistic coverage in the new medium of print. His successor Louis XII, while enjoying more success in the Italian wars, at the same time contributed to material prosperity by reducing taxes and beginning the reform of justice, and he was rewarded with a laudatory biography by Seyssel and the title of 'father of his country' (*pater patriae*, characteristically rendered by Michelet as 'Père du Peuple'). Francis I, because of his better publicised support of the humanist programme, especially the founding of regius professorships in Latin, Greek and Hebrew (the basis of the future Collège Royal, later Collège de France), was immortalised as 'the restorer of good literature'; and he presided over the first phase of French humanism and the early stages of the Reformation, which acted first to supplement and enrich, and then to qualify and to undo, the cultural and political achievements of the Renaissance as Michelet viewed it.[17]

The key figure in the alliance between humanism and royalism was Guillaume Budé, who represented both the Italianate tradition of *bonae litterae* and the French legal tradition. As a public official Budé served both the monarchy (as *maître des requêtes*) and the city of Paris (as *prévot des marchands*); as a scholar he championed the cause of 'encyclopaedic' humanism – 'philology' was his term – on many levels.[18] He was the greatest Hellenist of his day (Erasmus not excepted), having established his reputation with the publication in 1508 of his *Annotations on the Pandects*, and sealing it with his seminal *Commentaries on the Greek Language* of 1529, the foundation of the great (and still authoritative) thesaurus of Greek, published a generation later by Henri Estienne. In the first of these works, Budé set out to do for the classic text of Roman law what Erasmus was doing for the New Testament, namely, to correct the text and to interpret it in literary and historical terms. In the course of this pioneering commentary on Romano-Byzantine law, Budé offered comparative discussions on French institutions (such as the parlement of Paris, the royal archives and his own office) in order to show their parity with, or superiority to, corresponding Roman legal creations; and he continued this celebration of French culture in other works, including his study of Roman coinage (the *De Asse* of 1515), his *De Studio litterarum* of 1527 and his *Philologia* of 1530.[19] In his own vernacular effort, the posthumously published *De l'Institution du Prince*, Budé praised the new invention of printing 'as the restoration (*instauration*) and perpetuation of antiquity', and he was instrumental in encouraging Francis I to found and to fund the 'trilingual college'. Despite his devotion to classical antiquity, Budé sided with the Moderns against the Ancients (as he sided with his own *patria* against that of the Italians). He remarked: 'Since in our age we see letters restored to life, what prevents us from seeing among us new Demosthenes, Platos, Thucydides, Ciceros, etc., not only imitators but emulators of these?'[20]

Transcending the classical heritage was indeed on the minds of French scholars of this generation, and perhaps the most venturesome critic of antiquity was Petrus Ramus, who, according to legend, called into question everything that Aristotle had ever written. Ramus' reach may well have exceeded his grasp, but his famous 'Method', derived from humanist rhetoric and associated with the 'new learning' of evangelical religion, offered a systematic alternative to the scholasticism reigning in the universities. 'Ramism' became the rage, especially in Protestant circles, because of its practical and mnemonic value (and hostility to Aristotle), and it was perhaps the dominant doctrine in France before Cartesianism.[21]

In the two generations after Budé 'philology', too, was expanded, not only in classical, biblical and legal scholarship, but also in the study of the relics and monuments of native culture. Budé's work on Roman law was pursued on a more professional level by Jacques Cujas, François Baudouin, and their colleagues at the University of Bourges, while their younger disciples, many of them also graduates of this stellar law school, turned the methods and insights of philology towards medieval studies – Pierre Pithou towards the publication of French chronicles, for example, Antoine Loisel and Louis Le Caron to the French legal tradition, and Etienne Pasquier towards the recovery of French institutions and culture in a more general sense.[22] Although the basic impulse for these investigations into the national past was a scholarly one, intended to beat the Italians at their own game, there were also practical motives, as the arguments of Louis Le Caron suggest: 'Frenchmen, you have enough examples in your own histories without searching those of the Greeks and the Romans.' In another context and addressing King Charles IX, he declared: 'You are subject to the laws neither of the Greeks nor of the Romans, and your magistrates do not apply them except insofar as they find them reasonable.'[23] For humanists like Budé, Pasquier, and Le Caron, as well as Romantics like Michelet, the upshot of the French Renaissance was a declaration of political as well as cultural independence.

Modernisation and vulgarisation

What these efforts suggested was a shift not only from ancient to modern concerns, but also from classical language to the vernacular. Le Caron, for example, began his career with a learned Latin commentary on the law of the Twelve Tables and ended it by charging his patriotic colleagues ('amateurs de leur patrie') to follow his example in the dedication 'to research and restoring to light the ancient books of their language for its decoration'.[24] Le Caron's major work, his *Pandects of French Law* (1587), began as a translation of the Digest but finally turned into a treatise which, combining the lessons of legal humanism with the practical aims of Seyssel, described and celebrated the 'French Republic', its origins and legal structure, within the framework of Roman law. Much the same can be said of Etienne Pasquier's *Interpretation of the Institutes of Justinian* (written about 1607), which also developed into a study of comparative law, language and institutions, designed likewise to show the humanity and liberality of French institutions, and hence their superiority to those of ancient Rome. Even more interesting was the *Institutes of Customary Law* (1602) by Pasquier's friend Antoine Loisel, who, while following the order of Justinian's famous textbook of civil law, sought the 'spirit' of French society in its own provincial customs, maxims, proverbs, and even literary sources.

But the vernacularising of the Budean heritage can best be seen in the work of another of Le Caron's contemporaries, Louis Le Roy, who was Budé's first biographer (1540) and a royal professor of Greek. Le Roy was a pioneering translator of Plato and Aristotle in the early years of the civil wars and an advocate of religious reconciliation. In his masterwork, *The Vicissitude or Variety of Things in the Universe* (1575), he celebrated Budé's encyclopaedic agenda and the wonders of printing in a context that upheld not only the party of the Moderns against the Ancients, but also the vernacularists against the classicists; indeed he went so far as to give his lectures in French at the 'Trilingual College'. Le Roy's book has been regarded both as 'the first history of civilisation' and as an early expression of the idea of progress, and it is true that he exhorted his contemporaries 'to transmit [the fine things restored or recently invented] to those who come after us just as we have received them from our ancestors'.[25] And, he added, 'the road is open'. Yet it should be added that Le Roy saw continued cultural advance not within mutable and corruptible national traditions, but only in the larger framework of universal history.

'Vernacular humanism' was the programme of the intellectual avant-garde in France in the second half of the sixteenth century, and the often under-appreciated work of translation was of fundamental importance. As early as 1510 Claude de Seyssel had sought 'to enrichen, to magnify, and to make public' the French language through his translations (via the Latin of Valla and others) of Thucydides, Xenophon, Eusebius and other ancient historians, although these works were not published until after his death.[26] Other contemporaries defended French from the charge of 'barbarism' (for example, Jean Lemaire de Belges in 1511) and attempted to 'decorate' the language through translators (Geoffroy Tory in the 1520s), and in 1540 the great scholar-printer Etienne Dolet published his work on 'the way to make good translations from one language to another'. The monarchy itself, for its own purpose, was touched by this vernacularist enthusiasm, and in 1539 Francis I issued a famous ordinance ordering all legal instruments and transactions (*registres, enquestes, contrats, commissions, sentences, testaments*, etc.) to be expressed 'in the maternal French language and none other'.[27] Charles Dumoulin's commentary on this edict – and other works by him, including a small treatise on the origins of the French monarchy – appeared in French as well as Latin versions. The master of the art, however, was Jacques Amyot, and no less a translator than Montaigne 'gave him the palm' for his patriotic efforts of adorning the French language with his renderings of Plutarch and others.

The *locus classicus* (or *anti-classicus*) of vernacular humanism was Joachim DuBellay's *Defense and Illustration of the French Language* of 1549, which transposed to France the old arguments devised by Italian scholars on behalf of the *volgare*. Despite Budé's doubts that French was useful for much more than vulgar pursuits like hunting, DuBellay asserted that French was indeed capable of treating literary, historical and even philosophical subjects.[28] Defences of the vernacular continued throughout the period of the civil wars and inevitably became politicised. In 1579 the Huguenot, Henri Estiènne, followed the trail blazed by Budé in the study of Greek, but he also wrote treatises protesting Greek and 'Italianising' influences on the French language. Not only words like 'assassin' but the practice itself, he suggested, had been brought into France by the Machiavellian followers of Queen Catherine de Médicis (a libellous biography of whom has also been attributed to Estiènne).

Three years after the appearance of DuBellay's work Estiènne Pasquier, though an enthusiast for the 'legal humanism' of Cujas, wrote a letter to the great classical scholar Adrien Tournèbe arguing the case for the use of French over Latin (as Cicero had preferred Latin over Greek), and a generation later (in 1586) Pasquier placed this letter at the head of his own collection of familiar, historical and literary epistles.[29] Retrospectively, Pasquier associated himself with the great 'fleet' of poets launched at this time – especially the Pléiade, but including Le Caron and other professionals – who were just beginning to promote the vernacularist cause in a concrete way (and beyond the conventions of the old school of *Rhetoriqueurs* and the newer one of Marot) by transferring, or transmuting, into French the forms and values of classical literature. Ronsard – 'prince of poets' as Dumoulin was 'prince of legists' – was captain of this fleet; and (in his office of *historiographe du roi*) he contributed to the political as well as poetical aspect of vernacular humanism with his epic survey of national history, his *Franciade*, illustrating again the persistence of the myth, the 'open boundaries between history and fiction' in the sixteenth century.[30]

The spirit of French culture

History was indeed the key to the formation of French identity in the sixteenth century, which was a seminal age of historical research, reconstruction and, in Michelet's word, 'reconstruction'. Again there are deeper roots, particularly in the long tradition of official historiography, centring at first on the chronicles of St Denis (first in Latin, then in French) and popular historians like Nicolas Gilles, who published a semi-legendary study of the origins of the French in 1492; but the humanist phase began with the work of Robert Gaguin and especially Paolo Emilio, *historiographe du roi*, whose *De rerum gestis francorum* (Paris, 1516) was revised, continued, translated and imitated for generations. The Italian-style, Livian history of 'Paule-Emile' was expanded and amplified by later royal historiographers, including Bernard du Haillan, François de Belleforest, Jean de Serres and other 'artisans of glory' (as Orest Ranum has called these court historians), who may have been Catholics (like Belleforest) or Protestants (like De Serres), but who served above all the Gallican tradition and the 'grand monarchy'.[31] Most comprehensive was du Haillan's *De l'Estat et succes des affaires de France* (1570) and *Histoire de France* (1576), which adopted Claude de Seyssel's scheme of four ages of monarchy, and which included the history of laws, institutions and society, as well as political and military matters. Drawing upon familiar medieval sources and the best of modern literature, and claiming to recount a *vraye histoire*, Du Haillan devoted himself, at the very height of the civil wars, to celebrate the 'fortune and virtue', the 'destiny' and the 'glory' of France.[32]

Historical reconstruction went beyond the old genre of political narrative in the style of Livy and Leonardo Bruni, for it depended on exploitation of documentary sources and the formation of a national – in most cases royalist – canon. Publication of medieval chronicles (beginning with Gregory of Tours in 1516) was followed by legal and ecclesiastical records, and then arrangement in an order that was at once, chronological, argumentative and dramatic. The purpose was to assemble material that represented both 'monuments' and precedents (*preuves*) to enhance the 'grandeur' and to promote the 'augmentation' of the monarchy. The 'memory' of the monarchy lay in the *trésor des chartes*, the registers of the Parlement, and various libraries, and this was where the process of historical and ideological canon-formation began. A major figure in this process was Jean du Tillet, chief archivist (*greffier*) of the Parlement of Paris, whose charge of reordering the archives for legal purposes led to the publication of his *Recueil des roys de*

France (1577).[33] This book, in effect the first 'documents pour servir à l'histoire de France', joined a brief narrative to a comprehensive inventory of the main legislative, ecclesiastical and diplomatic records of the monarchy. Du Tillet's brother, also named Jean, and Bishop of Meaux, published a continuation of Paule-Emile's history and *editiones principes* of various medieval texts, including the – national and in this sense ancestral – Law of the Salian Franks. As the first Jean du Tillet argued, one did more honour to the French by stressing Frankish origins than by repeating the old Trojan legends. Many other works, whether of a primarily scholarly and antiquarian or primarily technical and practical character, appeared in these years of religious conflict for 'the defense and illustration' of the French monarchy.

The most comprehensive and sensitive attempt to place the 'spirit' of France in perspective was undoubtedly the *Recherches de la France* of Estiènne Pasquier, who worked on his collection of antiquarian essays from 1557 until his death sixty years later.[34] In the early books Pasquier studied the problem of the Gallo-Franco-Roman origins of France and, like most historians since Paule-Emile, rejected the theory of Trojan origins. Pasquier also treated the history of the major institutions of the monarchy ('le faict de nostre police), including the Parlement, the Chambre des Comtes (on which he himself served as advocate), the chief officers of the crown and the Gallican church. Later he explored the history of language, literature, learning and the University of Paris (which he defended in 1564 in a famous suit against the Jesuits), including the faculties of law, theology and 'humanité'. To this task Pasquier brought both the techniques of humanist scholarship and the habits of legal argumentation, which required written 'proof' for demonstration of fact or the exposure of falsehood. In this pious dedication to 'French antiquities', an enterprise in which he was followed (and, as he feared, plagiarised) by others, most notably Claude de Fauchet, Pasquier hoped to serve both historical truth (*la vérité historiale*) and national glory (*la gloire de son pays*) in ways that were neglected by the likes of Paule-Emile.

By the late sixteenth century the scholarly and vernacularist avant-garde had become an intellectual establishment. In 1583, La Croix du Maine celebrated, in *Les Bibliothèques françoises*, the some 3,000 'men and women who wrote and composed works of their own or made translations into French', which was ten times as many as the number of Italian authors (he estimated) since the time of Dante, Petrarch and Boccaccio.[35] In his dedication to Henri III, La Croix noted two reasons for compiling his catalogue. One was to get to know the learned men of his own day, such as Pasquier – the learned advocate of the court of the parlement, Latin and French poet, historian and orator – and Le Roy – royal reader and philosopher, great historian and orator – not to forget Montaigne, Rabelais and other luminaries of the first degree. La Croix continued: 'The other reason is to show the great honour and praise brought to France (and consequently the King and sovereign Prince thereof) for her wealth of men learned not only in Hebrew, Greek, and Latin but also in French.' In this intellectual elite the legal profession played an increasingly prominent part (as suggested by the surviving libraries of lawyers, as well as the number of published works), and the tradition of royal legists was celebrated more particularly by Antoine Loisel, who cast his secular hagiography in the form of an antiquarian dialogue named, appropriately, after his lifelong friend and collaborator, *Pasquier* (1607).[36]

The new learning

The phrase 'new learning', more often than not, suggested not humanism but what in France was called 'the so-called reformed religion' (*religion pretendue reformée* – 'RPR'), and by La Croix de Maine's time these ideas had created an irreparable division in the republic of French (and of European) letters. In his last major work Budé himself had announced *The Transition from Hellenism to Christianity* (Paris, 1535), but he had no sympathy with the heresies already attracting members of his own family and given systematic expression the next year by Calvin. La Croix included Calvin in his catalogue, but he added that he 'would not give him here more ample mention for fear of the hostility of the men who would not want an account of his works . . ., [which were] in the catalogue of books banned and prohibited by the Council of Trent' (vol. I, 467). Pasquier himself had recognised 'Papisme' and 'Huguenotterie' (the current terms of abuse) as the twin threats to Gallican unity – threats, respectively, of Italian and of German origin – and by the time La Croix's *Bibliothèques* was published, six wars had been fought over 'the question of religion', which by then had also become the 'political question'. This brings us to the second of Michelet's great 'electric currents', which had an even more shaping impact than the Renaissance on French politics, society, culture and, in general, the search for national identity.[37]

The Reformation entered France by way of 'Lutherist' ideas in the 1520s, although to be sure there was an earlier movement of Christian humanism and evangelical 'pre-reform' (as it used to be called) associated especially with Jacques Lefèvre d'Etaples, who promoted the Erasmus programme by translating the New Testament into French. To Lefèvre the gospel represented the fulfilment of the renaissance of learning. 'Why may we not aspire to see our age restored to the likeness of the primitive church, when Christ received a purer veneration?' he asked, celebrating the restoration of the 'three languages' necessary for biblical study, and the almost simultaneous discovery of 'new lands' in which the message of the word of Christ might be spread further.[38] Lefèvre and other champions of what has been called the 'evangelical revolution' tried to carry on this missionary task in France, but within a few years the new faith had been driven underground or into exile, Lefèvre himself leading the movement into German and Swiss refuges, over which Farel and Calvin would later preside.

The 'roads to heresy' were many in the second quarter of the sixteenth century – sermons, pamphlets (translations from Luther as well as Erasmus), iconoclasm, missionary activity and, finally, ecclesiastical and political organisation in centres like Zurich, Basel and, of course, Geneva.[39] Still another factor was the example of, and publicity around, martyrs like Louis Berquin (executed in 1529 for possession of heretical literature); but not until 1535 did Francis I begin a consistent policy of persecution. The immediate occasion was the famous affair of the placards, in which posters denouncing the 'horrible abuse of the mass' were distributed in Paris and other French towns, including the chateau of Amboise, where the king was staying; but the underlying reason was royal outrage that the 'sacramentarians' had presumed not only to blaspheme but also to defy authority and to threaten the principle of Gallican unity which was integral to the monarchy. The king had 400 suspects imprisoned, nine burned at the stake, and had their tongues cut out – he even tried to abolish printing by edict and took the unprecedented step of transferring the task of 'pursuing' and 'exterminating' the foreign pest from the Sorbonne to the Parlement. From that time on, heresy became a civil crime and was punished even more systematically, by confiscation as well as execution, under Henry II (1547–59).

It was in this atmosphere of religious ferment and growing intolerance that Calvin, after a conventional humanist education, was converted to the new religious ideas and himself fled the university into an exile that he expected would be temporary. In the first edition of his *Institution of Christian Religion* (1536), he defended his sacramentarian comrades and appealed to Francis I not to listen to papist calumny but to accept the 'pure doctrine' of the gospel as the basis of the true, and French, religious tradition.[40] But the king would not listen, and Calvin spent the rest of his life in exile, exhorting his spiritual brothers and sisters – and then his confessional children – either to reject popery (to the point of martyrdom, if not active resistance'), or to flee the French 'Babylon' and to join him in the Genevan 'Jerusalem'. The successive editions of the *Institution* and his many polemical works reflected Calvin's theological development and the formation of his own self-defining historical perspective, while his polemics and organisational successes in Geneva revealed his emergence as a leader of an international network of churches – 'Calvintern', as Robert Kingdon termed it – stretching across Europe from Scotland to Poland, but concentrated especially in France and the Netherlands.[41] Yet Calvin remained a Frenchman, one of the forgers indeed of the literary vernacular, and looked always to the monarchy as the natural basis of his spiritual mission, as did his successor Theodore Beza and, of course, his 'Huguenot' following in France. Unfortunately, the historical 'canon' developed by the outlawed members of the RPR came to be based not on conventional historiography but on martyrology, not on the triumphant progress of the grand monarchy, but rather on the roll-call of holy victims who consented to serve the faith by this ultimate act of 'testimony', and who were given a place of honour in Jean Crespin's *Histoire des martyrs*, which celebrated another kind of historical perspective and cultural 'identity'.[42]

From religious dissent to civil war

What Nürnberger called the 'politicization of French protestantism' was a complex process spanning a generation – from the evangelical revolution of the 1520s to the outbreak of civil war in 1562, and it was associated with long-standing feudal rivalries, as well as with foreign notions of a purified faith.[43] In the 'new learning' associated with Luther and other magisterial reformers, the university community was deeply implicated, but, by the 1550s, heresy had come to infect all three of Claude de Seyssel's 'estates', including a few of the leading noble families (whose business continued to be, of course, risking life and fortune in military ventures). Censorship, inquisition and the policy of 'extermination' (in the language of the royal edicts) could not stem the new ideas nor the rising tide of social violence; and political polarisation seemed to make armed-conflict inevitable. In 1559 the accidental death of Henry II – leaving the monarchy in the hands of Catherine de Médicis, with her four under-aged sons – created a constitutional crisis and brought the neo-feudal rivalries to a head. The Catholic party was an instrument of the Guise family, with Francis, the second duke, heading the military establishment, and his brother Charles, the Cardinal of Lorraine, the leading figure in the Gallican hierarchy; the opposition centred on the 'princes of the blood', Antoine de Navarre (with his estranged Protestant wife, Jeanne d'Albret) and the Prince of Condé. The lines of division continued over a generation of bloody feuding, exchanged assassinations and full-scale wars, with attendant out-bursts of propaganda and efforts of legitimation in terms of French political and religious tradition.

Last ditch efforts to head off armed conflict were unsuccessful. The Colloquy of Possy (1561) brought Calvin's spokesman Beza into confron-tation with Catherine and the Cardinal of Lorraine, but reconciliation or compromise was far from the minds of the major participants either then or after the model Edict of Pacification of January 1562.[44] Beza demanded 'liberty of conscience', the government demanded submission to authority. In his address, the chancellor, Michel de l'Hôpital, begged his countrymen to stop their name-calling ('papist' and 'Huguenot'), but events and emotions were outrunning the hopes of irenic pacifiers (who seemed to be hypocrites to the Huguenots and traitors and heretics to the Catholics, to judge at least from the pamphlets). So the parties were formed, irreconcilable and yet both taking their stand on devotion to the monarchy, true religion, and French nationality; and both the pamphlet and the shooting wars began in earnest in April 1562.

The turning-point of the civil wars came with the massacres of St Bartholomew a decade later.[45] From then on the wars became international in scope, as the Netherlands and Spain were drawn in, and the propaganda became radically political. The Huguenots were led to justify not only active resistance but, in effect, revolution, in the sense at least of rejection of a tainted sovereignty that had justified the atrocities of 1572. The Huguenot line of argument, derived from Calvin's *Institution*, as well as the dilemma created by the crisis of 1559, was based not only on 'liberty of conscience', but also on notions of limited monarchy similar to the view of Claude de Seyssel (whose work was revived in the context of civil war and in the interests of convoking the Estates General to 'bridle' an intemperate and popish monarchy). Historically, there was insistence on the essentially Germanic provenance of French society, implying especially the traditional rejection of Roman 'tyranny', modern as well as ancient. The classic formulation of this modern myth was François Hotman's *Francogallia* of 1573, which envisaged and tried to document an 'ancient constitution' of the French monarchy, analogous to the idealised 'primitive church' preached by his mentor and spiritual 'father' Calvin and, more recently, by Beza, Calvin's disciple and Hotman's comrade-in-exile.[46] The Catholic position, at least as characterised by Hotman, was an 'Italogallic' image of French tradition that was quite as corrupt as its papist archetype. In any case the Huguenot position, as Beza too argued, implied not martyrly surrender but active resistance to tyranny and constitutional reorganisation through the Estates General.

In reality these partisan extremes, which drew on all of the hyperbolic weaponry of rhetoric and ingenuity of legal argument, and which have been so fascinating to historians of political theory, do not do justice to the complexities of the religious and constitutional predicament of late sixteenth-century France. Another product of St Bartholomew was the emergence, or re-emergence, of a moderate group which proposed to end the fighting by legal and secular (and some would add, 'Machiavellian', a term coined just in this connection) means – by reason of state, we might say, rather than by demands of conscience. This was the position of the party of the *Politiques*, who came (after the death of Henry III, last of the Valois) to support Henry of Navarre and eventually to support his re-conversion to Catholicism in 1594. Perhaps the most comprehensive philosophical expression of the *politique* position was Jean Bodin's *Republic* of 1576, which was directed in part against the subversive views of Hotman and other 'monarchomachs' (as they

would later be called), especially against ideas of limited or divided sovereignty. For Bodin, sovereignty (equivalent to Roman *maiestas*) was indivisible, inviolable, perpetual – a conceptual capstone of the complex modern
state, with attendant social structure, which was France.[47] While claiming to
travel further down Machiavelli's 'new route' to a science of politics, Bodin
also offered a conservative view of French government and society which gave
systematic legal and, in a sense, sociological form to the 'grand monarchy'
described by Seyssel and contemporary historians like du Haillan and
Pasquier and fought over by the religious parties.

Withdrawal and recovery

In the ideological pandemonium of the later sixteenth century, the choices for
coping with a 'world-upside-down' (a topos of contemporary pamphlet
literature) were not only right and left – orthodoxy or heresy, obedience or
resistance – or somewhere in between, but also withdrawal above, or below,
the fray. The *vita activa* celebrated by 'civic humanists' of the earlier
Renaissance seemed less promising to later generations. This was in effect the
conclusion of Michel de Montaigne and his late friend Etienne Boétie, whose
search for identity took them not into the national past, or into the ferociously
divided present, but rather into the private realm of moral philosophy.[48]
Ironically, and much to Montaigne's disgust, La Boétie's essay on *Voluntary
Servitude* (probably written before 1550) was widely regarded as a resistance
tract, in part because it was first printed in a collection of post-St Bartholomew Huguenot pamphlets; but in fact La Boétie's more subtle argument was
that the ultimate grounds of 'tyranny' was to be found in political structures
and social 'custom' in general. In the midst of confessional and constitutional
enthusiasms, French culture also displayed elements of philosophical criticism, scepticism and alienation from pressures of national tradition: this
joining of moral acuity and political passivity also became part of French
intellectual tradition.

   Critical withdrawal was reinforced by ideological exhaustion and the
experience of near total war. A generation of civil war left France, in the last
decade of the sixteenth century, with a divided society, a broken economy,
and most of the institutions, described by Seyssel and developed by the last of
the Valois kings, in disrepair; and the incidence of famine, epidemics and
popular revolts made the predicament of the nation worse. Yet the accession
of Henry IV in 1594 (after his celebrated re-conversion), which represented
the major triumph of the *Politiques*' programme, was followed by an
extraordinarily rapid recovery, politically and institutionally. The Parlement
and the Gallican church were restored, the Edict of Nantes (1598) provided a
legal settlement for the conditional recognition of the Huguenots, and a large
outpouring of legislation signalled a massive effort by the king and his

government to reorder society and reform the body politic and restore it to good health. As an Italian ambassador wrote in 1598, Henry IV – Henry the Great – 'rose like a phoenix from the ashes of that huge kingdom . . ., [and] now it is he alone who can put power and wisdom to work to revive hopes – which had almost vanished for a while – of restoring his country to its former splendor'.[49]

Charles de Loyseau's *Traité des offices* of 1610 replaced the work of Seyssel as the standard description, and quasi-official public image, of the French polity. Like Seyssel, Loyseau praised the richness and complexity of the social structure of France and concluded:

Thus, by means of these multiple division and subdivisions, there is made from many orders a general order, and of several estates a well regulated state, in which there is a beautiful harmony and consonance, a correspondence and rapport from the lowest to the highest, in such a fashion that by means of order an innumerable number converge in unity.[50]

The 'highest' level, of course, referred to political sovereignty; and following Bodin and other 'Politiques' – that is, those who understood *la science politique* – Loyseau praised this principle as 'the form that gives being to a state'. To judge from political theory as well as political reality, then, the 'grand monarchy of France' seemed to be entering another phase – national expansion and political absolutism – and soon another phase of international conflict as well.

Culturally, Minerva and Mars continued to keep company, along with the muses; the French philosophy and natural science were about to join language, literature and philosophy in a new position of dominance in the European republic of letters. As Richelieu and the Bourbon dynasty built on the achievements of the last of the Valois kings, so Descartes and the major figures of French classicism and historical scholarship stood on the shoulders of giants like Ramus, Montaigne, Rabelais, Ronsard, Cujas, Pasquier – and at least surreptitiously Calvin – and other survivors (or victims) of the times of trouble. The Renaissance left its mark and its legend, for the rest of the old regime, and itself enjoyed a revival in the age of Michelet; and its story – crossed confusedly with that other 'electric current', the Reformation – continues to be told, if not to be explained, and to inform the intellectual and cultural aspects of what Braudel called 'the identity of France'.[51]

NOTES

1 F. Braudel, *L'Identité de la France* (Paris, 1986), vol. II; and cf. C. Beaune, *Naissance de la nation française* (Paris, 1985). For a recent bibliography on historical background as well as major authors see R.C. La Charité, *A Critical Bibliography of French Literature* (Syracuse, N.Y., 1985).
2 W.F. Church, 'France' in O. Ranum (ed.), *National Consciousness, History, and*

Political Culture in Early-Modern Europe (Baltimore, Md., 1975), 43–66; and cf. G. Atkinson, *Les nouveaux horizons de la Renaissance française* (Paris, 1935).

3 R. Folz, *Le Légende et la mémoire de Charlemagne dans l'empire germanique mediéval* (Paris, 1950), and M. Bloch, *Les Rois thaumaturges* (Strasbourg, 1924).

4 F.O. Martin, *L'Histoire de la coutume de la prévôté et vicomté de Paris* (Paris, 1922), vol. I, 25.

5 J.H.M. Salmon, *Society in Crisis; France in the Sixteenth Century* (London, 1975), with further bibliography, and H.A. Lloyd, *The State, France and the Sixteenth Century* (London, 1983); cf. F. Braudel (with E. Labrousse) in *Histoire économique et sociale de la France* (Paris, 1970), vol. I, M. Wolfe, *The Fiscal System in Renaissance France* (New Haven, Conn., 1972), and H. Hauser, *La Modernité du XVIe siècle* (Paris, 1963).

6 C. de Seyssel, *The Monarchy of France*, trans. J.H. Hexter and ed. and intro. D.R. Kelley (New Haven, Conn., 1981), 36; and cf. J.S.C. Bridge, *A History of France from the Death of Louis XI* (Oxford, 1936), vol. V, *France in 1515*, and P.S. Lewis (ed.), *The Recovery of France in the Fifteenth Century* (New York, 1971).

7 Seysell, *The Monarchy of France*, 51; and cf. V. Martin, *Le Gallicanisme et la réforme catholique* (Paris, 1929).

8 Seysell, *The Monarchy of France*, 54; and cf. F.O. Martin, *Histoire du droit français* (Paris, 1948), J.J. Shennan, *The Parlement of Paris* (London, 1968), and R. Delachenal, *Histoire des avocats au parlement de Paris 1300–1600* (Paris, 1885).

9 Seysell, *The Monarchy of France*, 56ff; cf. R. Doucet, *Les Institutions de la France au XVIe siècle* (Paris, 1948), and J. Russell Major, *Representative Government in Renaissance France* (New Haven, Conn., 1980), W.F. Church, *Constitutional Thought in 16th-century France* (Cambridge, Mass., 1941), and E. Schalk, *From Valor to Pedigree: Ideas of Nobility in France in the Sixteenth and Seventeenth Centuries* (Princeton, N.J., 1986).

10 F. Simone, *The French Renaissance: Medieval Tradition and Italian Influence in Shaping the Renaissance in France*, trans. H. Hall (London, 1969); R. Mandrou, *Introduction à la France moderne* (Paris, 1961); I.D. McFarlane, *A Literary History of France*, vol. I, *Renaissance France 1470–1589* (London, 1974); Y. Giraud and M.R. Jung, *Littérature française: La Renaissance* (Paris, 1972–4); and W.L. Gundersheimer (ed.), *French Humanism 1470–1600* (New York, 1969).

11 L. Febvre and H.J. Martin, *L'Apparition du livre* (Paris, 1958); E.L. Eisenstein, *The Printing Press as an Agent of Change* (Cambridge, 1978); and A. Claudin, *Histoire de l'imprimerie en France au XVe et XVIe siècle* (Paris, 1900).

12 L. Le Roy, *The Vicissitude or Variety of Things* (1575), trans. J.B. Ross and M.M. McLaughlin (eds.), *The Portable Renaissance Reader* (New York, 1958), 91–2; and see H. Baron, 'The *Querelle* of the ancients and the Moderns as a problem for Renaissance scholarship', *Journal of the History of Ideas*, 20 (1959), 3–22, and H. Gillot, *La Querelle des anciens et des modernes en France* (Paris, 1914).

13 J.M. Michelet, *Histoire de France*, vol. VII, ed. R. Casanova, in *Oeuvres complètes*, ed. P. Viallaneix (Paris, 1978), 51, 122; and, in general, see W.K.Ferguson, *The Renaissance in Historical Thought* (Boston, Mass., 1948).

14 R. Filhol, *Le Prémier Président Christofle de Thou et la réformation des coutumes* (Paris, 1937).

15 C. Dumoulin, *Oratio de concordia et unione consuetudinarium Franciae* and *La première partie du Traicté de l'origine, progrez, et excellence du royaume et monarchie de France*, in *Opera omnia* (Paris, 1681), vol. II, 690 and 1034. See also D.R. Kelley, 'Civil science in the Renaissance: jurisprudence in the French manner' in *History, Law, and the Human Sciences* (London, 1984), and 'Fides Historiae: Charles Dumoulin and the Gallican view of history', *Traditio*, 22 (1966), 347–402.

16 J. Ferrault, *Insignia percularia christianissimi Francorum regni* ([Paris], 1520); C. de Grassaille, *Regulium Franciae libri duo* (Paris, 1545); and J.H. Franklin, *Jean Bodin and the Rise of Absolutist Theory* (Cambridge, 1973), ch. 1.

17 R.J Knecht, *Francis I* (Cambridge, 1982).

18 G. Budé, *Annotationes in quatuor et viginti libros Pandectarum* (Paris, 1535), and *Commentarii graecae linguae* (Paris, 1529); and see especially D.O. McNeill, *Guillaume Budé and Humanism in the Reign of Francis I* (Geneva, 1975), and D.R. Kelley, *Foundations of Modern Historical Scholarship: Language, Law and History in the French Renaissance* (New York, 1970), ch. 2.

19 G. Budé, *De Philologia libri II* and *De Studio litterarum recte et commode instituendo* (Paris, 1532), 158ff; and cf. F. Simone, *La Coscienza della rinascita negli umanisti francesi* (Rome, 1949), S. Kinser, 'Ideas of temporal change and cultural process in France', in A. Molho and J. Tedeschi (eds.), *Renaissance Essays in Honor of Hans Baron* (Florence, 1971), and A. Lefranc, *Histoire du Collège de France* (Paris, 1893).

20 G. Budé, *De l'Institution du Prince* (Paris, 1547), 63; and see Claude Bontems, Léon-Pierre Raynaud and Jeanne-Pierre Brancourt, *Le Prince dans la France des XVIe et XVIIe siècles* (Paris, 1967), 77ff.

21 W.J. Ong, *Ramus, Method, and the Decay of Dialogue* (Cambridge, Mass., 1958).

22 Kelley, *Foundations*, with further references, and G. Huppert, *The Idea of Perfect History* (Urbana, Ill., 1970).

23 L. le Caron, *Responses et decisions du droict françois* (Paris, 1637), 'Avant-propos', and *Panegyrique . . . au Roy Charles VIIII* (Paris, 1566); see D.R. Kelley, 'Louis Le Caron Philosophe' in *History, Law, and the Human Sciences*.

24 L. Le Caron, *Le Grand Coustumier de France* (Paris, 1598), preface; and see Kelley, *Foundations*, chs. 9–10.

25 Le Roy, *Vicissitude of Things*, 92; and see W.L. Gundersheimer, *The Life and Works of Louis Le Roy* (Geneva, 1967).

26 F. Brunot, *Histoire de la langue française*, vol. II (Paris, 1927); and cf. C.-G. Dubois, *Mythe et langage au XVIe siècle* (Bordeaux, 1970). L. Le Caron, *La Philosophie* (Paris, 1556), dedication: 'Je di, et l'ai tousjours soustenu, que nostre langue n'est pauure mais aussi plus riche que la Grecque, Latine, ou autre estranger, tant brave soit elle.'

27 F. Isambert (ed.), *Recueil général des anciennes lois françaises* (Paris, 1821–33), vol. XII, 622–3 (15 August, 1539), and C. Dumoulin, *Commentaire sur l'ordonnance du grand roy François en l'année 1539* (Paris, 1637).

28 J. DuBellay, *La Défense et illustration de la langue française*, ed. L. Humbert (Paris, n.d.), ch. 11, and Estiènne, *Dialogues du nouveau langage françois italianisé*, ed. P. Ristelhuber (Paris, 1885).

29 E. Pasquier, *Choix de lettres sur la littérature, la langue et la traduction*, ed. D. Thickett (Geneva, 1956).

30 H. Chamard, *Histoire de la Pléiade* (Paris, 1939), and P. de Nolhac, *Ronsard et l'humanisme* (Paris, 1921).

31 O. Ranum, *Artisans of Glory: Writers and Historical Thought in Seventeenth-Century France* (Chapel Hill, N.C., 1980), ch. 1, and C.-G. Dubois, *La Conception de l'histoire en France au XVIe siècle* (Paris, 1972).

32 B. du Haillan, *De l'Estat et succes des affaires de France* (Paris, 1570), and *Histoire de France* (Paris, 1576); cf. *De la Fortune et vertu de la France* (Paris, 1576); and see P.M. Bondois, 'Henri II et ses historiographes', *Bulletin Philologique et Historique* (1925), 135–49.

33 J. du Tillet, *Recueil des roys de France, leur couronne et maison* (Paris, 1577); and cf. Kelley, *Foundations*, ch. 8.

34 E. Pasquier, *Les Recherches de la France* (Paris, 1622); and D. Thickett, *Bibliographie des œuvres d'Estiènne Pasquier* (Geneva, 1956), and *Estiènne Pasquier (1529–1615), the Versatile Barrister of 16th-Century France* (London, 1979); also J. Espiner-Scott, *Claude Fauchet, sa vie, son œuvre* (Paris, 1938).

35 La Croix du Maine, *Les Bibliothèques françoises*, ed. R. de Juvigny and Du Verdier (Paris, 1772), 'Epistre au . . . Henry III' (following the bibliography).

36 A. Loisel, *Pasquier ou dialogue des advocats du parlement de Paris*, ed. A. Dupin (Paris, 1844).

37 D.R. Kelley, *The Beginning of Ideology: Consciousness and Society in the French Reformation* (Cambridge, 1981), with further references; and see P. Polman, *L'Elément historique dans la controverse réligieuse du XVIe siècle* (Gembloux, 1932), and P. Joutard (ed.), *Historiographie de la réforme* (Neuchâtel, 1977).

38 J. Lefévre, *Commentaria iniatorii in quatuor Evangelia* (Paris 1522), trans. Ross and McLaughlin, *Renaissance Reader*, 85; and see A. Renaudet, *Préréforme et humanisme à Paris pendant les premières guerres d'Italie* (Paris, 1953).

39 E. Droz, *Les Chemins de l'hérésie* (Geneva, 1970–6); *Aspects de la propagande religieuse*, ed. E. Droz (Geneva, 1956); and, on the affair of the placards, G. Berthoud, *Antoine Marcourt* (Geneva, 1973); more generally, E.G. Leonard, *A History of Protestantism*, trans. H. Rowley (London, 1965–7); P. Imbert de la Tour, *Les Origines de la Réforme* (Paris, 1905–48); and the co-operative work, R. Mandrou *et al.*, *Histoire des protestants en France* (Toulouse, 1977).

40 For Calvin, as for other magisterial authors, see the critical bibliographies in La Charite (cited above, n. 1); also F. Wendel, *Calvin: The Development of his Religious Thought*, trans. P. Mairet (London, 1963), and most recently W.J. Bouwsma, *John Calvin: A Sixteenth Century Portrait* (Oxford, 1988).

41 R. Kingdon, *Geneva and the Coming of the Wars of Religion in France, 1555–1563* (Geneva, 1956); *Geneva and the Consolidation of the French Protestant Movement, 1564–1572* (Geneva, 1967); and J.H.M. Salmon, *Renaissance and Revolt: Essays in the Intellectual and Social History of Early Modern France* (Cambridge, 1987).

42 J. Crespin, *Histoire des martyrs*, ed. D. Benoit (Toulouse, 1885–9), and D.R. Kelley, 'Martyrs, myths and the massacre: the background of St Bartholomew' in A. Soman (ed.), *The Massacre of St Bartholomew* (The Hague, 1974).

43 M. Yardeni, *La Conscience nationale en France pendant les guerres de religion (1559–1598)* (Louvain, 1971), V. de Caprariis, *Propaganda e pensiero politico in Francia durante le guerre di religione* (Naples, 1959), and J.H.M. Salmon, *The French Religious Wars in English Political Thought* (Oxford, 1959); also R. Nürnberger, *Die Politisierung des französischen Protestantismus* (Tübingen, 1948).

44 D.O. Nugent, *Ecumenism in the Age of Reformation: The Colloquy of Poissy* (Cambridge, Mass., 1974); H.O. Evennett, *The Cardinal of Lorraine and the Council of Trent* (Cambridge, 1930); and M. Turchetti, *Concordia o tolleranza? François Bauduin (1520–1573) e i 'Moyenneurs'* (Geneva, 1584).

45 R. Kingdon, *Myths about the St Bartholomew's Massacres* (Cambridge, Mass., 1988), F.J. Baumgartner, *Radical Reactionaries* (Geneva, 1975), and S. Mastellone, *Venalità e machiavellismo in Francia (1572–1610): all'origine della mentalità politica borghese* (Florence, 1972).

46 F. Hotman, *Francogallia*, ed. R. Geisey and trans. J. Salmon (Cambridge, 1972), J.H. Franklin, *Constitutionalism and Resistance in the Sixteenth Century* (New York, 1969), and D.R. Kelley, *François Hotman, A Revolutionary's Ordeal* (Princeton, N.J., 1973); see also P. Ronzy, *Un Humaniste italianisant, Papire Masson (1544–1611)* (Paris, 1924).

47 Bodin, *Les Six Livres de la Republique* (Paris, 1576), vol. I, 8; and especially H. Denzer (ed.), *Verhandlungen der internationalen Bodin Tagung in München* (Munich, 1973).

48 See N.O. Keohane, *Philosophy and the State in France: Renaissance to the Enlightenment* (Princeton, N.J., 1980); E.F. Rice, Jr, *The Renaissance Idea of Wisdom* (Cambridge, Mass., 1958); L. Febvre, *The Problem of Unbelief in the Sixteenth Century: The Religion of Rabelais*, trans. B. Gottlieb (Cambridge, Mass., 1982); R.H. Popkin, *The History of Skepticism from Erasmus to Descartes* (New York, 1964); and H. Busson, *Le Rationalisme dans la literature française de la Renaissance* (Paris, 1957). For the vast literature on Montaigne, Rabelais, and others, see La Charité, *Critical Bibliography*.

49 Report of Pietro Duodo to the Venetian Senate, 1598, in J.C. Davis (ed.), *Pursuit of Power* (New York, 1972), 264.

50 C. de Loyseau, *Traité des offices*, cited in Keohane, *Philosophy and the State*, 127.

51 See above, n. 1. And see now, above all, Denis Crouzet, *Les Guerriers de Dieu: la violence au temps des troubles de religion, vers 1525–vers 1610*, 2 vols. (Paris, 1990).

EIGHT

_____ ॐ _____

ENGLAND

DAVID STARKEY

'Methought,' wrote Thomas Starkey in about 1530, 'when I first came into Flanders and France that I was translated, as it had been, into another world: the cities and towns appeared so goodly, so well builded, and so clean kept.'[1]

The student of the Renaissance must try to recover that sense of wonder at another, new world – however devalued, dog-eared or doubtful it seems to have become. It was not only a physical new world of course. England, indeed, was rather slow to imitate the new styles in architecture, and even slower to adopt the new techniques in the other visual arts like painting and sculpture. Still less was it the New World on the other side of the Atlantic. A visionary like Sir Thomas More might perceive some of the implications of the great discoveries at the beginning of the century; but it took until the time of Shakespeare at the end for the awareness to become at all general. What Starkey was responding to were the political, social and cultural differences that separated England from the apparently more advanced countries of the continent; he was also, and above all, reacting to that 'other country' of the classical past, where they did things even more differently, which he had encountered in mind, thanks to his studies in that most advanced contemporary country, Italy.

But Starkey and his contemporaries were not content, Miranda-like, merely to admire. Instead they wanted to apply their knowledge. Like those other seers of alternative worlds in the nineteenth century, they were determined to build a new Jerusalem in England's green and pleasant land – or a new Rome or a new Athens. And they understood the means. As Starkey told Cromwell, he had consciously prepared himself for 'a politic life', and now that it was clear that Henry VIII was 'so set to the restitution of the true common weal' he wanted to come home and join in.[2] These endeavours made the Renaissance an age of reform as well. But conscious reform also stimulated an awareness of what was being changed. The result, paradoxically, was a deeper understanding of tradition. That was not the only paradox. A better understanding of Latin produced a greater sensitivity about

English; a greater awareness of Rome, old and new, led to a deeper commitment to England. That indeed was probably the most important effect of the Renaissance: it not only took place within a national context, it shaped the very idea of nationhood itself. At the beginning of our period, an idea of English nationhood was just formed; at the end, the English nation had emerged – so it thought – as the predestined vehicle of God's purpose upon earth.

There are, declared the English delegation to the General Council of the Church at Constance in 1416, three elements to nationhood: race or 'blood', 'territory' and 'language'.[3] The English race, happily, is a mongrel that defies analysis. But territory and language, which are susceptible to historical treatment, tell opposite stories. As a territory England was already old: it had an unbroken political history since at least the Norman Conquest in 1066, and the limit of legal memory stretched back to the beginning of the reign of Richard I in 1189. It was also an unusually centralised and well-governed kingdom, with the result that it was probably more aware of itself as a unity than any other area of comparable extent in Europe. But if England were old, English was comparatively new: it had 'not continued in one form of understanding two hundred years', as Bishop Gardiner contemptuously observed in the middle of the sixteenth century.[4] It was not, indeed, until the second half of the fourteenth century that English had emerged as an official language in its own country. Legal and parliamentary proceedings and wills in the vernacular all first appear then. But, even so, it continued to share the stage with Latin and (increasingly bastardised) French for centuries more. Its victory as a literary language, which dates from the same time, was more absolute – not least because because its first task was to translate the existing French and medieval Latin literature into the language of common speech.

In the case of the greatest of this first generation of English writers, Geoffrey Chaucer, his sources for translation extended further, to the contemporary Italian writers Petrarch and Boccaccio. He was familiar with their work at first hand, and may indeed have met the writers themselves, thanks to two visits he had paid to Italy on diplomatic business. Moreover his adaptations match, if they do not exceed, the original in spirit. Chaucer, particularly in *Troilus and Criseyde*, the story of which comes from Boccaccio's *Filostrato*, is remarkably aware of cultural and linguistic variations – whether in time and place, or as between individuals. This has led some critics to hail Chaucer as England's first Renaissance poet. But the sources of his insights do not seem to have been Renaissance at all: his awareness of cultural relativism came, not from contemporary Italians, but from the great author of late antiquity, Boethius, whose *De Consolatione Philosophiae* he translated into English prose; while his 'individualism' was, it will be argued, an authentically native characteristic. Indeed, I would go further and suggest that Chaucer consciously turned away from the Latin, or 'Renaissance' side of Petrarch and Boccaccio. This seems the only possible reading of *The Parliament of Fowls*. The introductory section of the poem begins with an accurate and elegant translation of a classical tag; it continues with the first description of the Renaissance in English (this 'newe science' which comes out of 'olde bokes'), and concludes by giving a fully Renaissance reading of Cicero's *Dream of Scipio* from the *De Republica* as an encomium on statesmen 'that lovede commune profyt'.[5] But the poem now turns: the poet nods off over Cicero's elevated sentiments and his sleep transmutes the orator's political themes into fairy matter: a parliament, but of birds, debating not patriotism, love of country, but love indeed. In other words, Chaucer had seen the new world of 'civic humanism' but preferred the old, though still lively, realm of courtly love.

If Chaucer were late medieval England's greatest creative intelligence, then Henry V (1413–22) was certainly her greatest king – indeed, he is arguably England's greatest king *tout court*. And he was similarly indifferent to the voices of novelty from Italy. Instead he determined, consciously and effectively, to realise the highest ideals in his own culture. A king had two jobs: to rule justly and to fight gloriously. He excelled at both. At home there was reform; abroad his stunning victories at Harfleur and Agincourt, and his no less bold diplomacy, brought him within a whisker of realising the dream of his ancestors and uniting the crowns of England and France into a dual monarchy. All this sounds like the mere culmination of dynasticism; instead Henry saw himself, and was seen, as the first servant of his realm and people. He was hailed as an emperor, the worthy successor of Constantine and Justinian; but the English were also God's chosen people, and their victories were the work of His hand. Indeed, it is Henry's Englishness which, in reality as well as in Shakespeare's marvellous recreation, is his most striking characteristic. It was on his explicit orders that the English delegation at Constance insisted on their claim to great nation status (with the force of England's arms making their elaborate academic analysis irresistibly convincing); and he was the first English king to use English for his own official correspondence. This was a matter of example as well as practicality, and his lead in using 'the common idiom' was quickly followed by important groups of his subjects, like the London Brewers in their Company records.[6] Finally, he saw the continued development of English as a literary language as a matter of national pride and status also. This is made clear by John Lydgate's note that Henry had commissioned his composition of the *Troy Book* because he wanted 'the noble story' to be freely available 'in oure tonge, . . . as in latyn and frensche it is'.[7] Wars, Henry clearly understood, are fought with words as well as weapons.

But the words were traditional ones: the source of Lydgate's *Troy Book* was the compilation of the thirteenth-century Italian Guido della Colonna, not Homer or Virgil; while the texts invoked to support England's national claims were the Old Testament and Roman law and so were older still. This complacent insularity is easily understood and, so long as England were winning, there was no need to change it. Indeed, it is important to remember that early fifteenth-century Italians were at least as likely to be influenced by England as the other way around. The all-conquering king of England was the flower of European chivalry and aspirant Italian princelings, like the Gonzaga rulers of Mantua, were proud to wear his livery. But with Henry V's untimely death at the age of only thirty-five problems began. At first, under the leadership of the King's two brothers, John, Duke of Bedford in France, and Humphrey, Duke of Gloucester in England, the English held their own. But when Henry VI (who had been only nine months old at his father's death) assumed power, things fell apart: first France was lost; then England collapsed into the faction fight known as the Wars of the Roses. Between 1461 and 1485 there were five kings of three different dynasties. And only one, Edward IV, died in his bed and he had been dethroned for a time.

To confront this national crisis there emerged two policies: one was for war with France, at first to continue it, subsequently to renew it; the other was for peace and domestic reform. Now on the defensive, the English were more susceptible to foreign ideas and the proponents of both policy options in turn drew on the Renaissance. First, and for long uniquely, was the war party. In part this was an accident of those very Renaissance things, personality and patronage. Humphrey of Gloucester, the Protector of England, longed to cut a figure on the European stage and clearly saw the role of Renaissance prince as the most glamorous. His collection of books became the nucleus of Oxford university library; he employed successive Italian humanists as his secretary, and he commissioned books in Italy and England (including Latin translations of *The Politics* and *The Republic*). What has not been sufficiently emphasised, however, is that this literary patronage was intended to bolster the arguments of the war party, of which Gloucester was leader. The subjects alone make this plain. Tito Livio Frulovisi, one of his Italian secretaries, wrote a Latin *Life* of Henry V and the *Humfroidos*, an epic account of Gloucester's martial exploits in France in 1435–7; while one of his English clients, Nicholas Upton, who oscillated between the careers of don, soldier and cleric, produced the *De Officio Militari*.

But the most important and creative contribution was the work of William of Worcester. He came from the same stable as Upton, except that he combined his soldiering with the other role of 'gentleman bureaucrat'; while his connections with the war party lay through service to Bedford rather than Gloucester. In 1451, in the immediate aftermath of the English defeat in France and the first outbreak of domestic disorder in Cade's rebellion,

Worcester began the *Boke of Noblesse*. He attributed the English collapse to
two factors: the first was national sin; the second was national disunity. The
remedy for the first was to be found in Christian teaching; for the second, in
Cicero's theory and practice of *respublica*. 'It is for to remember among all
other things,' Worcester noted, that 'every man after his power and degree
shuld principally put him in devoir [i. e. duty] and labour for the advancing of
the common profit.'[8] With this the Renaissance had really arrived in England:
Cicero was to be its favourite author, and 'commonwealth' (the more usual
form) its key word. The contrast between Chaucer, who shied away from a
political application of Cicero, and Worcester, who rejoiced in it, establishes
the chronology precisely. Worcester's linkage of the Ciceronian ideal of the
subordination of the individual to the collective good with Christian concepts
of sin and redemption was also to become universal. On the other hand, his
view that the proper goal and measure of the moral and political unity of a
nation were success in war was partisan.

And the linkage of 'commonwealth' language and war (in what we should
call 'militant', as opposed to 'civic', humanism) lasted so long as the war party
itself did. The *Boke of Noblesse* was reworked twice, for presentation to
Edward IV and Richard III. One of Edward's leading supporters, Walter
Blount, Lord Mountjoy, commissioned a translation of Upton's *De Officio
Militari*; while the only manuscript known to have been produced for Richard
III as king was a translation of the classical treatise on war by Vegetius. Most
interesting, however, is the case of another major supporter of Edward IV's,
John Tiptoft, Earl of Worcester. He was the first English nobleman to study in
Italy. On his return to England, he became Constable. This was the chief
military office of the realm, with responsibility both for jousts and tournaments, for which he issued the definitive rules, and for state trials and
executions, which he conducted with exemplary barbarism. But he was just as
active with the pen as with the sword: he made English translations of
standard works by Cicero and Caesar, as well as a treatise on nobility by
Buonaccorso, which argued (what was not yet a commonplace) that true
nobility lay in virtue rather than blood.

The English, who thought that there was more blood than virtue in
Tiptoft's own career, found the man an unwelcome puzzle. This was partly
because the mood had changed. There were still gestures to war, but more and
more the party of peace and domestic reform was in the ascent. It is, however,
important to distinguish two, radically different, stages. The first centres on
Sir John Fortescue, Chief Justice of England and councillor of Henry VI. His
Lancastrian loyalties (and his eventual willingness to compromise them) he
shared with William of Worcester. Otherwise the two men were polar
opposites. For Fortescue was a little Englander: the solution to England's
problems could only be found at home, by domestic reform based on native
tradition.

The fact that Fortescue wrote his most important work, *The Governance of England*, in exile in France only sharpened his insularity. The work is usually interpreted simply as a blueprint for solving the king's financial problems (and hence, Fortescue argues, his political ones as well) by building up the landed revenues of the crown, rather than by instituting permanent general taxation. This was seen as the English way, as opposed to the French way of taxation. More revealing, however, is to investigate the social attitudes implicit in Fortescue's argument. There is only one reference to morality, and that is when he boasts of the high number of hangings in England as proof of Englishmen's courage and appetite for wealth, even if they have to rob for it. There is also only one reference to religion, and that is of the same ilk. Previous kings, Fortescue says, have used their lands to found monasteries, but the king who creates a permanent landed endowment for the crown 'shall then have founded an whole realm'. And like a monastery, the realm will sing its founder's praises: 'We shall now more enjoy our own good; ... Of his alms it is that we have all that is in our own.'[9] In other words, 'God bless the king for abolishing taxes!'.

But abolishing taxes is tantamount to abolishing government: endowed monarchy is 'privatised' monarchy, ruling over a realm where not it but private property is supreme.[10] The purpose of government is thus not to make men good, but to guarantee them free enjoyment of their goods. And the test of good government is not the 'commonwealth', but a wealthy commons: Fortescue compares the prosperous yeomen of England with the poverty-striken peasants of France, and concludes that English government is 'better' in just such measure as its people are individually richer. This, in a startlingly modern fashion, reduces politics to political economy. But it is also old. For the individualism that characterises Fortescue's thought has been seen as inherently, even aboriginally, English by Alan MacFarlane in his immensely suggestive book, *The Origins of English Individualism*. It surfaces in Chaucer; it was entrenched in Fortescue's professional discipline of Common law. It also stood at the opposite pole to the 'commonwealth' doctrine of Worcester.

Nevertheless, the future was on the side of 'commonwealth'. At first there was a middle ground, in which the new communitarian language was used to describe the old individualistic position. Fortescue himself resorts to this device in the brief abstract of *The Governance* which he prepared for the Lancastrian Prince Edward in 1471. So does Edward's supplanter, the Yorkist Edward IV, in the speech he gave to Parliament in 1467. This defends a Fortescuean fiscal policy in the 'commonwealth' idiom: leaving money in the pockets of his commons would benefit the commonwealth. The perversion, or rather inversion, of language is transparent.

In 1485 the dynasty changed yet again as Henry VII, the first Tudor king, seized the throne. The broad outlines of policy remained constant, however.

But within this continuity there were two important shifts. First, Fortescuean fiscal policies were taken to such a pitch of effectiveness that the monarchy became markedly stronger. And second, the king's judicial powers were exploited to a novel extent: partly to bridle the over-mighty, and partly to extract money from everybody (but especially the rich for they had more of it). Fortescue himself had been insouciant about the moral obligations of government, but that was because he had a modest view of its purposes. On the other hand, Henry VII's apparent contempt for even the values of justice sat ill with the much greater ambitions of his rule.

There were two solutions to the problem. The first was to reduce government once more to Fortescuean limits; the second was boldly to bolster the 'New Monarchy' with the 'New Learning'. Both were tried in the vehement reaction which followed the king's death in 1509. The first was the official line. It was loudly proclaimed but quickly abandoned. The second was mooted by Edmund Dudley, Henry VII's principal legal and fiscal agent. He had been arrested soon after his master's death and while he was imprisoned in the Tower awaiting execution on trumped up charges of treason, he wrote the *Tree of the Commonwealth*. This has had a bad press from historians, who have concentrated on the stale allegory of its form to the exclusion of the real innovativeness of its contents.

For Dudley moved morality to the centre of politics. The commonwealth itself is seen as a moral order of mutual interdependence; while within it the monarch's role ceases to be passive, as in Fortescue, and becomes supremely active. Ideally Christian charity should bind the members of every estate to fulfil their own duties and respect the rights of others. But if charity fails (and Dudley is sure that it has), then it is the king who must step in and by rigorous justice make men both good Christians and good citizens whether they will or no. Dudley was well aware that this represented an incursion of royal power into an area usually reserved for the church and he answered the obvious objections. Would not the king be assisting 'the bishops, curates or preachers'? 'Forsooth none of them', came the reply; instead 'he assisteth his maker and Redeemer of whom he hath all his power and authority . . . over all his subjects, spiritual and temporal'.[12] In other words, Dudley was calling for an ethical reformation to be brought about by an ethical royal supremacy.

This seems to stand the traditional judgement on its head and turn Dudley from a thinker of no originality into a mould-breaker. That would be absurd. Directly Dudley can have influenced nobody (The *Tree of the Commonwealth* was not printed until 1859); instead he stands as a representative of his *milieu* in the high legal and political circles of early Tudor government. Clearly that *milieu* was more influenced by the Renaissance than we have tended to think. The conventional account of the dissemination of the Renaissance in England goes something like this. The Renaissance made slow headway in fifteenth-century England: most humanistic activity remaineo ᵥ work of foreigners; conversely, any Englishman who wished to advance beyond an elementary level had to study abroad, especially in Italy. Not till the last decades of the century, with the generation of John Colet, William Grocyn and Thomas Linacre, did Englishmen catch up with continental standards of scholarship, and only then was a self-sustaining English literary Renaissance possible. This seems to me to err in both the chronology of change and its agents.

It does so because it exaggerates the importance of the 'professional' scholar. Professional scholars were important in Italy. There there was a real profession – that of notary – from which they sprang, and plenty of opportunities for employment in the chanceries of popes, princes and cities for the more politically ambitious. And from this involvement with the real world of affairs sprang real books, like Bruni's *Laudatio* of Florence. The sincerity of this 'civic humanism', around which scholarly debate has raged, is immaterial; what matters is its undoubted intellectual weight and influence. None of this applied to England. There there were only two outlets for professionals: the not fully distinct careers of churchman and teacher. The literary output of churchmen was light-weight (typical was Thomas Chaundler's wonderfully incongruous adaptation of Bruni's *Laudatio* to argue the superiority of the cathedral city of Wells to its rival Bath within the joint diocese of Bath and Wells); while teachers produced either textbooks – or pupils! Some of these pupils were the next generation of professionals; most were not. The point, therefore, is that the key figure of the English Renaissance of the fifteenth century was the same as that of the sixteenth: the gentleman amateur, who wrote in English though he was inspired by Latin. Every text that we have mentioned so far belongs to this category; while every author, with the possibly significant exception of Fortescue, had studied at Oxford.

Oxford, indeed, was the cradle of this amateur lay humanism of the fifteenth century. This should prompt us to look again at its facilities – like the university library, founded by Gloucester and augmented by a large bequest from Tiptoft of Latin books 'to encourage students to acquire a more classical latinity'.[13] The same motive was also prominent in the foundation of Magdalen College and School in 1455. The statutes provided for at least two or three undergraduates to devote themselves 'so long to grammatical and poetical and other humane arts that they could not only profit themselves but be the Masters and ushers of Magdalen College School. Those holding the posts included John Stanbridge, Robert Whittinton and William Lilly. They composed grammars and *vulgaria*, or translation exercises. These presented the new intellectual fashions – like 'commonwealth' or Cicero-worship – in the predigested form of textbooks throughout the ages. And they were soon to reach a vastly wider audience through printing.

None of this was enough to produce a continental-class scholar (though it laid decent foundations for one). But it was quite sufficient to turn out a literate politician or administrator, capable of reflecting critically on what he was doing and well able to put his thoughts on paper. Nor did things change with the first generation of English scholars who enjoyed a continental reputation. All were friends of Erasmus and he exhausted even his fecund ingenuity in making excuses for their failure to publish: Grocyn had weak eyesight, Linacre was too perfectionist, and so on. The truth seems to be that they wrote nothing because they had nothing to say. Instead, like their predecessors, they were educators and editors. And they too found their fulfilment in a great pupil: Thomas More, who was another amateur. More took the intellectual tensions, which had reduced his teachers to silence, and turned them into the basis of his own creativity. He added a generous measure of psychological tension as well: between sex, religion and politics. The result was the first two masterpieces of the English Renaissance: *The History of Richard III* and *Utopia*.

The two (as the rediscovery of the original Latin text of *Richard III* makes clear) were conceived and written within three years (1513–16) and should be treated together. The first, *Richard III*, deals with politics in More's own world. These were characterised, he felt, by false values and a belief in appearances. In such a society the successful politician must be a dealer in appearances also: that is, he must be an actor. Hence More's repeated use of the language of the theatre: Richard III was a consummate actor, who 'could adopt any role'; England was a 'stage', politics 'a regal tragicomedy' and the English people, programmed to respond to convention, a too-complaisant audience.[15] But if history shows us drama, then it is the fiction of *Utopia* that must restore us to reality. Contemporary European states, More argues, are not commonwealths at all because private property has destroyed 'public welfare' (*'publicum commodum'*). In Utopia, however, communism has cut off the root of private selfishness. So not only is Utopia 'the best country in the world', it is 'the only one that has any right to call itself a commonwealth ("respublica")'.[16] It is also, by another paradox, the only one to embody a Christian mode of life even though it has not received Christianity.

More is, therefore, an early example of the English intellectual's dislike of his own country. His favourite targets are things of which his fellow countrymen were inordinately fond, like the legal system and hanging. He also sets the dialogue of Book 1 of *Utopia* in Antwerp, which was not only in a different country but represented the different, and More would have thought superior, values of burgher society as opposed to the aristocratic ostentation of England. Finally he wrote in Latin. He never translated *Utopia*, though he

did begin a translation of *Richard III*. It was not a success. Some of the best
passages refused to go into English, and even the form changed as an elegant
Latin essay became a messy English chronicle. He abandoned the miscege-
nated work incomplete. There is an important corollary to all this. If you see
more wrong than right in your country, you will not be keen on fighting for it:
in other words, More's pacificism, too, was a function of his sense that
'patriotism was not enough'.

Or indeed, perhaps, that it was nothing at all. This, after all, was the line
taken by Erasmus's punningly titled *Encomium Moriae* or *The Praise of Folly*
(or *More*), which had been written up in More's house and was dedicated to
him. Here love of country appears as one of the infinite varieties of self-love ('a
kind of common self-love'), each of which is more foolish and absurd than the
rest.[17] But there is a deeper source. More had delivered a series of lectures on
St Augustine's *City of God* in about 1501, and he followed Augustine in
distinguishing sharply between the moral authority of state and church: the
former was conditional, the latter absolute. This meant that an English
parliament could err: 'much people may sometime believe one man's lie';
while a general council of the church was infallible, since 'the good assistance
of the spirit of God is according to Christ's promise as verily present and
assistant as it was with His blessed apostles'.[18] Only towards the end of his
career, with the Divorce and the break with Rome, was More forced to spell
out the difference between the spiritual and the temporal powers in such
uncompromising terms. But nothing suggests that his views had ever been
fundamentally different. He had lived, as he died, 'the king's good servant, but
God's first'. Which means in turn, an apologist would say, that it was not so
much that More did not love his native land, but that he loved Christendom
more.

I would concede the point. But though the phrasing be kinder, the effect was
the same. And it was to make More a sharp break in the history of the
Renaissance in England. Moreover, in this respect at least, More was typical
of his generation. No new humanist works appeared to justify Henry VIII's
resumption of Henry V's war against France in 1513; instead works of the
fifteenth-century war party, like Lydgate's *Troy Book* or the *Life* of Henry V
were republished in print or manuscript. On the other hand, the marriage and
peace treaties of late 1518 were immediately celebrated with elegant *Orations*
by two of the leading lights of the circle of court humanists, Cuthbert Tunstall
and Richard Pace. This radical shift of attitude also coincides, of course, with
the moment at which England first acquired the full technical apparatus of
Renaissance scholarship. Was this then the 'real' Renaissance?

Scholars of very different persuasions have agreed that it was. For one side,
More's radicalism represents a moment when the ills of England could have
received a cure commensurate to the seriousness of the disease. But the

: of politics and the Protestant Reformation meant that the moment
ragically quickly. For the other side, More's repudiation of the values
vn culture was the representative act of a Renaissance which sought to
a living (if rather battered) native tradition with a neo-classicism that
was both alien and still-born. From this threat England was rescued either by
chance or 'Constellation', according to C. S. Lewis, or by the Protestant
Reformation, according to John King. The value-judgements indeed are
opposite, but the narrative is the same. When extremes meet, the moderate
man turns elsewhere: quite simply, More and his generation were no more
'typical', 'representative' or 'real' than any other, and they have only
appeared so because of the curiously amputated chronology which has begun
the Renaissance in 1509, with the accession of Henry VIII, and ended it in
1540, with the fall of Thomas Cromwell.

We can go further: More was not even typical of these three chosen
decades. The touchstone, once again, is the attitude to nationhood. The
principal writers of the 1530s all focused on this question, and all took the
opposite side to More. First was Sir Thomas Elyot, whose *Book Named the
Governor* was published in 1531. Elyot himself came from the same stable as
More. He was a lawyer, administrator and self-taught amateur scholar. His
book parallels *Utopia* too. The latter was the most brilliant work of the
English Renaissance; the former was the most influential. *Utopia* argued that
Renaissance values and Englishness were contradictory; *The Governor* that
they were complementary. Indeed, Elyot's central purpose was to incorporate
Renaissance learning within the educational programme of the English upper
class. To do that he had first to show that the Renaissance was compatible
with England – and, indeed, with class. This meant confronting More
directly. He began with a statement of his fundamental commitment. This
was not to the greater body of Christendom, like More's, but 'to my natural
country'. From this everything else flowed: he would write in English, 'in our
vulgar tongue', which More had found himself unable to do; and he would
locate his 'just public weal', not in the never-never land of Utopia, but in the
here-and-now of 'mine own experience . . . in [the] daily affairs of the public
weal of [Henry VIII's] most noble realm'.[19]

But what precisely of the 'justice' of the English commonwealth? More had
seen a gulf between ideal and real that could only be leapt over by irony; Elyot
(who was not a genius and therefore was not content with paradox) saw only
a problem to be solved by translation. More (like everybody else) translated
'*respublica*' as 'commonwealth'. And – as words alone show – the proper
social system of a *common*wealth was *commun*ism. But, Elyot pointed out,
the translation is wrong: '*respublica*' is a *public* weal. This in turn implies a
society stratified by degree and differentiated by the ownership of private
property – just as Rome had been and England was. Elyot lost the battle over

the word but won the point of substance: 'commonwealth' remained the current term, but it now meant what Elyot understood by 'public weal'.[20]

So Elyot reconnected the Renaissance to England. But his England remained a vague concept, with little sense of the particularity of place, history or institutions. This next step on the road to reality was taken by Thomas Starkey, in his *Dialogue between Pole and Lupset*. More had set his Utopian dialogue in the least English of places: an urban garden in the Netherlands; Starkey chose the most English: Bisham Abbey in Berkshire, the seat and sepulchre of Reginald Pole's ancestors, the Montagu Earls of Salisbury. And Pole's interlocutor, Thomas Lupset, launches the dialogue by invoking both the place and the attendant ancestral shades: 'this place of Bisham, whereas the image and memory of your old ancestors of great nobility shall, as I trust, stir and move your heart and mind.'[21] This is another fundamental difference from More. In *Utopia*, aristocratic values are the prime obstacle to change; in Starkey, the only hope of change rests on a reformed aristocracy. But to invoke aristocracy is to invoke history. In More, English political history provides no more than the *mise-en-scène* for Richard III's 'regal tragicomedy'; in Starkey, it becomes the source of the wisdom of 'our old ancestors, the institutors of our laws and order of our realm', who had established the office of Constable to bridle the tyrannical tendencies of kings.[22] Here Starkey's sense of history develops into a conception of an English constitution which is itself the product of specific historical development. Starkey must have got the details of all this from reading English sources, historical and antiquarian. But the concept is derived from the sophisticated humanist reworking of the history and institutions of Venice, with which he was familar at first hand.

So far, we have looked only at the effect of the Renaissance on political thought. The concentration may seem excessive. But, in fact, political thought is almost synonymous with prose in this period.[23] To put it the other way around, prose was the vehicle in which 'gentlemen bureaucrats' expressed themselves about their natural business of governing. The other vehicle of self-expression was verse. This is usually seen as the medium for emotion rather than reflection. In fact, the main theme of poetry in the English Renaissance was its deployment for the same political purposes as prose, but by a better class of person.

The history of English Renaissance verse begins where we stopped our account of political thought: that is, with the recovery of a specifically English tradition. The year was almost the same too: 1532. Then, within a short space of each other, there appeared two luxury editions of the first generation of English poets: Chaucer and his contemporary John Gower. Both editions were humanist, both were semi-official. The Chaucer was prefaced with an important essay on language. This traced the development and maturation of the great European languages. Maturity was identified with two things: regularity, which meant that a language could be reduced to 'a grammar or rule ordinary';[24] and literature, in which the rules were put at the service of invention. The preface to the Gower develops the idea of literature as a normative source for language. It does so as an important and early contribution to the controversy about the use of 'ink-horn terms' or new words imported into English from the classical and romance languages. The preface takes a middle line: borrowings were permissible when really necessary; otherwise, the usage of 'our most allowed old authors' (like Gower himself) should be followed.[25] Here we can see classicism shaping both the idea of an English classic, and of pure English itself. It was a great English classicist who put it most succinctly: Chaucer, Roger Ascham wrote in the *Toxophilus* (1545), was 'our English Homer'.[26]

Some writers went much further. The rule of thumb is that a Ciceronian in Latin became a John Bull in English. The classic example (in every sense of the word) was Sir John Cheke, one of Edward VI's tutors. In his specimen translation of St Matthew's gospel, he pointed the way to a comprehensive re-teutonisation of English: 'proselyte' became 'freshman'; 'crucified', 'crossed'; and – nicest of all – 'lunatic', 'mooned'.[27] Here authenticity teeters on the edge of absurdity, not to say lunacy (or 'mooning'). Some languages, like French under the impact of the neo-classicism of the *Grand Siècle*, crossed the barrier and paid the price of fossilisation. English remained mongrel and thrived.

And it is in the context of this debate about language and literary tradition that we must place the two great poets of the early sixteenth century, Sir Thomas Wyatt and Henry Howard, Earl of Surrey. Most modern criticism (following the Elizabethan assessment) emphasises their novelty: both experimented with new forms and new metres: while Surrey, in a creative life of less than a decade, perfected the sonnet, invented blank verse and successfully imposed a new metrical regularity on English. All this is true. But contemporaries saw another side. 'I take them best English men, which follow Chaucer and other old writers', wrote one critic in 1544, and made Wyatt chief of these followers.[28] Surrey, Wyatt's elegist and poetic heir, agreed and claimed that Wyatt had 'reft Chaucer the glory of his wit'.[29] In fact, there is no contradiction in the two judgements: Wyatt and Surrey innovated in form – that is they were Renaissance – but remained traditional – that is English – in vocabulary and poetic diction.

And with Surrey, the more radical innovator, the attachment to England was the more marked. It showed itself in his use of English place-names: 'Norfolk', 'Surrey', 'Windsor' echo through his verse and resonate with time as well as place. This is the poetic equivalent of Starkey's invocation of Bisham, and, like Bisham, it implies an aristocratic, that is a political, role for verse. Wyatt's greatest work, Surrey thought, was his translation of the

Penitential Psalms, because it offered 'a mirror clear' in which 'Rulers' might see the 'bitter fruit' of sin and repent.[30] Similarly his own unfinished translation of the *Aeneid* used – it is now powerfully argued – the death of Troy and its rebirth in Rome as an implied metaphor for the renewing of England in himself and his great family.

The accident of politics eliminated first Surrey and then his family from the enterprise. But his vision was still realised, if in the hands of others. Central to his concept of renewal was war. And it was in the renewal of war – first the threat and then the actuality – from 1539 that we see all the themes of this essay drawn together. In striking contrast to the first wars of Henry VIII's reign, humanists flocked to the flag. 'Only take an English heart unto thee and mistrust not God', exhorted Tunstall from the pulpit; 'Let us fight this one field with English hands and English hearts', echoed the Paduan-educated Richard Moryson in his *Exhortation*.[31] What had happened?

The first thing is the Reformation. Reform had often been promised; now at least Henry VIII's break with Rome seemed to be about to turn the hope into reality. But it would be reform in one country, and conformable to the spirit of that country. The shift shows clearly in the proposals for law reform. Everybody agreed that English law needed codification. Starkey proposed to go the whole hog and adopt Roman law. A few years later, at the beginning of the war scare, two unpublished tracts by Moryson and John Hales took a very different line. English law was peculiar to the English; Roman law to the Romans: 'so is not one law meet for all people, nature is so diverse.'[32] Instead, therefore, codification should take the *form* of Roman law but preserve the *spirit* of English. And it would be as easy to do this, Moryson asserted, as 'for an English tailor to make of an Italian velvet an English gown'.[33] Reform by itself was not enough, however, to shift the lingering scholarly resistance to fighting. Indeed, domestic reform was seen as an alternative to foreign war. Both Moryson and Hales linked their proposals for law reform to Henry VIII's great scheme of coastal fortification, which he had begun in 1539. The former would strengthen the kingdom internally; the latter externally, and together they would enable happy England to hold aloof from war.

The Reformation, in so far as it was a Protestant phenomenon, also strengthened the aboriginal Christian revulsion from war. The proto-Protestant Thomas Becon, for example, entitled the first, 1542 edition, of his war tract, *The New Policy of War*, and the second, 1543 edition, *The True Defence of Peace*. The crisis of conscience is obvious. Yet finally it was Protestant theology which opened the way to a conscientious patriotism that could embrace war, and even rejoice in it. The ground had been prepared by the shift of Renaissance thought to particularity. Starkey had emphasised the importance of time and place; Moryson drew the obvious conclusion and proclaimed that, 'Peace is to be refused when time forceth men to war'.[34] This smacks of opportunism (Moryson's writing usually does). The element of conscience was supplied by Edward Walshe in a little-noticed tract, *The Office and Duty in Fighting for Our Country*, which he claims to have 'pronounced . . . at several times unto his fellows militing at the siege of Boulogne' in 1544. His argument rests on his view of the operations of 'the high institution and providence of God'. By this God 'hath ordained and constituted each man to live under the powers of the earth . . . not under such powers as we our selves shall choose or desire'.[35] In other words, it is God that has willed us to be English. This makes patriotism a Christian as well as a natural duty; it also makes nations the vehicles of God's providence. We can now see clearly the intellectual foundations of the national Church of England. They combined this theological doctrine of Providence (and Incarnation too) with the Ciceronian sense of the moral unity of the commonwealth, which had expressed itself in a virtual theory of supremacy as early as Dudley in 1509.

More had set himself to combat this view. He lost, as he did comprehensively on everything else. The rejection was completed in the next generation when the Renaissance recovered the native English tradition of Fortescue. In his *Discourse of the Commonweal* (1549), Sir Thomas Smith deploys Fortescue's individualistic political economy; while his *De Republica Anglorum* (printed in 1583) reproduces his predecessor's positivistic account of English political and social institutions and his pride in their uniqueness. Here the repudiation of More is explicit: his *De Republica Anglorum*, Smith boasted, was not one of those 'feigned common wealths' or 'vain imaginations', like Plato's or More's; instead it was real: 'so as England standeth and is governed at this day the 28 of March *anno* 1565.'[36] Time and place indeed!

Smith was also a pioneer of that most paradoxically English thing: the classical country house. The visual Renaissance came late to England. In the early sixteenth century, Renaissance and vernacular elements would be freely combined in the same building; in the 1540s, in the high Protestant-aristocratic circles of the Seymours and the Dudleys, there was a brief burst of purist classicism, as in Somerset House; but under Elizabeth there was reversion if not outright reaction. Buildings blended both native and foreign styles; while there was something of a Gothic revival. Both before and after the 1540s the mixture of styles has been interpreted as the result of ignorance and muddle. Our account of the literary Renaissance suggests another possibility. Might the mixture have been intentional? After all, when Wolsey and Henry VIII put Italian terracotta roundels of Roman emperors on the red brick of Hampton Court, they were only doing architecturally what Wyatt and Surrey practised in their verse. Similarly, when the Elizabethans built houses whose design was rigorously symmetrical and coherent (that is Renaissance) but whose architectural vocabulary was vernacular, they were applying to the letter Moryson's prescription for law reform: make an English gown with Italian velvet.

Nor really did things change in substance in the early seventeenth century with Inigo Jones's vastly more sophisticated and informed classicism. Jones thought a thoroughgoing classicism appropriate to a small, new building like the Queen's House at Greenwich. But when it came to restoring a grand, old building, like St Paul's, once more a blending of styles was suitable. In other words, Jones wanted an English classicism: he gave it English roots when he interpreted Stonehenge as a circular temple in the Tuscan order; while his insistence that exteriors be 'solid . . . masculine and unaffected' laid the foundations for a 'quintessentially English' style.[37]

Jones' enterprise, in fact, was the same as Starkey's. Both learned in Italy but wanted to practise in England. Jones envisaged a national classicism; Starkey a national humanism. In neither case were their patrons the beneficiaries. Jones' hopes for an English Palladianism were realised, not by the monarchy of Charles I, but by the Whig aristocracy of Hanoverian England. They found in its restraint the perfect architectural expression of their preference for ordered and moderate government, as opposed to the Baroque follies of absolute monarchy. Similarly, Starkey's vision of a reformed aristocracy was not fulfilled by the Poles, tainted as they were by both Catholicism and Yorkist blood; nor by the Howards (though Surrey remained a powerful example through to the seventeenth century, when Inigo Jones painted a magnificent architectural setting for his portrait at Arundel). Instead it was achieved by the Protestant nobility of Elizabethan England. They combined an English sense of the claims of lineage and chivalry with a Roman awareness of the obligations of public office and the demands of military service. And they sought to exercise this double role in the preservation of liberty at home and the Protestant religion abroad. It is much the same formula as that of the Whig aristocracy, and it is no accident, for the Elizabethans were their ancestors.

NOTES

1 T. Starkey, *A Dialogue between Reginald Pole and Thomas Lupset*, ed. K.M. Burton (London, 1948), p. 92.

2 S.J. Herrtage (ed.), *England in the Reign of Henry VIII: I, Starkey's Life and Letters*, Early English Text Society Extra Series, vol. XXXII (London, 1927), x, lxviii.

3 Cited in J.W. McKenna, 'How God became an Englishman' in D.J. Guth and J.W. McKenna (eds.), *Tudor Rule and Revolution* (Cambridge, 1982), 33.

4 J.A. Muller (ed.), *The Letters of Stephen Gardiner* (Cambridge, 1933), 289.

5 F.N. Robinson (ed.), *The Works of Geoffrey Chaucer*, 2nd edn (Oxford, 1966), 311.

6 Cited in K.B. McFarlane, *Lancastrian Kings and Lollard Knights* (Oxford, 1972), 119

7 Cited in D. Pearsall, *John Lydgate* (London, 1970), 125.

8 [William of Worcester], *The Boke of Noblesse*, ed. J.G. Nichols, Roxburghe Club, vol. LXXVII (London, 1860), 56–7.

9 Sir J. Fortescue, *The Governance of England*, ed. C. Plummer (London, 1885), 155–6.

10 The idea of 'privatisation' in this context is borrowed from P.R. Coss, 'Bastard feudalism revised', *Past and Present*, 125 (1989), 63.

11 Fortescue, *Governance*, 115.

12 E. Dudley, *The Tree of the Commonwealth*, ed. D.M. Brodie (Cambridge, 1948), 33.

13 A.B. Emden, *A Biographical Register of the University of Oxford to A.D. 1500*, 3 vols. (Oxford, 1959), vol III, 1878.

14 Cited in M. Dowling, *Humanism in the Age of Henry VIII* (London, 1986), 10.

15 D. Kinney (ed.), *In Defense of Humanism*, Yale Edition of the Complete Works of St Thomas More, vol. xv (New Haven, Conn. and London, 1986), 325, 483.

16 Sir T. More, *Utopia*, ed. and trans. P. Turner (Harmondsworth, 1965), 128, and n. 46.

17 D. Erasmus, *The Praise of Folly*, ed. H. Gross (n.p. 1979), 60.

18 Cited in A. Fox, *Thomas More: History and Providence* (Oxford, 1982), 178.

19 Sir T. Elyot, *The Book Named the Governor*, ed. S.E. Lehmberg (London, 1962), xiii.

20 *Ibid.*, 2.

21 Starkey, *Dialogue*, 21.

22 *Ibid.*, 165.

23 I owe this insight to Robert Barrington of the Department of History and Civilisation, European University Institute, Florence.

24 W. Thynne (ed.), *The Works of Geoffrey Chaucer*, introduced by W.W. Skeat, fac. edn (London, n. d.), xxiii.

25 Sir J. Gower, *Confessio Amantis*, ed. T. Berthelet (London, 1532), sig. aa ii (v).

26 Cited in C.S. Lewis, *English Literature in the Sixteenth Century Excluding Drama*, Oxford History of English Literature, (Oxford, 1954), vol III 281.

27 Cited in *ibid.*, 283.

28 J. di Porcia, *The Preceptes of Warre*, trans P. Betham (London, 1544), sig. a vii.

29 H. Howard, *Poems*, ed. Emrys Jones (Oxford, 1964), 27.

30 *Ibid.*, 29.

31 Cited in G.R. Elton, *Policy and Police* (Cambridge, 1972), 190, 205.

32 J. Hales, An oration in commendation of the lawes . . . , B[ritish] L[ibrary], Harley MS 4990, fo. 21v.

33 R. Moryson, ['Treatise on the codification of common law'], BL, Royal MS A 18 L, fo. 24.

34 S.J. Frontinus, *The Strategemes, Sleyghtes, and Policies of Warre*, trans. R. Moryson (London, 1539), sig. a vi.

35 E. Walshe, *The Office and Duety in Fightyng for Our Country* (London, 1545), sigs a iii (v), b ii (v) – b iii.

36 Sir T. Smith, *De Republica Anglorum*, facs. edn (Menston, 1970), 118.
37 J. Harris and G. Higgott, *Inigo Jones: Complete Architectural Drawings* (London, 1990), 17, 56.

FURTHER READING

This chapter has tried to revise the English Renaissance in both chronology and content. A consequence has been to leave out much that might have been expected, like Shakespeare and Gloriana. The reading list indicates my dissent from some key authorities, picks out some recent work which points in new directions, and fills in some gaps.

The main targets are: R. Weiss, *Humanism in England during the Fifteenth Century*, 3rd edn (Oxford, 1967), which presents English humanism as a quest for professionalism; C.S. Lewis, *English Literature in the Sixteenth Century Excluding Drama*, Oxford History of English Literature, vol III. (Oxford, 1954), which argues for the incompatibility of the Renaissance and English tradition but only shows that Lewis disliked the literature he read; and J.K. McConica, *English Humanists and Reformation Politics* (Oxford, 1965), which tries to fit all early Sixteenth-century humanism under the umbrella of 'peace and love' Erasmianism.

New approaches to the fifteenth century are: J.W. McKenna, 'How God became an Englishman' in D.J. Guth and J.W. McKenna (eds.), *Tudor Rule and Revolution* (Cambridge, 1982) and G.L. Harris (ed), *Henry V: The Practice of Kingship* (Oxford, 1985). These both stress the role of nationhood. A. Fox, *Thomas More: History and Providence* (Oxford, 1982) asks the right questions but offers the wrong answers; D. Kinney (ed.), *In Defense of Humanism*, Yale Edition of the Complete Works of St Thomas More, vol. XV (New Haven, Conn. and London, 1986), prints the text of *Richard III* which corrects Fox. Radical reassessments of the relationship between nobility, chivalry and the Renaissance are given by W.A. Sessions, *Henry Howard, Earl of Surrey*, Twayne's English Authors Series (Boston, Mass., 1986) and R.C. McCoy, *The Rites of Knighthood*, The New Historicism: Studies in Cultural Poetics, ed. Stephen Greenblatt, vol. VII (Berkeley, Calif., 1989). Greenblatt's own *Renaissance Self-Fashioning: from More to Shakespeare* (Chicago, Ill. 1980), like F.A. Yates, *Astraea: The Imperial Theme in the Sixteenth Century* (London, 1975) or R. Strong, *Splendour at Court: Renaissance Spectacle and Illusion* (London, 1973) stress the medium rather than the message – perhaps because they do not take the message seriously enough. M. Girouard, *Robert Smythson and the Elizabethan Country House*, new edn (New Haven, Conn., and London, 1983) and J. Harris and Gordon Higgott, *Inigo Jones: Complete Architectural Drawings* (London, 1990) both reconnect Rennaissance architecture to the idea of national tradition – the former implicitly, the latter explicitly.

—————————————— ⟐ ——————————————

NINE

HUNGARY

TIBOR KLANICZAY

The origins of the Renaissance in Hungary

There hardly was a country with more favourable conditions for the reception of the Italian Renaissance than Hungary. In the fourteenth century the Neapolitan Anjou (Angevin) dynasty ruled the country, whose policy was involved in the affairs of Italy in more ways than one. Louis the Great (1342–82), led campaigns to Naples (1347 and 1350), fought a victorious war against Venice (1378–81), and strengthened control over the Dalmatian coast; Hungarian mercenary troops on Italy's soil became a frequent occurrence, and an Italian traders' colony was established in Buda, the capital, while Hungarian students frequently attended the universities of Bologna and Padua. The ever-increasing cultural contacts facilitated the constant flow of material and spiritual values between Italy and Hungary.[1] This process gained momentum under the rule of King Sigismund (1387–1437), especially when, in 1410, he became the ruler of the Holy Roman Empire, and his royal seat, Buda, had become one of the centres of European policy. Of the first generation of Italian humanists Filelfo and Traversari spent months, Branda Castiglione and Giuliano Cesarini years, while Pier Paolo Vergerio nearly three decades (1417–44), in Hungary; Poggio Bracciolini was to have received a promising position at the court, but eventually he did not come to Hungary. This was the country where Filippo Scolari (Pippo Spano), famous from Andrea Castagno's portrait, had a brilliant career, and it was in Hungary where Masolino painted some of his works, paintings that have not come down to us, unfortunately. The historical sources also testify to a constant influx of Italian bishops and other church dignitaries, of surgeons, physicians and bankers, who settled down in Hungary. Giovanni da Serravalle translated the *Divina Commedia* into Latin for King Sigismund, and Vergerio translated Arrianos' *Anabasis Alexandri* for him. When Sigismund was in Italy between 1431 and 1433, touring Italian towns at the occasion of his coronation as emperor, his retinue already found the world of the Renaissance *in statu nascendi.* János Hunyadi (*c.* 1407–56), later to become the great military leader and statesman, was hired by the Viscontis at this time.[2]

This, of course, was only the potential reception of the Renaissance: Hungary's society was still leading very much a medieval life with no sign, at the beginning, of openness towards the new type of learning. When Petrarch chanced to read one of Louis the Great's charters worded in a barbaric Latin, he remarked despisingly that the King of Hungary had better hire good scribes instead of spending his money on bloodhounds.[3] On his arrival in Austria, decades later, as secretary to Frederick III, Enea Silvio Piccolomini complained to Cesarini, who chanced to be at Buda at the time, saying that it was 'as foolish a thing to look for Rome in Austria as it is to inquire about Plato among the Hungarians'.[4] A humanist, however, did not have to come from Italy to feel without equals in learning and aspiration in Hungary: the greatest of Hungary's humanist poets, Janus Pannonius (1434–72), who had spent eleven years in Italy, complained in 1458 that, 'this barbaric land compelled him to use barbarous words, and if Virgil or Cicero came to see the country, they would fall silent too'.[5]

On the other hand, this was also the time when Matthias Hunyadi (Matthias Corvinus) succeeded to the throne, and it was largely due to him that the Italian Renaissance in Hungary quickly became a reality. He was the son of János Hunyadi (at the time of his accession dead for two years), who had staved off the Turkish conquest of Hungary for seventy years and secured the country's integrity with his victory at Belgrade in 1456.[6] It was this victory that had obviously allowed the Renaissance to flourish in Hungary, and it was in the person of Matthias that Europe saw the first-ever ruler outside Italy to have received a sound humanist education.

Vergerio, author of the first humanist treatise on pedagogy – *De ingenuis moribus et liberalibus adolescentiae studiis* (1400–02) – did not live and work in Hungary for such a long period without some success: however slowly, his teachings began to bear fruit. It was on the basis of his principles that Enea Silvio Piccolomini wrote his *De liberorum educatione*, a work which he composed for the infant King Ladislaus V in 1451. The first Hungarian humanist, Johannes Vitéz (*c.* 1408–72) was also Vergerio's follower, and they jointly organised the first learned humanist *cenacolo* in Buda in the early 1440s. The same Johannes Vitéz was one of the associates of János Hunyadi and also educator of the young King Matthias, who was himself the embodiment of the new type of learning and human ideals. As heir to enormous wealth and the son of a glorious father, Matthias Corvinus this *homo novus* among European monarchs who had been brought up under the influence of humanist pedagogy, must have been literally predestined for the role of the Renaissance ruler.[7]

The age of Matthias Corvinus

Under the shadow of expansionist Turkish policy and threatened by the German king who contested for Hungary's crown, Matthias needed the most modern means available if he was to achieve his goals.[8] These included a strong centralisation of power, new taxation policies, a permanent army, as well as humanist propaganda and the splendour of a Renaissance court. Johannes Vitéz, who had been Matthias's teacher and was now his chief chancellor, understood that efficient diplomatic ties – especially with the Holy See and the Italian states – could only be kept up in a humanist 'coat-of-arms'. He himself had set an excellent example in his epistles and orations.[9] He was also perfectly aware that the state's future politicians and highest-ranking officials had to be provided with the best possible education, and that is why he sent those under his patronage – including his nephew, the poet Janus Pannonius – to learn from the best Italian masters, such as Guarino da Verona. In this way a humanist chancellery was created from those who had received the best Italian education, and by now Petrarch himself would not have found fault with the writings that they were producing. Political argumentation in correspondence and orations, laudatory prose and poetry in praise of the king, the urging of Europe's nations to Christian solidarity against the Turks, the rewriting of the history of the nation in the spirit and style of humanism – these were some of the themes of the new humanist literature just being born in Hungary. The demand for humanist literature started to attract men of letters from other countries, mainly from Italy, such as Galeotto Marzio, Antonio Bonfini, Bartolomeo Fonzio, Aurelio Brandolini Lippo, Francesco Bandini and many others, all of whom served the king for different lengths of time. Hungarians, Croatians, Italians, Germans, and Poles together had made up this humanist elite who, besides serving the king, were beginning to shape their own lives in constant debate and argument, studying the ancient authors and taking part in symposia modelled on antique and Italian patterns. In addition to propagandistic writings, humanist poetry was now beginning to accommodate personal lyrical poems, especially in the work of Janus Pannonius.[10]

For all that, books – mainly those by the ancient authors – were needed. These were also available: already Vergerio had transferred his excellent library to Buda. Johannes Vitéz was to become Hungary's first humanist bibliophile, who established a library at his bishop's seat at Várad and later at his archbishop's palace at Esztergom and who, in the little free time that he had, devoted himself to the emendation of ancient scientific texts together with Galeotto Marzio and the German astronomer, Regiomontanus.[11] The greatest achievement, however, was the king's: he founded what came to be known as the *Bibliotheca Corvina*, a library of world renown, on which a host of humanists, scriptors, illuminators and book-binders worked in the work-shops of Buda and in the *bottegas* of Florence, on the king's order. This great cultural centre of Renaissance Hungary (destroyed in the sixteenth century) became one of the major seats of learning in central Europe, with its enormous quantities of ancient literary works and humanist writing.[12]

The library frequently hosted learned meetings and discussions, modelled on Lorenzo de' Medici's and Marsilio Ficino's Academia Platonica. The *coetus Ungarorum*, according to Konrad Celtis' term, can be considered a branch of the Academy at Florence, largely due to the fact that its main organiser had been Ficino's associate Francesco Bandini, who himself had spent fourteen years at Buda. The great Florentine master himself did not accept the invitation to come to the court, but he did send all of his works, some of them dedicated to the king and Hungarian humanists. The dominant trend of early humanism in Hungary became neo-Platonism: Plato was now being discovered in Pannonia too, and it was his spiritual influence as well as the works of Plotinus, Ficino and the hermetic writings that permeated the finest poems of Janus Pannonius and other authors.[13]

The humanist spirit of Matthias's court took root in the artistic soil of the Quattrocento, especially from 1476 onwards, when the king married the daughter of the King of Naples, Beatrice of Aragon. The Gothic royal castle of Buda was partially rebuilt, and new Renaissance wings were added to it. According to Vasari, Chimenti Camicia was in charge of the reconstruction and alteration project, and it was also he who built the famous hanging gardens of the palace, based on the Urbino model. The king intended to have the town of Buda restructured altogether, and for that purpose he asked Bonfini to translate Filarete's *De Architectura* from Italian into Latin, [14] but he did not have time enough to create the ideal city. He did, however, spend a good deal of time decorating and embellishing his royal palace. Benedetto da Maiano, Giovanni Dalmata and Ercole de' Roberti worked personally in Buda, and many other artists got commissions from him: Andrea Mantegna painted his portrait; Filippino Lippi made the altarpiece of the palace chapel; Antonio Pollaiuolo designed the drapery for his throne and Verrocchio made the bronze relief for one of the palace gates. Actively engaged in the work were the best illuminators of the time, such as Attavante degli Attavanti, Gherardo and Monte di Giovanni and many others. Mention has to be made of the king's summer palace at Visegrád, the ruins of which can still be seen today, as well as of the famous court ensemble and choir, about which Bartolomeo de' Maraschi, the leader of the papal choir, remarked that it was second only to his own.[15]

Antonio Bonfini wrote of King Matthias that 'he strove to transform Pannonia into a second Italy'.[16] He certainly did everything in his power to make his country – especially his royal court – equal in rank to the Italian

Renaissance centres. How did contemporary Hungarian society respond to all this? Could it appreciate, and was it in a position to act upon the king's initiative? Obviously enough, many people despised foreign ways and customs, frowned upon the exorbitant spending, and looked upon all that was happening with incomprehension. Matthias had to protect Miklós Báthory, Bishop of Vác (c. 1440–1506) from the scorn of the lords in his court when he was immersed in his Cicero, instead of chatting away with the others while waiting in the ante-chamber.[17] Matthias was, however, first and foremost a politician, and cultural innovation was not an end in itself to him, even though he was an ardent supporter of the Renaissance. When it was necessary he knew how to be a shrewd statesman. He won the favour of the nobility, who were hostile towards anything foreign, by supporting and propagating the cult of the supposed Hun origin of the Hungarians. Matthias, in this way, did not mind the nobility welcoming the second Attila in his person, while the humanists glorified in him the new Hercules. On the one hand, the person with whom he spent the most time discussing matters of philosophy was the Epicurean and atheist Galeotto Marzio; on the other, he assumed the role of defender of Christianity and the church, carrying on crusades against the infidel Turks and the heretic Czechs. He supported the mendicant orders – the Franciscans in particular – and had churches erected for them, in Gothic style, giving an enormous impetus to the late efflorescence of Gothic art in Hungary too. At the time of his death in 1490, his country was one where the upper elite was the adherent of, and actively engaged in, Renaissance and humanist culture, but the bulk of the society still lived according to the standards of a traditional medieval culture.[18]

Expansion of Renaissance culture and political catastrophe

The emergence of humanism and the quick prevalence of the Italian Renaissance in Hungary led to a coexistence of the old and the new type of culture in the decades that followed Matthias's death. It turned out that ever broader strata of the society were showing a strong sensitivity towards Renaissance values. Obviously, it was mainly the aristocrats' courts and those of the large noble families and the prelates that quickly developed into seats of Renaissance learning and culture: palaces and churches were being built, old buildings were being transformed and medieval cathedrals were receiving new, additional chapels in the style of the Renaissance. In the early sixteenth century, Renaissance tabernacles were appearing in small villages, and many noblemen were having Renaissance tombstones made even in the most remote parts of the country. Most of these were no longer the works of Italian masters, even though their presence could still be felt in the major centres. Beside the leading Italian artists, more and more Hungarian masters had been working in the workshops of Matthias's court, but now these were spreading their activities all over Hungary.[19] All this activity was closely related to the changes in the political sphere: Matthias had enormous revenues, thanks to his strong central power and the efforts of his associates as well as his severe taxation policies, while the kings who followed him to the throne – Wladislas II (1490–1516) and Louis II (1516–26) of the Jagello dynasty – did not have the necessary power and capabilities, which meant that the state became poor because revenues remained in the hand of the privileged classes of the society. The country however benefited from this change since more and more prelates, magnates and wealthy burghers could afford to spend money on architecture and the arts. This explains how such gems of the Renaissance as Tamás Bakócz's – the Archbishop of Esztergom's (1442–1521) – chapel was built.[20] Humanist learning was also gaining ground, with the *studia humanitatis* becoming the core of both secular and clerical education at schools, the Greek language being introduced in several places, and more and more authors writing in the humanist spirit.[21]

One special feature of the Renaissance in Hungary was that it attained a height right at the beginning, during the reign of Matthias, which it was never to achieve again. An extraordinarily lucky historical situation made possible this brilliant start, but the conditions that could have sustained it were lacking. This unique example, however, was sufficient to secure the adequate spread of humanist learning and Renaissance taste. In the decades that followed Matthias Corvinus's reign, the country's political orientation had also changed: contacts with Italy had remained, but those with Austria, Bohemia and Poland were now more important than before, if only because humanist teachings had got a strong foothold in these countries too by the year 1500, and the Vienna and Cracow universities had become the major central European bases of humanist thought. Hungary was now looking to these regions, partly for dynastic reasons: Wladislas II and Louis II were also Kings of Bohemia, with their closest relatives on Poland's throne, and with a double bond of matrimony tying them to the Habsburgs of Austria. A cosmopolitan humanist central Europe was beginning to take shape: humanists from Hungary joined with their colleagues from Austria and Bohemia under the aegis of Konrad Celtis' *Sodalitas litteraria Danubiana*; the leading personality from whom they were expecting guidance, however, was no longer Ficino, the Italian, but the greatest European thinker north of the Alps – Erasmus of Rotterdam.[22] In 1526 the humanist officials at the court at Buda, short of money but full of expectations, were now looking towards the Dutch scholar. Many of them carried on correspondence with Erasmus, and their enthusiasm was shared by the young Hungarian and Bohemian king, Louis, as well as his wife, Mary of the Habsburg dynasty, who also had leanings towards the teaching of Luther. The learned gatherings at Buda, and

Hungary's Renaissance court, however, were not to be long-lived: in a few
months' time the independent Hungarian kingdom and state would come to
an end. Suleiman the Magnificent had a decisive victory over the king's army
in the battle of Mohács on 29 August 1526. The king himself died on the
battlefield and the sultan captured Buda, admired and ransacked Matthias's
palace, destroyed the Bibliotheca Corvina, taking as booty some of the books
as well as some of the sculptures outside the palace including the colossal
Hercules symbolising the king. Erasmus consoled the young widowed queen,
who was fleeing from Buda castle, by writing for her his *Vidua christiana* and
Luther by dedicating to her his *Vier tröstliche Psalmen.*

The political consequences are well-known: the military catastrophe
brought with it not only the plundering of the greater part of the country, but
also the political partitioning of Hungary. In one part, the country's mightiest
baron, John I of Szapolyai (1526–40), in another, Ferdinand I (1526–64), the
younger brother of Charles V was crowned king. Neither of the two could get
the upper hand over the other. Ferdinand and his successors were only able to
keep power over the western and northern part of the country, while John and
those who succeeded him established power in eastern Hungary. It was here
that the Hungarian principality of Transylvania evolved, under Turkish
tutelage. Finally, the occupation of Buda in 1541 meant Turkish rule in the
middle part of the country. Hungary was split into three for 150 years. What
could the fate of the Renaissance be in these circumstances?

The survival of the humanist tradition and the victory of Reformation

Destruction was immense: many new Rennaissance works of art and a great
part of Hungary's medieval buildings and institutions was destroyed. The
royal court ceased to function in its earlier form, and the same happened to
the bishops' seat (that had been made into magnificent centres of humanist
learning), either because they were taken by the Turks, or had to be converted
into military strongholds, or because they were terminated by the triumphant
Reformation. Continuity was only observable in western, northern and
eastern cities and in barons' courts in these regions, which were less seriously
affected by the warfare. Social development in towns, however, was rather
slow in fifteenth century Hungary, and the middle class were leading their
lives according to medieval standards as late as the early sixteenth century,
which meant that they were not a dynamic force promoting the new type of
culture. The aristocracy, on the other hand, suffered severe losses in the war,
with the majority having fallen either at Mohács or having died in the
decades to follow. It took more than a quarter of a century before a new
aristocracy was born from talented and unscrupulous individuals, one that
was receptive to a higher brand of culture. In want of a suitable social basis

and institutional background, there was only one stratum of society that could become the repository of humanism and Renaissance values – the intellectuals.

Under the reign of King Matthias and his successors, the rapid flourishing of the economy, administration and education had enormously increased the demand for professional people. This had meant an accelerated increase in the number of church clericals, and even more so in the number of secular intellectuals.[23] An important circumstance for the spread of humanism was that a significant part of these people had attended foreign universities. The universities of Hungary, founded by Louis the Great, Sigismund and Matthias, had not survived, and by the sixteenth century not a single one remained in Hungary. Higher education was coming from abroad, and this practice assumed great proportions. In the fifteenth century, for example, about 5,500 people attended foreign universities from a country with a population of 3.5 million. Only the well-to-do could afford Italy or Paris, but from the late fifteenth century onwards, people were already importing a humanist education from the less remote universities of Vienna and Cracow. From the 1530s, Wittenberg took the leading role in that respect, where students from Hungary became staunch adherents not only of the Reformation, but also of Melanchthon's humanist ideals concerning education. Towards the end of the century, Heidelberg replaced the ever-more orthodoxical Wittenberg as a centre of learning for Hungarian Protestants, to be followed, in the next century, by Dutch and English universities. In the mean time, the attraction of the Italian universities did not wane; worthy of mention here are the universities of liberal Padua, which Protestants could also attend, and Rome, notably the Collegium Germanicum-Hungaricum, where the supporters of Catholic restoration received an excellent education. However disadvantageous it was for the country to have no university from the people's point of view, the fact that Hungarian students had to go abroad did have advantages: students required first-hand information about the most important achievements in science and scholarship, and could be present at the birth of the most up-to-date intellectual and religious doctrines.[24]

The intellectual stratum in the age of the Renaissance was, of course, extremely diversified. Those in the highest layer (made up mainly of people that had attended Padua University) were in top administrative posts either in the Habsburg-ruled part of the country or serving the prince of Transylvania; but in either case they remained devoted to humanist Latin literature. The fields in which they created lasting values were poetry and, in particular, historiography. The two new capital cities which substituted for Buda Pozsony in north-west Hungary (today, Bratislava in Slovakia) and Gyulafehérvár in Transylvania (today, Alba Iulia in Romania) – saw major intellectual academic centres emerging, but these could not compensate for

Matthias's capital.[25] Those sixteenth century Hungarian humanists whose work was appreciated by the whole of Europe and the scholarly world at large had to go abroad sooner or later: this is how Johannes Sambucus (1513–84), the philologist and author of emblem books, went to work in Vienna,[26] while Andreas Dudich, the philologist and philosopher (1533–89), continued his work in Poland.[27] The same is true, unfortunately, for other outstanding figures of the cultural élite: Valentin Bakfark (1507–76), perhaps the greatest lute player and composer of the century, had his successes in Poland, France and Italy, and was able to publish his work abroad only.[28]

It is the middle layer of the intelligentsia, whose members first went to Cracow and later chiefly to Wittenberg to study, to whom the credit goes for the introduction and dissemination of the Reformation in Hungary. The country, including the parts under Turkish rule, was 90 per cent Protestant by the end of the sixteenth century. Everywhere, the emergence of the Reformation was closely tied to the intellectual fermentation produced by the Renaissance and Humanism, but this was particularly true in the case of Hungary, where it was not only a religious movement but had also a social political, cultural and national character. The merits of the Reformation in the improvement of the nation's cultural and educational level can hardly be exaggerated. It was within the framework of the Reformation that schools in the smallest villages were organised and the spread of literacy began. In the cities, people with a humanist education were establishing excellent secondary schools, which sometimes provided, in addition to the *artes*, theology and philosophy at a level comparable to foreign universities. The leading figures of the Reformation wrote and published textbooks, and foreign books were reprinted for these schools, for example the minor works of Erasmus. The children were taught Greek and Roman classics. They were encouraged to perform plays especially written for them. Printing presses were needed to provide all this material, and for this sponsorship was obtained from the local authorities and individual aristocrats.[29] Theological debates, both written and oral, were going on, not so much between Catholics and Protestants as might be expected, but between particular reformist trends, each and every one of which was now gaining ground and finding adherents in Hungary. Besides the suporters of Luther, Melanchthon, Zwingli and Calvin, the more extreme movemens were present, such as anabaptism, anti-trinitarianism, and Judaising sect (Sabbatarians) that rejected the New Testament.[30] In the literary field, those religious reformers whose careers are worthy of mention include Péter Melius Juhász (1536–72), organiser of the Calvinist church in Hungary; István Szegedi Kis (1504–72), who wrote his Latin theological works in the Turkish-ruled part of the country and published them in Geneva and Basle; Ferenc Dávid (*c.* 1510–85), the leading figure of anti-trinitarianism and the founder of the Unitarian church; and Péter Bornemisza (1535–85), Lutheran minister, and outstanding playwright of his time.[31]

The rise of Hungarian literature

One of the novelties of this literature, however, was that the majority was written in the vernacular, not in Latin. The first written text in Hungarian (i.e. Magyar) dates back to the twelfth century, but the role of the vernacular had only been secondary up to the sixteenth century. This did not change during the humanist period, only beginning to alter with the collapse following the battle of Mohács. National aspirations, however, were already in evidence in the Latin-language literature, not as an antithesis to humanist cosmopolitanism but rather intricately interwoven with it. Johannes Vitéz, Janus Pannonius and the historians of King Matthias had been unswerving in their patriotism, devoutly serving Hungaria – or Pannonia, to use the humanists' term. In face of constant threat, this nationalistic-patriotic fervour was especially emphasised in their literature, leading to the creation of myths of a particular kind. This was how, in the battles against the Turks, the image of the country as the 'bastion of Christianity' was born, while the confrontation with the German empire revitalised the Hun myth about the origins of the Hungarians. Later, after the battle of Mohács and under the influence of the biblicism of the Reformation, the ideology of a Hungarian-Jewish historical parallelism appeared: both were a chosen people, punished by God for their sins, to be relieved of their suffering only if they regained their faith. The cult of Attila, characteristic of a great and powerful nation, was replaced by the image of a small nation being threatened from many sides, and this latter image badly needed the cohesion provided by a unified national language.

Even the Italophile King Matthias had not been insensitive to the Hungarian language and the old traditions. As Galeotto Marzio tells us, Hungarian 'heroic sagas', and love-songs were often sung on special occasions in the king's court, alongside the international, 'modern' Burgundian-Flandrian music.[32] In his charters the king reproached Emperor Frederick III, for his wish to extirpate 'the Hungarian language', while István Werböczy (1458–1541), the eminent jurist, when acting as envoy for Louis II in Venice in 1519, made his opening speech before the Doge in Hungarian, in spite of his excellent Latin. This cult of language and its role in the country's literature was even more emphatic in the decades after the battle of Mohács, when it served as a defensive reflex for the nation. To this was added the stress of the Reformation on the vernacular languages, one of the most effective means against the old church. The new religious teachings had to be got across to the widest masses, who spoke no Latin. Hungarian became the language of the service and the scriptures had to be available to the people in vernacular. Several partial bible translations had been made before, but the publishing of a complete Hungarian Bible was a task for the Reformation to carry out, a patriotic undertaking and a humanist achievement at the same time. The first complete New Testament in printed form appeared in 1541, the work of

János Sylvester, who used Erasmus's text. He made an excellent translation and, to facilitate his work, wrote and published the first grammar of the Hungarian language. The year in which Sylvester wrote that 'the nation could now be proud of reading God's message in Hungarian' was the year when the Turks occupied Buda.[33]

This was the beginning of the sudden proliferation of works in Hungarian: actively engaged in it were not only learned humanists and protestant theologians, but also village teachers, scribes and office clerks in cities and towns, the entire lower stratum of the educated people. The dominant genre – besides translations of the Bible, treatises on theology, religious polemics and devotional books – was poetry of all kinds. Much in demand during the Reformation, a host of liturgical hymns, rewordings of Luther's chants, paraphrases of psalms, didactic and satirical poems, as well as a vast number of versified chronicles were written. In the middle of the century, these latter had become the predominant genre, an interesting amalgamation of medieval (partly oral) tradition, new religious ideals and vulgarised humanist learning. A variety of themes appeared in versified form, ranging from books of the Bible (mainly the Old Testament), old Hungarian sagas, motifs from Hungarian history (including the deeds of János Hunyadi and Matthias), the events of the wars against the Turks, the heroic defence of the border fortresses, to some of Boccaccio's stories, the *Aeneis* and Enea Silvio Piccolomini's *De duobus amantibus*. The form of these versified chronicles did not resemble the poetry of the Renaissance. The content, however, showed a strong affinity, with its unity of humanist, Reformation and national ideals. The valour of those fighting the Turks was praised in terms of the Renaissance concepts of *humanitas* and *virtus*: the love-stories rejoiced over the lovers overcoming social inequalities; the story of the prodigal son appeared in a colourful form to suit Renaissance tastes; and the figure of Judith and those of the Maccabees manifested as national heroes. The prose and the drama of the age were written in a similar vein: the play *Magyar Elektra* by Péter Bornemisza (1558) and the fables and short stories by preacher, writer and printer Gáspár Heltai (+ 1574) are cases in point.[34]

The second efflorescence of Hungarian Renaissance

The victory of the Reformation and the flourishing of the new Hungarian literature compensated for the slowing down of the Renaissance advance that had once been so vigorous. This also facilitated the second efflorescence of the Renaissance, on an unprecedented scale, when the country could take breath after the series of political and military crises. This took place during the last decades of the sixteenth century. As a result of the mutual recognition of the status quo (1570) between the Habsburg king and the Hungarian prince of

Transylvania; as well as of the fragile peace treaty (1568) with the Turks, a period of relative consolidation followed, to last several decades. The major beneficiary of this process was the new aristocracy, which, by fair and unfair means alike, had accumulated enormous economic and political power during the troubled years following the battle of Mohács. The wealth of some of the aristocracy compared with that of smaller Italian or German princes. These people were genuine creatures of the age of the Renaissance: they often changed allegiance between the two Hungarian rulers, betraying first one and then the other; they exploited the peasants and oppressed them, yet at the same time they fought heroically against the Turks, risked their lives in battle leading their underlings' troops against the enemy, initiated modern business enterprises and, most importantly, were not at all insensitive to culture. These new magnates sent their sons to the universities of Italy and Germany, led a Renaissance way of life in their fortresses (which also served as strongholds against the Turkish threat), tried to obtain for their libraries the best of contemporary Italian and French literature, and, on special occasions, displayed everything that had once been characteristic of the Renaissance splendour of the royal court. The royal court no longer existed but about twelve aristocrats substituted their own seats for it, and although they could not compete with the king's court, they still preserved the values of Renaissance culture for later centuries.[35]

The eminent scholar, Johannes Sambucus, published the most complete edition of Janus Pannonius' poetry in 1569. A year before, he had published Antonio Bonfini's *Rerum Hungaricarum decades*, to be translated by Gáspár Heltai into Hungarian after a few years. Several works written in the humanist era of Matthias similarly saw the light in this period. The aristocrats tried to obtain some of the relics that had once been in the king's possession, and to emulate his interest in Italian art and culture. The Italian orientation was especially strongly felt in the court of the Transylvanian princes. Since 1571, the Hungarian princes of Transylvania had come from the Báthory dynasty, the founder – Stephen Báthory – later becoming King of Poland. In his time, the prince's court at Gyulafehérvár (Alba Iulia) very much resembled an Italian court, but the similarity became even more striking in the reign of his nephew and successor, Sigismund Báthory. Foreign diplomats, travellers and envoys often wrote in surprise that all the leading politicians of his country spoke Italian, and sometimes they used Italian in their private correspondence. Sigismund Báthory was mainly enthusiastic about music: he had an Italian orchestra and choir, and he himself played several instruments besides composing music.[36]

The 'renaissance of the Hungarian Renaissance' was not, however, confined to the courts aristocrats. In the regions a safe distance away from the areas controlled by the Turks, nobles and aristocrats built mansions and castles one after the other, in the towns rich burghers competed with one another in decorating their houses in Renaissance style. The most spectacular development, however, was in literature: the new works written in the epic poetry genre in the last decades of the century already showed the hallmarks of the Renaissance, and bespoke a literary language brought to perfection. This was the time for the genuine adaptation and assimilation of Latin and Italian Renaissance poetry into Hungarian, in which no small role was played by the first real classic of Hungarian poetry, Bálint Balassi (1554–94).

Educated by the Protestant writer Péter Bornemisza, Balassi was also a member of the new aristocracy, who spent years fighting the Turks in several fortresses along the border, and was well versed in traditional Hungarian poetry. His readings, however, included mainly works by Latin humanists and Italian Renaissance poets, and his own poems created what could be called the Hungarian version of Petrarchism. His cycles of love-lyrics and his pastoral play testify to a fully matured poetic language, and his disciple, the poet János Rimay (c. 1570–1631), rightly said of him that the language of his works had reached the summit of eloquence. Balassi created a synthesis of the poetry-writing tradition of the time: his poems, on the life of the common warrior fighting the Turks, display the rigidly closed composition of Renaissance poetry. In the tradition of the religious poetry of the Reformation, he wrote the gems of Hungarian religious verse in the spirit of the psalm paraphrases of Théodore de Bèze and George Buchanan, which are unsurpassed even today.[37]

The country's history did not make it possible for the Hungarian Renaissance to come up to the highest European standards in the fine arts, music, philosophy, science and scholarship, notwithstanding the promising beginnings. This was not to be. It was only in poetry, written in the isolated Hungarian language and hardly understood outside the country, that the Hungarians excelled. This explains why the Hungarian Renaissance is given so little credit in Europe's intellectual circles. Its significance from the nation's point of view, on the other hand, can hardly be over-emphasised: this was the period when the foundations of Hungarian national culture were laid down. The greatest monarch of Hungary's history is Matthias, that Renaissance king whose example remained one of the sources of the national consciousness for centuries. At the same time, while the most calamitous and tragic era in Hungarian history is the sixteenth century, it was this same period which forged a national identity which has remained one of the strongest points of Hungarian culture.

NOTES

1 D. Dercsényi, *Nagy Lajos kora* (Budapest, 1941); *Gli Angioini di Napoli e di Ungheria* (Rome, 1974); *Louis the Great. King of Hungary and Poland*, ed. S.B.

Vardy, G. Grosschmid and L.S. Domonkos, (New York, 1986).

2 H. Horváth, *Zsigmond király és kora – König Sigismund und seine Zeit* (Budapest, 1937); E. Mályusz, *Zsigmond király uralma Magyarországon* (Budapest, 1984); L. Beke, E. Marosi, and T. Wehli (eds.), *Művészet Zsigmond király korában. 1387– 1437*, 2 vols. (Budapest, 1987).

3 T. Kardos, *Studi e ricerche umanistiche italo-ungheresi* (Debrecen, 1967), 37–8.

4 'In Austria vero dementis est querere Romam, aut Platonem apud Hungaros vestigare' in *Fontes Rerum Austriacarum* ii. Abt. Dipl. et Acta LXI, 152.

5 *Ad Galeottum Narniensem* in: Jani Pannonii, *Opera Latine et Hungarice*, ed. S.V. Kovács (Budapest, 1972), 242–9.

6 Cf. J.M. Bak and B.K. Király (eds.), *From Hunyadi to Rákóczi. War and Society in Late Medieval and Early Modern Hungary* (New York, 1982).

7 T. Klaniczay, G. Török and G. Stangler (eds.), *Schallaburg '82. Matthias Corvinus und die Renaissance in Ungarn* (Vienna 1982).

8 K. Nehring, *Matthias Corvinus, Kaiser Friedrich III und das Reich* (Munich 1975).

9 J. Vitéz de Zredna, *Opera quae supersunt*, ed. I. Boronkai, (Budapest, 1980) (Bibliotheca Scriptorum Medii Recentistique Aevorum S.N., III).

10 J. Huszti, *Janus Pannonius* (Pécs, 1931); J. Horváth, *Az irodalmi műveltség megoszlása.Magyar humanizmus* (Budapest, 1935); T. Klaniczay, *Mattia Corvino e l'umanesimo italiano* (Rome, 1974); T. Kardos and S.V. Kovács (eds.), *Janus Pannonius (Tanulmányok)* (Budapest, 1975); R. Manselli, *Umanesimo ungherese ed umanesimo europeo: primo tentativo d'un bilancio* in T. Klaniczay (ed.) *Rapporti veneto-ungheresi all'epoca del Rinascimento* (Budapest, 1975); 43–50; M.D. Birnbaum, *Janus Pannonius, Poet and Politician* (Zagreb, 1981).

11 Z. Nagy, *Ricerche cosmologiche nella corte umanistica di Giovanni Vitéz* in *Rapporti veneto-ungheresi* . . . 65–93; K. Csapodi-Gárdonyi, *Die Bibliothek des Johannes Vitéz* (Budapest, 1984).

12 Cs. Csapodi and K. Csapodi-Gárdonyi, *Bibliotheca Corviniana. The Library of King Matthias Corvinus, King of Hungary* (Budapest, 1969); Cs. Csapodi, *The Corvinian Library. History and Stock* (Budapest, 1973).

13 J. Huszti, 'Tendenze platonizzanti alla corte di Mattia Corvino' in *Giornale critico della filosofia italiana*, 9 (1930), 135–62, 220–87.

14 The Corvinian manuscript still exists in the Biblioteca Marciana (Venice).

15 J. Balogh, *A művészet Mátyás király udvarában*, 2 vols. (Budapest, 1966); Td., *Die Anfänge der Renaissance in Ungarn* (Graz, 1975); R. Feuer-Tóth, *Renaissance-Baukunst in Ungarn* (Budapest, 1981); Klaniczay, Török and Stangler (eds.), *Schallaburg '82* . . .; B. Rajeczky (ed.), *Magyarország zenetörténete I. Középkor* (Budapest, 1988), 106–32.

16 'Pannoniam alteram Italiam reddere conabatur.' In A. de Bonfinis *Rerum Ungaricarum Decades*, ed. I. Fógel, B. Iványi, L. Juhász, vol. IV/1, (Budapest, 1941); 135 (Bibliotheca Scriptorum Medii Recentisque Aevorum).

17 Cf. G. Martius Narniensis, *De egregie, sapienter, iocose dictis ac factis regis Mathiae*, ed. L. Juhász (Lipsiae, 1934), 34 (Bibliotheca Scriptorum Medii Recentisque Aevorum).

18 Cf. T. Klaniczay, *L'ambiente intellettuale di Galeotto Marzio in Ungheria* in *Umanesimo e Rinascimento a Firenze e Venezia* (Firenze, Olschki, 1983), vol. III, (Miscellanea di studi in onore di Vittore Branca, III).

19 Cf. Klaniczay, Török and Stangler (eds.), *Schallaburg '82*, 560–694.
20 J. Balogh, 'La cappella Bakócz in Esztergom' in *Acta Historiae Artium* (Budapest), 3 (1956), 1–197.
21 I. Mészáros, *XVI. századi városi iskoláink és a 'studia humanitatis'* (Budapest, 1981).
22 I. Trencsényi-Waldapfel, *Erasmus és magyar barátai* (Budapest, 1941); Á. Szalay-Ritoók, *Erasmus and die ungarischen Intellektuellen des 16. Jahrhundert*, in A. Buck (ed.), *Erasmus und Europa* (Wiesbaden, 1988), 111–28.
23 G. Bónis, *A jogtudó értelmiség a Mohács előtti Magyarországon* (Budapest, 1971); E. Mályusz, *Egyházi társadalom a középkori Magyarországon* (Budapest, 1971).
24 Gy. Székely, *Le rôle des universités hongroises du Moyen Age et des études universitaires à l'étranger dans la formation des intellectuels de Hongrie* in J. Le Goff and B. Köpeczi (ed.) *Intellectuels français, intellectuels hongrois, XIIIe-XXe siècles* (Budapest-Paris, 1985), 53–64; T. Klaniczay, *Les intellectuels dans un pays sans universités (Hongrie: XVIe siècle)*, in Le Goff and Köpeczi, 99–109.
25 T. Klaniczay, 'Le mouvement académique à la Renaissance et le cas de la Hongrie', *Hungarian Studies*, 2 1986, 13–34.
26 H. Gerstinger, *Johannes Sambucus als Handschriftensammler*, in *Festschrift der Nationalbibliothek in Wien* (Vienna 1926), 251–400; E. Bach, *Un humaniste hongrois en France. Jean Sambucus et ses relations littéraires*. (Szeged, 1932); E. Várady, 'Relazioni di Giovanni Zsámboky (Sambucus) coll'umanesimo italiano', *Corvina* (Budapest), 15 (1935), 3–54; A. Buck, *Leben und Werk des Joannes Sambucus (Zsámboky János)* in J. Sambucus, *Emblemata*, fac. edn (Budapest, 1982); I. Téglásy, *A nyelv-és irodalomelmélet kezdetei Magyarországon (Sylvester Jánostól Zsámboky Jánosig)* (Budapest, 1988).
27 P. Costil, *André Dudith, humaniste hongrois, 1533–1589* (Paris, 1935); C. Vasoli, 'Andreas Dudith-Sbardellati e la disputa sulle comete', in *Rapporti veneto-ungheresi . . .*, 299–323.
28 O. Gombosi, *Der Lautenist Valentin Bakfark. Leben und Werke (1507–1576)* (Budapest, 1967).
29 M. Bucsay, *Geschichte des Protestantismus in Ungarn* (Stuttgart, 1959); T. Klaniczay, 'Réforme et transformations culturelles en Hongrie', in *Les Réformes: enracinement socio-culturel* (Paris, 1985), 233–8.
30 A. Pirnát, *Die Ideologie der siebenbürger Antitrinitarier in den 1570er Jahren* (Budapest, 1961); R. Dán and A. Pirnát (eds.), *Antitrinitarianism in the Second Half of the 16th Century* (Budapest-Leiden, 1982); R. Dán, *Az erdélyi szombatosok és Péchi Simon* (Budapest, 1987).
31 I. Nemeskürty, *Bornemisza Péter az ember és az iró* (Budapest, 1959); T. Bartha (ed.), *A máscdik helvét hitvallás Magyarországon és Méliusz életműve* (Budapest, 1967) (Studia et Acta Ecclesiastica, II); G. Kathona, *Fejezetek a török hódoltsági reformáció történetéból* (Budapest, 1974); M. Balázs, *Az erdélyi antitrinitarizmus az 1560-as évek végén* (Budapest, 1988).
32 Martius Narniensis, *De egregie* 18.
33 J. Balázs, *Sylvester János és kora* (Budapest, 1958).
34 T. Klaniczay, '*A magyar reformáció irodalma*' in, *Reneszánsz és barokk* (Buda-

pest, 1961), 64–150; B. Varjas, *A magyar reneszánsz irodalom társadalmi gyökerei* (Budapest, 1982).

35 T. Klaniczay, 'La haute aristocratie, principal soutien de la Renaissance et du baroque en Hongrie' in *Renaissance, maniérisme, baroque* (Paris, 1972), 224–34; A.R. Várkongi (ed.), *Magyar reneszánsz udvari kultúra* (Budapest, 1987).

36 E. Kastner, 'Cultura italiana alla corte transilvana nel secolo XVI', *Corvina*, (1922), 40–56.

37 S. Eckhardt, *Balassi Bálint* (Budapest, 1941); T. Klaniczay, 'Réalité et idéalisation dans la poésie pétrarquiste de Bálint Balassi', *Acta Litteraria* 8 (1966), 343–70; I. Bán, 'Il petrarchismo di Bálint Balassi e le sue fonti veneziane e padovane' in V. Branca (ed.), *Venezia e Ungheria nel Rinascimento* (Firenze, 1973); A. Di Francesco, *A pásztorjáték szerepe Balassi Bálint költöi fejlödésében* (Budapest, 1979).

TEN

POLAND

ANTONI MĄCZAK

Only in Italy has the Renaissance – no matter how defined – been treated as a genuine, native phenomenon. When looking for it in other countries (with the possible exception of the Burgundian circle), the first question used to be about Italian influences. The Renaissance civilisation in a European periphery raises the question of cultural, and in particular artistic, transplants. But the discussion in terms of a dichotomy of Italian influences on the one hand, and native elements of Renaissance civilisation on the other, can easily mislead the student of the period, and surely this is not the only way of interpreting the Renaissance in the north.[1]

The influence of Italy, as well as that of other countries prominent in the sphere of fine arts and of letters, is difficult to overestimate. However, in each country the resultant of various cultural factors was different. The new attitude to the classical antiquity was but a part of the cultural restructuring of the sixteenth-century Latin Europe to which it gave a new identity and a new sense of unity. Like Italy of the Quattro and Cinquecento, each society drew both from its own past and from foreign influences. This is particularly clear if we understand the Renaissance not only as an artistic and intellectual trend or style, but as a civilisation including systems of power and authority.

The Renaissance: what's in a name? This question asked with a country like Poland in mind may get answers very different from the ones given by the students of the Italian scene. In each case particular problems should be considered. From the Polish perspective they may be as follows:

- Was the Renaissance the determinant of a period?
- How were Italian (and also German, Netherlandish) influences merged with local traditions, and how were Renaissance symbols understood and interpreted there?
- What did this country bring to the common treasury of the Renaissance civilisation?

There are arguments for regarding the Renaissance as an eponym of a period. This period has been sometimes delineated very broadly, roughly between about 1500 and the 1650s. While the mid–1650s were a major break in Polish political and economic history because of devastating invasions of Russians, Swedes and Transylvanians, the trend now is for a more restricted approach. A recent Renaissance volume of a history of art in Poland embraces the period 1500–1640, but its authors try meticulously to distinguish between works they attribute to the Renaissance (including Mannerism), and to the Baroque.[2] The late Professor Jan Białostocki in his lucid synthesis of the art of the Renaissance in eastern Europe, i.e. in Hungary, Bohemia and Poland, hardly reached beyond the first quarter of the seventeenth century.[3] He underscored diverse asynchronisms:

Humanism – even in Italy, its place of origin – precedes by a few generations the crystallization of artistic phenomena that we classify as Renaissance style. The art of Renaissance was born in Italy; and it took more than a hundred years before it spread all over the Continent . . . before the new merged with the old into an acceptable formula - new enough to satisfy the need for fashionable modernity, yet old enough not to be felt as something foreign.

According to Białostocki, 'in the east, in Hungary, Slovakia or Poland, we can meet the Renaissance – at least in the early stages of its development – in a more original, pure form' than in contemporary France, Germany, Spain and England where late Gothic style was reaching its climax. Adam Miłobędzki writes: 'Pure Renaissance architecture in its Tuscan version was adopted by only two European countries: Hungary and then Poland.'[4] But it was a particular merger of both styles that was characteristic for Poland. The Renaissance art came there as highly elitist: the king and the highest ecclesiastical lord were the first patrons. At that time it was just a transplant of 'pure, original' foreign civilisation. But in one or two generations, Renaissance art would become generally accepted and transformed according to current local needs and tastes.

So the preliminary answer to the above question may be as follows. The Renaissance art, initially known only to a small minority of Poles and created there by foreign hand, became an instant success and already by the second generation, before the middle of the sixteenth century, was privatised by the upper classes. It would shortly be introduced into popular art as well. Active attitude and the taste of patrons were possibly even more important for the development of Polish versions of the Renaissance style than the talents of native artists. All works of art that enriched the national landscape are regarded without much discussion as the national heritage. This was also the case in the early stage of the Renaissance in Poland when, for example – the Sigismund chapel in Cracow – a true masterpiece by any European standards – was designed by Italian masters and hewn in stone by mostly Italian and Hungarian craftsmen, the only noticeable native contribution being the acceptance of the design by the king himself.[5] This is not an unusual attitude both today and in the past. Giovanni 'di Bologna' (or Giambologna) was for example, in his lifetime completely absorbed by his Italian environment and regarded – by foreign visitors at least – as an Italian. And for that matter, Georg Friedrich Handel is now as English as Henry Purcell. Yet in the case discussed here, this was not a balanced exchange of talents and artistic ideas.

Early Renaissance art made Poland particularly and directly indebted to Italy (to Florence but also Venice). Only in painting and particularly in the casting of bronze was the German influence in the early sixteenth century a dominating factor; bronze plaques and slabs from the Vischers' workshop are visible in most prominent places in Cracow churches (156; 158; 161–3). Later, up until the end of the eighteenth century, Poland became a Promised Land for artists from the Lombard Lake District.[6] The active presence of foreign artists remained a constant factor in early modern Polish civilisation at least until the end of the period. And yet, while few Polish artists got any recognition abroad, already around the middle of the sixteenth century there emerged a true native talent, Jan Michałowicz, who was able to absorb and to transform the Italian artistic message.

Particularly characteristic of Renaissance art in Poland was the influence of patrons, chiefly a substantial gentry and magnatery, but also town patriciates. In some later and larger artistic programmes, it is possible to trace a sort of enchantment with works of art that they had seen abroad; this however would be more characteristic of the Baroque.[7] The special demands of lesser sponsors were also important: they compelled artists to follow patterns familiar to them. The Sigismund Chapel and the early tombs created in Cracow, as well as the courtyard arcades of the Wawel Castle were examples of the new artistic style and were reproduced in various scales all over the country.

Already, by mid-century, Renaissance art in Poland was developing clear individual styles. While it constantly drew from foreign sources (Italian, German, Netherlandish), it preserved its identity. Possibly both the timing of Italian influences on Poland and some unfathomable traits of social psychology contributed to the spread of mannerist art. This particular trend would become characteristic of the art on the Vistula and prepare a triumph of Baroque there.

Another peculiarity of the Polish Renaissance was its rural character. Destructions and reconstructions in the subsequent centuries changed the balance: only a few noble residences would resist the portentous challenges of time. One reason for this was that in the sixteenth century stone and brick made up probably less than one per cent of the architecture in Poland. What remains and dominates our image of that art, are tombs and altars in churches, as well as town halls.

Italian urban art had been adapted to the tastes of the nobles, but it also left its imprint on the cities before they became enveloped in the long-term crisis of the seventeenth century. In towns it reflected the growing awareness of urban ruling groups, chiefly merchants who would be plagued by the economic depression somewhat later than the artisans. Town halls, urban parochial churches were being rebuilt, often with visible traces of earlier, Gothic constructions. Direct Italian influence was visible on a greater scale only in Cracow and Poznań, while numerous town houses were being rebuilt and redecorated according to the pattern set by Cracow's principal public buildings. The blossoming of the grain and timber trades in the later sixteenth and early seventeenth centuries also brought about a rebuilding of some towns directly connected with the Baltic: Gdańsk, Elbląg and Toruń. These centres, chiefly Protestant, were greatly influenced by the northern Mannerism; the Italian influence was mostly indirect.[8]

Eventually, this coexistence of rather a somewhat provincial eclecticism of the three styles from the Gothic to the early Baroque, became characteristic of the Polish milieu. Many churches remained partly Gothic, but their constructions were modified by Renaissance chapels and their interiors enriched by, often splendid, sepulchres. These would remain the most characteristic trait of the Polish Renaissance. The likeness in stone of Sigismundus Augustus was located above that of his royal father in the Sigismund Chapel (104, 202), such a 'double-decker' became the fashion with wealthy noble families; the idea itself was older, however (109).[9] If room was available, a family sepulchre could occupy a large space of a wall with its numerous pilasters and arcaded niches. There were even places made for children and babies: some Polish parents seemed to have been particularly prone to commemorate offspring. The great demand for such art found an answer in almost serial production of sculptures by Italian ateliers.[10] Such 'mass-production' tended to level tastes but eventually the quality of that sepulchral art remained impressive indeed. However, it would be wrong to conclude that the general trend was towards uniformity. Both the principal Italian artists and their Polish patrons early on appreciated Manneristic attitudes and decorations. But 'disharmonious, unclassical, incorrect, and unrestrained' forms, as Białostocki described them, coexisted with charmingly quiet, almost sentimental ones (344–61). It was the latter style and taste which eventually dominated sepulchral art. In the Renaissance, Poles did not die: they were merely sleeping and dreaming. Unlike the Valois at St Denis, they never displayed their raw bones and worms did not trouble their bodies or souls. Only a gust of wind raised their fluttering robes or mantles (202–5; but 195).[11]

It would only be a slight exaggeration to suggest that the Polish Renaissance was split according to social classes. The art sponsored principally by the nobility had its roots in Florence. The often flamboyant gable parapet, a decoration most characteristic of town halls and many houses (in fact for a few noble residences as well), came directly from Bohemia and Moravia (235–57; 269; 276). The urban art in the north of the country in the later sixteenth and the early seventeenth century was, however, primarily influenced by Dutch artists. The Gdańsk Armoury, built (1602–05) by Anton van Opbergen [313–15], was strikingly similar – if less extravagant in its construction and decorations – to the Exchange building in Copenhagen and other public constructions from Christian IV's times.

In one sense, Protestantism, the German ethnic identity of the ruling groups in the cities of Royal Prussia, as well as the interaction between merchants who worked their commerce around the Baltic, were creating a special artistic style which strongly influenced the Renaissance in Poland. The ancient capital of the Teutonic Order, Marienburg, later a seat of a royal governor and centre of a royal estate, was given a vast new Renaissance and later a Baroque decoration which, however, did nothing to destroy the core thirteenth/fourteenth century construction. What was being built anew did not always conform to acknowledged contemporaneous Italian principles of art. Local masters were sometimes influenced by their surroundings; in some parts of the country, like Masovia, parochial churches graciously combined elements of the old and new. Eventually a simple, local type of church was created, usually with one nave and Gothic proportions; distinctive decorations were employed on the gable covering the façade outside the church, and this was followed through internally on the vault. Inspiration might have come from collegiate churches built by Bernardo Morando in Zamość (after 1587–1600) and by Giambattista of Venice in Pułtusk (1560) (275, 330), but the original patterns were imaginatively developed and, eventually, in the first half of the seventeenth century, became the dominant style in central Poland, giving it a unique artistic character.

The coexistence of various styles remained characteristic for Polish architecture and each century added its heritage on top of its predecessors. This is why the Renaissance, while hailed by art historians, has been rather put in the shadow by the quantitatively dominant Baroque architecture. It must be stressed, however, that the Renaissance contributed much to its fast and complete triumph. It was the style alone however that would create an artistic unity of the country and would broaden the western influence on the Ruthenian, and primarily Orthodox, parts of it. The Counter-Reformation – the Jesuits as well as the mendicant orders of St Francis – being the crucial factor.

However, in order to answer the question whether the Renaissance determined a period of the country's history, one has to consider other facets of that life-style. First of all, this is the question of the 'Renaissance state'.

A Renaissance state

It sounds like a paradox but Poland–Lithuania may be regarded as one of the most accomplished Renaissance states, as this term is understood by J.

Russell Major.[12] True, the problem in itself is rather ambiguous because scholars found no consensus about the very notion of the 'Renaissance state'. Professor Major discusses chiefly the France of the Valois kings and stresses its decentralised, consensual structure with representative assemblies playing the crucial role. To such Renaissance administrative-political structures he contrasts the modern state, which is basically absolutist. On the other hand, Federigo Chabod approaches the same general question of the 'Renaissance state' from the Italian perspective, Italy as it was in those days, composed of small states with their old and strong urban ruling elites, as well as with bureaucratic administrative systems which had been introduced there by the Spaniards (Chabod's analytic studies concentrated on Milan).[13]

Now, if France of the later Valois, if Milan, Venice la Serenissima, as well as Naples under the Spanish Habsburg rule, are all to be regarded as Renaissance states, it is not easy to find the common denominator for them all. It may even be concluded that the term does not correspond to a definable reality. However, it is useful to have a term for socio-political structures in which feudal relationships were losing their medieval importance, while the structure of professional bureaucratic administration was only in its prime. Most important for that period, and for the forthcoming power relationships in each particular country, was the nature of post-medieval elites, the role of city patriciates as royal officers, as well as the fate of representative assemblies. Possibly not a roughly uniform solution, but rather the very struggle for identity of the state, was characteristic of what may be called specifically Renaissance power structures. At the risk of a rather gross oversimplification of the Polish constitution, it is possible to say that Poland of the early sixteenth century had drawn somewhat extreme conclusions from common Latin-European dilemmas.

The Kingdom of Poland (since the union of Lublin with the grand duchy of Lithuania in 1569, it had been called the Commonwealth) was an immense *Ständestaat* of almost one million square kilometers (400,000 square miles) and about 11 million inhabitants. Its coherence was neither principally based upon personal ties of *La Féodalité*,[14] nor upon the servants of the crown. Since at least 1501–6 Poland, and since 1569 both parts of the Commonwealth, were one *corpus politicum* with a double corner-stone: the king and the two-chamber diet (Polish: *Sejm*). Unlike the French estates, the *Sejm* met rather regularly, at least once in two years. Provincial parliamentarism, developing during the second half of the fifteenth century, created regional patriotism but only in a few cases (Royal Prussia since 1454/1466, small parts of Silesia) was such political identity based on the awareness of deep historical traditions. In the mid-sixteenth century it was generally understood by the deputies that they represented the country (the nation) as a whole, and not their particular constituencies.[15] In this (and only in this) sense, could the Polish parliamentary system of the Renaissance have satisfied Edmund Burke. It is commonly known, however, that this principle so dear to the politically self-conscious and militant gentry, in particular in the third quarter of the sixteenth century, would be interpreted in a quite opposite manner by their grandsons.[16]

Was that constitutional system directly associated with the Renaissance? There are arguments for that.

Feudal ties had never been very strong and formal in Poland, and the kings of the originally Lithuanian Jagiellon dynasty had to strengthen their disputable rights to the Polish throne and to satisfy the Polish nobles' growing political awareness.[17] The long century of the Jagiellons in east-central Europe ended with the battle of Mohács (1526). Their country of origin, Lithuania, never became a sound dynastic power-base and, finally, as the true victors over the Jagiellons on the international scene (Bohemia and Hungary) emerged the Habsburgs, and on the domestic (Polish-Lithuanian), the nobility.

The latter competitor may be easily misinterpreted, however. During the fifteenth century the estate of the nobility in Poland (but not yet in Lithuania) was given allodial property rights (*possessio iure militari*) which became a strong foundation of civic rights and political independence of that numerous estate. What may be well compared to the habeas corpus – the principle of *Neminem captivabimus nisi iure victum* – was bestowed upon the nobility in a set of statutes as early as 1425–34. In the sixteenth century the nobles could, and did, identify themselves with the nation and the state, developing a quite mature (and in a sense modern) notion of citizenship: unlike their counterparts in many European monarchies, they stressed their *citizen*-and not *subject*-status. The price of these freedoms was to be paid by other prospective political elites – first of all by urban patriciates. It is all too easy to underscore the relatively broad franchise in Poland. At least equally important is the fact that the urban elites were not included in it, and that the upward mobility of the peasantry had been successfully blocked by the statute of 1492 and subsequent royal rulings in which the king (Sigismund I) declined to judge in cases between lords and their serfs (1520). Nevertheless, in the sixteenth and still in the early seventeenth century, the church offered an avenue of advancement for capable and ambitious commoners: bishops were among the principal dignitaries of the Commonwealth and built up their clerical clienteles.

The kings had the right to appoint numerous officers and dignitaries; according to a common estimate of the epoch, up to 40,000 posts, a rule-of-thumb figure which ought not to be taken for granted but which vividly manifests the interest and emotions of the public.[18] Yet the king's freedom of choice was strictly limited by the local self-government of the nobility and by the emerging power of the magnates. In most countries endowed with representative assemblies in early modern Europe, the political polarisation between the prince and the estates was blurred by the system of recruitment of officers. They were socially hardly discernible from the members of the assembly, and often formed a particular, if still informal, estate, or at least had a split identity, with loyalties divided between the prince and their peers.

This was also true of civil officers in Poland but – what was decisive – the kings here were not able to develop their own bureaucracy, here illustrating the 'Renaissance state' of the Italian type as Chabod saw it. Their early attempt to create judicial officers responsible only to the king failed early, and both the fiscal and the judiciary branches of the government became dependent upon the *Sejm* and/or upon the local self-government of the nobility.

A similar trend has been observed in France of the early Valois: each new office originally created to strengthen the king's grip over his subjects and over other already existing offices tended to change itself into a property (or rather leasehold). In Poland–Lithuania all local administrative and judicial officers became so-called 'county *terrestres* officers', i.e. officers representative of their county assemblies of the nobility and partly responsible to an assembly. Most of them were appointed by the king from four nominees of their peers, or upon suggestion of the assembly; *ius indigenatum* was very strictly observed.

Royal power in the provinces was limited by the sheer size of the country and its feeble communications system. This gap was filled by the richest stratum of the nobility, later called the magnatery. The strictly egalitarian ideology and pharaseology of the nobles in Poland–Lithuania was a cover for deep inequalities. A local power-base – that is, a power-base with country assemblies combined with landed wealth – created the position of a magnate house; for all practical purposes peers were created that way. A great noble with a strong local power-base could successfully demand high posts and favours from the king. The latter in turn needed officers loyal to him but also influential with the local gentry.[19]

This all too general description of power networks in Poland shows some traces familiar to a student of French history of that age. Royal power there was deeply shattered during the wars of religion, when aristocratic factions seemed much stronger. However, the outcome of that crisis was eventually different from the fate of the power system in Poland. A few points may be mentioned in this connection. Unlike the *noblesse de robe*, in Poland nobles were not created by virtue of holding office: it was a noble's social status that made him eligible for officers and dignities. Unlike in the west, the commoner or the city could participate in the power game only through the influence of money. The non-noble remained an outsider in the *corpus politicum* of the Commonwealth. Contemporary observers seriously discussed the Polish phenomenon; only in the following century, or for that matter, after the unfortunate reign of Henri Valois, would they wonder about its uniqueness and strangeness.

While it would be difficult to find direct links between the Polish 'democracy of the nobles' and Antiquity, leaders of the gentry at least since the middle of the sixteenth century were profoundly aware of, and interested in, such analogies. At that time everybody in Europe seemed to discover and exhibit with much enthusiasm his ancient roots. Respective myths gained wide currency in Poland as well ('Sarmatian' origins of the Polish nobility), while from the mid-fifteenth century Ruthenian-Lithuanian nobles elaborated their own Trojan myth; particular noble families from Lithuania cultivated their separate Roman ancestors. This was a not uncommon method of cultural modernisation. Another example of the link between current politics and the classical tradition, was a book entitled *De Senatu romano*, written by a future chancellor and *Hetman* (Polish supreme army commander), Jan Zamoyski, during his early studies at Padua University.[20]

More important than these trivialities of classical erudition were the observations of an anonymous visitor who wrote, in English, 'A relation of the state of Polonia and the united provinces of that Crowne, anno 1598'.[21] The authorship of this treatise is disputed: the editor sees in him Sir George Carew who had indeed visited Poland that year. On the other hand, a distinguished authority, Professor Stanisław Kot, argued for William Bruce, a Scottish scholar who spent long years in the country and had been teaching in Zamość where he could observe Chancellor Zamoyski rather closely. The author, it should be noted, was well informed and obviously close to the chancellor. A hypothesis which seems most probable (while it cannot be proven) is that it was Carew who commissioned a detailed report on the country, and possibly subjected the report to some copy-editing. Bruce's style and/or his Scottish spelling cannot be traced, but the text is strongly Zamoyski-oriented and clearly reflects a long-term familiarity with the country and the chancellor's faction. It also contains numerous allusions to England, so cannot be regarded as a simple translation.

In one of the most spirited chapters of the treatise, the anonymous author compares the Polish polity to the 'Germania' of Tacitus and even to the ancient Roman civic virtue. The common denominator of the ancient and current Polish polities was for him the patron–client relationship:

For that is the common bande of unity between the riche and the poore, bothe by that meanes participating in the benefittes of the lande, the one by commaunde, and the other by dependency of the Commaunders trencher, besides the correspondency of patrone, and Cliente, imitating in that the auncient Rommane state, which by that order was united and kepte in mutuall amity, the Patricians being the patrones of the Plebeians, counselling them, following theire suites, pleading theire causes, and defending them in all cases without fee or reward, and on the other syde the Clientes observing, honoring and with greate respecte wayting on theire patrons.[22]

In the next paragraph, the anonym underscores the analogy with the Germanic tribes: 'Tacitus description of the Germane traynes dothe most aptly expresse the Polish.' This comment sounds rather strange because the author was by no means an uncritical observer of Polish politics. He comments with true insight:

In Polonia the condition bothe of suche as serve, and of others, which lyve uppon small revenewes without dependency, is farre better then in Lithuania, being neyther so servile, nor so subjecte to the injuries of the potent. . . .[23]

The principal value of the Polish polity, as the author saw it, was that 'thys dependency makes that the multitude is not so easely drawne to the factions divorces, which some troublesome spirites seeke for the conversion of confusion of the State. . . . ' This was a concern very characteristic of the period.

Alluding to the Aristotelian classification of power systems, the author in question defines the Polish system of rule – with some hesitation – as 'Aristocraticall', and twice compares it to Venice. By '[a]bsurde articles which of a father of the realme make the kinge a pupill', the nobles 'clipt the eagles wynges' and 'seeke dayly to make hys condition worse then any free subiect'.[24] With such opinion the anonymous author anticipates the polity that would develop in the seventeenth century. However, this leads him to a comparison of the King of Poland with the Doge.[25] His elegant, erudite criticism reflects the viewpoint of King Stephen and his principal minister Zamoyski. It is very much in the Renaissance style that our author tries to classify the Polish polity in Aristotelian terms:

. . . some would inferr that this is a Democracy, seeing the Summum Imperium is chiefly in the Nobility, which maketh an huge multitude, those not being excluded, whoe for theire poverty are but serving men.[26]

He also classifies whatever he had learned about Polish history in the same way.

So the political class in Poland drew conclusions from the modern ideas of state. One may even comment that the magnatery shared in practice, if not in theory, that 'predatory' attitude towards the state which Professor Jack Hexter discovered in the political thought of Machiavelli.[27] The result would eventually astound the rest of Europe.

One of the curiosities the anonym touched in his 'Relation', was the multitude of religions in Poland. This was included by him into internal 'inconveniences and dangers of thys state'.[28] He comments 'for religion there is not in any countrey such variety, but that seems better to mainteyne the common peace, then yf the lande were devided into twooe bodies of religion, as France is.' Yet he hails Chancellor Zamoyski for his tolerance, 'whoe seeing the strength of the Common Wealthe to be devided into 3 mayne bodyes of great bulke, viz. Catholikes, Protestantes, and Greekish, knowes

that yf by pursuite, or depression any parte should be mooved to take armes
. . . there would follow the ruine of the State.[29]

Renaissance and the Reformation

Much of the discussion concerning the mutual relationship between the
Renaissance and the Reformation in European countries can be related to
Poland as well. The Reformation has left fewer direct traces on Polish
civilisation than the Counter-Reformation: Catholicism eventually became
very strongly interconnected with Polishness and with the defence of Polish
national identity.

The Reformation, which had already arrived in Poland already by the early
1520s, became a dominating religious and intellectual force during the
following half century.[30] Protestantism – roughly, Calvinism among the
nobility in Poland, Lutheranism among nobles and burghers in Royal Prussia,
and the Polish brethren chiefly in Little Poland – never took violent forms; the
nobility was not given to dogmatic discussion and, until later times, religious
disputes hardly disrupted local communities. Violence by the fanatical mob
would be introduced as a political tool by the Counter-Reformation only,
from the 1570s.

The general problems of the Reformation cannot be discussed here unless
they touch directly on the Renaissance. But in fact, the Reformation was in
many respects an important cultural and innovative factor. Various social
mechanisms were active here. First, after few edicts against the heretics, not
strongly enforced, both the last Jagiellon kings were tolerant of Protestanism;
from the mid-century onwards the Augsburg Confession (but not the
Reformed, that is, Calvinist one) was made legal and equal to Catholicism in
Royal Prussia; Sigismund Augustus even toyed with the idea of a national
church. This made the Commonwealth a haven for persecuted Protestants
and many of them came – Stancari, Blandrata, Fausto Sozzini and some
members of the Czech Brethren being outstanding examples of that immigration. The influx of Protestants increased Poland's contacts with most
intellectually active regions of Europe. It also widened the sphere of western
influence in the country: Lithuanian magnates were mighty and dedicated
patrons of Protestantism. Secondly, confessional competition visibly
enhanced the development of education. Schools based on the Strasbourg
model of Johann Sturm were founded in Protestant centres under the
patronage of great nobles, and in major Prussian towns where they served
both their communities and the landed gentry. Several decades later Catholics
developed two independent networks: Jesuit colleges, chiefly for the gentry,
and seminaries for future priests.

Generally speaking, confessional struggle contributed to the development of literacy and intellectual awareness in Poland. This happened on several levels and in many areas: Protestant ministers in the later sixteenth century were more often than not better educated than the Catholic parochial clergy: this was at least partly due to the influence of German universities, including Königsberg (founded 1544) and schools in Royal Prussia.

Journeys abroad were becoming fashionable with the more substantial gentry; a grand tour became a necessary part of the curriculum for the sons of magnates. Confessional preference dictated countries and universities to be visited which included Ingolstadt or Altdorf and Leiden or Louvain/Leuwen, but Paris and Padua were everybody's favourites. King Stefan Batory, Chancellor Jan Zamoyski and his secretary, a historian, Reinhold Heidenstein – each of them from a different background – were all 'Paduans': that school became the Alma Mater of Polish youth in of the later Renaissance era. Foreign travel was important for the development of the Renaissance spirit. Sadly the universities and schools in Poland could not compete either in learning or in prestige and popularity with any of the major foreign centres of learning. The national university in Cracow (founded 1364 but active from 1400) had declined and by the sixteenth century was in a state of crisis. The Jesuit college in Vilna and the Zamość Academy created by Chancellor Zamoyski were similarly ill-equipped to attract students.

Confessional struggle was also strongly connected to parliamentary politics. The election crisis, of 1572–6 contributed greatly to political interest and awareness amongst the gentry. This has been confirmed by a massive production of pamphlets, mostly manuscript, collected and transcribed with interest into family records.

The confessional triangle mentioned by the anonym, that of Catholics, Protestants and Orthodox or Greek Christians, was a unique phenomenon of the Commonwealth. It is very plausible that neighbourly coexistence and mutual understanding between Catholics and Orthodox nobles in the borderlands of Poland and Lithuania taught them elementary lessons of tolerance which became principles of parlimentary polity in the second half of the sixteenth century.[31]

In a long-term perspective, and particularly in comparison with the following century, the Renaissance state in Poland achieved a delicate equilibrium. In 1505, the Chamber of Deputies in the *Sejm* had formally overcome the domination of the Senate and by the 1560s was co-operating well with the king. Principles of parliamentary polity set deep roots in the *corpus politicum*. Citizenship was virtually limited to the nobility which set up a working self-government with a secure rule of law. Inside the estate the domination of the upper stratum seemed seriously hampered. During the later sixteenth century growing western demand for Polish grain and timber secured economic prosperity; economic thinkers were mostly optimists, even if they stressed the need for a more consistent foreign trade policy. Notwith-standing anti-urban legislation, many royal towns enjoyed their share in the economic boom and some private ones became thriving centres of landed estates.

This picture however, does not reflect a true state of affairs. The Polish counterpart of Jean Bodin and Jędrzej Frycz Modrzewski (c. 1503–72) advocated alternatives: a stronger royal power, more chances for commoners and, in certain critical cases, like punishment for manslaughter, equality before the law.[32] However, arguing for a strong monarchy would mean political disaster. Even the Jesuits, after an initial setback, changed their attitude and began flattering the gentry. The latter seemed to be the principal winner on the Parliament's floor; they were, however, neither winning in the country's economy nor in county diets.

The final failure of the Renaissance state in Poland was caused by what might be called a contradiction between the egalitarian legislation and political freedoms of the noble estate, and inequality of economic chances between various strata of landowners.[33] The rule by patronage would not save the Commonwealth from factions and civil wars, and factors which still need to be analysed hampered the development of a Polish version of the Jacobean 'rule by the pen'. The domination of the magnatery was enhanced politically by the shattered authority of the sovereign since the free elections, and eventually led to a wide gap between the egalitarian political phraseology and a growing dependence of the gentry upon the magnatery.

Jacob Burckhardt's enthusiasm for the modernity of the Renaissance in Italy has been widely criticised recently.[34] Much of the argument fits Poland as well, but the relationship between the old and the new here took rather particular forms.

The Renaissance in Poland might be presented as an essay in the solution of problems concerned with ethnic-cultural diversity. While the Italian scene was divided into numerous states but in respect of language relatively uniform,[35] the Renaissance culture in the Commonwealth was founded upon a manifold ethnic infrastructure. Polish language and manners were both gaining ground in the Ruthenian and Lithuanian east and struggling with the traditionally dominant German influence in the towns. One is tempted to risk the conclusion that some borderland milieux were likely to have a culturally fruitful soil. Nicholas Copernicus (1475–1543), a scion of a Toruń (Thorn) family originating from Silesia, was exposed to influences from both Germany and Poland – and profited greatly from his studies at Cracow before visiting Italy. Like the whole Varmia/Ermland chapter he was loyal and dedicated to the Polish *raison d'état*. His person and manifold achievements (including a treatise on money with an early formulation of the 'Gresham's Law') show, or rather symbolise, the potential of urban society and its openness to intellectual influences. Ruthenian and oriental (Armenian and other) contributions to the Polish Renaissance were of a different nature. Polish historians agree with Stanisław Grzybowski that long coexistence there of diverse ethnic traditions, and particularly Orthodox and Catholic confessions, contributed to the spirit of tolerance for dissident views and customs.[36]

We have stressed the coexistence and mutual influence of various artistic styles but there were different factors which shaped the literature of Renaissance Poland. Czesław Miłosz wrote: 'to me [the] history of Poland and of its literature seems extravagant and full of incongruities: a Slavic nation whose writers, up to the Renaissance, used only Latin . . . ; a refinement of taste, which produced lyrical poetry comparable to that of Elizabethan England, combined with irony and brilliance but always threatened by drunken torpor and parochial mumblings.'[37] The Renaissance signified both the refinement of Latin and direct contacts with humanists all over Europe (Erasmus was very popular among Cracow intellectuals), and the development of a literary Polish language. The chief works of scholarship were in Latin, of course, like Copernicus' *De Revolutionibus Orbium Coelestium* (1543), Modrzewski's *De Republica emendanda . . .* (1554) and Wawrzyniec (Laurence) Goślicki's *De Optimo Senatore* (1568). There was also an abundant correspondence in Latin of which that of the diplomat, Johannes Dantiscus, was probably the largest.

While Latin – in which, according to common European wisdom, each Pole excelled – built bridges to the intellectual west, the printing-press opened a market for the vernacular. Principal Polish writers published poetry in both languages; a Protestant, Mikołaj Rej (1505–69) enjoyed writing in his native tongue and coined a saying: 'Let the neighbouring nations know that Poles are not geese, but have their own language.' The vernacular literature struggled in the first half of the fifteenth century with inadequacies of vocabulary and with spelling, but already around the middle of the century it was helping to establish a national identity.

Jan Kochanowski (1530–84), both courtier and sincere laudator of the country life, became the symbol of the age. He travelled throughout Germany, Italy, France and was fluent in many languages. He freely translated the Psalms (*David's Psalter*), availed himself of George Buchanan's poems, and often alluded to Horace, while choosing themes from the *Iliad* in his works. The lyrics of his *Laments* which describe the death of his beloved daughter are as moving today as they were in his own period. He also enjoyed composing short verse, which was sometimes obscene, and often directed at his contemporaries. An accomplished contemporary of *la pléiade*, he might also well have written laudatory verse for Thomas Coryat's *Crudities* had he not died too early! In contrast, the next generation got, in Mikołaj Sęp

Szarzyński (1500–81), 'a kind of a metaphysical poet' who was a precursor of
Polish literary Baroque and in his poetry greatly resembled John Donne:[38]

> You, who want to find Rome in Rome, pilgrim,
> are unable to find Rome in Rome itself . . .
> Today in vanquished Rome, unvanquished Rome
> . . . lies buried

The second half of the Renaissance age in Poland was as intellectually intense
as it was politically dramatic. In 1566 appeared *The Polish Courtier* of Łukasz
(Lucas) Górnicki (1527–1603). This was a free translation of *Il libro del
corteggiano*, adapted to suit Polish conditions and the lifestyle of the Polish
court. Shortly thereafter, during the first free elections of the kings and the
confessional struggles, massive production of political pamphlets, in prose
and verse, testified to the growing literacy of the gentry. The numerous pirate
editions of Jan Kochanowski's poetry signified growing demand for his
poetry and for literature in the vernacular in general. The pace of progress
during this period was faster than in any time previously or thereafter, but it
still could not be compared with that of contemporary England, France,
Germany or Spain either in the quantities of books and pamphlets which were
printed in or the variety of literary *genres*. In particular theatre in Poland
developed slowly.

However, Poland's greatest triumph was in its influence upon the East. The
first book in Old Slavonic appeared in Cracow in 1491, followed by books in
Ruthenian. The availability of the printing press increased the attractiveness
of the Polish language and contributed in part to the Polonisation of the
Ruthenian and Lithuanian nobility in eastern parts of the Commonwealth.
However, this proved in the end to be a mixed blessing and contributed to
dramatic national conflicts from the mid-seventeenth until today.

NOTES

1 In the final stage of preparation for this chapter I profited from conference papers
   whose proofs Professor Samuel Fiszman kindly gave me for inspection: J.
   Białostocki, 'Renaissance sculpture in Poland and its European context: some
   selected problems'; A. Miłobędzki, 'The Renaissance and local "modi": architecture under the last Jagiellons in its political and social context' in S. Fiszman (ed.),
   The Polish Renaissance in Its European Context (Bloomington and Indianapolis,
   1988). The reader may turn to that volume chiefly for literary matters. For general
   information about Poland, see J.K. Fedorowicz *et al.* (eds.), *A Republic of Nobles.
   Studies in Polish History to 1864* (Cambridge, 1982); also A. Mączak, H.
   Samsonowicz and P. Burke (eds.), *East-Central Europe in Transition. From the
   Fourteenth to the Seventeenth Century* (Cambridge, 1985).
2 H. and S. Kozakiewicz, *Renesans w Polasce* [The Renaissance in Poland], 1st edn
   (Warsaw, 1976), 2nd edn (Warsaw, 1987).

3 J. Białostocki, *The Art of the Renaissance in Eastern Europe. Hungary, Bohemia, Poland* (Ithaca, N.Y., 1976), the following quotations from 1f. Figures in brackets in the text and in notes refer to illustrations in that well-documented book.

4 Miłobędzki, 'Architecture' 291.

5 King Sigismund to the burgomaster John Boner, 1517: 'There has been here an Italian with a model of a chapel he is going to build for us and which we like very much'. H. and S. Kozakiewicz, *Renesans w Polsce*, 37.

6 Białostocki, 'Renaissance sculpture' in Fiszman, *Polish Renaissance*, 281; Miłobędzki, 'Architecture' cit. in *Polish Renaissance*, 291.

7 An outstanding case is the collegiate church in Nieśwież Lithuania, a Baroque-style church under construction at the same time as the building was commissioned by Prince Michael Casimir Radziwill, a Calvinist recently converted by the Jesuits, who had visited Rome during his pilgrimage to the Holy Land.

8 Białostocki, *The Art of the Renaissance*, 82f 311; 313–15; 320. Cf. there comments on the notion of northern Mannerism. Cf. also his comments on houses of wealthy grain-merchants in Kazimierz on the Vistula, 'Renaissance sculpture' in Fiszman, *Polish Renaissance*, 287.

9 More on tomb sculptures in Białostocki, 'Renaissance sculpture in Fiszman, *Polish Renaissance*; H. Kozakiewiczowa, 'Renaissance nagrobki piętrowe w Polsce' [Renaissance double-decker tombs in Poland], *Biuletyn Historii Sztuki*, 18 (1955), 3–47.

10 See H. Kozakiewiczowa, 'Spółka architektoniczno-rzeźbiarska Bernardina de Gianotis i Jana Cini' [Architectural-sculptural firm of Bernardino de Gianotis and Giovanni Cini], *Biuletyn Historii Sztuki*, 212 (1959), 151–74.

11 Białostocki, 'Renaissance sculpture' in Fiszman, *Polish Renaissance*, 288.

12 J.R. Major, 'The Renaissance monarchy: a contribution to the periodization of history', *The Emory University Quarterly*, XIII, 2 (June 1957), 112–24; *Representative Government in Early Modern France* (New Haven, Conn., 1980).

13 F. Chabod, 'Esiste uno stato del Rinascimento?' [1957–8] in his *Scritti sul Rinascimento* (Turin, 1981), 591–623.

14 A. Mączak, 'Vicissitudes of feudalism in Poland' in P. Thane, G. Crossick and R. Floud (eds.), *The Power of the Past. Essays in Honour of Eric Hobsbawm* (Cambridge and Paris, 1984), 283–7.

15 This is one of the principal theses of Konstanty Grzybowski's path-breaking monograph of the *Sejm* in the reign of Sigismund Augustus (1548–72): *Teoria reprezentacji w Polsce epoki Odrodzenia* [Theory of Representation in Poland at the time of Sigismund Augustus], (Warsaw, 1956).

16 This is the question of *liberum veto*, a procedure based on a noble principle but in political reality a virtually anarchic one; in the seventeenth eighteenth century the *liberum veto* became a tool in the hand of many a magnate faction leader. See W. Konopczyński, *Le Liberum veto* (Paris, 1930).

17 See n. 13 and also Fedorowicz, *et al.*, *A Republic*.

18 Cf. C.H. Talbot (ed.), 'Relation of the state of Polonia and the united provinces of that crown anno 1958', *Elementa ad Fontium Editiones* (Rome) 13, 1965. This treatise will be discussed below.

19 These relationships have been presented by the author in 'The conclusive years.

The end of the sixteenth century: the turning point of Polish history?' in E.I. Kouri and T. Scott (eds.), *Politics and Society in Reformation Europe. Essays for Sir Geoffrey Elton on his Sixty-Fifth Birthday* (London, 1987).

20 However, Carolus Sigonius with whom Zamoyski had studied, boasted to Jacques Auguste de Thou that *he* was its author.

21 Talbot, 'Relation', 86.

22 *Ibid.*, 86

23 *Ibid.* 87

24 *Ibid.* 39, 60, 61.

25 Yves Durand was only formally right when he did not classify Poland as a republic. Cf. *Les Republiques au temps des monarchies* (Paris, 1973). Incidentally, Talbot, 'Relation', buttresses our argument that the late sixteenth century was a period decisive for the subsequent two prepartition centuries. See above, n. 19.

26 Talbot, 'Relation', 39.

27 J. Hexter, *The Vision of Politics on the Eve of Reformation* (New York, 1973) 150–72.

28 Talbot, 'Relation' 129.

29 *Ibid.*, 130.

30 For a general overview, see J. Tazbir, *A State without Stakes* (Warsaw, 1973); cf. also G. Schramm, *Der polonische Adel und die Reformation 1548–1607* (Wiesbaden, 1965).

31 The first historian who elaborated this theme was Stanisław Grzybowski. Cf. his 'Mikołaj Sienicki, Demostenes sejmów polskich' [A Demosthenes of the Polish Parliament], *Odrodzenie i Réformaçja w Polsce*, 2 (1957).

32 J. Frycz Modrzewski, *Opera omnia*, ed. C. Kumaniecki (Warsaw, 1953–); his principal treatise was *De republica emendanda . . .* (1551).

33 The political rhetorics of that period need a detailed study but it may be symptomatic that in the later sixteenth century when the sovereign as the supreme authority was mentioned, the Commonwealth was added as well.

34 Cf. P. Burke, *The Renaissance* (Atlantic Highlands, N.J., 1987).

35 We are aware of a gross simplification: see C. Dionisotti, *Geografia e storia della letteratura italiana* (Turin 1971), 163. It seems, however, acceptable in order to stress the nature of cultural diversity of both the countries in question.

36 See n. 28, above.

37 C. Miłosz, *The History of Polish Literature*, 2nd ed. (Berkeley, Calif. 1983), xvi ff.

38 *Ibid.*

ELEVEN

ℬ

BOHEMIA AND MORAVIA

JOSEF MACEK

Any attempt to place the Renaissance into the context of Czech history must take into consideration that the period of the fifteenth and sixteenth centuries, during which the first signs of the Renaissance and Renaissance humanism appeared in Bohemia and Moravia, was deeply influenced by the Czech Reformation. It became the determining factor with regard to all political, social and cultural developments.

Hussite revolution, Czech Reformation and Renaissance humanism

From the end of the fourteenth century the kingdom of Bohemia had witnessed a reform movement which culminated in the person of Jan Hus (1369–1415) and turned into the Hussite Revolution in 1419.[1] Although its purpose was not the overthrow and abolition of the existing social order, its armed struggle against the Roman church and the latter's exercise of secular governmental authority had shaken the whole of central Europe and generated a series of profound ecclesiastical and social reforms during 1419–27. Church possessions were forcibly secularised, prelates deprived of political power and the majority of monasteries in Bohemia and Moravia dissolved. Ecclesiastical landed property passed into the hands of the nobility and burghers and, church life fell under the direct control of the lay community. An Utraquist church was created, independent from Rome, which had its own clerical system of administration (consistory), but the supreme authority for the Utraquists were the estates of the realm, consisting of representatives drawn from the upper and lower nobility, and the burghers. Even in individual parishes it was the lay community which decided on the fate of church property and the appointment or discharge of the priests. While the Utraquist church, on the one hand, introduced the Czech language into its liturgy and tried to maintain the apostolic succession by accepting the consecration of its priests, first from its own elected archbishop (Jan Rokycana), and afterwards from foreign (mainly Italian) bishops, the newly founded Union of Czech Brethren (*Unitas fratrum*), on the other hand, broke with Rome and constituted itself as an independent church at the end of the fifteenth century. It was precisely within the latter faction of the radical Czech Reformation movement that the Taborite tradition continued, recalling the chiliastic experiment of 1420 to establish at Tábor in south Bohemia a Christian community of wholly equal believers, in the true spirit of the apostolic church of Jesus.[2]

The coexistence of three churches in the kingdom of Bohemia would last until the rebellion of the Bohemian estates and the Battle of the White Mountain (1618–20). The appearance of Martin Luther and the development of the German and Swiss Reformation movements gave the Czech Reformation new impulses. Recent studies, however, have shown that the German Reformation influenced the Czech lands more significantly only after the second half of the sixteenth century. The so-called neo-Utraquism, which radicalised religious and cultural life in Bohemia around 1500–20, did not represent an echo of Lutheranism, but a renovative force of the Czech Reformation and a revitalisation of domestic Hussite traditions.[3]

Despite all attempts at Christian universalism and international co–operation, the Czech Reformation – the target of five crusades – found itself gradually isolated from mainstream European cultural development. More-over, from the Hussite revolution until the end of the fifteenth century, the trade blockade of Bohemia remained in force and it was not until 1495 that Pope Alexander VI gave his consent that merchants were to be allowed to enter Bohemia and develop commercial activities without the fear of being punished by the church.[4]

Although many a merchant did business, in spite of prohibitions imposed by the church, trade links between Bohemia and the surrounding countries of western and southern Europe were undermined nevertheless. It is equally true that the stereotype, 'a Czech equals a heretic' played a negative role whenever Czech tradesmen, travellers, students or diplomats met foreigners, and contributed to Bohemia's isolation.[5]

Of course the Hussites themselves also contributed, of course, to the isolation of the Czech Lands from their European neighbours. The Hussite messianism transformed itself gradually into an ideological barrier behind which Czech Utraquism was threatened, as a way of life, to become either a regional curiosity or to degenerate into a musty provincialism. For example, a negative feature of Utraquist towns was that the guilds admitted only those craftsmen who publicy honoured the chalice. A similar tendency prevailed at schools, especially at the University of Prague where only those scholars who had sworn on the chalice could become Masters.

In vain did King Vladislav, in response to his counsellors, members of the Royal Chancellery, try to revive the University by inviting adherents of

Renaissance humanism as professors. The University of Prague finally turned down these proposals in 1509.[6] The Masters of Prague University came to look at the arrival of Catholic humanists as a threat to the privileges of the Utraquist church. Whereas the University of Cracow in Poland was becoming a basis for the spread of Renaissance humanism at the end of the fifteenth century the University of Prague remained stagnant and carried on teaching the obsolete curriculum of the Middle Ages. The number of its Bachelors was declining and their outlook was becoming narrower. Student numbers were also falling and those who remained came almost exclusively from Czech Utraquist towns.[7] The students from Moravia usually headed for the Universities of Vienna or of Cracow, and the sons of the Czech nobility and of burghers from Catholic towns (Plzeň, Budějovice, Cheb) preferred to go to Leipzig. If they could afford it, they would study at Italian universities (Bologna, Padua). Although the cultural isolation of Bohemia became less restrictive during the sixteenth century, the cultural life of the country was affected by it nevertheless. The message of the Renaissance entered the kingdom of Bohemia mediated through the church filter, as it were, and often delayed.

I have tried to sketch some of the obstacles put into the way of the advance of humanism from Italy by the Czech anomaly, the Hussite Revolution,[8] and the Czech Reformation. By Renaissance humanism I understand a cultural trend founded on the full and complex appreciation of classical antiquity. Scholars, artists and intellectuals were no longer satisfied with scraps and fragments of the legacy of Greece and Rome that were taken over by scholasticism and the Gothic art. They desired a complete renovation of classical knowledge and its creativity. Applying advanced linguistic methods to the study of newly discovered sources, they tried to integrate the classical cultural legacy into the contemporary world and transform it into a living and stimulating inspiration for creative work and a way of life.[9]

The first contact between Bohemia and the Renaissance (as defined above) took place during the reign of Charles IV when Cola di Rienzo and Petrarch visited the imperial court in Prague.[10] The Czech milieu, however, was not yet ready to receive Renaissance impulses. After a brief echo in the Latin work of the imperial chancellor Jan of Středa, Renaissance humanism vanished from the kingdom of Bohemia. The growing reform movement, the Hussite Revolution and the subsequent five crusades against Bohemia sealed off the Czech Lands from the sources of the Italian Renaissance almost hermetically.

During the era of Jiří of Poděbrady (1453–71), thanks to the temporary calm and the diplomatic mission of Aeneas Silvius Piccolomini, the disrupted cultural links with the cultural centres of Europe began to be restored. During his struggle against the Pope, while developing the ideas of 'conciliarism', King Jiří himself relied on the help of German humanists, especially

Gregorius of Heimburg,[11] and some Czech humanists who had been educated in Italy.[12] Names like Prokop of Rabštejn and Jan of Rabštejn became prominent among the scholars who sought also in classical literature models of religious tolerance and endeavoured to learn from it. Even at the University of Prague there were several cautious attempts. Thus Šimon of Slaný tried to interpret the works of Virgil and Livy, albeit in the light of the religious and moral thinking of his time.[13] Yet again, the eruption of a new crusade in 1467 nipped this promising trend in the bud.

Latin (Catholic) and Czech (Utraquist) humanism

Only during the Jagiellonian era, especially after the conclusion of the Peace of Olomouc in 1479, did Renaissance humanism begin to spread more successfully in Bohemia and Moravia. It has been suggested that the years from the end of the fifteenth century up to the 1520s should be considered the most favourable period for the development of the Renaissance and humanism.[14] I accept this view and would like to elaborate why it could be so. The most important factor was the cessation of wars and the fact that Bohemia was returning to Europe. Political, economic, commercial and cultural links were being restored. The exhaustion from long wars was strengthening the ideas of religious tolerance. The longing for the return to pre-revolutionary conditions was reinforced by the fact that the country was ruled by a Catholic monarch and that a section of the nobility returned to Catholicism. All these factors helped to relax old and ossified ideas about the cankerous 'pagan sciences and arts', thereby opening the gates for novel cultural and artistic impulses.

However, scholars and artists in Bohemia and Moravia could not disentangle themselves from the ties they had with the Czech Reformation. Whoever we notice among the Czech humanists of the Jagiellonian era, it is impossible to overlook how the country's complicated religious and political situation was reflected in their work. And how the two conflicting principles of government, embodied in the monarch and the estates respectively, had divided the humanists into two camps and absorbed their creative energy. As a rule, one speaks of two kinds of humanism – Latin and Czech (i.e. linguistically Czech) – during the Jagiellonian era. Sometimes the terms Catholic and Utraquist humanism are used.

The most conspicuous representative of the so-called Latin humanism was Bohuslav Hasištejnský of Lobkovice (1461–1510), who was originally an Utraquist but later became a zealous Catholic. Bohuslav Hasištejnský (who studied in Bologna and Ferrara) wrote in Latin and educated his pupils in the same language though he also tried Greek. For his library he collected mostly works by Roman classical writers. He developed into an outstanding Latin scholar whose poems – most of them published posthumously – reached an extraordinarily high standard.[16] In his works of prose Hasištejnský tried to understand the essence of the state of the human soul, and occasionally referred to classical authors. At the same time, of course, he quoted from the Bible and admitted that he respected Christian writers and philosophers more than he did Seneca and Pliny – he was afraid to become alienated from Christian principles. In his work, *De veterum philosophis*, Hasištejnský speaks contemptuously of classical thinkers, ignores the heroes of antiquity because they were pagans, and magnifies instead the Christian saints. Hasištejnský even warned his humanist friend Jan Šlechta to be wary of the fundamental ideas of classical culture, and composed his works rather as a mosaic of quotations from ancient authors.[17]

Augustin Käsenbrod (1467–1513), son of a German burgher from Olomouc in Moravia and known as Augustinus Olomucensis, also wrote his works in Latin.[18] His defence of poetry actually belongs to Italian humanist literature, although it was written by a Moravian author.[19] At the same time, this ardent admirer of the legacy of antiquity wrote a tractate against the Waldenses and against the *Unitas fratrum*. It was not enough for him to be involved in polemics with the Czech Brethren; he exploited his position in the Royal Chancellery to incite King Vladislav to persecute this radical stream of the Czech Reformation. The Olomouc humanist's reputation was further sullied by his defense of instigators of an anti-Jewish pogrom in České Budějovice in 1502. It was the town of Olomouc which around 1500 became the seat of the infamous inquisitor (*hereticae pravitatis*), Heinrich Institoris, who also joined the fight against the Czech Reformation and thus became a leader of the vanguard of the Counter-Reformation movement.[21]

Another Latin humanist worth mentioning was Racek of Doubrava (†1547).[22] He studied in Bologna and Padua and wrote a popular compendium on how to compose letters, in which he fully admitted to be a follower of classical literary authorities. But the same Racek was also the author of a theological pamphlet against Luther's tractate addressed to the town councillors of Prague. He also polemicised against the Reformation in his commentary on the Epistle of Saint Paul to the Galatians.

The ideological foundation for the humanist writing in the Czech language was the Czech Reformation. It would be a mistake to regard Renaissance humanism as conductive to the effort of creating Czech texts. From the end of the fourteenth century the use of the Czech language became customary not only among men of letters and in the offices of the king and the nobility but also in learned disputations and theological tractates (for example, in the works of Petr Chelčický). Take Viktorín Kornel of Všehrdy, a builder's son from Chrudim. After parting with the militant Catholic and his former friend Hasištejnský in 1494,[23] he announced a programme of Czech humanism not as a novelty of cultural life but as a challenge to the literary activities of humanists, who were predominantly Latin-writing Catholics. Thus the Czech language was given the same status as the more thoroughly studied Latin of the ancient writers.

Although certain doubts have been expressed in the past as to whether Kornel's writings were inspired by the ideas of humanism,[24] it is now recognised that Kornel knew the works of ancient writers well and that, for example, he was influenced by the thinking of Dante, whose authority he acknowledged. [25] In his main work he followed the models of classical antiquity.[26] His conception of man is close to that of the Ancients, and in all his writings the idea of religious tolerance predominates. He considers the Republic prior to Caesar to be the apogee of Roman history. It was Caesar and the emperors who had broken the law and usurped the right to make decisions regarding matters of the state without the participation of the citizens.[27] At the same time, Kornel Všehrd remained a Czech Utraquist who continued to be inspired by the idea of earlier Czech literature. However, in the subsequent edition of his principal work, *Knihy devatery* (Ninefold Books), he omitted quotations from authors such as Pliny, Homer, Plautus, and even from Plato,[28] and retained only references to genuine Christian authorities and the Bible.

During the first burst of Renaissance humanism in Bohemia, the Czech authors profited from Latin translations made by Italian humanists (Marsilio Ficino, Francesco Petrarca, Giovanni Pontano, Giannantonio Campano, Filippo Beroaldo, Aeneas Silvus Piccolomini, Lorenzo Valla, Pico della Mirandola and others). It is characteristic that more detailed direct translations from the works of classical authors were not available, so deeply rooted was the fear of 'pagans' among the followers of the Czech Reformation. It must not be forgotten that to Jan Rokycana Aristotle was a pagan against whom one should be guarded,[29] and that the writer and bishop of the *Unitas fratrum*, Jan Blahoslav (1523–71), who had a good knowledge of antiquity, held Ovid for 'an excellent master of Satan's work'.[30] After all, it was as late as 1555 that the young theologians of the *Unitas fratrum*, which meant so much to Czech culture especially during the sixteenth century, had seriously begun to study Latin![31]

Thus antiquity, that is the works of classical authors, was reaching the Czech milieu mostly through the intermediary of Italian humanists. There were exceptions, such as the translation of Seneca's maxims and wisdom. Seneca, next to Virgil, was respected and regarded as a thinker close to Christianity. This was the reason why as early as 1433 Seneca's maxims were translated into Czech; a second translation was published at the beginning of the sixteenth century.[32] Even more important was the Czech translation of Plato's *Republic*. The text, now lost, is mentioned by Jan Blahoslav.

Quotations from Plato appear in Czech literature as early as the fourteenth century, but most of these are excerpts from anthologies of poems (*florilegia*) and from the works of G. Burley.[33] Between 1484 and 1494 the scribe Matyáš, who worked in Zaječice in the Chrudim region for Jan of Kunčí, translated Plato's *Republic* into Czech and dedicated it to the outstanding Moravian politician, Ctibor Tovačovský of Tovačov.[34] If Blahoslav's information is correct, the Czech language must have been the first among national languages into which this work of Plato was translated. The scribe Matyáš, who was an Utraquist, must certainly have used the Latin version of Plato by M. Ficino, which had been available since 1483–4. This, of course, was rather an exception and Viktorín Kornel of Všehrdy in a letter to the priest Jíra complained that 'perhaps we still do not possess' any Czech translations of classical authors.[35]

An outstanding personality among humanists writing in Czech was Řehoř Hrubý of Jelení (†1514).[36] Hrubý's major contribution lies in the translations of classical authors, including the works of Cicero. He relies on Cicero in his *Napomenutí k Pražanům* (Warning to the Citizens of Prague), in which he definitely sides with the Utraquist burghers against the Catholic nobility and recalls Jan Žižka of Trocnov as a model and example. In Hrubý's work, for the first time, not only do we come upon expressive compassion for the subjected peasants, but also upon explicit defence of their rights suppressed by feudal authorities.[37] The humanist orientation overcomes the aristocratic barrier and acquires forms foreshadowing the modern conception of humanism. Thanks to Hrubý Czech literature could claim to have been enriched, as the first in Europe, by a translation of Erasmus' *Encomium moriae* into a national language (1513).

In his translations Řehoř Hrubý aimed to prove the capability of the Czech language in contributing to the rise of intellectual standards. At the same time Hrubý was concerned with substantiating the ideological foundation of Utraquism. This was why he translated from the early patristic literature in which the early church is distinctly portrayed. Hrubý had explicitly to defend the 'heathens' before the radical Utraquists[38] to whom he belonged, not only because of his severe criticisms of the Roman papacy, his resistance to scholasticism (including, for example, Thomas Aquinas) and his determination to separate the Utraquist church from Rome,[39] but also on account of his warm reverence for the revolutionary Hussite tradition. However, the Utraquist humanist did not shut his eyes to other Christian countries and explicitly emphasised the feeling of closeness to 'western countries', that is, to the countries of western Europe.[40]

It was due to Řehoř Hrubý's financial backing that Václav Písecký (1482–1511), an outstanding authority on Latin and Greek, was able to study in Italy.[41] The prematurely deceased scholar paid tribute to the Czech language in the introduction to his translation of a speech attributed to the Greek orator Isocrates. But Písecký was not only a Czech patriot; he was also a defender of the Czech Reformation. During 1510–11 at the University of Bologna, he conducted a disputation with an Italian Dominican monk in which he defended the communion in both kinds.[42] Even this remarkable Renaissance humanist could not escape from the influence of the Czech Reformation. In vain he fought the conservative Utraquists who dominated the University of Prague, and failed to carry through its reform in the spirit of humanism.

From the mid-sixteenth century the country, in which the Czech Reformation was in conflict with the Roman church (strengthened by the arrival of the Jesuit order in 1533) and in which the Estates and especially the free towns were gradually forced out of the political scene, could no longer serve as a platform for the growth of Renaissance humanism. Latinising humanism was socially too exclusive and sterile: it degenerated into sheer formalism and provincial versification.[43] One of the most significant Latin humanists of the second half of the sixteenth century was Matouš, known as Collinus (1516–66), the son of a burgher from Kouřim.[44] Already his studies at Wittenberg and the relationship with his teacher Phillipp Melanchthon give an indication of his spiritual orientation. With the latter's assistance, Collinus became a professor at Prague University where he lectured on moral precepts on the basis of the writings by Virgil, Cicero and Ovid (*Fasti*). Collinus was also interested in the works of Plautus and Terentius. It was probably on account of his merit that Prague saw the first presentation of *Miles gloriosus* by Plautus. Collinus also tried his hand at interpreting Homer but his Greek was rather poor. Collinus devoted most of his energy to the struggle for putting through the radical aims of the Czech Reformation. He continued in the earlier Hussite tradition and he is classed among those who represented the so-called left Utraquism.[45]

For Catholic humanists, the situation was no different. Their work reflected the confrontation with the Czech Reformation. The most significant personality of the first half of the sixteenth century was the prelate Jan Dubravius (c. 1486–1553). He was Bishop of Olomouc, a feudal landlord and a prolific writer of texts[46] that included a compendium on the raising of fish (carp). His Latin work *Theriobulia* (1520) follows closely the Czech work *Nová rada* (New Council, 1394) by Smil Flaška of Pardubice and this in itself detracts from the originality of its Renaissance style.[47] As a follower and supporter of King Ferdinand I, Dubravius opposed not only the estates, but also the Czech Reformation. It cannot be ignored that his literary production includes interpretations of Psalms which contain attacks on advocates of the Reformation. Dubravius was also politically active against Lutherans and the *Unitas fratrum*.

A German humanist who came from Bohemia was Mattheus Aurogallus Golthan (1490–1543). He was the son of a burgher from Chomutov and was noted for his knowledge of Greek and Hebrew.[48] Having tried and failed to gain a position in Bohemia, Golthan left for Wittenberg where he eventually became rector of the university. To the Czech environment this Renaissance humanist was lost although in his work he, too, paid tribute to Jan Hus and Jan Žižka of Trocnov. Jan Honorius (1498), another German from Bohemia who came from Loket, prepared the first complete edition of Horace but he did so in Germany after leaving Bohemia.[49] The Moravian humanist Wolfgang Heiligmaier, the son of a German burgher from Jemnice, proved himself at the University of Vienna. Only after his conversion to Lutheranism and marriage, however, did he come to live in Moravia. Another native of Jemnice, the humanist and lawyer Leonard Dobrohost became rector of the University of Vienna in 1524.[50] It was certainly not accidental that the talents of followers of Renaissance humanism were brought to full fruition in places situated outside of the kingdom of Bohemia.

It has not been my intention to present a history of Renaissance humanism in the Czech lands and, indeed, the brief scope of this survey does not allow it. I have endeavoured, however, by way of a few sketches of leading personalities, to demonstrate the obstacles which the Renaissance encountered in Bohemia. In addition, I have tried to show how Renaissance humanism as a whole succumbed to the ideological programme and practical interests of the Czech Reformation.

There should be no doubt that due to these specifically unfavourable conditions, Renaissance humanism did not become a stimulating cultural tendency and remained a rather marginal phenomenon in Bohemia and Moravia. For the same reason the Czech milieu produced no personalities who could assert themselves and leave their mark on the development of humanism in Europe at large. Not even the eminent educationalist Jan Amos Komenský (Comenius, 1592–1670) could become such a figure. As a person and through his work, Komenský essentially belongs to the Czech and European Reformation rather than to the European Renaissance.

Poetry, prose and drama

The above outline of Renaissance humanism in Bohemia makes it clear that, from the end of the fifteenth century, Czech writing was not developing under the banner of the Renaissance. I shall now try to demonstrate that Czech poetry, prose and drama were rather a part of the cultural trend influenced by the Reformation.

There is still a great deal of misunderstanding and ignorance in attempting to separate the Renaissance from the Middle Ages categorically. It is, for instance, erroneous to consider the erotic tones in poetry or the cult of the naked female body merely as pronounced manifestations of the Renaissance. Such attempts interpret the poetry of Hynek of Poděbrady as a typical Renaissance phenomenon, because he appears to celebrate physical love, the beauties of nature and the naked female body.[51] But all these themes were already well known in Old Czech lyrical poetry of the fourteenth century and in German poetry of the first half of the fifteenth century, which served as a source of inspiration to the Czech poems attributed to Hynek.[52]

A similar mistake is made when Hynek's prosaic work is described as being composed in the Renaissance style, because the author modelled himself on Giovanni Boccaccio and introduced the so-called Boccaccio stories into Czech.[53] It should not be forgotten that Hynek of Poděbrady (if he indeed was the author) translated Boccaccio from German and, moreover, he did it selectively. The selection clearly betrays Hynek's feudal knightly bias which rejects Boccaccio's burgher mentality. Whereas the Florentine author gives prominence to a burgher, the Czech version has a noble. Indeed, the Czech adaptor of Boccaccio's work obviously finds enjoyment in making fun of a burgher. In the Czech text the nobility of spirit is replaced by the cult of hereditary knighthood. Thus the works of Hynek of Poděbrady do not celebrate the spirit of the Renaissance. On the contrary, they belong to the tradition which revered the medieval knightly culture repudiated by the Hussite Revolution, but reappearing in the kingdom of Bohemia by the end of the fifteenth century.

Nor is it possible to regard laicisation and secularisation of culture in the Czech Lands as significant contributions of symbols of the Renaissance. Already Archbishop Jan Rokycana, the influential adviser of King Jiří, had encountered critical voices which demanded that priests should not meddle in public affairs and politics. In Bohemia, as it is known, in the wake of the Hussite Revolution prelates ceased to be members of the Estates and landed property of the church was considerably curtailed. This did not, however, mean that faith or religion were taking a back seat in struggles of ideological and cultural life.

I have attempted to classify publications which appeared in print in Bohemia between 1480 and 1526, and I find that more than 60 per cent of the total output produced by printing shops were publications with an educational and religious content.[54] Among the so-called secular literature the largest proportion – about 17 per cent – was taken up by acts and ordinances of the Diet, followed by calendars and texts relating to current affairs. Only about 8 per cent of prints could be classified as Renaissance literature: they comprised editions of writings by foreign, mainly Italian, humanists, Renaissance and classical authors. Thus laicisation of themes does not come conspicuously into view in printed publications which are entirely dominated by the Czech Reformation. In spite of the fact that church administration passed into the hands of laymen, religious faith remained the fundamental component of the socio-psychological structure of all strata forming the Czech society during the sixteenth century. There is no trace in the Czech Lands of atheism which, for example, may be found in the Italian Renaissance.

To call the Utraquist burgher, translator and printer, Mikuláš Konáč of Hodiškov (+1546), a Renaissance writer is not possible.[55] No doubt, there are many Renaissance elements adorning the works of Konáč, but more characteristic of his spiritual orientation is what he translated from Petrarch. Konáč was not interested in Petrarch's lyrical work in which the great Italian poet celebrated earthly love or the beauties of nature, nor was he taken in by Petrarch's praise of Brutus. What he preferred was to translate Petrarch's mystical work 'Seven Penitent Psalms from Petrarca, the Remarkable Poet, Pious and Godly Man'. In this way the Czech reader could familiarise himself, on the threshold of the sixteenth century, with those aspects of the poet's work which seemed to affirm the moral programme of the Czech Reformation. A similar function fulfils Konáč's translation of Savonarola's 'Interpretation of the Psalms' (1514).[56]

If we take another example, the moralising composition by Vavřinec Leander Rváčovský (1525–90), we can see that it presents a blend of two worlds, the world of classical mythology and biblical allegory.[57] His *Masopust* (Carnival) is a critique of vices and sins, as fostered by the Czech Reformation since the fifteenth century. We find a similar tendency in the works of Šimon Lomnický of Budeč (1552–c. 1622) who belonged to the medieval prose tradition, also through his versification of the fourteenth century work by Gualter Burley about the deeds and morals of ancient wise men. Likewise, we can hardly call Mikuláš Dačický of Heslov (1555–1616) a Renaissance poet. Written in the spirit of the Reformation, his work is directed against the Roman church and its clerics. The religious and political orientation of other authors, such as the bishop of the *Unitas fratrum* Jan Blahoslav[58] or one of the executed leaders of the rebellious Bohemian estates, Václav Budovec of Budov (1551–1621),[59] also testifies to the fact that they were, by and large, followers and defenders of the Czech Reformation to whom the Renaissance was of marginal or incidental cultural interest. Even the so-called light literature, published during the second half of the sixteenth century, indicates the topics which the Czech reading public favoured; they included earlier medieval stories about Alexander the Great and Griselda, together with new themes such as the fairy Mélusine, the Roman emperor Jovian, or Doctor Faustus.[60]

Distinct Renaissance elements are to be found only in the so-called *Frantova práva* (Frank's Rights, 1518), an entertaining piece of prose that contains strong non-religious tone and the praise of frivolous worldliness. But within the context of Czech light literature this work remains an exception.[61] A parallel collection of light hearted stories connected with King Jiří's jester, Paleček (Little Thumb) reflects, on the contrary, the influence of the *Unitas fratrum*. It contains moralistic and didactic reading-matter, which is among the best of its kind. It remains, however, completely committed to the ideology of the Czech Reformation.[62]

Remarkable humanist elements are manifested in a versified disputation regarding the faith between a Roman, a Czech (i.e. an Utraquist) and a 'Picard' (i.e. a member of the *Unitas fratrum*). It is significant that the person who judges and wins is a scholar ('a wise man') who pretends to be superior to the contesting religious parties. The scholar defends the virtue of justice and recommends tolerance. The significance of tolerance is already brought out at the beginning of the disputation, not only on account of the fact that all participants are Christian, 'but also because they are human beings'.[63] The idea of religious toleration anchored in the Act of Coexistence between the Roman and Utraquist churches (1485) was also passionately defended by Prokop of Jindřichův Hradec, a member of the *Unitas fratrum*. His tractate, recently discovered, testifies to the fact that ideas of religious tolerance were growing not only out of Renaissance humanist roots, but were also fruits of the Hussite Reformation.[64]

It is more than retrograde to attempt to assign writings on Czech history to Renaissance literature. The Czech translation of Aeneas Silvius' *History* is characterised by the intention of mitigating its Catholic anti-Hussite bias. The historical writings carry a clear ideological message. This is typical of those writers defending the Czech Reformation (Bartoš the Scribe, M. Kuthen), as well as of Václav Hájek of Libočany, the author of the *Česká kronika* (Czech Chronicle), an entertaining work in the spirit of Counter-Reformation.[65] It is when we compare this type of literature or the so-called historical calenders (Adam of Velselavín, Prokop Lupáč) with the works of Niccolo Machiavelli or Francesco Guicciardini,[66] that we recognise immediately how Czech historiography of the sixteenth century differed methodologically and formally from the Renaissance writing of history.

The Czech Reformation also left its mark on scientific literature. Whether the endeavour to develop scientific knowledge related to medicine (Jan Černý – an active defender of the *Unitas fratrum*),[67] botany, mineralogy, mining or other fields, it was customary to refer not only to ancient authorities and personal observations and experience, but also to quote from typically medieval compendia and encyclopaedia.[68] At the same time, authors of translations from these predominantly Latin and German texts could not avoid being influenced ideologically by the Reformation or Counter-Reformation respectively. This applies even to Mikuláš Klaudyán who was a physician and member of the *Unitas fratrum*, and the author of the first map of Bohemia (1518).[69] This first modern map of Bohemia with its sketches of mountains, rivers, towns and castles is incorporated into a religious-political text which promotes the principles of the Reformation. The combination of a map with a religious pamphlet is a truly eloquent testimony of how the Renaissance approach was woven into the ideological structure of the Reformation.

While in the sphere of emerging natural sciences the traces of Renaissance influence were more extensive and conspicuous, in the history of the Czech theatre they were only marginal. The staging of Plautus' *Miles gloriosus* in Prague (1535) led to strife between the town councillors and the university. The principal actor spent three days in prison and the Utraquist leaders imposed a strict ban of all future 'pagan plays'.[70] When, in 1548, Collinus tried to restage the Plautus comedy, he had to append a prologue in which he defended his decision and admitted the difficulties accompanying the presentation of a classical play in Utraquist Prague. Collinus and other authors were one-sided in emphasising the didactic and moralistic aspects of the plays by Plautus and Terence.[71] Even so, Greek and Roman dramatic works did not succeed in breaking into the Czech theatre. If Konáč of Hodištov wanted to write a play, he reached for the Bible to present Judith of the Old Testament to the spectators. At the end of the sixteenth century, the typically medieval plays on themes like the resurrection of Christ or the three Mary's were revived. Pavel Kyrmezer, a Slovak playwright active in Moravia, directed the popular comedy about the rich man and Lazarus. Tobiáš Mouřenín of Litomyšl (†1625) wrote moralistic plays often based on German texts.[72]

The above historical outline of prose, poetry and drama confirms that in the history of Czech literature the period between 1450 and 1600 cannot be called the Age of the Czech Renaissance. True, Renaissance impulses were finding a way into artistic production, as much as Renaissance elements and affinities are traceable in the works of humanists, but, notwithstanding the few exceptions, a genuine Czech Renaissance literature never materialised. Czech prose, poetry and drama, and scientific literature were marked by the ideology of the Czech Reformation as well as Counter-Reformation.

In fact, in Bohemia the Renaissance notion of art as a creative act did not become established until well into the sixteenth century. In old Czech the word *umění* (art) still suggests merely 'skill' or 'ability'. It is this sense that the word *umění* is employed in 1506 to label the 'skill' exercised by the town executioner,[73] and in 1491 to describe the 'ability' to prognosticate.[74] Painters and sculptors were still looked upon as artisans and were therefore organised into guilds. There were guilds which ruled out the admittance of children of pipers and fiddlers into apprenticeship. According to the older mode of thinking, these artistic performers were still classified as people living on the margins of the society, such as executioners, barbers and Jews.[75] In 1516, for instance, certain fiddlers were prosecuted for having played at a feast: they were taken for dangerous vagabonds and criminals.[76] Until the sixteenth century the vocabulary of Old Czech does not contain the words 'muse' or 'genius': the classical concepts associated with the creative act were quite foreign to the Czech milieu. Nor was the genuinely aesthetic approach to works of literature appreciated. There is no evidence that, as in Renaissance Italy, artists were honoured in public (coronations of poets).

Fine arts and architecture

There have also been attempts in the history of the fine arts to characterise the period from the second half of the fifteenth century until the end of the sixteenth century as the Age of the Renaissance. In particular, those historians who disregard the detailed analysis of style and ignore continuity tend to incorporate the fine arts mechanically into the history of economic and social developments, and consider the Renaissance as an early bourgeois art movement. For them early bourgeois art is to be found not only in Italy, but also north of the Alps. They argue that artworks, commonly known as Late Gothic, were in reality nothing else but Renaissance art.[77] Such a confusion of terms not only hinders the advance of research but undermines, in general, the evaluation of works of art and the understanding of the principal features of creativeness in the production of architects, sculptors and painters. As far as the fine arts in Bohemia and Moravia are concerned, such views have no relevance whatsoever and a recent comprehensive survey of Late Gothic art in Bohemia demonstrates this clearly.[78]

The fine arts do not reflect mechanically contemporary social and political conditions, but constitute a specific, essential part of culture and mentality. Even the late Gothic had its own aesthetic theories in which not only the role of God as the creator of the beauties of nature was underlined, but also as that of the creator of talents, the mediator, the artist (*artifex*), who places these beauties before the human society.[79] Thus the artist – an inhabitant of the earth – is able to depict realistically natural things, plants, human beings, and also objects produced by man, such as buildings, jewels and weapons. Therefore, Late Gothic realism is not in conflict with faith and religion, nor with the church. It is this kind of artistic perception which prevails in the lands north of the Alps.

In the Czech Lands the situation was no different. The Czech Reformation turned the attention, above all, to the ethical and religious conceptualisation of the world and man, and thereby impeded the spread of the classical legacy in central Europe. In the sphere of the fine arts it was primarily the theory and practice of Hussite iconoclasm, already from the first decades of the fifteenth century, which were undermining the evolution of the creativity of painters and sculptors, indebted as they were to the Hussite radical view of idolatry. Traces and manifestations of Hussite iconoclasm still persisted at the beginning of the sixteenth century. In the dialogue which Mikuláš Konáč wrote in 1515, the 'Picard' (that is the representative of the radical wing of the Reformation) criticises the Utraquist for worshipping idols, pictures and sculptures in the church.[80] The confrontation was confined not only to verbal and learned polemics. In 1504, a Prague tailor pulled down a statue of Christ and, together with another artisan, flogged the wooden sculpture shouting: 'To the woods, to the woods!' In this way the point was made that the statue was no more than ordinary wood which had no place in a church.[81] Such manifestations of fading iconoclasm hardly constituted a favourable milieu for the fine arts in general, and for works of arts with secular motifs even less.

It is certainly true that its secularisation and laicisation of the fine arts was not exclusively due to the Renaissance.[82] Nevertheless, it was the Italian Renaissance that prominently highlighted secular themes in paintings and sculptures, whose share in western Europe increased from 15 per cent in the fourteenth and fifteenth centuries to 35 per cent in the sixteenth century.[83] A more detailed examination of the Italian art of that time reveals the contribution of the Renaissance more fully. Whereas in 1420 only about 5 per cent of paintings carried secular motifs, by 1530 the number increased to 20 per cent of the total.[84] If we try to compare this trend with the composition of paintings in the Czech Lands during 1450–1550,[85] we immediately perceive profound differences. Before 1500 there is not a single picture with a secular theme, if the epitaph motif with the figure of the kneeling donor is excluded. Between 1500 and 1550 we find among 223 surviving and classified pictures only four portraits of nobles and one picture known as 'The Death of Lucretia' (1525). This means that secular themes comprise less than 3 per cent of the work of painters, and even if pictures with religious themes are taken account of which carry the painted figure of the secular donor (five nobles and three burghers), the number does not exceed 6 per cent. The overwhelming majority of paintings was fully and unequivocally concerned with the celebration of the Virgin Mary, Jesus Christ, the Saints and biblical episodes. This comparison, I would argue, reveals once again the difference between the orientation in the work of artists in the Czech Lands and, for example, in Italy and the Netherlands. It constitutes another proof how the Czech Reformation consistently turned the attention of painters and sculptors to religious themes. Moreover, orders to produce large paintings continued to be placed almost exclusively by church institutions and prelates.

But even regarding the nature of religious themes, the Czech Lands and the countries of southern and western Europe contrasted sharply. It is known that the figure of Eve inspired creative artists and that, for example, the theme of the so-called nursing Madonna offered an opportunity to pay homage to female beauty. However, the nursing Madonna theme – fairly widespread in Italy and the Netherlands – disappeared from Czech painting and sculpture completely from about 1450 to 1550. True, at the beginning of the sixteenth century the Utraquist priest Martin of Žatec harshly condemned the blasphemous comments about the Virgin allegedly achieving her objectives by baring her breasts and displaying her beauty.[86] But we cannot find a single naked female body represented in a painting or sculpture in Bohemia and Moravia between the end of the fifteenth and the mid-sixteenth centuries. Only the picture *Death of Lucretia*, influenced by Renaissance models, constitutes an obvious attempt to portray the beauty of the naked female body.[87]

It was the power and ideology of the Czech Reformation which in the Czech Lands prevented the establishment of the Renaissance as a distinct period of art. In the most recent collection of studies on the Renaissance in Bohemia the editor in his preface rightly stresses that the trend of historical development prevented 'central Europe from truly taking the Renaissance road'.[88] We know that this was essentially due to the Czech Reformation. The Renaissance is not conceived of as an era, but rather as an 'artistic system with formal contents'.[89] The development of the fine arts in the Czech Lands was dependent on the influx of Italian artists or on the journeys of domestic artists to Italy. This is why one speaks about the penetration of the Renaissance into central Europe or direct transplantation of this style into central and eastern Europe.[90] Doubtless, in this process, a mediating role was played by the court of Matthias Corvinus generating new impulses which saturated not only the kingdom of Bohemia, but also Poland.[91]

The implantation of the Renaissance in the artistic milieu of the kingdom of Bohemia was accomplished gradually, especially after the accession of King Ferdinand I. The influence was primarily in the field of architecture. Renaissance elements and tendencies were finding their way into Late Gothic art, for example the Renaissance windows of 1493 in the Gothic Vladislav Hall at Prague Castle. Similarly, landscapes began to appear in pictures of the Crucifixion and biblical settings included portraits of real people and Gothic and Renaissance scripts mix together (for example *incunabula*). It is impossible to separate the Renaissance style from Late Gothic art by a firm dividing line, because the Czech environment managed to transform even explicitly Renaissance impulses and adapt them to the older domestic tradition. It is not an accident that there was an attempt to call these particular art forms the 'Late Gothic Baroque'.[92]

Whereas under the Jagiellonians a few Renaissance architectural elements, diffusing to Bohemia and Moravia from Hungary, make an appearance in Prague and elsewhere (Castle Tovačov), under Ferdinand I a royal garden planned in pure Renaissance style is laid out in 1534. It also housed Belvedere, the first stylistically immaculate Renaissance summer-house in central Europe built by Italian architects (after 1538).[93] In a similar way Maximilian II and Archduke Ferdinand become patrons of Renaissance architecture. Only afterwards did the principals of great noble families follow suit and invite Italian artists to build ostentatious castles for them (for example at Litomyšl, Opočno, Moravská Třebová, Bučovice, Jindřichův Hradec and Telč). After the middle of the sixteenth century even burghers began to build in a more conspicuous Renaissance style. But in town architecture the Renaissance does not manifest itself in such a pure form as it does in castles.[94] One speaks of a popular style (appealing to the layman) and of the so-called Czech Renaissance characterised by the fact that edifices were adorned by paintings. The houses, town-halls and hospitals of Czech and Moravian towns are decorated in the Renaissance style (for example, Olomouc, Český Krumlov and Telč). During 1544–54 the first Renaissance churches and congregation halls of the *Unitas fratrum* were also erected at Brandýs nad Labem and Mladá Boleslav. The ideological orientation of the *Unitas fratrum*, inspired as it was by the early church, found its expression in the ground-plan of the building: it is a pseudo-basilica.[95] If in the history of the Czech fine arts one comes very early across references to the so-called Mannerism, the question arises whether the Reformation and Counter-Reformation did not contribute to the change in style of town architecture at the end of the sixteenth century.

As in architecture, so in sculpture strong Renaissance impulses reached Moravia from Hungary. Among the first Renaissance sculptures in the Czech Lands were portrait medallions of Ladislav of Boskovice and his wife Magdalena of Dubé at the castle in Moravská Třebová.[96] It is assumed that the medallions were made by a Florentine sculptor who worked in Buda. It was predominantly the Late Gothic style, however, which prevailed in sculpture until the mid-sixteenth century. Naturally, the style gradually improved with more accurate imitations of the human body's anatomy and also by ornamentations derived from Renaissance principles of art.

As for painters, they remained by and large traditionalists and committed to the Late Gothic style until the second half of the sixteenth century. In the same way as the word *báseň* (poem) meant 'invented' or 'false story', the word *malovaný* (painted) signified in Old Czech an 'unreal' or 'imaginary' person as late as the beginning of the sixteenth century. If Petr of Rožmberk is not to have soldiers and money, he will be a mere *malovaný haitman* (painted captain): not a real holder of one of the highest offices of the state.[97] In Jagiellonian Bohemia painters were prosperous craftsmen organised with shieldmakers in guilds. In 1520 when town armies took the field against the nobility, a painter accompanied the troops to watch over the shields and pavises.[98] The generally low social esteem in which painters were held was constructed to the same way the guilds isolated themselves ideologically by not admitting anyone who refused to take the oath on the chalice and was not an Utraquist.[99] The Catholic nobles, on the other hand, showed no respect for the Prague guild of painters and invited artists from abroad.

With regard to mural and panel painting artists tried to improve on their representations of men and landscapes. The wall decorations in castles of nobles evoke chivalrous pursuits (tournaments and hunting) or revive medievally moulded classical motifs such as the Judgement of Paris. The human figures in the paintings of the so-called Smíšek Chapel of the Church of St Barbara in Kutná Hora have a realistic appearance although the experts believe that the artist did not come from Italy, but from the Danube basin or from the Rhineland.[100] Not even the murals in the chapel of St Wenceslas in Prague can be unequivocally classified as works created exclusively in the Renaissance style. The blending of Gothic and Renaissance elements is also acknowledged in the work of the so-called Master of Litoměřice. Only after 1520 do we notice in a Gothic sea a slow increase of a few islands of Renaissance painting.[101] This was largely due to the creativeness of the anonymous painter, known by the initials I.P., who had extensive knowledge of the works of Dürer and Mantegna. Only after the middle of the sixteenth century can we observe a more conspicuous spread of classicising themes in sculptures and mural paintings. Yet again they are located primarily in architectural works commissioned by the Habsburgs – for example the summer house Hvězda (Star) near Prague – and by the high nobility.

Renaissance elements are also in evidence in miniature painting. Painters illuminated prayer-books for Utraquist as well as Catholic churches. Patronage was confined largely to burghers and members of choir fraternities. Only in Moravia, largely in monasteries, is there a concern for the embellishment of written texts.[102] The Utraquists, the opponents of the Roman Church, also affected the sphere of miniature painting. In 1470 the illuminator Václav Střet became a fugitive from the 'heretic plague' by leaving Bohemia.[103]

Only a few miniaturists, especially in Moravia, employed the Renaissance style in their decorative and ornamental artwork. Here again, however, the question arises as to whether it is possible to consider the use of perspective or a knowledge of the human body (as in the case of the hymn-book by the Master of Litoměřice). We know that in various places artists, who favoured the realistic method, acquired this kind of knowledge. The influence of the Italian Renaissance appears more conspicuously in graduals and antiphonaries from Olomouc, Brno and Louka near Znojmo, with explicitly direct references to the influence of paintings by Pisanello and Mantegna, and mediated by the Buda court of King Matthias Corvinus.[104]

It was also from Hungary that samples of Italian Renaissance majolica reached Moravia and Bohemia.[105] However, the motif on tiles built up into the so-called 'knightly stoves', showing knights fighting in a tournament, is a further proof for the revival of Gothic knightly culture, at the end of the fifteenth century (though the Renaissance technology and patterns were imported from Hungary). A similar stylish decoration on the stove in the knights' hall of the castle at Jindřichův Hradec, containing biblical motifs, can be attributed to the influence of Late Gothic art from the Danube basin as well.[106] Altogether it is difficult to decide, and among the experts there is no agreement, which particular detail still relates to the so-called Late Gothic and which already to the Renaissance period. The same lack of consensus exists concerning wood-carvings in church stalls as well as decorations of church bells, in particular in relation to the appearance of herbaceous ornaments, regarded as a Renaissance element.[107] It is enough to point to the herbaceous motif in the sculptural decoration of the royal rostrum at the St Vitus Cathedral in Prague, thought to be a typically Late Gothic work, to realise the uncertainty in the interpretation of what is and what is not 'Gothic' any more.

In conclusion, I would like to go back to the fundamental question which keeps returning. Among historians, historians of art and historians of literature, there is no agreement on what constitutes the essence of the Renaissance in Bohemia. Very often the notion of the Renaissance is mixed up with an entire era of Czech and European history respectively. Alternatively, the term Renaissance is associated with an artistic style or it becomes the label for a specific cultural movement. I have tried to indicate that it is doubtless erroneous to conceive the period of Czech history during 1450–1550 or 1500–1600 as the Age of the Czech Renaissance. The known political, religious, social and economic realities in Bohemia and Moravia during this period lead us to the conclusion that the kingdom of Bohemia lived under the sign of Reformation from the fifteenth century. If that era has to be characterised by one word then let it be the 'Reformation' rather than the 'Renaissance'. The whole world of culture and arts and the mentality of the population were distinctively marked by the Reformation, and not by the Renaissance. The Reformation and the Renaissance cannot be equated; it is impossible to put one particular cultural form of a social epoch above another.

It was the Czech Reformation, which, in its ideological, political and social totality, erected barriers against the cultural and artistic transformations emanating from the Italian Renaissance. As far as the Renaissance in the Czech Lands is concerned, it is only possible to speak of an artistic style and of a cultural movement which, together with humanism, gradually found their way to Bohemia. The Renaissance elements and tendencies may be observed in the fine arts, especially after the middle of the sixteenth century. But they remain rather peripheral and do not replace or remove the Reformation,[108] the core of prevailing ideological activity. These mutual relationships between the Reformation and the Renaissance appear clearly in the history of Czech literature, as well as in the history of fine arts (especially architecture). The Renaissance advances to Bohemia and Moravia from Italy and Hungary, descending down the social pyramid: from the monarchs' court through the nobility to the burghers. Here the movement acquires characteristic features, suggesting the power of domestic traditions and the milieu into which the Renaissance was transferred.

NOTES

1 For detailed explanation, see J. Macek, *Jean Hus et les traditions hussites* (Paris, 1973), 15–203. The transition from revolt to revolution is analysed in H. Kaminsky, *A History of the Hussite Revolution* (Berkeley, Calif., 1967), 3.

2 Macek, *Jean Hus*, 204–88.

3 W. Eberhard, *Konfessionsbildung und Stände in Böhmen 1478–1530* (Munich and Vienna, 1981), especially 144–50. I have reached the same conclusion in my synthesis of Czech history for the years 1471–1526 (still in manuscript form).

4 H. Schenk, 'Die Beziehungen zwischen Nürnberg und Prag von 1456–1500' in I. Bog (ed.), *Der Aussenhandel Ostmitteleuropas 1450–1650* (Munich and Vienna, 1971), 193.

5 Macek, *Jean Hus*, 209.

6 F. Hrejsa, *Dějiny křesťanství v Československu* (Prague, 1948), vol. IV, 178.

7 F. Šmahel and M. Truc, 'Studie k dějinám university Karlovy v letech 1433–1622', *Historia* (Prague-Universita Karlova), 2 (1963), 17 ff. For a comparison between the universities of Prague and Cracow, see, J. Macůrek, 'Humanismus u nás a v Polsku do Bílé Hory' in *Humanistická konference* (Prague, 1966), 108–9.

8 F. Šmahel, *La Révolution hussite, une anomalie historique* (Paris, 1985), 7–13.

9 I have defined my own conception of humanism and the Renaissance in J. Macek, *Il Rinascimento Italiano* (Rome, 1981). An excellent overview of different opinions on the Renaissance and humanism has been attempted by J. Ludvíkovský in the volume, *Humanistická konference*, 5–47. For more details on the main problems of the Renaissance in Bohemia, see J. Macek in *Studia comeniana et historica* (Uherský Brod, 1988).

10 A. Molnár, 'Cola di Rienzo, Petrarca e le origini della reforma hussita', *Protestantesimo*, 19 (1964), 214–23.

11 F.G. Heymann, *George of Bohemia, King of Heretics* (Princeton, N.J., 1965); O. Odložilík, *The Hussite King: Bohemia in European Affairs, 1440–1471* (Rutgers, N.J., 1965), 180–1.

12 F. Šmahel, 'Humanismus v době poděbradské', series *Rozpravy ČSAV* (Prague, 1963), 73–6.

13 R. Urbánek, 'První utrakvistický humanista Šimon ze Slaného', *Listy filologické*, 65 (1938). Recent research has, however, established, that even Šimon of Slaný had not been original in the search for humanist terms, but found them in the work of Aeneas Silvius Piccolomini; see A. Fialová and J. Hejnic, 'Jiří z Litoměřic a jeho Oratio ad studiosos', *Listy filologické*, 102 (1979), 143.

14 J. Kolár, 'Vztah české literatury 14.–16. století k italské kultuře humanismu a renesance', *Slavia*, 52 (1983), 28.

15 J. Hejnic and J. Martínek (eds.), *Rukověť humanistického básnictví v Čechách a na Moravě* (Prague, 1969), vol. III, 170–203. This is the fundamental work for the understanding of the life and work of Czech humanists.

16 J. Martínek, 'Bohuslaus von Lobkowicz und die Antike', *Listy filologické*, 103 (1980), 25–8.

17 See the letter from Hasištejnský to B. Adelmann of 1509. In *Antika a česká kultura* (Prague, 1978), 223–4. For more details, see Martínek, 'Bohuslaus von Lobkowicz', 25–8.

18 See Hejnie and Martínek, *Rukověť*, vol. I, 111–16.

19 K. Svoboda, 'Augustina Olomouckého "Dialog na obranu básnictiví"', *Listy filologické*, 69 (1942), 26.

20 J. Janáček, *Doba předbělohorská 1526–1547* (Prague, 1968), vol. I. 1, 243.

21 See A. Molnár 'Protivaldenská polemika na úsvitu 16.století', *Historická Olomouc a její současné problémy* (Olomouc, 1980), vol. III, 153–74.

22 See Hejnic and Martínek, *Rukověť*, vol. II, 84–8.

23 The motive for the break between Kornel and Hasištejnský was Kornel's appeal to the citizens of Prague in 1493 in which the former criticised one of Hasištejnský's poems. See J. Martínek, 'Výzva Pražanům z roku 1493 přičítaná Všehrdovi', *Listy filologické*, 104 (1981), 53–65.

24 See J. Jakubec, *Dějiny literatury české* (Prague, 1929), vol. II. 2, 572.

25 P.M. Haškovec, 'Dante a Všehrd', *Časopis Matice moravské*, 55 (1921), 52–64.

26 E. Pražák, 'Knihy devatery jako dílo literární', *Právně-historické studie*, 7 (1961), 297–8.

27 Martínek, 'Výzva Pražanům' 63.

28 F. Čáda, *Právně-historické studie*, 7 (1961), 97–8.

29 R. Urbánek, *České dějiny* (Prague, 1930), vol. III. 3, 685. Also the Utraquist Jan Bechyňka considered Cicero as a mere pagan in 1500 (see J. Bechyňka's papers in the National Museum of Prague, MS IV h 45, fo. 28a).

30 P. Váša, *Pochodně zazžená* (Prague, 1949), 14. (This is a quote from Jan Blahoslav's *Musica*, published in Olomouc in 1558, in which a theory of music was attempted.)

31 A. Molnár, *Českobratrská výchova před Komenským* (Praha, 1956), 190.

32 K. Hrdina, 'Seneca v nejstarších českých překladech', *Český časopis filologický*, 2 (1944), 147–59.

33 E. Jeauneau, 'Plato apud Bohemos', *Medieval Studies*, 41 (1979), 161–214.

34 E. Pražák, 'Český překlad Platonovy Politeie z 15.století', *Listy filologické*, 9 (1961), 102–8.

35 *Ibid.*, 107.

36 See the essential monograph by E. Pražák (ed.) *Řehoř Hrubý z Jelení* (Prague, 1964).

37 Řehoř Hrubý z Jelení, *Napomenutí k Pražanům* (1513); Pražák, *Řehoř Hrubý*, 145.

38 Eberhard (*Konfessionsbildung*, 103) has placed Hrubý among the 'left Utraquists'.

39 Pražák, *Řehoř Hrubý*, 83, 87.

40 See Hrubý's introduction to his translation of Erasmus' *Encomium moriae* in *ibid.*, 98.

41 Hejnic and Martínek, *Rukověť*, vol. IV 185–8.

42 For Písecký's letter, see B. Ryba, 'Horatius v Čechách předhumanistických', *Listy filologické*, 60 (1933), 115–26, 273–87, 436–40. It is significant that the earlier edition of Písecký's correspondence by J. Truhlář has not included this particular letter to Michal of Stráže; the letter was found not to be humanist.

43 Janáček, *Doba předbělohorská*, vol. I, 244–5.

44 Hejnic and Martínek, *Rukověť*, vol. I, 415–51.

45 R. Urbánek, 'Novoutrakvisticky humanista Matouš Kollin z Chotěřiny a starší tradice husitská', *Časopis společnosti přátel starožitností českých*, 64 (1956), 1, 70; W. Eberhard, *Monarchie und Widerstand. Zur ständischen Oppositionsbildung im Herrschaftssysytem Ferdinands I. in Böhmen* (Munich, 1985), 280, 314.

46 Hejnic and Martínek, *Rukověť*, vol. II 74–84.

47 J. Dubravius, *Theriobulia. Rada zvířat*, ed. M. Horna and E. Petrů (Prague, 1983), 31.

48 Hejnic and Martínek, *Rukověť*, vol. I, 116–17.

49 B. Ryba, 'Horatius v Čechách předhumanistických', *Listy filologické*, 63 (1936), 33.

50 O. Králík, 'Moravský humanista Wolfgang Heiligmaier', *Listy filologické*, 72 (1948), 191–202.

51 See, for example, Z. Tichá in the introduction to *Veršované skladby Neuberského sborníku* (Prague, 1960).

52 This has been demonstrated again, for instance, by P. Trost, 'Zwei tschechischen Minnereden', *Wiener Slawistisches Jahrbuch*, 17 (1972), 289–94; and in his polemical articles against Z. Tichá, in *Slovo a slovesnost*, 37 (1976), 289–94; *Česká literatura*, 21 (1973), 481–6.

53 See the introduction by A. Grund to the edition of *Boccacciovské rozprávky* (Prague, 1950), 19. Grund even considers Hynek of Poděbrady the first poet of the Czech Renaissance.

54 For my analysis I have used information available in *Knihopis českých a slovenských tisků od doby nejstarší až do konce 18.století*, published in Prague since 1925.

55 The fundamental monograph is by M. Kopecký, *Literární dílo Mikuláše Konáče z Hodištvova* (Prague, 1962), who has also edited Konáč's *Pravidlo lidského života* (Prague, 1961).

56 Kopecký, *Literární dílo Konáče*, 36–7. Kopecký, however, draws the wrong conclusion and takes Konáč' typical medieval perspective of man and of the world for 'Baroque poetry' (66).

57 See J. Hrabák (ed.), *Dějiny české literatury* (Prague, 1959), vol. I, 351–4.

58 *Ibid.*, 363–78.

59 N. Rejchrtová, *Václav Budovec z Budova* (Prague, 1984).

60 Hrabák, *Dějiny*, vol. I, 363–78.

61 'Frantova práva' was published, together with other moralistic satires from the Reformation period, by J. Kolár, *Frantové a grobiáni. Z mravokárnych satir 16.věku v Čechách* (Prague, 1959). In his introduction J. Kolár makes a clear

distinction between 'Frantora práva' and the other satires, in which 'the prevailing tones are closer to medieval than Renaissance thinking' (18).

62 R. Urbánek, 'Jan Paleček, šašek krále Jiřího a jeho předchůdci v zemích českých' in *Příspěvky k dějinám starší české literatury* (Prague, 1958), 5–89.

63 *Rozmlouvánie o vieře*, old print (1511); new edn (Prague, 1928).

64 A. Molnár, 'Neznámý spis Prokopa z Jindřichova Hradce', *Husitský Tábor*, 6–7 (1985), 423–48.

65 F. Kutnar, *Přehledné dějiny českého a slovenského dějepisectví* (Prague, 1973), vol. I, 60f.

66 I have tried to show Machiavelli's methodological contributions in my book, *Machiavelli e il machiavellismo* (Florence, 1980), 51–91.

67 J. Černý, *Knieha lékařská, kteráž slove Herbář aneb Zelinář*, ed. Z. Tichá (Prague, 1981).

68 See, for example, transcripts of the encyclopaedia by Vincent of Beauvais preserved in a Czech manuscript of the fifteenth century. See P. Spunar, 'Encyklopedie 13.století a jejich znalost v Čechách', in *Umění 13.století v českých zemích* (Prague, 1983), 593.

69 See especially M. Bochatcová, 'Höltzels Einblatt mit der Klaudianischen Land- karte Böhmens' in *Gutenberg Jahrbuch 1975*, 106–12; and K. Kuchař, *Mapy českých zemí do poloviny 18.století* (Prague, 1959).

70 F. Černý (ed.-in-chief), *Dějiny českého divadla* (Prague, 1968), vol. I (ed. A. Scherl) 103.

71 M. Kopecký, *Pokrokové tradice v české literatuře od konce husitství do Bílé Hory* (Brno, 1979), 42.

72 *Dějiny českého divadla*, vol. I, 111–39. The authors, however, have erroneously referred to a 'humanistic theatre'. They are right, of course, when they stress that a Renaissance drama, such as Machiavelli's *Mandragora*, was completely alien to the Czech theatre of the sixteenth century (110).

73 J. Charvát (ed.), *Staré letopisy české* (Prague, 1940), no. 736 (LM).

74 *Ibid.*, no. 656 on the year 1491.

75 Ż. Winter, *Děviny řemesel a obchodu v Čechách v XIV. a XV. století* (Prague, 1906), 685.

76 *Archiv český*, vol. XIV (s.a.) 288–9.

77 E. Ullmann, 'Zum Problem der Renaissanceliteratur in der Kunstgeschichte', in R. Weimann, W. Lenk and J.J. Slouka (eds.), *Renaissanceliteratur und Frübür- gerliche Revolution* (Berlin and Weimar, 1976), 195–296.

78 J. Krása (ed.), *Pozdně gotické umění v Čechách* (Prague, 1978).

79 E. Assunto, *Die Theorie des Schönen im Mittelalter* (Cologne, 1963), 118–20.

80 Kopecký, *Literární dílo M. Konáče*, 56–7.

81 W.W. Tomek, *Dějepis Prahy* (Prague, 1894), vol. X, 207–08.

82 A. Chastel, 'Y a-t-il une éstetique de la Renaissance?' in L. Gerevich (ed.) *Actes du colloque sur la Renaissance* (Paris, 1958), 24.

83 According to P.A. Sorokin, 'The western religion and morality of today' in *Internationales Jahrbuch für Religionssoziologie* (1966), vol. II; cited by Kopecký, *Pokrokové tradice*, 20.

84 P. Burke, *Die Renaissance in Italien. Sozialgeschichte einer Kultur zwischen Tradition und Erfindung* (Berlin, 1984).

85 I have carried out this comparison on the basis of the catalogue of Czech paintings between 1450–1550 as printed in J. Pěšina, *Česká malba pozdní gotiky a renesance* (Prague, 1950).

86 Martin ze Žatce, *Knížky proti ošemetné poctě a pokryté svatých z roku 1517*, National Museum Library, signature 37 D 29, fo. D4.

87 Pěšina, *Česká malba*, no. 214.

88 J. Neumann (ed.), *Die Kunst der Renaissance und der Manierismus in Böhmen* (Prague, 1979), 48.

89 *Ibid.*, 8.

90 J. Białostocki, *The Art of the Renaissance in Eastern Europe*, (London 1976); J. Kropáček, 'On the penetrating of the Renaissance into central Europe in 1400–1510' in *Actes du XXIIe Congrés International d'histoire de l'art* (Budapest, 1972), 639–44; J. Vacková, 'Reflets de l'italisme dans la peinture en Bohéme vers 1500' in *Actes du colloque*, 645–8. See also the introduction in the book of F. Seibt, *Renaissance in Böhmen* (Munich, 1985).

91 L. Gerevich, *The Art of Buda and Pest in the Middle Ages* (Budapest, 1971), 126ff.

92 J. Pěšina, 'Studie k pozdně gotickému baroku', *Památky archeologické (historie)*, 6–8 (1940), 68–81.

93 J. Krčálová 'Die Renaissancearchitektur in Böhemen' in *Kunst der Renaissance*, 50.

94 *Ibid.*, 118.

95 *Ibid.*, 129.

96 *Ibid.*, 11.

97 *Archiv český*, vol. VIII, 220–1.

98 K. Chytill, *Malířstvo pražské XV. a XVI.věku a jeho cechovní kniha Staroměstská z let 1490–1582* (Prague, 1906), 8, 17–18.

99 *Ibid.*, 19.

100 Preface to *Kunst der Renaissance*, 11–12.

101 *Ibid.*, 12.

102 K. Chytill, *Vývoj miniaturního malířství za doby králů rodu jagellonského* (Prague, 1896), 36.

103 *Památky archeologické*, 33 (1923), 165.

104 Chytill, *Vývoj miniaturního malířství*, 40.

105 Z. Smetánka and O. Topolová, 'Die älteste böhmische Keramik mit Zinn-Bleiglasur', *Památky archeologické*, 58 (1967), 499–544.

106 T. Durdík, Z. Smetánka and M. Soudný, 'Keramická plastika z hradu v Jindři-chově Hradci', *Památky archeologické*, 73 (1982), 230. The model for the so-called stove' in Moravia is Buda. See P. J. Michna, 'Archäologische Nachweise der mährisch-ungarischen Beziehungen im 15.Jahrhundert', *Folia archeologica*, 25 (1974), 183, 190–1, 202.

107 L. Ulčák and P. Šrámek, 'Zvonařství na severní Moravě v 15.–18.století', *Památky a příroda*, 10 (1979), 589–90.

108 J. Ludvíkovský wrote that the effort to apply the term Renaissance to an entire historical period in the land of Hus and Comenius encounters serious difficulties. See the volume *Humanistická konference*, 589–90. F. Šmahel argued similarly 'Husitství-humanismus-renesance' in *ibid.*, 61.

(All dates are AD unless otherwise stated)

Abbate, Niccolò dell', *see* Dell'Abbate
Abbe, Derek van, 115
Ackerman, J., 54
Aeneas Sylvius, *see* Pius II
Aesop (620–*c*.560 BC), 78
Agricola, Rudolf (Roelof Huysman; 1442–
   85), Dutch humanist, 10, 78, 104
   De inventione dialectica, 77–8, 106
Agrippa von Nettesheim, Cornelius (*c*.1486–
   1535), German humanist (occult
   studies), 110
Alberti, Leone Battista (1401–72), Venetian
   painter and humanist scholar, 32, 34, 94
   Descripto urbis Romae, 43
Alexander III, the Great (356–323 BC), king
   of Macedon 336–323 BC, 97, 207
Alexander VI (Rodrigo Borgia; *c*.1430–1503),
   pope 1492–1503, 47, 198
Alfonso I (Alfonso V of Aragon; 1385–1458),
   king of Aragon, Sicily, and Naples, 71
Altdorf, university of, 191
Altdorfer, Albrecht (1480–1538), German
   artist, 95, 96
   The Battle of Issus, 96–7
Americas, spread of Italian Renaissance art
   to, 11
Amsterdam, 63, 80, 84, 85, 86, 87
Amyot, Jacques (1513–93), translator of
   classics into the French language, 133
anatomical studies, influence on art, 22, 96,
   214
Androuet de Cerceau (Ducerceau), Jacques
   (1510–84), 10
   Livre d'Architecture, 12
Angoulème, 17
antiquity/ancients, *see* classics
Antoine de Bourbon, duc de Vendôme
   (assumed title 'king of Navarre';

d.1562), 138
Antonello de Messina (*c*.1430–79),
   introduced oil paints into Italy, 59
Antwerp, 17, 72, 77, 79
Apuleius, Lucius (2nd cent. AD), *The
   Golden Ass*, 44, 101
Aquinas, St Thomas (*c*.1225–74), 25, 47, 114,
   203
   Thomism, 103
Arabs, as disseminators of new knowledge, 1
architecture
   Baroque, 54, 55, 84, 181, 182, 183, 184
   Byzantine, 54, 55
   Gothic, 21, 22, 54, 181, 183, 210, 212, 214,
   215
   literature on, 12, 22, 43, 167
   *see also under countries, towns and
   individual architects*
Arcimboldo, Giuseppe (1533–93), Milanese
   artist working in Prague, 10
Aretino, Pietro (1492–1556), satirical writer
   from Arezzo working in Venice, 60, 61, 62
Arezzo, 23, 27, 34, 37, 60
Ariosto, Ludovico (1474–1533), Italian poet,
   9, 10, 62
Aristides (*c*.530–468 BC), *Panathenaicus*, 29
Aristotle (384–322 BC), 24, 48, 105, 111, 114,
   131, 132, 189, 202
   Ethics, 24, 25
   Politics, 24, 25, 29, 30–1
Arrian (2nd cent. BC), *Anabasis Alexandri*,
   164
arts, visual, *see* architecture; painting;
   sculpture
Ascham, Roger (1515–68), 13–14
   Toxophilus, 158
Athens (5th cent. BC), 29
Attavante degli Attavanti (fl. 1480),
   Florentine illuminator working in Buda,
   167

Attila (c.406–53), king of the Huns c.433–53, 173

Augustine, St (d. 604), 1st archbishop of Canterbury, City of God, 155

Augustus (63 BC–AD 14), Roman emperor 27 BC–AD 14, 4, 28, 82

Aurelius, Cornelius (1462?–1531), Dutch humanist, 81

Austria, 71, 72, 76, 165, 169
   see also Habsburgs

Averlino, Antonio di Pietro, see Filarete

Avignon, humanism in, 8

Bakfark, Valentin (1507–76), Hungarian composer/musician, 172

Bakócz, Tamás (1422–1521), archbishop of Esztorgom, 169

Balassi, Bálint (1554–94), Hungarian poet, 176

Balbi, Girolamo (d. after 1530), Venetian humanist teaching in Vienna, 103

Bandini, Francesco (fl. 1477), Italian writer associated with Platonic Academy, 166, 167

barbarians, 14

Barbo, Pietro, see Paul II

Baron, H., 56

Baroque, see architecture

Basel (Basle), Reformation in, 137, 172

Batavia, renamed in 1619 (formerly Jakarta), 15

Batavians/Batavian myths, 81, 83, 87

Báthory, Miklós (c.1440–1506), bishop of Vác, 168

Báthory, Sigismund, see Sigismund III

Báthory, Stephen (1533–86), prince of Transylvania c.1571–86 (king of Poland 1575–86), 175, 191

Baudouin (or Bauduin), François (1520–73), teacher at Bourges university, 131

Bavarians, origins of, 15

Beatrice of Aragon (d. 1508), 2nd wife of Matthias Corvinus, 167

Beavis of Hampton, writer of books on education, 62

Bebel, Heinrich (1472–1518), German humanist, 104

Becanus, Goropius, Origines Antwerpianae (1569), 79

Becon, Thomas (1512–67), Protestant divine
   The New Policy of War, 159
   The True Defence of Peace, 159

Belgium, see Low Countries

Belgrade, Turks defeated by Hungary (1456), 165

Bellay, Joachim du, see DuBellay

Belleforest, François de (1530–83), French

Catholic historian, 134

Bellini, Gentile (c.1429–1507), Venetian painter (brother of Giovanni), 11, 55, 57

Bellini, Giovanni (1430–1516), 10

Bembo, Pietro (1470–1547), cardinal, 46

Beroaldo, Filippo the elder (1453–1505), Italian humanist, 202

Berquin, Louis du (1489–1529), Protestant martyr, 137

Bèze (Beza), Théodore de (1519–1605), Calvin's successor at Geneva, 137–8, 176

Białostocki, Jan, 181, 183

Bible, 74–5, 79, 102, 203, 207, 211
   as focus of theology studies at Protestant universities, 114
   in Hungarian, 173–4
   Luther's German translation, 98, 101
   New Testament, 136, 158, 172, 173–4, 201
   Old Testament, 15, 16, 46, 49, 79, 149, 174, 209

Biblioteca Corvina, Buda, Hungary, 166–7
   destroyed by Turks, 170

Biondo, Flavio (1392–1463), Roma instaurata, 43, 44

Blahoslav, Jan (1523–71), Czech theological writer, 202, 203

Blocke, Willem van der (fl. 1593), Netherlands architect, 11

Blount, Walter, 1st baron Mountjoy (d. 1474), 150

Boccaccio, Giovanni (1313–75), originator of classical revival in Florence, 21, 23, 28, 101, 127, 135, 147, 148, 178, 206

Bodin, Jean (1530–96), French political thinker, 141, 192
   Republic, 130, 139–40

Boece, Hector (1465?–1536), History of the Scots, 15

Boethius, Anicius Manlius Severinus (c.480–524), De Consolatione Philosophiae, 147

Bohemia and Moravia, 4, 169, 183, 186, 197–219
   arts and architecture, 181, 200, 210–15
   classics, 201, 202–4, 207, 209
   Counter-Reformation, 201, 208, 209, 213
   Hussite Revolution (1419), 197–200, 203, 204, 206, 208, 210–11
   Italian influence, 202, 203, 211
   Latin and Czech humanism, 197, 200–5
   literature (poetry, prose, and drama), 201, 205–10
   relations between Renaissance and Reformation, 197–216
   see also Church of the Brethren; Utraquists

Bologna, 10, 11, 23, 47
  university of, 164, 199, 200, 201, 204
Bologna, Giovanni da (or Jean Boulogne;
  1529–1608), French sculptor working in
  Florence, 8, 181–2
Bonapace, Vettore (fl. 1442), Venetian
  teacher, 62
Bonfini, Antonio (c.1427–1502/5), Italian
  scholar working in Hungary, 166, 167
  Rerum Hungaricum decades, 175
Borgia family, 147
Borgia, Rodrigo, *see* Alexander VI
Bornemisza, Péter (1535–85), Hungarian
  Lutheran minister, 172
  Magyar Elektra, 174, 176
Botticelli, Sandro (1444–1510), 45
Bourbon dynasty, 138, 141
Bourges, university of, 131
Bracciolini-Poggio, Giovanni Francesco, *see*
  Poggio Bracciolini, Giovanni Francesco
Bramante, Donato (1444–1514), architect in
  Urbino, 45, 94
Brant, Sebastian (1458–1521), German
  humanist author, 104
  Narrenschiff, 108
Braudel, Ferdinand, 123, 124, 128, 141
Brederode, Gerbrand Adriaensz (1585–1618),
  Dutch poet/playwright, 84, 85, 86
Bruce, William (fl. 1598), Scottish scholar in
  Poland, 188
Brueghel, Pieter *the younger* (1564–1638), 10
Brunelleschi, Filippo (1377–1446), Italian
  architect, 21–2, 23, 45, 94
Bruni, Leonardo (1370–1444), chancellor of
  Florence, 23–5, 28–9, 30–1, 34, 56, 101,
  134
  *Dialogue to Pietro Paulo Vergerio of
    Istria*, 24
  History of the Florentine People, 24, 27
  Introduction to Moral Doctrine, 25
  Laudatio, 153
  Panegyric to the City of Florence, 29
Bruno, Giordano (1548–1600), Italian
  philosopher, 50
Brutus the Trojan, 15
Buchanan, George (1506–82), Scottish
  humanist poet, 176, 193
Buda (now Budapest), 213, 214
  humanists in, 165, 166–7
  Italian traders in, 164
  sacked by Turks (1526), 170, 174
Budé, Guillaume (1467–1540), French
  humanist, 10, 128, 130, 132, 133
  publications, 130–1, 136
Bugenhagen, Johann (1485–1558), German
  Protestant reformer, 115

Burckhardt, Jacob (1818–97), Swiss
  historian, 5, 56, 192
Burdach, Konrad, 102–3
Burgkmair, Hans *the elder* (d. 1531),
  German artist, 95, 96
Burgundian territories, 2, 36, 70, 81, 180
Burgundy, ducal house of, 36, 70, 71–2, 75–6
  taken over by Habsburgs, 72, 76
Burke, Edmund (1729–97), 185
Burley, Walter (1275–1345?), classics scholar,
  203, 207
Busche, Hermann von dem (1468–1534),
  Westphalian humanist, 104, 112, 115,
  116
Byzantine, *see* architecture
Byzantium, *see* Constantinople

Cade, John (d. 1450), rebel leader, 149
Caesar, Gaius Julius (100–44 BC), 14, 28, 47,
  81, 87, 150, 202
Caliari/Cagliari, Paulo, *see* Veronese
Calvin, John (1509–64), 99, 136, 137, 138,
  141, 172
  Institution of Christian Religion, 137, 139
Calvinists, 81, 98–9, 190
Cambiaso, Luca (1527–85), Genoese painter,
  10
Camerarius, Joachim (1500–74), German
  classicist, 114, 115
Camicia, Chimanti (fl. 1476), Italian
  architect of Buda castle, 167
Camões, Luis de (c.1524–80), Portuguese
  poet, *The Lusiads*, 15
Campagna, Girolamo (c.1549–after 1626),
  Venetian sculptor, 60
capitalism, 3
Caravia, Alessandro (1503–68), Venetian
  goldsmith/heretic, 62
Carew, Sir George (d. 1612), visit to Poland
  (1598), 188
Carpaccio, Vittore (c.1455–c.1525), Venetian
  painter, 55
Carthage, 27
Casola, Pietro (1427–1507), Milanese
  pilgrim/writer, 61
Castagno, Andrea del (1423–57), Italian
  painter, 164
Castiglioni, Baldassare (1478–1529), 11, 164
  Il Cortegiano, 11, 13
Castillejo, Cristóbal de (c.1494–1550),
  Spanish poet, 14
Catherine de Medici (1519–89), queen of
  Henry II of France, 13, 133, 138
Catholic Church/Catholics, 9, 13, 102, 110–
  13, 125, 159
  in Bohemia and Moravia, 197–9, 200, 203,

Catholic Church/Catholics (*cont.*)
204, 207–8, 214
in France, 136–40
in Poland, 190, 191, 193
see also Counter-Reformation; inquisition;
papacy; Reformation
Catholic universities, 113, 114
Cato *the elder* (Marcus Portius Cato; 234–
149 BC), 78
Cellini, Benvenuto (1500–71), at court of
Francis I, 10
Celtis, Conradus (1459–1508), German
humanist/poet, 10, 92, 96, 104, 106, 115,
116, 167
importance to German Renaissance, 108
criticizes monasteries, 110
founds College of Poets and
Mathematicians at Vienna, 111
Ludus Dianiae, 109
Quattuor Libri Amorum, 108
Rhapsodia, 109
Sodalitas litteraria Danubiana, 169
Černý, Jan (fl. 1500), Czech writer on
science, 208
Cesarini, Giuliano (1389–1444), Italian
diplomat in Hungary, 164, 165
Chabod, Federigo, 185, 187
Charlemagne (742–814), Frankish king, 1st
Holy Roman Emperor 800–14, 123, 124
Charles IV (1316–78), Holy Roman Emperor
1355–78, 102, 104, 199
Charles V (1500–58), Holy Roman Emperor
1519–55, king of Spain 1516–56, 71, 72,
73, 98, 129, 170
Charles VIII (1470–98), king of France 1483–
98, invades Italy, 130
Charles IX (1550–74), king of France 1560–
74, 129, 131
Charles I (1600–49), king of England 1625–
49, 161
Chartier, Roger, 8
Chaucer, Geoffrey (1340?–1400), 14, 147–8,
150, 151, 157–8
The Parliament of Foules, 148
Troilus and Criseyde, 147
Chaundler, Thomas (1418?–90), dean of
Hereford, 153
Cheke, Sir John (1514–57), classics scholar,
13–14, 158
Chelčický, Petr (c.1390–c.1460), Czech
moralist, 201
Chigi, Agostino (1465–1520), Roman
banker/arts patron, 44
Christian II (1481–1559), king of Denmark
1513–23, patron of foreign artists, 11–12
Christian IV (1577–1648), king of Denmark

1588–1648, patron of foreign artists, 12
Christianity, 3, 113, 166
Catholic/Protestant controversies, 17, 72,
73, 80–1, 93, 112–13, 136–40
see also Catholic Church; Counter-
Reformation; Protestants; Reformation
Chrysoloras, Manuel (?1350–1415), teacher
of Greek at Florence, 23, 24
Church, Catholic, *see* Catholic Church
Church, Eastern Orthodox, 191, 193
Church of the Brethren (*Unitas Fratrum*),
198, 201, 202, 203, 204, 208, 209, 213
Church of England, 159–60
Cicero, Marcus Tullius (106–43 BC), 3, 4, 23,
24, 26, 31, 43, 50, 57, 61, 78, 100, 101,
104, 106, 148, 150, 153, 160, 165, 168,
203, 204
De officiis, 25, 28, 30
De oratore, 24, 33
Familiar Letters, 28
Cimabue, Giovanni (c.1240–1302),
Florentine artist, 14
Civil Wars, French (1562), 138
classics/classical revival
studied in schools, 31–6, 62, 77–8, 165,
171, 190
in universities, 108–16
see also Florence; Greece; Hebrew; Latin;
Rome; *and under countries and classical
authors*
Claudian (c.370–404), 21
Colet, John (1467?–1519), dean of St Paul's,
10, 153
Collège Royal (later Collège de France), 130
Collegium Germanicum-Hungaricum, Rome,
171
Collinus (Matouš; 1516–66), Czech Latin
humanist, 204, 209
Colloquy of Possy (1561), 138
Cologne, university of, curriculum reform,
112–13
Colonna, Guido della (c.1215–c.1285),
Italian poet, 149
Colonna, Otto, *see* Martin V
Colonna, Pompeo (c.1479–1532), Roman
revolutionary, 48
Comenius (Jan Amos Komenský; 1592–
1670), Czech educationist, 205
Commynes, Philippe de (1447–1511), French
ambassador to Venice, 59, 60
Condé, Henry I de Bourbon, prince de
(1552–88), 138
Constance, General Council of the Church
(1416), 147, 148
Constantine I, the Great (c.280–337), Roman
emperor 307–37, 148

Constantinople, 11, 55
  Sack of (1204), 55
Coornhert, D.V. (1522–90), Dutch humanist,
  79
Copenhagen, 12
  architecture, 184
  university, 11
Copernicus, Nicolaus (1473–1543), studies at
  Cracow, 192–3
  De revolutionibus orbium coelestium, 193
Corbinelli, Antonio (d. 1425), Florentine
  aristocrat, 33
Cornelis (Cornelisz) van Haarlem (1562–
  1638), Dutch Mannerist painter, *Fall of
  the Titans*, 12
Cortesi (Cortese), Paolo (1465–1510),
  humanist scholar employed by the
  papacy in Rome, 44, 47
Cortona, 27
Coryat, Thomas (?1577–1617), *Crudities*, 193
Counter-Reformation, 50, 54–5, 77, 87, 185,
  190, 201, 208, 209, 213
Cracow, 194
  architecture, 181, 182, 183, 193
  university, 169, 171, 191, 192, 199
Cranach, Lucas *the elder* (1472–1553), Saxon
  court artist, 95–6, 97, 98
Crespin, Jean (d. 1572), *Histoire des martyrs*,
  138
Cromwell, Thomas, earl of Essex (1486?–
  1540), 146, 156
Crotus Rubeanus (fl. 1510), Erfurt humanist,
  112
Cujas, Jacques (1522–90), scholar at Bourges
  University, 131
Czechoslovakia/Czechs, *see* Bohemia and
  Moravia

Dačický of Heslov, Mikuláš (1555–1616),
  Czech writer, 207
Dalmata, Giovanni (fl. 1476), Italian
  architect working in Buda, 167
Dante Alighieri (1265–1321), 32, 35, 135
  influence on Czech humanists, 202
  Divina Commedia, 164
Dantiscus, Johannes (fl. 1550), Polish
  diplomat, 193
Darius III (d. 330 BC), king of Persia (336–
  330 BC), 97
Dati, Gregorio (1362–1435), Florentine
  historian, 29
Dávid, Ferenc (c.1510–85), Hungarian
  founder of Unitarian Church, 172
De Certau, Michel, 8
Dell'Abbate, Niccolò (1512–71), artist from
  Modena, 10

Delorme, Philibert (1515?–70), French
  architect, 10
Demosthenes (c.384–322 BC), 109, 114
Denis, St (d. 258?), patron saint of France, 134
Denmark, Renaissance in, 11–12
Descartes, René (1596–1650), 141
  Cartesianism, 131
discovery and exploration, 70, 84, 128
Dobrohost, Leonard (fl. 1524), Moravian
  humanist/lawyer, 205
Dolet, Etienne (1509–46), French scholar/
  printer, 133
Domenichi, Domenico de' (1416–78),
  Venetian humanist, 45
Dominici, Giovanni (c.1356–1419),
  Florentine dominican preacher, 32–3, 34
Donatello (Donato de Nicolo di Betto Bardi;
  1386–1466), Florentine sculptor, 22, 45
Dondi dell'Orologio, Giovanni (Johannes ab
  Horologio; 1318–89), Paduan humanist,
  43
Donne, John (1572–1631), 194
DuBellay (Du Bellay), Joachim (1522–60),
  *Defense and Illustration of the French
  Language*, 14, 133
Dubravius, Jan (c.1486–1553), Catholic
  bishop of Olomouc, 204
  Theriobulia, 204
Dudich, Andreas (1533–89), Hungarian
  philologist/ philosopher, 172
Dudley, Edmund (1462?–1510), lawyer/
  supporter of absolute monarchy, 160
  Tree of the Commonwealth, 152
Dudley, Robert, earl of Leicester (c.1531–88),
  82
Dufay, Guillaume (c.1400–74), Burgundian
  composer, 45, 70
Dumoulin, Charles (1500–66), French legist,
  129, 133
Dürer, Albrecht (1471–1528), 10, 12, 61, 95,
  96, 97–8, 99, 214
  The Four Apostles, 98
Dutch East India Company, 15
Dutch Renaissance, *see* Low Countries

economics, new, 1, 3
  in Florence, 31–2
education
  in schools, 31–6, 37, 62, 77–8, 114–15, 154,
  165, 171, 190
  see also under university towns
Edward IV (1442–83), king of England 1461–
  70/1471–83, 149, 150, 151
Edward VI (1537–53), king of England 1547–
  53, 158
Edward, prince of Wales (1453–71), 151

Egypt, ancient, 15, 49
Elias, Norbert, 3
Elizabethans, 160–1, 193
Elyot, Sir Thomas (1490–?1546), *Book named the Governor*, 157–8
Emilio (Paule-Emile), Paolo (d. 1529), French historian, 16, 134, 135
Engels, Friedrich (1820–95), 1–2
England
  architecture, 160–1
  economics, 151
  humanism in, 4, 13–14, 146–63
  idea of nationhood, 14–15, 16, 147, 156
  influence of Italy, 13, 146, 147, 149, 153
  literature (historiography), 147–61
  monarchy, 148–52, 161
  poetry, 157–9
  political thought, 146–57
  printing, 154
  Reformation, 156, 159–60
  vernacular supersedes Latin, 14, 146–8
  wars with France, 148–9, 155
  Wars of the Roses, 149–50
Enlightenment, 1, 2, 6–7, 63
Erasmus, Desiderius (1466?–1536), 10, 46, 63, 71, 73, 128, 130, 136, 137, 154, 174, 193
  contacts with Hungary, 169–70, 172
  influence on Italian Renaissance, 61–2
  interest in education, 77
  importance to European Renaissance, 78–9
  portraits of, 95, 96
  split with Luther (1525), 113
  Enconium Moriae, 155, 203
Erfurt, university of, 111, 114
  curriculum reform, 113
Erik XIV (1533–77), king of Sweden 1560–9, patron of arts, 11
Eschenbach, Wolfram von, *see* Wolfram von Eschenbach
Estienne, Henri (1528–98), French humanist printer, 13, 14, 16, 130, 133
Etruscans, 17, 28, 49
Eusebius of Caesarea (c.260–340), 132
Eyb, Albrecht von (1420–75), German theologian, 103, 104
  Margarita poetica, 101
Eyck, Jan van (c.1385–1441), 7, 71
  innovations in fabrication of paint, 70

Farel, Guillaume (1489–1565), French religious reformer, 137
Fauchet, Claude de (1530–1602), French historian, 135
Ferdinand I (1503–64), king of Bohemia and Hungary 1526–64, Holy Roman

Emperor 1556–64, 170, 204, 212–13
Ferrara, 25, 70
  university of, 200
Ferrault, Jean (fl. 1550), French legist, 129
feudalism, 2, 3, 5
Fichet, Guillaume (fl. 1450–1506), rector of Paris University 1467, 127
Ficino, Marsilio (1433–99), revives Platonic philosophy, 25–6, 34, 103, 110, 167, 169, 202, 203
Filarete (Antonio di Pietro Averlino; c.1400–c.1469), *De architectura*, 167
Filelfo, Francesco (1398–1481), scholar at Rome University, 43, 164
Finariensis, Petrus Antonius (fl. 1450), Italian lecturer at Basel/Heidelberg, 103
Finland, 11
Fioravanti, Aristotele (fl. 1470), architect from Bologna working in Moscow, 11
Flaška, Smil, *Nová rada* (1394), 204
Flemish, *see* Low Countries
Florence, 2, 6, 7, 14, 17, 21–41, 42, 45, 53, 54, 55, 56, 63, 73, 153, 167, 213
  arts, 21–2
  classical revival, 21–41
  early history, 17, 21, 28
  education, 31–6
  influence on Polish art, 183–4
  letters/thought, 23–4, 25–6
  neoplatonism (Platonic Academy), 3, 25, 110, 167
  political system, 25, 26–31
Floris V (1254–96), count of Holland, 83, 87
Floris, Frans (1516–70), Flemish painter, 10
Fonzio, Bartolomeo (fl. 1470), Italian writer working in Hungary, 166
Fortescue, Sir John (1394–?1476), lord chief justice of England, 150–1, 152, 153, 160
  The Governance of England, 151
Foscari family of Venice, 58
Foscari, Francesco (c.1372–1457), doge of Venice 1423–57, 57
Fouquet, Jean (c.1420–c.1480), French painter of miniatures, 10
France, 123–45, 146
  civil war (1562), 138
  classical revival, 130
  Enlightenment, 6–7
  Gallic Church, 125
  historiography, 14–15, 16, 123–4, 134–6
  humanism, 4, 127–8, 130, 134–6
  Italian influence, 10, 127, 128
  anti–Italianism, 13
  law, 125–6, 129–30, 131, 132–3
  literature, 9, 14, 102, 127–8
  modernisation, 131–4

monarchy, 124–7, 129, 130, 134, 139–41, 187
nationhood/origins, 15, 123–4, 130
political theory, 128–31, 136–41
printing, 127–8, 129, 130–1, 137
religion/Reformation, 128, 136–40
universities, 127, 130
vernacular supersedes Latin, 13, 14, 131–4, 135, 136
wars with England, 148–9, 155; with Italy, 130
Francio the Trojan, 15
Francis I (1494–1547), king of France 1515–47, 10, 124, 129, 130, 131, 133, 137
Francis II (1544–60), king of France 1559–60, 129
Frankfurt an der Oder, university of, 111
Franks, 15, 135
Carolingian/Merovingian dynasties, 123
Frederick I 'Barbarossa' (c.1123–90), Holy Roman Emperor 1155–90, 109
Frederick III (1415–93), Holy Roman Emperor 1440–93, 92, 103, 165, 173
Frederick II (1534–88), king of Denmark 1559–88, 12
Frederick Hendrik, prince of Orange (1625–47), 86–7
Freiburg im Breisgau, university of, 107, 109, 112
French Revolution (1789–99), 16, 123, 129
Frulovisi, Tito Livio (fl. 1420), Italian secretary to Humphrey of Gloucester, Humfroidos, 149

Gabrieli, Andrea (c.1520–86) and Giovanni (1557–1612), Venetian composers/organists, 61
Gaguin, Robert (c.1425–1502), French historian, 134
Galileo Galilei (1564–1642), 26
Gama, Vasco da (c.1460–1524), 15
Gansfort, Wessel (1420–89), Dutch humanist, 78
Garcilaso de la Vega (c.1503–36), Spanish poet, 14
Gardiner, Stephen (1483?–1555), bishop of Winchester, 17
Gdansk, architecture in, 183, 184
Geneva, 137, 172
Genoa, 35, 37
Geoffrey of Monmouth (1100?–54), bishop of St Asaph, 15
George of Poděbrady, see Poděbrady, Jiří of
Germany, 2, 12–13, 92–122, 166
arts, 93–9, 181
classical revival, 92–3, 100–1, 102–9

education
schools, 114–15
universities, 102, 103–7, 108, 110, 111–12, 113
German language, 99, 100–1, 108
history, 92–3
humanism/humanists, 102–13
role in religious reform, 110–11, 112
influence of Italy, 61, 92, 94, 96, 100–1, 102, 103, 104, 105, 111
anti-Italianism, 13
influence on Poland, 182, 192
literature, 99–102, 106–7, 108–9, 111–13
nationhood, 15, 17, 111
printing, 108, 109, 113
Reformation, 7, 93, 94, 98–9, 102, 113, 114–16
Ghent, as refuge for Protestant dissidents, 72–3
Ghiberti, Lorenzo (1378–1455), Florentine sculptor, 22, 45
Ghirlandaio (1449–94), Italian painter, 45, 70, 95
Ghislieri, Michele, see Pius V
'Giambologna', see Bologna, Giovanni da
Giles (Gilles) of Viterbo (c.1465–c.1532), vicar-general of Augustinian order, 47, 48
Gilles, Nicolas (fl. 1492), French historian, 134
Giorgione (c.1478–1510), founder of Venetian school of painting, 59
Giotto (Giotto di Bondoni; c.1266–1337), 22
Goedeke, Karl, 116
Goes, Hugo van der (c.1440–82), Flemish painter, 70
Golthan, Mattheus Aurogallus (1490–1543), Bohemian classicist, 205
Goltzius, Hendrik (1558–1617), Dutch painter, 10
Górnicki, Lukasz (1527–1603), Polish poet, The Polish Courtier, 194
Goslicki, Wawrzyniec, De optimo senatore (1568), 193
Gothic, see architecture
Gower, John (1325?–1408), English poet, 157–8
Grassaille, Charles de (1495–1582), French legist, 129
Gratius, Orwin (fl. 1518), Cologne humanist, 112–13
Great Schism (1378–1417), 27, 45, 125
Greece, ancient, 1, 3, 9, 21, 29, 49, 93, 101, 205
language, 23–4, 102, 114, 115, 130, 138
literature, 43, 78, 109, 114, 127

Greece, ancient (*cont.*)
    see also under individual
    writers/philosophers
Gregorius of Heimburg (fl. 1460), German
    humanist working in Bohemia, 200
Gregory of Tours, St (538–94), 134
Gresemund, Dietrich *the younger* (1475–
    1512), *Dialogue on the Seven Liberal
    Arts*, 107
Grien, Hans Baldung (1484–1545), German
    artist, 95, 96
Grimani family of Venice, 58
Grocyn, William (1446?–1519), English
    Greek scholar, 10, 153, 154
Groot, Geert (1340–84), Dutch teacher, 77
Groot (Grotius), Hugo de (1583–1645),
    Dutch lawyer/scholar, 80, 81, 84
Grünewald, Matthias (d. 1528), German
    artist, 95, 98
Grzybowski, Stanislaw, 193
Guarino da Verona (1374–1460), Italian
    poet, 166
Guicciardini, Francesco (1483–1540), 208
    History of Italy, 16, 26
Guise family of Lorraine, France, 16, 138
    Francis (1519–63), 2nd duke of Lorraine,
    138

Habsburg, Austrian dynasty, 15, 76, 107,
    129, 169, 171, 174, 185, 186, 214
    take over house of Burgundy, 72, 76
Haillan, Bernard du, 140
    De l'estat et succès des affaires de France
    (1570), 134
    Histoire de France (1576), 134
Hájek of Libočany, Václav (b. 1553), Czech
    chronicler, 208
Hales, John (1584–1656), Protestant scholar,
    159
Handel, Georg Friedrich (1685–1759), 182
handwriting, development of, 23
Hasištejnský, Bohuslav (1461–1510), Czech
    humanist scholar, 200–1
    De veterum philosophis, 201
Hebrew language, 102, 109, 112, 114, 115,
    130, 205
Heemskerk, Maerten Jacobsz (often called
    Maerten van Veen; 1498–1574), Dutch
    painter/architect, 10
Hegius, Alexander (1433–98), *Invective
    against the Modes of Signifying*, 107
Heidelberg, university of, 103, 105–6, 109,
    171
Heidenstein, Reinhold (fl. 1580), Polish
    historian, 191
Heiligmaier, Wolfgang (fl. 1500), Moravian

humanist, 205
Heinsius, Daniel (1580–1655), Dutch
    classicist/writer, 80, 84
Heltai, Gáspár (fl. 1574), Hungarian writer,
    174, 175
Henry V (1387–1422), king of England 1413–
    22, 148–9, 155
Henry VI (1421–71), king of England 1422–
    61/1470–71, 149, 150
Henry VII (1457–1509), king of England
    1485–1509, 151–2
Henry VIII (1491–1547), king of England
    1509–47, 95, 146, 155, 156, 159, 160
Henry II (1519–59), king of France 1547–59,
    129, 137, 138
Henry III (1551–89), king of France 1574–89,
    139, 187
Henry IV (1553–1610), king of France 1589–
    1610, 140–1
Hermelink, Heinrich, 103
'Hermes Trismegistus' (Hermetic books;
    *c.*3rd cent. AD), 49
Hesiod (8th cent. BC), 101
Hexter, J.H., 36, 189
Heynlin, Jean (*c.*1430–96), Swiss scholar at
    Paris University, 127
Hippocrates of Cos (*c.*460–*c.*370 BC), 109
historiography, 4, 15–17
    see also under countries
Hochstraten, Jacob von (fl. 1513),
    theologian/inquisitor at Mainz, 112–13
Holbein, Hans *the elder* (*c.*1465–1524), 10
Holbein, Hans *the younger* (1497/8–1543),
    95, 96
Holy Roman Empire, 3, 17, 71, 92, 93, 129, 165
Homer (8th cent. BC), 101, 109, 114, 149,
    202, 204
    Iliad, 86, 193
Honorius, Jan (fl. 1498), Bohemian classicist,
    205
Hooft, Peter Corneliszoon (1581–1647),
    Dutch statesman/ writer, 81–3, 84, 85,
    86, 87
    Geeraert van Velzan, 83
    Nederlandsche Historien, 81–2
Hoogewerff, G.J., 72
Horace (65–8 BC), 100, 193, 205
Hotman, François (1524–90), *Franco-Gallia*,
    14, 129
Howard, Henry, earl of Surrey, (1517?–47),
    English poet, 158–9, 160
Hrubý of Jelení, Řehoř (fl. 1514), Czech
    classicist, 203
Huguenots, 137, 138, 139
    St Bartholomew's Day massacres (1572),
    139, 140

humanism/humanists, 3, 5
    complex role in Renaissance, 4
    importance of publishing in vernacular,
        79–90, 106
    as national scholars/historians, 13–18
    importance of universities, 104–5
    increasing aggressiveness, 110–13
    role in religious reform, 110–11
    social background, 104
    see also classics; and under countries and
        humanists
Humphrey, duke of Gloucester (1391–1447),
    149, 153
Hungary, 3, 164–79, 186, 212
    architecture, 167, 168, 169, 181
    art, 181
    Biblioteca Corvina, 166–7
    education, 165, 171
    cultural interchanges with Italy, 164, 166,
        168, 169, 175
    literature, 166–7, 171, 172, 173–6
    in Middle Ages, 165, 168
    music, 167, 175
    nationalism, 173
    philosophy, 167, 168
    politics, 164, 166, 169–70
    Reformation, 170–2, 173, 174
    society, 168, 170–1
    vernacular supersedes Latin, 173–4, 176
    universities, 171
    wars with Turks, 165, 166, 168, 170, 173,
        174–5, 176
Hunyadi, János (c.1407–56), Hungarian
    military leader, 165, 174
Hunyadi, Matthias, see Matthias Corvinus
Hus, Jan (1369–1415), founder of Czech
    Reformation, 197, 205
Hussite Revolution (1419), 197, 198, 199,
    203, 204, 206, 208, 210–11
Hutten, Ulrich von (1488–1523), German
    humanist, 104, 105, 115
    attacks Roman Catholic Church, 111,
        112–13
Huygens, Constantin (1596–1687), Dutch
    statesman/poet, 84, 85, 86
Hyma, Albert, 103

Iceland, 11
imperialism, 4
Industrial Revolution (c.1760–c.1840), 16
industry, 3
Ingolstadt, university of, 92, 106, 107, 111,
    113, 191
Innocent VII (Cosimo Gentile de'Migliorati;
    1336–1406), pope 1401–6, 43
inquisition

    Czech, 201
    German, 112
    Roman, 50, 55
    Spanish, 73
Institoris, Heinrich (fl. 1500), inquisitor at
    Olomouc, 201
Ireland, influence of Italian Renaissance on,
    11
Isaak, Heinrich (c.1450–1517), Flemish
    musician, 8
Islam, architectural tradition, 12, 49
Italian Renaissance
    reception abroad, 1–5, 6, 7–13
        cross-cultural exchanges, 7–9, 10, 18,
            102–3, 106, 108, 111, 127, 128, 146, 149,
            153, 161, 164–5, 180, 181, 182, 199, 211,
            214
        anti-Italianism, 13–14, 18
    Italian language, 13, 14, 44
Italy, as origin of Renaissance, 2, 3, 6–20
    political situation (city states), 24–5, 185,
        192
    see also Florence; Rome; papacy; Venice
Ivan III (1440–1505), grand duke of Moscow
    1462–1505, 11
Ivan IV, the Terrible (1530–84), grand duke
    of Moscow 1533–84, and 1st tsar, 11

Jagiellonian dynasty of Poland-Lithuania,
    183, 186, 190, 200, 213
Jan of Kunčí (fl. 1484–94), Czech humanist,
    203
Jauss, H.R., 8
Jeanne d'Albret (1528–72), queen of
    Navarre, Protestant wife of Antoine de
    Bourbon, 139
Jesuits, 114, 135, 185, 190, 191, 192, 204
Jews, 49, 79, 112, 201
Jiří, king of Bohemia, see Poděbrady, Jiří
John I of Szapolyai, prince of Transylvania
    1526–40, 170
John III, king of Sweden 1569–92, 11, 12
Jones, Inigo (1573–1652), 10, 161
Jordanes, bishop of Croton (fl. 550), History
    of the Goths, 15
Josquin des Près (c.1440–1521), Flemish
    musician, 8, 45, 70
Juhász, Péter Melius (1536–72), organiser of
    Calvinist Church in Hungary, 172
Julius II (Giuliano della Rovere; 1443–1513),
    pope 1503–13, 47, 48
Justinian (483–565), Byzantine emperor 527–
    65, 129, 148
    system of law, 132
Justus of Ghent (c.1435/40–c.1480), Flemish
    painter, 10

Juvenal (c.60–c.130), 108

Karoch, Samuel (fl. 1450), German
    humanist/poet, 108
Käsenbrod (Augustinus Olomucensis),
    Augustin (1467–1513), Moravian
    humanist poet, 201
King, John, 156
Kingdon, Robert, 137
Kis, István Szegedi (1504–72), Hungarian
    religious reformer, 172
Klaudyán, Mikuláš (fl. 1518), Czech
    physician, 208–9
Kochanowski, Jan (1530–84), Polish scholar,
    193, 194
    Laments, 193
Konáč of Hodiškov, Mikuláš (fl. 1546),
    Utraquist burgher/writer, 207, 209, 210
Königsberg, university of, 191
Kornel of Všehrdy, V., see Všehrd
Kot, Stanislaw, 188
Krymezer, Pavel (fl. 1550), Slovak
    playwright, 209

La Boétie, Etienne de (1530–63), Voluntary
    Servitude, 140
La Croix du Maine, Les bibliothèques de
    France (1583), 135–6
Ladislas (1377–1414), king of Naples 1386–
    1414, 27
Ladislas V (1440–57), king of Hungary 1444–
    57, 165
Ladislas II (1456–1516), king of Bohemia
    1471–1516, 198, 201
    king of Hungary 1490–1516, 169
Ladislav of Bostovice (fl. 1500), Moravian
    nobleman, 213
Landsberger, Johannes, Dialogue for and
    against the Poetical Arts (1492), 106
languages, European, origins of, 15, 157–8
    Czech, 200, 201, 202–4
    Dutch, 13, 77, 79–80, 81, 85–6
    English, 146–8
    Flemish, 80
    French, 13, 14, 131–4, 135, 136
    German, 99, 100–1, 108
    Hungarian, 173–4, 176
    Italian, 13, 14, 44
    Polish, 193
    see also Greek; Latin
Lapo de Castiglionchio (c.1405–38), papal
    secretary, 46
Lassus, Orlando (c.1531–94), Flemish
    composer, 61
Latin, revival
    language, 4, 18, 33, 34, 43, 44, 78–80,

        100–1, 104, 106–7, 108, 112, 113, 130,
        133, 147–8, 154–5, 193, 200–1, 202
    literature, 9, 23, 24, 25, 43, 77, 99, 102,
        106, 107, 114–15, 116, 153, 171
    see also under individual Latin authors
Le Caron, Louis (fl. 1587), French legist,
    131–2, 133
    Pandects of the French Law, 132
Lefèvre d'Etaples, Jacques (c.1455–1536),
    French religious reformer, 10, 136–7
Leicester, earl of, see Dudley, Robert
Leiden, 81
    printing in, 81, 85
    university of, 80, 82, 85, 191
    as international centre of humanism, 80
Leipzig, university of, 111–12, 113, 114, 199
Lemaire de Belges, Jean (1473–c.1548),
    Belgian poet/historian, 133
Leo X (Giovanni de'Medici; 1475–1521),
    pope 1513–21, 46, 111, 113
Leonardo da Vinci (1452–1519), 10, 26, 45
Le Roy (Regius), Louis (fl. 1577), Greek
    scholar, 128, 132, 135
    The Vicissitudes or Variety of Things in
    the Universe, 132
Leto, Pomponio Guilio (1428–97), founder of
    the Roman Academy, 48
Lewis, C.S., 156
L'Hôpital, Michel de (c.1504–73), chancellor
    of France, 138
Lilly, William (1468?–1522), Oxford
    grammarian, 153
Linacre, Thomas (1460?–1524), 10, 153, 154
Lippi, Fra Filippo (c.1406–69), Italian painter
    working in Buda, 45, 167
Lippo, Aurelio Brandolini (c.1440–97/98),
    Italian writer, 66
Lisbon, 12
literature, see historiography; poetry; and
    under countries and individual writers
Lithuania, 186, 187, 190, 192, 194
Livorno, 27
Livy (Titus Livius; 59 BC–AD 17), 3, 24, 28,
    31, 134, 200
Locher, Jacob (called Philomusus; 1471–
    1528), Swabian humanist, 115, 116
    edits works of Horace, 109
    Historia de Rege Franciae, 109
Loisel, Antoine (1536–1617), French jurist,
    131–2
    Institutes of Customary Law, 132
Lombardo, Pietro (c.1435–1515), Antonio
    (c.1485–?1516) and Tullio (c.1455–
    1532), sculptors in Venice, 59–60
Lomnický of Budeč, Simon (1552–c.1622),
    Czech writer, 207

London, myth of origin of, 17
Longhena, Baldassare (1598–1682), Venetian
    architect, 54
Lorenzo the Magnificent, see Medici,
    Lorenzo de'
Lotto, Lorenzo (c.1480–1556), Venetian
    painter, 60, 62
Louis I, the Great (1326–82), king of
    Hungary 1342–82, 164, 165
  founds universities, 7
Louis II (1506–26), king of Hungary 1516–
    26, 169, 170, 173
Louis XII (1462–1515), king of France 1499–
    1515, 130
Louis XIV (1638–1715), king of France 1643–
    1715, 129, 130
Louvain
  printing in, 77, 78
  university of, 36, 77, 191
Low Countries, 2, 68–91
  architecture, 84
  art, 8, 12, 70, 84
  Chambers of Rhetoric, 85
  historiography, 80–3, 86–7
  humanism, 73–4, 77–88
  Italy, cross-cultural exchanges with, 70–1,
    72
  literature, 71, 73, 77–88
  in Middle Ages, 68
  music, 70
  nationhood, 71–7
  political history, 68
  religious controversies, 72–3
  Republic of the Seven United Netherlands,
    17, 68, 71, 76, 83
  scientific developments, 70, 84
  Spain, wars with, 71, 73, 74–6, 77, 79, 81,
    82, 83
  trade/industry, 72, 74
  urbanisation, 3, 84
  vernacular, importance of, 13, 77, 79–80,
    81, 85–6
  voyages of discovery, 70, 84
Loyseau, Charles de, Traité des offices
    (1610), 141
Lucian (c.120–c.180), 101, 109, 114
Lucretius (c.94–c.55 BC), De rerum natura,
    43
Luder, Peter (c.1415–c.1474), lecturer on
    poetry/rhetoric at Heidelberg, 103, 105–
    6, 108, 110, 115
Lupset, Thomas (1498?–1530), theologian,
    157, 158
Lusitanians, see Portugal
Luther, Martin (1483–1546), 3, 98, 101, 113,
    114, 138, 169, 170, 172, 174

effect on Czech Reformation, 198, 201
  praises classical learning, 115
  quarrel with Erasmus, 113
Lutherans, 95, 99, 102, 115, 136, 137, 190,
    204
Lydgate, John (1370?–1451?), Troy Book,
    148–9, 155
Lyons, 17, 130

Mabuse, Jan (c.1470/80–1533), Flemish
    painter, 12
MacFarlane, Alan, 151
Machiavelli, Niccolò (1469–1527), 4, 11, 12,
    13, 26, 35–6, 117, 140, 189, 208
  Discourses, 26
  The Prince, 125
  'Machiavellian', 139
Magdalena of Dubé (fl. 1500), wife of
    Ladislav of Boskovice, 213
magic/occult, 110, 115
Magnus, Johannes, All the Kings of the
    Goths and the Swedes (1554), 14
Maiano, Benedetto de (1442–97), Florentine
    architect in Hungary, 167
Major, J. Russell, 184–5
Mander, Karel van (1584–1606), Dutch
    painter, 10
  Schilderboeck, 70–1
Mandl, Johann (fl. 1450), lecturer on classics
    at Vienna, 103
Manetti, Bernardo (fl. 1420), Florentine
    patrician, 32, 33
Manetti, Giannozzo (1396–1459), humanist/
    theologian in Rome, 46
Mannerism, see painting
Manoel (Manuel) I (1469–1521), king of
    Portugal 1495–1521, 12
Mantegna, Andrea (1431–1506), Venetian
    painter/engraver, 60, 95, 96, 167, 214
Mantua, 25, 61, 96
Manutius, Aldus (c.1450–1515), Venetian
    printer/author, 61–2
Maraschi, Bartolomeo de' (fl. 1476), leader
    of papal choir, 167
Marcus Aurelius (121–180), Roman emperor
    161–180, 3
Marienburg, capital of Teutonic order in
    Poland, 184
Marlowe, Christopher (1564–93), Jew of
    Malta, 13
Martens, Thierry (c.1450–1534), Belgian
    printer/publisher, 78
Martial (c.40–104), 108
Martin V (Otto Colonna; 1368–1421), pope
    1417–31, ends Great Schism, 45
Martin of Žatec (fl. 1500), Utraquist priest, 212

Mary II (1662–94), queen of England 1689–94, 85

Mary of Burgundy (d. 1482), wife of Maximilian I, 72

Mary of Habsburg (1505–58), queen of Hungary and Bohemia, consort of Louis II of Hungary, 169, 170

Mary of Hungary, *see* Mary of Habsburg

Marzio, Galeotto (*c.*1427–*c.*1490), Epicurean/atheist philosopher in Hungary, 166, 168, 173

Masaccio (nickname of Tomaso di Giovanni di Guidi; 1401–*c.*1428), Florentine painter, 22, 45

Masolino (*c.*1383–*c.*1447), Italian artist in Hungary, 10, 164

Massys, Quentin (*c.*1466–1530), Flemish painter, 12

materialism, 1

mathematics, new, 3, 128

Matouš, *see* Collinus

Matthias Corvinus (Matthias Hunyadi; 1440–90), king of Hungary 1458–90, 170, 172, 173, 174, 175
  defends Christianity against infidels, 168
  founds Bibliotheca Corvina, 166–7
  influences Bohemia, 212, 214
  patron of Renaissance in Hungary, 165, 166–8, 169, 176

Matyàš (fl. 1484–94), translator of Plato's *Republic* into Czech, 203

Maurice, prince of Orange and count of Nassau (1567–1625), 82

Mauttherr, Philip (fl. 1450), lecturer on classics at Vienna, 103

Maximilian I (1459–1519), Holy Roman Emperor 1493–1519, 72, 105, 111

Maximilian II (1527–76), Holy Roman Emperor 1564–76, 213

Medici family of Florence, 16, 25, 26, 73

Medici, Catherine de', *see* Catherine

Medici, Giovanni de', *see* Leo X

Medici, Lorenzo de', the Magnificent (1448–92), 70–1, 167

medicine, 208

medieval, *see* Middle Ages

Mehmet II, *see* Mohammed II

Melanchthon, Philip (1497–1560), Luther's colleague at Wittenberg, 114, 115, 171, 172, 204

Mellissus, Paul (1539–1602), German poet, 102

Mendoza family of Seville and Toledo, 17

Mexico, influence of Italian Renaissance on, 11

Michalowicz, Jan (fl. 1550), Polish artist, 182

Michelangelo (1475–1564), 26, 45, 50, 95

Michelet, Jules (1798–1874), French historian, 128–9, 131, 134, 136, 141

Middle Ages, 15, 16, 23, 24, 42, 68
  Bohemia, 199, 205
  England, 147–8
  France, 123, 124, 129
  Germany, 99, 100, 101
  Hungary, 165
  education, 107, 114
  literature, 14, 102, 109, 134

Migliorati, Cosimo Gentile, *see* Innocent VII

Milan, 25, 27, 70, 73, 185

Milosz, Czeslaw, 193

Modrzewski, Jedrzej Frycz (*c.*1503–72), Polish jurist, 192
  De Republica emendanda, 193

Moerbeke, Willem van (*c.*1215–86), Dutch philosopher, 24

Mohács, battle of (1526), 170, 186

Mohammed II (1430–81), sultan of Turkey 1451–81, captures Constantinople (1453), 11

monarchy
  English, 148–52, 161
  French, 124–7, 129, 130, 134, 139–41, 187
  Polish, 186–7

Montaigne, Michel de (1533–92), 10, 127, 133, 135, 140, 141

Montecassino, 28

Montepulciano, 27

Monteverdi, Claudio (1567–1643), composer in Venice, 61

Morando, Bernardo (fl. 1587–1600), Italian architect in Poland, 10, 184

Moravia, *see* Bohemia and Moravia

More, Sir Thomas (1478–1535), 95, 146, 154, 156, 160
  The History of Richard III, 154
  Utopia, 154–5, 156, 157

Morelli, Giovanni (fl. 1600), Florentine writer, 32

Morosini family of Venice, 62

Moryson (Morison), Sir Richard (d. 1556), *Exhortation*, 159–60

Moscow, influence of Italian Renaissance in, 11

Mouřenín of Litomyšl, Tobiáš (fl. 1625), Czech playwright, 209

music, 2, 8, 45, 70, 167, 175

Muslim tradition, *see* Islam

Mussato, Albertino (1261–1329), Paduan scholar, 21

Mutian, Conrad (1471–1526), German neoplatonist, 104, 110

myths of origin (countries/peoples), 14–16, 17, 46–7, 207

in Dutch Republic, 81–2, 83
in France, 123–4, 130, 135
in Germany, 96–7
in Hungary, 173
in Poland, 188
see also nationhood

Nantes, Edict of (1598), 140
Naples, 6, 7, 25, 27, 185
Napoleon Bonaparte (1769–1821), emperor
  of France 1804–15, 76, 129
nationhood, concepts of, 3–4, 13–18, 80–2
  England, 14–15, 16, 147, 156
  France, 15, 123–4, 130
  Germany, 15, 17, 111
  Hungary, 173
  Low Countries, 71–7
Nebrija, Elio Antonio de (1444–1522),
  Spanish writer, 10, 18
Nero (37–68), Roman emperor 54–68, 10
Netherlands, see Low Countries
Neumarkt, Johann von (1310–80), Czech
  humanist, 102
New World, 1, 3, 5, 128, 146
Niavis, Paul (fl. 1480), German humanist,
  107
Niccoli, Niccolò (1364–1437), Florentine
  humanist, 23, 33–4
Noah, 15, 49
nonconformist sects, in Hungary, 172
Noot, Jan van der (1539/40–c.1595), Dutch
  poet, 71
Norway, 11

Obrecht, Jacob (c.1452–1505), Burgundian
  composer, 70
O'Donnell, Manus (d. 1564), Irish poet/
  politician, 11
Oldenbarnevelt, Jan van (1547–1619), Dutch
  statesman, 86
Olomouc, town in Moravia, 201, 204
Opbergen, Anton van (fl. 1602), Dutch
  architect in Poland, 184
Opitz, Martin (1597–1639), German poet,
  102
Orme, Philibert de l', see Delorme, Philibert
Ottoman Empire, Renaissance art in, 11
Ovid (43 BC–AD 17), 35, 101, 106, 202, 204
  Metamorphoses, 33, 44
Oxford, university of, 149, 153–4

Pace, Richard (1482–?1536), dean of St
  Paul's, 155
Pacher, Michael (c.1435–98), German
  painter, 94–5
Padua, 23, 53, 96

university of, 103, 164, 171, 188, 191, 199,
  201
paganism, in art, 46–9
Pahrs, Milanese family of architects, 11
painting, 2, 4
  Czech, 211, 213–14
  Flemish, 7, 8, 12
  Florentine, 22
  German, 94–9
  Hungarian, 164
  in Low Countries, 70–1
  Mannerist School, 12, 50, 54, 181, 183, 213
  religious, 47, 49, 54, 55, 61, 70–1, 94–9,
    211–12
  Venetian, 54–5, 59–60
  see also under individual artists
Palladio, Andrea (1518–80), Italian architect,
  6, 9, 54, 59
Pandolfino, Agnolo (1363–1446), Florentine
  philosopher, 33
Pannonia, see Hungary
Pannonius, Janus (1434–72), Hungarian
  poet, 165, 166, 167, 173
papacy/pope, 4, 13, 25, 54, 129
  Rome and, 45–50
  see also Vatican
Papal States, 8, 42, 49
Parenti family of Florence, 32
Paris, 123, 124, 130
  university of, 105, 127, 135, 191
Parker, Matthew (1504–75), archbishop of
  Canterbury, 14–15
Pasquier, Etienne (1529–1615), French
  historian, 125, 127, 131, 133, 136, 140, 141
  Interpretation of the Institutes of
    Justinian, 132
  Recherches de la France, 14, 135
patronage
  in Bohemia, 213–14
  in Denmark, 11–12
  in Florence, 25
  in Germany, 108, 111
  in Hungary, 164, 166–7
  in Poland, 182
  in Rome, 44
  in Venice, 56–8
Paul II (Pietro Barbo; 1417–71), pope 1464–
  71, 46, 47, 48
'Paule-Emile', see Emilio, Paolo
Pazzi, Andrea de' (fl. 1415), Florentine
  patrician, 32
Peñalosa, Francisco de (c.1470–1528),
  Spanish composer in Rome, 45
Perger, Bernard (fl. 1490), Viennese
  humanist, Nova Grammatica, 107
Pericles (d. 429 BC), 29

persecution, religious, 52, 55, 137, 138–9,
140, 190, 201
Persian Wars (499–448 BC), 29
Persius (34–62), 108
Peru, influence of Italian Renaissance art, 11
Perugia, 47
Perugino (c.1445–1523), master of Raphael,
11, 45, 46
Peruzzi, Baldassare (1481–1536), architect/
painter in Rome, 44
Peter, St (d. c.AD 67), 49
Petrarch (Francesco Petrarca; 1307–74),
Italian poet/Renaissance leader, 21, 23,
35, 42, 86, 101, 102, 127, 135, 147, 148,
165, 166, 199, 202, 207
Peuerbach, Georg (fl. 1450), humanist
lecturer at Vienna, 103, 106
Philip II (1527–98), king of Spain 1556–98,
10, 72, 73, 74, 76, 79, 82
Philip the Bold (1342–1404), lst duke of
Burgundy 1364–1404, 70, 71
Philip the Good (1396–1467), 3rd duke of
Burgundy 1419–67, 36, 71, 72
Piccolomini, Aeneas Sylvius, see Pius II
Pico della Mirandola, Giovanni, count
(1463–94), Italian philosopher/writer,
49, 110, 202
Piero della Francesca (also called Pietro
Borghese; c.1416–92), Italian painter, 45
Pinturicchio, Bernardino (c.1454–1513),
Italian painter, 47
Pirckheimer, Willibald (1470–1530), German
humanist, 104, 109, 114
Pisa, 27
Pisanello, Antonio (c.1395–c.1450), Italian
medallist, 214
Pisano, Niccolò (1220–84), Italian sculptor,
14, 21
Písecký, Václav (1482–1511), Czech classical
scholar, 203–4
Pistoia, 27, 34
Pithou, Pierre (1490–1554), French jurist,
125, 131
Pius II (Aeneas Sylvius Piccolomini; 1405–
64), pope 1458–64, 44, 103
as secretary to Frederick III, 165
diplomatic mission to Poland, 199
De duobus amantibus, 174
De liberorum educatione, 165
Pius V (Michele Ghislieri; 1504–72), pope
1566–72, 50
plague
in Rome, 50
in Venice, 54, 59
Plato (c.427–c.347 BC), 3, 25, 48, 49, 132,
167, 202–3

neoplatonism, 25, 48, 110, 167
Republic, 202–3
Platonic Academy, see Florence
Plautus (c.250–184 BC), 101, 106, 202, 204
Aulularia, 109
Miles gloriosus, 204, 209
Pliny the elder (23–79), 22, 28, 81, 201, 202
Plotinus (205–70), 167
Plutarch (c.46–c.120), 109, 133
Poděbrady, Hynek of (1452–92), Bohemian
poet, 206
Poděbrady, Jiří of (1420–71), king of
Bohemia 1453–71, 199–200, 206, 208
poetry, 3, 4, 114–15, 116, 157–9, 165, 166,
167, 174, 175, 176, 193–4, 201, 205–10
see also under individual poets
Poggio Bracciolini, Giovanni Francesco
(1380–1459), Italian humanist scholar,
23, 34, 42, 43, 164
On Nobility, 31
Poland, 16, 172, 175, 180–96, 212
architecture, 181
art, 180, 181, 182, 183–4, 193
cross-cultural influences, 180, 182, 191,
192, 194
education, 190–1
literature, 193–4
Polish language, 193
political situation, 184–90, 191–2
printing, 194
Reformation, 190–4
social structure, 183–4
Pole, Reginald (1500–58), cardinal, 157, 158
Politian (Angelo Poliziano; 1454–94),
Florentine poet/humanist, 25–6, 44, 50,
127
politics/political theory, 24–6
see also under countries
Pollaiuolo, Antonio (c.1432–98), Italian
painter/engraver, 95, 96, 167
Polo, Marco (1254–1324), 55
Pontano, Giovanni (c.1429–1503), Italian
lyricist, 9, 202
Ponzio, Giovanni (fl. 1410), scholar at Rome
university, 43
Portugal, 12
claim descent from Lusus (Lusitanians),
15–16
Postel, Guillaume (1510–81), French
philosopher, 50
Prague, 12, 211
architecture, 212–13, 214
classical revival in, 102–3, 209
university of, 198–9, 200, 204, 209
Prato, 27
Primaticcio, Francesco (1504–70), Italian

artist, 10
printing, 172, 194
  invention of movable type, 3
  makes texts accessible, 9, 61–2
  effect on Reformation, 137
  in France, 127–8, 129, 130–1
  in Germany, 101, 108
  in Low Countries, 77, 78, 85
Priuli family of Venice, 58
Prokop of Jindrichuv Hrdac (fl. 1484), Czech
  humanist writer, 208
Protestants, 9, 13, 79, 102, 131, 136–40, 156,
  161, 171, 172, 183, 184, 191, 198, 201,
  203
  universities, 113, 114
  see also Reformation
Ptolemy, Claudius (2nd cent. AD), 109
Purcell, Henry (1659–95), 182
Puttenham, George (d. 1590), The Art of
  English Poesie, 14
Pythagoras (c.560–c.480 BC), 48, 49

Quintilian (c.35–c.100), 33, 35, 101, 106
Quirini, Lauro (fl. 1441), Venetian humanist,
  25

Rabelais, François (c.1490–1553), 10, 135,
  141
Racek of Doubrava (fl. 1547), Czech
  Catholic scholar, 201
Raimondi, Marcantonio (c.1480–c.1534),
  Italian engraver, 96
Ramus, Petrus (1515–72), French humanist
  scholar (Ramism), 131, 141
Rantzau, Henrik (1526–98), Danish
  statesman, 12
Ranum, Orest, 134
Raphael (Rafaello Sanzio; 1483–1520), 10,
  44, 45, 46, 48, 60, 96
Ratgeb, Jorg (d. 1526), German painter, 98
Reformation, 5 n3, 7, 50, 93, 105, 113–14,
  115–16
  Czech, 197–200, 204
  English, 156, 159–60
  French, 123, 128, 130, 136–41
  German, 7, 93, 94, 98–9, 102, 113, 114–16
  Hungarian, 170–2, 173, 174
  Polish, 190–4
  see also Calvin, John; Luther, Martin
Regiomontanus, Johann (1436–76), German
  astronomer, 103, 166
Reimenschneider, Tilmann (1460–1531),
  Würzburg sculptor, 94, 98
Rej, Mikolaj (1505–69), Polish poet, 193
religion, see Christianity
Renaudet, Augustin, 103

Reuchlin, Johann (1455–1522), German
  humanist, 10, 104
  theological controversy with Cologne
  university, 112–13, 115
  publishes Hebrew texts, 109
  Augenspiegel, 112, 113
  De arte cabalistica, 110
  Henno and Sergius, 109
Rheims, myth of origin of, 17
Rhenanus, Beatus (1485–1547), German
  humanist historian, 15
Riario, Raffaele (?1460–?1521), cardinal, 45
Richard I (1157–99), king of England 1189–
  99, 147
Richard III (1452–85), king of England 1483–
  5, 150, 154, 157
Rienzo (Rienzi), Cola da (c.1313–54), Italian
  revolutionary, 48, 102, 199
Rimay, János (c.1570–1631), Hungarian
  poet, 176
Rinuccini, Cino (c.1350–1417), Florentine
  poet, 29
Rizzo, Antonio (1430?–1498?), sculptor in
  Venice, 59, 60
Roberti, Ercole de' (Grandi d'Antonio; 1450–
  96), Italian architect in Buda, 167
Rokycana, Jan (c.1397–1471), Utraquist
  bishop, 192, 202, 206
Roman Academy (founded c.1465), 47–8
Roman Catholic Church, see Catholic
  Church; Great Schism
Romanticism, 1, 2
Rome, ancient, 3, 4, 6, 9, 15, 18, 21, 27, 28,
  42, 87, 93, 100, 101, 147, 159
  architecture, 43–4, 46
  literature, 42–3, 109, 127
  see also Latin
  system of laws, 3, 131, 132, 149
  Roman Empire, 4, 14, 55, 124
  Roman Republic, 5, 21, 202
Rome, Renaissance, 6, 7, 10, 21, 25, 35, 53,
  54
  antiquity, revival of, 42–52
  architecture, 10, 43, 44–5
  Christian/pagan themes in art, 43, 46–9
  literature, 46
  music, 45, 70
  painting, 44, 46, 48, 50
  plague (1522), 50
  Sack of Rome (1527), 50
  sculpture, 45
  university of, 43, 48
  see also Latin; papacy
Ronsard, Pierre de (1524/5–85), 86, 133–4,
  141
  Franciade, 15, 17, 134

Rosselli, Cosimo (1439–1507), Florentine
    painter working on Sistine Chapel, 45
Rosso, Fiorentino (Giovanni Battista di
    Gaspare; 1494–1540), Italian painter, 10
Roswitha of Gandersheim (c.935–c.1000),
    German nun/playwright, 109
Rovere, Francesco della, see Sixtus IV
Rovere, Giuliano della, see Julius II
Rudolf II (1552–1612), Holy Roman
    Emperor 1576–1612, 12
Rufus, Jacobus Publicius (fl. 1467), Italian
    humanist at Leipzig and Erfurt, 103
Russia, influence of Italian Renaissnce on,
    11, 12
Ruthenia, 192, 193, 194
Rváčovský, Vavřinec Leander (1525–90),
    Czech writer, 207

Sachs, Hans (1494–1576), Nuremberg
    cobbler/songwriter, 99, 101
Sallust (86–c.34 BC), 28
Salutati, Coluccio (1331–1406), chancellor of
    Florence, 21, 23, 25, 28, 29, 30–1, 33
Sambucus, Johannes (1513–84), Hungarian
    philologist, 172, 175
Sangallo, Antonio da (1485–1546) and
    Giuliano da (1445–1516), Florentine
    architects in Rome, 45
Sanmichele, Michele (1484–1559), Veronese
    sculptor in Venice, 60
Sansovino, Jacopo (1486–1570), Italian
    architect, 10, 45, 54, 59
Sarpi, Paolo (formerly Pietro) (1552–1623),
    Venetian ideologue, 57, 62–3
satire, humanist, Letters of Obscure Men
    (1513), 112–13
Savelli, Paolo (fl. 1400), Venetian nobleman,
    57
Savello, Antimo (fl. 1511), Roman
    revolutionary, 48
Savonarola, Girolamo (1452–98), Florentine
    Dominican monk and religious
    reformer, 47, 207
Saxl, Fritz, 44
Saxo Grammaticus (c.1150–c.1205), History
    of the Kings of the Danes, 15
Saxons, origins of the, 15
Scandinavia
    nationalism/myths of origin, 15
    Renaissance in, 9, 11–12, 13
Schongauer, Martin (c.1450–90), Alsatian
    painter/engraver, 95
science, new, 1, 3, 5, 70, 79–80, 128, 166, 208
Scolari, Filippo (fl. 1500), portrait by
    Castagno, 164
Scorel, Jan van (1494–1562), Netherlandish

    painter, 10, 71
Scotland
    myth of Scots' descent from Scota,
        daughter of an Egyptian pharoah, 15
    Renaissance in, 6, 11
sculpture, 8, 9, 22, 70, 94, 182, 211, 213
    see also under countries and individual
        sculptors
Seneca, Lucius Annaeus (c.4 BC–AD 65), 77,
    78, 87, 101, 106, 201, 202
Serlio, Sebastiano (1475–1554), Italian
    architect, 6, 9, 10, 11, 12
Serravalle, Giovanni de (fl. 1432), translator
    of Divina Commedia into Latin, 164
Serres, Jean De (c.1540–98), French
    Protestant historian, 134
Seville, 17
Seyssel, Claude de (c.1450–1520), French
    historian, 130, 132, 134, 138, 139, 140,
    141,
    Monarchy of France, 124–7
Sforza family of Milan, 73
Shakespeare, William (1564–1616), 146, 148
Shearman, John, 50
Shute, John (fl. 1550–70), English architect, 10
Sigismund (1368–1437), king of Hungary
    1387–1437, Holy Roman Emperor
    1411–37
    patron of scholars, 164–5
    founds universities, 171
Sigismund I (1467–1548), king of Poland
    1506–48, 186
Sigismund II Augustus (1520–72), king of
    Poland 1548–72, 183, 190
Sigismund III (Báthory) (1566–1632), king of
    Poland 1587–1632, 175
Signorelli, Luca (c.1442–1523), Italian
    painter, 45
Šimon of Slaný (fl. 1450), Czech humanist,
    200
Sinan Bey (Mimar Sinan; 1489–1588),
    Ottoman architect, 11
Sixtus IV (Francesco della Rovere; 1414–84),
    pope 1471–84, 44
Šlechta, Jan (fl. 1480), Czech humanist
    scholar, 201
Slovakia, 181
Sluter, Claus (c.1350–c.1405), Dutch
    sculptor, 70
Smith, Sir Thomas (1513–77)
    De Republica Anglorum, 160
    Discourse of the Commonweal, 160
Sophocles (497/496–406/405 BC), 87, 114
Sorbonne, 125, 137
Spain, 6, 8, 139
    Castilian language, 18

Italian influence on architecture, 12
origins/ancestry, 17–18
poetry, traditional, 14
wars with Low Countries, 71, 73, 74–6, 77, 79, 81, 82, 83
Spiegel, H.L. (1549–1612), Dutch humanist, 79
Spitz, Lewis, 116
Sprangler, Bartolomäus (1546–1627), Flemish artist, 10
Stanbridge, John (1463–1510), Oxford grammarian, 153
Starkey, Thomas (1490?–1538), 147, 159, 161
Dialogue between Pole and Lupset, 157, 158
Steinhöwel, Heinrich (1412–78), physician/ classicist at Ulm, 101, 103
Stephen Báthory, see Báthory
Stevin, Simon (1548–1620), Dutch scientist, 79–80
Stoss, Veit (1438?–1533), Nuremberg sculptor, 94
Strasbourg, 17
Gymnasium, 114, 190
Středa, Jan of (fl. 1350), imperial chancellor of Bohemia, 199
Střet, Václav (fl. 1470), Czech illuminator, 214
Strozzi family of Florence, 29
Sturm, Johannes (1507–89), German Protestant educationist, 114, 190
Suleiman I, the Magnificent (c.1494–1566), sultan of Turkey 1520–66, 170
Sulla, Lucius Cornelius (138–78 BC), 28
Surrey, earl of, see Howard, Henry
Sweden
nationalism, 14
Renaissance in, 11
Swicker, Paul (fl. 1450), Viennese humanist, 103
Switzerland, Renaissance in, 6
Sylvester, János (fl. 1541), translates Bible into Hungarian, 174
Szarzynski, Mikolaj Sep (1500–81), Polish poet, 193–4

Tábor, town in south Bohemia, Christian chiliastic community (Taborites, 1420), 198
Tacitus, Publius Cornelius (d. 276), 81, 86, 87
Germania, 15, 188–9
Historiae, 28–9, 82–3
Tagliente, Giovanni Antonio (fl. 1524), Libro maistrevole, 62
Tasso, Torquato (1544–95), Italian poet, 10

technology, 3, 58–9
Terence (c.185–159 BC), 106, 109, 204, 209
Eunuchs, 109
Theocritus (c.310–c.250 BC), 114
Thomas, St/Thomism, see Aquinas
Thou, Christofle de (1508–82), French Reformation leader, 129
Thucydides (c.460–c.400 BC), 29, 132
Tibaldi, Pellegrino (1527–c.1582), Italian artist, 10
Tillet, Jean du (d. 1570), French scholar/ archivist, 125
Recueil des roys de France, 134–5
Tintoretto, Jacopo Robusti (1518–94), 60–1
Paradise, 54
Tiptoft, Jean, earl of Worcester (1427?– 1470), 150, 153
Titian (Tiziano Vecelli; c.1487/90–1576), 10, 57, 58, 59–60
Assumption of the Virgin, 54
Torrigiano, Pietro (1472–1522), Italian sculptor, 10
Tory, Geoffroy (c.1480–1533), French printer/engraver, 133
Tournèbe, Adrien (fl. 1580), French classical scholar, 133
Tovačovský, Ctibor (fl. 1438), Moravian politician, 203
Transylvania, 170, 171, 175
Traversarius, Ambrosius (?1386–1439), Italian scholar in Hungary, 164
Trent, Council of (1545–63), 114, 136
Trithemius, Johann von (pseud. of J. van Heidenberg; 1462–1516), German historian, 15
interest in magic/occult, 110
Trojans/Trojan myths, 15, 87, 135, 148–9, 159, 188
Tübingen, university of, 107, 112
Tunstall, Cuthbert (1474–1559), bishop of London, 155, 159
Turks/infidels, 165, 166, 168, 172, 173, 174–5
defeat Hungary (1526), 170
Tuscany, 17, 27, 53, 63
architecture, 21, 181
education, 35
see also Florence

universities, 104–5, 110–11, 127, 130, 171, 175
curriculum reform, 113–14
see also university towns
Upton, Nicholas (1400?–1457), De officio militari, 149, 150
urbanisation, 84, 182–3
Urbino, 10, 45

Utraquists, 197, 198, 199, 200, 202, 203, 204, 208, 209, 210, 214
Utrecht, Union of (1579), 76

Valerius Maximus (fl. AD 30), 106
Valla, Lorenzo (1405–57; Italian philologist), 43, 46, 127, 132, 202
Valois dynasty of France, 140, 141, 185, 187
   tomb at St Denis, 183
Vasari, Giorgio (1511–74), *Lives of the Painters*, 14, 26, 50, 56, 70, 167
Vatican, 60
   Borgia apartments, 47, 49
   library, 43
   Raphael's *School of Athens*, 48–9
   Sistine Chapel, 45, 46, 49
Vegetius (fl. 400), 150
Veldenaer, Johann (fl. 1447–83), Louvain printer/engraver, 77
Vendramin family of Venice, 58
Venice, 2, 6, 7, 10, 11, 17, 25, 48, 53–67, 157, 173, 185, 189
   architecture, 54–5, 57, 59
   book trade/printing, 61–2
   classical revival, 53–5
   cross-cultural contacts, 59–60, 61, 62–3, economy, 59, 60
   music, 61
   painting, 54–5, 59–61
   plague epidemics, 54, 59
   politico-social structure, 56–63
   technology, 58–9
Vercingetorix (d. 46 BC), chieftain of the Arveni (Gallic tribe), 14
Vergerio, Pier Paulo (fl. 1400–44), bishop of Capodistria in Hungary 1417–44, 164, 166
   De ingenuis moribus et liberalis adolescentiae studiis, 165
Vergil, Polydore (c.1470–c.1555), Italian humanist historian, 15, 16
vernacular, *see under countries*
Verona, 23, 53, 60
Veronese, Paul (real name Paul Caliari/ Cagliari; 1528–88), 60
   The Apotheosis of Venice, 54–5
Verrocchio, Andrea del (1435–88), Florentine sculptor, 167
Verstegen, Richard (fl. 1565–1620), 16
   Restitution of Decayed Intelligence, 14
Vicenza, 53
Vida, Marco Girolamo (?1485–1566), *Christiad*, 46
Vienna, 103
   Congress of (1815), 76
   university of, 103, 106, 107, 109, 110, 169,

171, 172, 199, 205
Vilna, Jesuit College, 191
Virgil (Publius Vergilius Maro; 70–19 BC), 23, 33, 77, 78, 101, 106, 149, 165, 200, 202
   Aenead, 46, 159
Vischer, Peter *the elder* (1460–1529), Peter *the younger* (1487–1528), and Hermann (1486?–1517), Nuremberg sculptors in bronze, 94, 182
Visconti family of Milan, 27, 165
Visconti, Giangaleazzo (1351–1402), duke of Milan, 27
Visscher, Roemer (1547–1620), Dutch poet, 85
Vitéz, Johannes (c.1408–72), lst Hungarian humanist, 165, 166, 173
Vitruvius Pollio (fl. 1st cent. BC), 22
Vladislav, *see* Ladislas
Vogel, Walther von der (c.1160/70–c.1230), German lyric poet, 99
Vondel, Joost van der (1587–1679), Dutch poet, 71, 82, 83, 85, 86–7
Vries, Adriaen de (fl. 1634–50), Netherlandish painter, 12
Všehrd, Viktorín Kornel (c.1460–1520), Czech humanist, 201–2, 203

War of the Eight Saints (1375–78), 27
Wars of the Roses (1455–85), 149–50
Weckherlin, Georg Rudolf (1584–1653), German poet, 102
Werbőczy, István (1458–1541), Hungarian jurist, 173
Westfalen, Jan van, *see* Veldenaer, Johann
Weyden, Rogier van der (c.1400–64), Flemish painter, 7, 70
White Mountain, Battle of the (1620), 198
Whittinton, Robert (fl. 1519), Oxford grammarian, 153
Willaert, Adriaan (c.1490–1562), Flemish composer, 8, 61
William of Moerbeke, *see* Moerbeke, Willem van
William of Savona (fl. 1450), Italian scholar in Vienna, 103
William of Worcester, *see* Worcester
William the Silent, prince of Orange (1533–84), 74, 76, 79, 81, 82, 85
   murder of, 81, 82
William of Orange (1650–1702), William III of Great Britain 1689–1702, 85, 87
William I (William VI of Orange; 1772–1843), king of the Netherlands 1815–40, 76
Wimpheling (Wimfeling), Jacob (fl. 1480–

1500), German humanist, 103, 104, 107, 110, 113, 116
  Germania, 14, 17
  Isidoneus Germanicus, 107
  Stylpho, 109
Wittenberg, univerity of, 171, 172, 204, 205
Wladislas II, *see* Ladislas
Wolfram von Eschenbach (*c*.1170–*c*.1220), German poet, *Parzival*, 100
Wolsey, Thomas (1475?–1530), cardinal, 160
Worcester, William of (1415?–1482?), 149–50
  Boke of Noblesse, 150
Wyatt, Sir Thomas (1503?–1542), English poet, 158–9, 160
Wyle, Niklas von (1501–78), German classicist scholar, 101, 103

Xenophon (*c*.430–355 BC), 132

Zamosc, Poland, 184, 188
  Academy, 191
Zamoyski, Jan (1542–1605), Polish chancellor, 189, 191
  De Senatu romanu, 188
Zechinelli, Francesco (fl. 1500), Venetian mercer, 62
Žižka, Jan (*c*.1376–1424), Hussite military leader, 203, 205
Zuccaro Federico (1543–1609), Italian artist, 10
Zurich, 137
Zwingli, Huldreich (1484–1531), Swiss Protestant reformer, 98–9, 172

KRAUSKOPF LIBRARY

940.21 R29p   STACKS
/The Renaissance in national context

3 1896 00044 8187